# HIDEOUS PROGENY

**FILM AND CULTURE   JOHN BELTON, EDITOR**

COLUMBIA UNIVERSITY PRESS - NEW YORK

ANGELA M. SMITH

# HIDEOUS PROGENY

## DISABILITY, EUGENICS, AND CLASSIC HORROR CINEMA

COLUMBIA UNIVERSITY PRESS
*Publishers Since 1893*
New York    Chichester, West Sussex
cup.columbia.edu

Library of Congress Cataloging-in-Publication Data

Smith, Angela M.
Hideous progeny : disability, eugenics, and classic horror cinema /
Angela M. Smith.
        p. cm. — (Film and culture)
Includes bibliographical references and index.
ISBN 978-0-231-15716-2 (cloth : alk. paper) — ISBN 978-0-231-15717-9 (pbk. :
alk paper) — ISBN 978-0-231-52785-9 (ebook)
1. Horror films—History and criticism.     2. People with disabilities in
motion pictures.     3. Grotesque in motion pictures.     4. Eugenics in
motion pictures.     I. Title.

PN1995.9.H6S585     2012
791.43′6164—dc23                              2011040542

Columbia University Press books are printed on permanent and durable
acid-free paper.
This book is printed on paper with recycled content.
Printed in the United States of America

c 10 9 8 7 6 5 4 3 2 1
p 10 9 8 7 6 5 4 3 2 1

References to Internet Web sites (URLs) were accurate at the time of writing.
Neither the author nor Columbia University Press is responsible for URLs that
may have expired or changed since the manuscript was prepared.

An earlier version of chapter 1 appeared as "Monsters in the Bed: The Horror-
Film Eugenics of *Dracula* and *Frankenstein*," in Susan Currell and Christina
Cogdell, eds., *Popular Eugenics: National Efficiency and American Mass Culture in
the 1930s* (Athens: Ohio University Press, 2006).

*Design by Shaina Andrews*

FOR
# MATT
WHO ALWAYS JUMPS AT THE SCARY PARTS

# CONTENTS

# LIST OF ILLUSTRATIONS

# ACKNOWLEDGMENTS

*Hideous Progeny* was made possible by several generous institutions and individuals. During my Ph.D. studies and dissertation writing, I received a fellowship from the New Zealand–United States Fulbright Foundation, fellowship and research funding from the University of Minnesota Graduate School, and teaching assistantships and conference funding from the University of Minnesota's Department of English. I received invaluable archival assistance from Ned Comstock, of the University of Southern California Film Archives, Carlos Noriega of the Warner Bros. Film Archives, Barbara Hall of the Margaret Herrick Library at the Academy of Motion Picture Arts and Sciences, Rob Cox and Valerie Lutz of the American Philosophical Society Library, and the staff of the Library of Congress Newspaper Reading Room.

My graduate studies also benefited from the wisdom, enthusiasm, and guidance of several professors, including Ellen Stekert, who first introduced me to disability studies; Paula Rabinowitz, Jani Scandura, and Jigna Desai, who were engaged and critical committee members; and my adviser, John Mowitt, who unfailingly inspired me with his ideas, generously shared his immense knowledge, and enthusiastically responded to my work. My writing was also much the better for the input of the members of my Feminist Studies dissertation-writing class in spring 2000 and the members of John Mowitt's dissertation-writing class in spring 2001.

In my many years writing this book, I have drawn on the financial and intellectual support of Massey University and Victoria University of Wellington, both in New Zealand, and Richmond University, in Virginia. More recently, at the University of Utah, I benefited from the time and intellectual community provided by a fellowship at the Tanner Humanities Center. My colleagues in the University of Utah's Department of English and the Gender Studies program have been unstinting in their support and encouragement, and *Hideous Progeny* was greatly improved by the astute readings and suggestions of Kathryn Stockton, Stuart Culver, Nadja Durbach, Howard Horwitz, Jessica Straley, and Richard Preiss. I am also grateful to Ian Conrich, who encouraged and helped publish my horror-film writing at critical stages, and to Robert McRuer, who read the partially completed manuscript and provided timely encouragement and advice. And I am indebted to the wonderful staff at Columbia University Press, especially Jennifer Crewe, Associate Director and Editorial Director, editorial assistant Asya Graf, and my copyeditor Roy Thomas.

For much of this book's development, I was a long way from my New Zealand home and family. But the fact that I have any argumentation skills at all is thanks to my very smart and always contrary brothers, Jared and Greg. And the fact that I have spent so long thinking, reading, and writing about a subject as impractical as horror movies is entirely due to the models of wide-ranging intellectual curiosity provided by my parents, Marilyn and Kel, and their unquestioning support of all the travels, academic and geographic, I have undertaken. So, thank you, Smiths.

Finally, I would like to thank my own not-at-all hideous progeny, Eamon and Jack, whose lives are still so new as I complete this book, and my husband Matt, who has—through all the vampires, monsters, and mad doctors—been a patient reader and listener, a voice of wisdom, a passionate ally, an unstinting source of laughter, and a soul-mate.

# HIDEOUS PROGENY

# INTRODUCTION

## DISABILITY, EUGENICS, AND CLASSIC HORROR CINEMA

n December 1931, Colonel Jason S. Joy, administrator of Hollywood's Production Code, was a little anxious. Writing to Paramount executive B. P. Schulberg about the forthcoming film *Dr. Jekyll and Mr. Hyde*, Joy wondered whether local censors would "overlook the horrors that result from the realism of the Hyde make-up," and warned, "[W]e cannot estimate what the reaction will be to this, or to other horror pictures." A few days later, Joy expanded on his concern in a memo to Will Hays, president of the Motion Picture Producers and Distributors of America:

> Perhaps it would be wise to obtain an early estimate of the audience reaction and critical opinion concerning *Dracula* and *Frankenstein* by Universal; *Dr. Jekyll and Mr. Hyde* by Paramount; and *Almost Married* by Fox, all of which are in distribution or about to be distributed. Paramount has another "gruesome" picture about to be put into production [*Island of Lost Souls*] and Metro-Goldwyn-Mayer has *Freaks* which is about one-half shot. Is this the beginning of a cycle that ought to be retarded or killed? I am anxious to receive your advice."[1]

The movies Joy lists, with the exception of the obscure *Almost Married*, are now familiar as early examples of the American horror-film genre, which Joy already perceived as members of a discrete class. He describes the films in terms that anticipate later definitions of horror film as a "body genre" that uses images of damaged or deformed bodies to affect viewers physically.[2] *Gruesome* derives from the Middle English "gruen," meaning "to shudder," while *horror* stems from the Latin word "horrēre," meaning "to bristle," and denotes "[a] painful emotion compounded of loathing and fear; a shuddering with terror and repugnance . . . the feeling excited by something shocking or frightful."[3] The gruesome bodies *in* the films—like the horrific Hyde—thus conflate with the gruesome body of the genre itself, whose potentially disturbing effects seem to warrant censorial intervention: the "retarding" or "killing" of an incipient and deformed genre.

In considering whether to delimit or dispense with this aberrant strain of films, Joy used rhetoric that resonated with the discourse of American eugenics, a set of theories and practices that sought to promote species or racial health by identifying the genetically "superior" and encouraging their reproduction, while diagnosing the genetically "inferior" and preventing or inhibiting their reproduction. Joy's comments imply three eugenic assumptions. First, although his concern is with cultural texts rather than actual persons, Joy's focus in the letter to Schulberg is nonetheless on a "realistically" deformed individual, Hyde, whom he views as symptomatic of a deeper and innate problem with the generic body. Joy's words thus reflect eugenic interpretations of individual bodily differences as proof of internal, genetic aberrations. Second, the threat posed by such deviance and its likely reproduction is measured in its effect on the social body. Like propagandists for eugenic ideas, Joy assumes that presumably normal members of the public *naturally* react negatively—with shuddering and repugnance—to visible deformities and disabilities. Such reactions ostensibly confirm such traits as self-evidently "bad" and register the likely physiological harm such deviance may cause the nation. Third, in querying whether horror movies ought to be somehow inhibited or destroyed, Joy affirms the eugenic imperative to protect America by identifying the defective body, corralling it, and, in extreme instances, disposing of it.

Joy's "eugenic" response to horror films reminds us that the genre emerged out of a culture used to assigning pathological meanings to certain body and behavioral traits, and thus justifying the institutionalization, sterilization, and even elimination of certain individuals. Accordingly, *Hideous Progeny* challenges scholars' tendency to overlook the genre's disability politics, arguing that eugenic assumptions about bodily form and biological inheritance were vital to the formation of classic horror's visual and narrative conventions. As *Hideous Progeny* uncovers the films' pervasive and often "ableist" exploitation of unusual bodily forms, however, it also demonstrates that the films complicate, diffuse, and even vilify eugenic messages. Moreover, as *Hideous Progeny* moves from horror-film plots and iconography to formal and technical elements and on to audience reception, it increasingly discovers less a reductive abhorrence of visible and behavioral difference than a fascination with and desire for the frisson of embodied vulnerability, an attraction to physical variation and mutability, and a passion for discomfort and distress that undercuts eugenic assumptions about the "normality" of the American public.

In order to illuminate the connections between eugenic thought and classic horror films, this introduction presents some disability-studies perspectives on cultural narratives before proceeding to a brief summary of American eugenics as a disability discourse premised on pathological interpretations of people who were physically or mentally impaired, non-white, non-"Nordic," or poor. The introduction then posits the genre of eugenic film and its disability politics as a cinematic link between eugenic discourse and 1930s horror films. Finally, in turning to the classic horror genre, the introduction contests conventional metaphoric readings of horror-film monsters and the concomitant marginalization of classic horror films, whose too-material bodies supposedly only enforce conservative cultural messages. *Hideous Progeny* argues that reading these films' monstrous bodies in relation to eugenics valuably uncovers a collision of cultural, social, and scientific forces that derive energy from exploitations and constructions of disabled bodies. In harnessing these forces, often in conflicting ways, horror films do not simplistically reveal the horrors of impairment or difference but question supposedly "natural" negative responses to unusual bodies and foreground the horrors of the eugenic enterprise itself. The classic horror film is thus both indebted to and traitorous toward eugenic thought, and by taking up eugenic narratives and icons—simplifying, individualizing, and rendering them in visceral form— it showcases eugenics' own discontinuities, fabrications, and perversions.

## DISABILITY

Joy's construction of the horror genre as a gruesome body drew on a long cultural tradition of interpreting unusual bodies as metaphors. Indeed, the term *monster*, deriving from the Latin *monstra*, meaning to show, display, or warn, presents aberrant bodies as symbols to be "read" for a disguised meaning.[4] Thus, in classical and medieval times, unusual bodies and behaviors were viewed as evidence of divine or otherwise unknowable forces and read as portents of good or ill or manifestations of "earthly malignancy and witchcraft."[5] Later eras sometimes contemplated physiological difference in terms of the endless and marvelous variety of forms, as in Ambroise Paré's *Of Monsters and Marvels* (1573), where "monsters" encompassed "conjoined twins, giraffes [and] hermaphrodites" and "became an index of Nature's fancy."[6] But the development of scientific discourse sought to explain and control extraordinariness in rational terms, from Francis Bacon's 1620 call to catalog "all prodigies and monstrous births of nature" to the actual catalog published in the 1830s by Isidore Geoffroy Saint-Hilaire.[7]

This developing view of bodily difference as a scientific and medical problem was consolidated in the nineteenth century, when the rise of statistical science established people with disabilities as biological deviations from a valorized norm.[8] Medical and scientific gazes construed external differences as empirical signs of the otherwise "ephemeral and intangible workings of the interior body," while pseudosciences such as physiognomy viewed "visible aberrancy and irregularity as indicative of moral nature."[9] Such approaches cemented what disability scholars have called the "medical model," which regards impairment as a pathology or flaw within an individual, requiring diagnosis and, if possible, cure or amelioration. As this perspective took hold, disabled people became problems in the medical world and objects of fear or pity beyond it.

In order to redress both ancient cultural stereotypes and the powerful medical model, disability activists and scholars have in recent decades drawn attention to the multiple, diverse, and unstable status of disability. Rosemarie Garland-Thomson has defined disability as

> an overarching and in some ways artificial category that encompasses congenital and acquired physical differences, mental illness and retardation, chronic and acute illnesses, fatal and progressive diseases, temporary and permanent injuries, and a wide range of bodily characteristics considered disfiguring, such as scars, birthmarks, unusual proportions, or obesity.

Rather than viewing these varied conditions as fixed and material facts, Garland-Thomson points out that disabilities are "never absolute or static," as they "fluctuat[e] over time," and "everyone is subject to the gradually disabling process of aging."[10] Further, activists and analysts promote a "social model" in which disability is seen not as a fixed quality inhering in specific bodies but as a *product* of the relationship between, on the one hand, individual bodies that have some kind of impairment and, on the other, often discriminatory societal, cultural, and environmental structures.[11] In other words, disability is often in the eye of the beholder. Accordingly, Lennard Davis presents disability as an interruption of culturally constructed and normalizing ways of seeing, "a disruption in the visual, auditory, or perceptual field as it relates to the power of the gaze."[12]

Representations of unusual bodies may thus reveal more about an era's cultural norms and self-image than they do about disabled individuals, even as they inevitably shape the latter's experiences and perceptions. David T. Mitchell and Sharon L. Snyder point out that in literary, cultural, and political texts, images of "[p]hysical and cognitive anomalies promise to lend a 'tangible' body to textual abstractions," through a process they call "the materiality of metaphor."[13] They refer to Antoine de Baecque's argument that in French Revolution–era cartoons, metaphors of disability conveyed "social and individual collapse." De Baecque writes, "bodily *topoi* —the degeneracy of the nobility, the impotence of the king, the herculean strength of the citizenry . . . the congenital deformity of the aristocrats, the bleeding wound of the martyrs—allowed political society to represent itself at a pivotal moment of its history." He continues, "One must pass through the [bodily] forms of a narrative in order to reach knowledge.[14] As Mitchell and Snyder note, while such corporeality appears to give validity and vitality to intangible historical formations, it also "embeds the body [and particularly the disabled body] within a limiting array of symbolic meanings."[15] Markers of deformity and woundedness are at once denigrated counterpoints to idealized or normative bodies and a means of access—at least for the nondisabled—to revelation, truth, and enlightenment.

Similarly, cultural narratives often use disability to generate a plot that ultimately reasserts and values normalcy. Lennard Davis writes of the novel, "From the typicality of the central character, to the normalizing devices of plot to bring deviant characters back into the norms of society, to the normalizing coda of endings, the nineteenth- and twentieth-century novel promulgates and disburses notions of normalcy and by extension makes of physical differences ideological differences."[16] Mitchell and Snyder present a similar conventional narrative structure dependent on normalization: difference is exposed, explained, and rehabilitated, often through cure, rescue, or extermination.[17] For example, in Hans Christian Andersen's *The Steadfast Tin Soldier*, the title character's missing leg generates the story, but his defective figure cannot exist beyond the conclusion, where his owner throws him onto a fire. Disability thus offers what Mitchell and Snyder call a "narrative prosthesis," "a crutch on which literary narratives lean for representational power, disruptive potentiality, and analytical insight" while "rarely taking up disability as an experience of social or political dimensions."[18] The overriding effect of such narratives is to strengthen and secure a norm: Davis asserts, "Normality has to protect itself by looking into the maw of disability and recovering from that glance."[19]

Accordingly, a disability-studies analysis operates in two directions at the same time—on the one hand, demanding consideration of the identities embedded in disabled bodies and, on the other, embracing disability as a shifting term that often eludes normative efforts to explain and contain it.[20] Careful study of bodily metaphors can thus uncover both the oppression of those marginalized due to physical or psychological impairment and the occasional incoherence or failure of efforts to naturalize dominant perspectives via disability tropes. Mitchell and Snyder contend that if we understand the literary as something *prosthetic*, which proffers our deficient bodies "the illusion of a fix upon the material world that they cannot deliver," certain textual uses of disability can also provide an "*accomplishment of a faulty, or at least imperfect, prosthetic function*" which "*make[s] the prosthesis show . . . [,] flaunt[s] its imperfect supplementation as an illusion.*"[21] Ato Quayson, building on these concepts, claims that "disability's rapid oscillation between a pure process of abstraction and a set of material conditions" generates an "aesthetic nervousness" in texts that is "coextensive with the nervousness regarding the disabled in the real world" and that inscribes in representations of disability "an ethical dimension that cannot be easily subsumed under the aesthetic structure." Consequently, certain representations call attention to and disrupt aesthetic uses of disability to anchor normative concepts of "wholeness" and "beauty," "thus holding out the possibility that the nondisabled may ultimately be brought to recognize the sources of the constructedness of the normate and the prejudices that flow from it."[22] We can take from these perspectives a dual focus on both the meanings attributed by expert and popular discourses to disability in a given historic and cultural moment and the failures of such discourses to render disability a static, explicable, and controllable entity. In particular, fictional uses of disability imagery—like those found in classic horror films—may "flaunt" the disability fictions that underwrite social privilege and inequality.

*Hideous Progeny* considers eugenics as a specific disability "fiction" or discourse. In keeping with its early-twentieth-century moment, eugenics developed a particular, pathological interpretation of visible or diagnosed impairments, casting disability as a matter of organic deviance requiring a medical or scientific fix, and extending this pathologization to other minority groups. Eugenics relied heavily on disability rhetoric, using imagery of visible impairment to concretize abstract concepts and authenticate processes of genetic heredity that could not, in the early twentieth century, be visualized or easily understood. It also used disability to construct a normalizing narrative, repeatedly iterating and describing imperfection, debility, and deviance in order to envisage and validate the "happy ending" of racial and species perfection. Classic horror films, in "flaunting" such eugenic and dysgenic imaginings, reveal eugenics' disability discourse as perverse and unstable, traversed by superstitious and unscientific concepts it claimed to have left behind, and obsessively fascinated with the deviance it claimed to abhor.

## EUGENICS

In the nineteenth century, medical and pathological narratives about disability served specific intellectual and social purposes. Social Darwinism, for instance, adapted Charles Darwin's evolutionary views to envisage species progression toward physical, intellectual, and cultural perfection. It used the notion of the "survival of the fittest" to justify social and economic inequalities as natural and beneficial to humanity and to imagine progression as the continued flourishing of social, economic, and racial elites over the savagery of "primitive" races and ethnicities.[23] But, according to the era's "degeneration theory," this proper course of development was under threat. Degeneration theory began as a pre-Darwinian notion that certain environments would lead inevitably to the weakening of species and thus coincided with the theory of Jean-Baptiste Lamarck that acquired conditions might be passed along to offspring. Post-Darwin, the idea of degeneration developed as an anxious underside to social Darwinism, its proponents arguing that the effects of civilization, industrialization, and modernization might in fact be weakening so-called superior races and classes. Evidence of such decay appeared in increasing rates of criminality, pauperism, and disease. Degeneration theorists imagined such damage becoming permanent and hereditary, producing increasing numbers of congenital degenerates and placing humans on a path of evolutionary regression toward physiological and social dysfunction.[24]

Disability tropes were central to this dark narrative and to proposed solutions that might protect the "natural" preeminence of the ruling class. The image of the degenerating, animalistic body legitimated the otherwise diffuse and abstract concept of degeneration. Witness criminal anthropologist Cesare Lombroso contemplating the skull of brigand Guiseppe Villela:

This was not merely an idea, but a revelation. At the sight of that skull, I seemed to see all of a sudden, lighted up as a vast plain under a flaming sky, the problem of the nature of the criminal—an atavistic being who reproduces in his person the ferocious instincts of primitive humanity and the inferior animals. Thus were explained anatomically the enormous jaws, high cheek bones, prominent superciliary arches, solitary lines in the palms, extreme size of the orbits, handle-shaped ears found in criminals, savages and apes, insensibility to pain, extremely acute sight, tattooing, excessive idleness, love of orgies, and the irresponsible craving of evil for its own sake, the desire not only to extinguish life in the victim, but to mutilate the corpse, tear its flesh and drink its blood.[25]

The pathological skull produces a horrific story of murder, corpse mutilation, and cannibalism, a social disruption resolved by the criminal's execution and autopsy. The skull ostensibly proves Lombroso's theory that criminal and immoral behavior are prompted by atavism or evolutionary regression; it is, he says, "not merely an idea" but fact, "revealed" in bone, facial features, and personality traits. Lombroso asserted that certain physical characteristics pointed to degeneracy and argued that those thus deemed congenitally deviant should be incarcerated or executed: consequently, the skull also anchors a broad pseudoscientific narrative bent on analyzing countless skulls, faces, and bodies in order to contain the degenerate threat they encode, reaffirm social norms, and secure species advancement.[26] In this way, Lombrosian science "passes through" bodily forms, quite literally looking into the "maw of disability" in order to consolidate its expert status and maintain social hierarchies.

Such narratives interpreted social, economic, and cultural factors in biological terms, asserting that recognition and tracking of visible and behavioral traits could enable the protection and improvement of humanity's "best." The development of eugenics in the nineteenth century upheld such notions but eschewed Lamarckianism, envisaging sexual reproduction as the singular determinative factor in biological merit. Francis Galton, Charles Darwin's cousin and the "father" of eugenics, called on statistical science to quantify physical, intellectual, and social attributes in books such as *Hereditary Genius* (1869), *Inquiries into Human Faculty and Its Development* (1883), and *Essays in Eugenics* (1909). He argued that "genius" and intelligence were hereditary and that accomplished individuals, families, and classes must multiply more rapidly to advance the human species. In *Inquiries*, he adapted the Greek term *eugenes*, meaning "good in stock, hereditarily endowed with noble qualities," to coin "eugenics," as "the science of improving stock . . . which, especially in the case of man, takes cognisance of all influences that tend in however remote a degree to give to the more suitable races or strains of blood a better chance of prevailing speedily over the less suitable than they otherwise would have had."[27]

Reduced to tracking heredity through external appearances and social accomplishments, Galton's eugenics could not fathom how traits were in fact passed on. But significant genetic discoveries were just around the corner: the work of German biologist August Weismann, for instance, displaced notions of the inheritance of acquired characteristics, instead positing the "germ plasm"—or gene—as the key to evolution and biological inheritance, while Austrian monk Gregor Mendel's 1865 paper on his experiments with sweet peas, rediscovered at the turn of the century, debunked the idea that parental characteristics were evenly blended in their offspring, instead noting the particularity of inherited traits and uncovering the work of dominant and recessive genes. These insights validated the idea of an innate biological force determining external characteristics and behaviors and would, in the United States, combine with Galton's call for manipulations of reproductive choices to form a specifically American eugenics.[28]

Notions of certain groups as biologically defective had circulated in the United States long before eugenics' official consolidation. Slavery had been justified on the grounds that African Americans were either less than human or degraded humans; in the late nineteenth century, post-slavery Jim Crow laws both punished and reproduced such perceived biological inferiority. From the 1880s, regional "ugly laws" depicted "unsightly" individuals as threats to the health and equilibrium of normal Americans, requiring that they remove themselves from public sight.[29] In 1883, Alexander Bell confirmed the self-evidently undesirable nature of disability, using his studies of deafness in Martha's Vineyard to posit deafness as a hereditary condition and to suggest that deaf people avoid marriage and procreation with one another.[30] In 1896, Connecticut legislated a similar sentiment, banning the legal union of "epileptic, imbecile, or feeble-minded" individuals in cases where the woman was of reproductive age.[31] In the same period, organizations opposed to the immigration of certain ethnic groups began to call for literacy tests, a move that anticipated eugenic justifications of ethnic discrimination on the grounds of intellectual inferiority.[32]

These instances reflected a growing sense that innate biological defects rendered certain people "unfit" for reproduction, that such defects were either obvious or could be elucidated through careful study, and that their bearers could justifiably be excluded from the public sphere and the national body. Several eugenic organizations were formed with the mission of identifying and eventually controlling the reproduction of such "defectives." In 1903, Harvard biologist Charles Davenport urged the American Breeders' Association (ABA) to establish a committee on eugenics, calling on its members to extend concerns with quality animal husbandry to human propagation. In 1904, Davenport became director of the Station for Experimental Evolution at Cold Spring Harbor, Long Island, an institution funded by the Carnegie Institution and focused on experiments in plant and animal breeding. In 1909, Davenport established the Eugenics Record Office (ERO), which, along with entities such as the Eugenics Research Association, the Michigan-based Race Betterment Foundation, the New York–based Galton Society, and the American Eugenics Society (AES), became the organizational face of American eugenics, at least until the closing of the ERO in 1939.[33]

The notion that a range of social ills could be explained in terms of genetic defect and contained by reproductive controls appealed to some of America's most influential scholarly and philanthropic figures. Eugenic associations counted among their members and supporters President Theodore Roosevelt, inventor Alexander Graham Bell, ichthyologist and Stanford University president David Starr Jordan, psychologist Henry Goddard, lawyer and naturalist Madison Grant, historian Lothrop Stoddard, sociologist Henry Pratt Fairchild, director of the American Museum of Natural History Henry Fairfield Osborn, and the ERO's managing director Harry Hamilton Laughlin, who eventually became an adviser to the House Committee on Immigration and Naturalization. The status of eugenics as a respected scientific enterprise was assisted by high-profile publications of monographs and articles in scientific and medical journals and by the presentation of eugenic concepts at medical conferences. Eugenic funding derived from wealthy and prestigious Americans such as the Carnegies, the Rockefellers, Mrs. E. H. Harriman, and cereal magnate John Harvey Kellogg. Thanks to such powerful support, eugenic ideas influenced federal and state legislation and permeated America's public sphere, appearing in town hall lectures, State Fair displays, school textbooks, university courses, newspaper columns, and even the scouting movement.

The eugenic doctrine so attractive to these notable Americans held that species and "racial" advancement depended on improving the nation's genetic health by propagating some kinds of bodies and delimiting the reproduction of others. Davenport's book *Heredity in Relation to Eugenics* (1911) defined eugenics as "the science of the improvement of the human race by better breeding."[34] Davenport explained that human traits were shaped by the presence or absence of certain genetic "unit characters" determined at conception, some of which produced positive or valuable traits while others inclined their bearers to congenital disease or debility. He wrote,

> The general program of the eugenist is clear—it is to improve the race by inducing young people to make a more reasonable selection of marriage mates—to fall in love intelligently. It also includes the control by the state of the propagation of the mentally incompetent. . . . It is the province of the new science of eugenics to study the laws of inheritance of human traits and, as these laws are ascertained, to make them known. There is no doubt that when such laws are clearly formulated many certainly unfit matings will be avoided and other fit matings that have been shunned through false scruples will be happily contracted." (*Heredity in Relation to Eugenics*, 4–5)

The ERO studied these "laws of inheritance" by training field workers to collect family pedigrees in order to track the surfacing or disappearance of particular traits within families. In this way, its founders hoped to uncover the workings of genetic determination and guide marital and reproductive practices. "Positive" eugenics used such data to publicize eugenic understandings of genetic heredity, critique the low birth rates of the "fit," and call on them to produce more children in the name of racial and national health. "Negative" eugenics used such data to support marital restrictions for those with conditions deemed genetically transmissible; justify the institutionalization and sterilization of individuals deemed feebleminded, criminal, degenerate, or otherwise deviant; support immigration restrictions against ethnic groups of ostensibly inferior stock; and underwrite anti-miscegenation laws, preventing a racial mixing considered damaging to the "fit."

Officially, eugenicists distinguished inner, genetic determiners from external and visible traits. Davenport warned, "A person who by all physical and mental examinations is normal may lack in half of his germ cells the determiner for complete mental development. . . . [N]o-one transmits to his progeny his somatic traits but rather the determiners in his germ plasm."[35] Still, since eugenicists could not see the gene, they had to deduce its presence, absence, or nature from genealogies that cataloged external and behavioral features across generations. At least one scholar notes a persistent faith in expert bodily interpretations: writes Marouf Hasian of the ERO's field-workers, "After a few weeks' training, [they] were thought to be able to tell at a glance whether someone had pure or tainted germplasm."[36]

Eugenic rhetoric thus remained dependent on the body exterior as a powerful "material metaphor" for mysterious genetic processes. The desirable stock of the "fit" was imagined in terms of whiteness, beauty, and physical fitness; embodied in the winners of the AES's "Better Babies" and "Fitter Families" competitions; invoked in books like Madison Grant's *The Passing of the Great Race* (1916), which described the progenitors of good American stock as "splendid conquistadores" of Nordic heritage with "absolutely fair skin" and "great stature"; and visualized in eugenic displays.[37] One such exhibit, at the American Museum of Natural History, portrayed "Our Face from Fish to Man," tracing "the evolution of the human face" through "sharks, reptiles, mammals, and apes," up to an "Australian bushman," peaking with "a faux marble bust of the Apollo Belvedere" meant to represent civilized man in the form of white "Nordic" Americans.[38] The 1921 Second International Congress of Eugenics also celebrated the ideal American with classical sculpture, featuring "a statue of a composite athlete sculpted from the measurements of the '50 strongest men of Harvard.'"[39]

This idealized eugenic body translated well to the mass media. As Snyder and Mitchell have noted, it coincided with the era's developing commodity culture, which promoted products with "legions of chubby white baby faces and athletic specimens from the physical culture craze of the early twentieth century. . . . These images of Caucasian wholesomeness functioned at all levels of mass-market culture as signs of racial purity and idealized national body types free of blemishes, defects, variations, or vulnerabilities."[40] The worship of bodily perfection suffused eugenically themed articles, like a 1922 New York newspaper piece headlined "Union of the Splendidly Developed Dancer Ruth St. Denis and Edwin Shawn, 'the Handsomest Man in America,' May Produce Results of Great Value to the Science of Race Betterment." Featuring images of the couple in dance poses, the article declared that their status as "almost perfect specimens of humanity" rendered the marriage of interest to "eugenic science, the science of rearing a finer race." It described in detail St. Denis's "beautiful figure" and "cultivation of her body" and Shawn's "manly beauty, . . . exquisitely graceful and symmetrical pair of legs, . . . [and] small but well proportioned head with regular features and a broad, smooth brow." Citing Davenport and his aim to "eliminate physical defects by preventing people from making marriages likely to perpetuate them," the text was more open than the eugenicist in embracing a physiognomic logic, insisting, "The perpetuation of physical beauty and health is one of the chief aims of eugenic science, being more important than any attempt to transmit special mental qualities. Investigation shows that children of fine physical development will, as a rule, be of superior mental attainments, as mental ability is usually associated with good physical stock." "[P]hysical beauty and health" were thus exalted as signs of worthy genetic material.[41]

These images of a better human species represented by white, attractive, and able bodies were irrevocably tied to visions of the lesser bodies that supposedly threatened racial advance: the non-Nordic immigrants disparaged by Grant; the "Australian bushman" contrasted to the Apollo Belvedere; the "defective" members of what the St. Denis article described, perhaps a little tongue-in-cheek, as "our poor, deformed race." Motivated by the belief that "[s]ociety must protect itself; as it claims the right to deprive the murderer of his life, so also it may annihilate the hideous serpent of hopeless protoplasm," official eugenics directed much of its energy toward identifying, representing in monstrous terms, and seeking to control the agglomerate body of America's and the world's "unfit."[42]

Eugenic doctrine and propaganda thus took up and augmented nineteenth-century medicalization and pathologization of unusual bodies and minds. In 1911, Laughlin and other ABA eugenic committee members developed a plan for "purging the blood of the American people of the handicapping and deteriorating influences of these anti-social classes," imagining the containment and eventual elimination of, as summarized by Edwin Black, "First, the feebleminded; second, the pauper class; third, the inebriate class or alcoholics; fourth, criminals of all descriptions including petty criminals and those jailed for nonpayment of fines; fifth, epileptics; sixth, the insane; seventh, the constitutionally weak class; eighth, those predisposed to specific diseases; ninth, the deformed; tenth, those with defective sense organs, that is, the deaf, blind and mute."[43] In selecting such groups as candidates for institutionalization and sterilization, the committee foregrounded the defective status of those with evident and ostensibly congenital conditions, including intellectual disability, epilepsy, mental illness, "weakness" or disease, deformity, and sensory impairments. Eugenicists cast the bearers of such impairments as costly burdens to the rest of America. In 1916, E. R. Johnstone declaimed, in his National Conference of Charities and Correction address, "When we view the number of the feeble-minded, their fecundity, and their lack of control, the menace they are, the degradation they cause, the degeneracy they perpetuate, the suffering and misery and crime they spread,—these are the burden we must bear."[44] Similarly, opthamologist Lucien Howe depicted blind people as useless, burdensome, and costly: "Now how much do these people cost us? . . . If we suppose that each one of them lives on the average of about 30 years that gives us a total of at least $37 millions to each generation. Now, who pays that money? When reduced to the best analysis you and I help to do so."[45] In arguing for having couples pay a bond if they produced blind progeny, Howe suggested this strategy as more palatable to the public than restrictions on racial or economic classes because "the blind constitut[e] a *natural* class in the eyes of the law."[46] This statement positions people with disabilities as the "natural" targets of eugenic measures; Howe also called for bonding couples against producing "insane or epileptic children."[47]

But eugenics was not content with identifying and controlling those already generally viewed as physiologically defective. As the ABA's categories suggest, eugenics mapped the purportedly obvious stigma of inherited defect, as "revealed" in visible disability, onto other "inferior" figures, including "criminals," "paupers," immigrants, and non-white people. The infamous early-twentieth-century "family studies," for instance, enumerated the troublesome traits of extensive family groups, such as the "Jukes" and the "Kallikaks," in impoverished rural areas, conflating instances of criminality, alcoholism, prostitution, and other "deviant" behaviors under the label of "feeblemindedness." Antisocial behaviors and IQ test results that often reflected poverty, lack of education, and low cultural status were viewed as signs of genetically transmitted intellectual impairments that justified sterilization.[48] Rhetoric of physiological impairment was also employed to demonize prospective immigrants, especially those from southeastern and eastern Europe, who supposedly threatened the "Nordic" stock of America's "best" classes. Madison Grant's *The Passing of the Great Race* (1916) asserted, "The great lesson of the science of race is the immutability of somatological or bodily characters, with which is closely associated the immutability of psychical predispositions and impulses." Accordingly, Grant associated racial "inferiority" with external (physical) and internal (moral, psychological, and intellectual) weakness, contending that since the Civil War, immigration to the United States had consisted of "a large and increasing number of the weak, the broken and the mentally crippled of all races," and declaring of the Mediterranean subspecies, "The stature is stunted in comparison to that of the Nordic race and the musculature and bony framework weak."[49] Eugenicists similarly used tropes of physical impairment to deplore race mixing; counter to research indicating that hybrid plants might be more vigorous, Davenport insisted that mixed-race progeny would be physically disharmonious:

he imagined the physical disastrousness of large teeth in a small jaw and worried that the combination of the "Negro's" long legs and white people's short arms would force those of mixed race "to stoop more to pick up a thing on the ground.'" He concluded elsewhere that "a hybridized people are a badly put together people and a dissatisfied, restless, ineffective people."[50]

Thus, eugenic efforts to control the unfit elaborated the disabling interpretations typically imposed on those with physical or sensory impairments, intellectual disability, or mental illness, projecting them also onto criminals, paupers, and certain ethnic and racial groups. Grant imagined a sterilization program that would begin with homegrown undesirables and extend ever outward: "This is a practical, merciful, and inevitable solution of the whole problem, and can be applied to an ever widening circle of social discards, beginning always with the criminal, the diseased and the insane, and extending gradually to types which may be called weaklings rather than defectives, and perhaps ultimately to worthless race types."[51] Such rhetoric took tangible form: many states passed anti-miscegenation statutes and prevented the marriage of people with certain conditions; medical professionals commonly authorized the long-term institutionalization of those deemed "feebleminded" or "insane," as well as those with blindness, epilepsy, and deafness; the 1924 Immigration Act fulfilled eugenic hopes for a diminishing of non-white and non-"Nordic" immigration; and the right of individual states to forcibly sterilize certain "defectives" was affirmed in the 1927 Supreme Court decision upholding Virginia's compulsory sterilization of Carrie Buck. Indeed, although eugenics' most extreme visions of population control did not eventuate in the United States, and although the "hardline" version of eugenics became increasingly discredited in the 1930s and was publicly replaced by a more moderate and environmental eugenic discourse, legalized compulsory sterilization continued as late as the 1970s (Lombardo 250).[52]

Eugenic discourse and practice in the first decades of the twentieth century thus exploited the ostensibly natural negative responses of "normal" Americans toward bodily and behavioral dysfunction to legitimate social and reproductive controls on various minority groups. In subsequent decades, activists and cultural critics challenging such racial, class, and ethnic oppressions—and other identity-based discrimination—have often similarly presumed the "natural" status of disability and fought to separate themselves from its material and degraded realm. Write Mitchell and Snyder,

As feminist, race, and sexuality studies sought to unmoor their identities from debilitating physical and cognitive associations, they inevitably positioned disability as the "real" limitation from which they must escape. . . . Formerly denigrated identities are "rescued" by understanding gendered, racial, and sexual differences as textually produced, distancing them from the "real" of physical or cognitive aberrancy projected onto their figures.[53]

Such strategies also appear in eugenic histories. For instance, Black writes, "The genuinely lame, insane and deformed were lumped in with the troubled, the unfortunate, the disadvantaged and those who were simply 'different,' thus creating a giant eugenic underclass simply labeled 'the unfit.'" He continues, "The eugenically damning classification [of feeblemindedness] certainly included genuine cases of severely retarded individuals who could not care for themselves, but it also swept up those who were simply shy, stuttering, poor at English, or otherwise generally nonverbal, regardless of their true intellect or talent."[54] These statements suggest that some subjects of the eugenic gaze were "genuinely" feebleminded or degenerate, perhaps appropriately located in the "unfit" underclass, while others were simply wrongly "swept up" by this classification. They thus replicate eugenic abjection of people with impairments and elide the fact that "actual" impairment, just like race or sex, can rarely be neatly and objectively separated from the textual and cultural constructions we are calling "disability." In this light, eugenics is a discursive machine that "produces" disability out of ethnic, racial, and class identities *in the same way* as it—like other pathologizing discourses—produce disability out of the identities and bodies of people with particular impairments.

To this extent, *Hideous Progeny* is interested in eugenic representations that might reveal the "produced" status of disability, both as historical documents that re-view eugenics as an unstable and incoherent discourse *and* as cultural texts that remind contemporary audiences of our continuing investments in and constructions of disability. For instance, since eugenic rhetoric legitimated itself with images of physical and visible aberrance in the popular sphere, we might expect that it also found a home in the cinema of the early twentieth century. In film, it would seem, eugenics could realize its visual logic, dramatizing through corporeal signs the ideal and deviant bodies on which its normalizing narrative depended. But cinematic eugenic propaganda was less than successful, with its explicit visualization making audience members uncomfortable not only with defective bodies—a discomfort eugenic films actively elicited—but also with eugenics itself. Thus, it is in the cinema that eugenic propaganda most dramatically *failed* in using dysgenic images to mobilize public support for negative eugenic practices. The story of the movie *The Black Stork* (1916) illuminates this public distaste for the eugenic drama, with responses indicating Americans' reluctance to take up a properly eugenic perspective on disabled figures. At the same time, the re-categorization of *The Black Stork* as a medical film registers Americans' willingness to allow eugenics to flourish out of the public view. Eugenic films of the 1910s and 1920s thus connect eugenic discourse to the 1930s horror film, which drags eugenic themes and images, costumed in fictional and sensationalistic form, back into the cinematic light.

## EUGENICS AT THE MOVIES

Like literary texts, films often depend on the elucidation and eventual destruction of disability. Genre films, in particular, present a formulaic narrative that indicates an established order, traces its disruption by some kind of deviance, and follows the typically successful effort to contain or destroy that deviance and restore order.[55] Such social or personal disruptions are often manifested in bodily form; the melodramas of early cinema, in particular, often relied on a physiognomic logic in which appearance reflected character and in which expressions and actions transparently conveyed thoughts, emotions, and motivations. Such conventions resonated with eugenic efforts to read exterior features as signs of innate genetic value.

And eugenic themes did find their way to American screens in the early twentieth century, in productions such as *Heredity* (1912), *The Second Generation* (1914), *Inherited Sin* (1915), and *The Black Stork*, aka *Are You Fit to Marry?* (1916, rereleased 1927).[56] *The Black Stork* (dir. Leopold and Theodor Wharton, Sherriot Pictures) was, as Martin Pernick's extensive study of the film informs us, "the most explicit depiction of negative eugenics to reach the silent screen." It was produced by Chicago surgeon Harry Haiselden to promote his practice of allowing disabled infants to die, an act for which he had received support from prominent eugenicists such as Davenport and Irving Fisher.[57] The movie depicts an engaged couple, Claude (Hamilton Revelle) and Anne (Elsie Esmond), who proceed with marriage despite being advised against it by a doctor, played by Haiselden himself. Because Claude carries a hereditary flaw, the couple subsequently produces a "defective" newborn; the doctor recommends they allow the child to die. As the mother agonizes over this decision, *The Black Stork* reveals the horror of a life of disability by presenting several disabled patients as "cripples" and anticipating for the newborn a life of crime and misery. The film, as its title indicates, also links physical and racial "inferiority," tracing the child's defect to his great-grandfather's sexual liaison with a slave woman. Swayed by this vision, Anne acquiesces to the baby's death. The doctor allows the boy to die, and "the infant's tiny soul leaps into the arms of a waiting Jesus."[58]

Haiselden's film displayed bodily impairment to make viewers shudder and thus, he hoped, to convince them of eugenics' validity. His appeal to the visible aligned with his belief that corporeal difference transparently registered inner, innate deviance. He initially asserted that the physical features and X-rays of an infant he had allowed to die did in fact indicate neurological damage, later contending more broadly "that virtually all physical defects were associated with eventual mental and moral defects, due either to common underlying hereditary causes or to the psychological effects of social ostracism," a belief supported by the film's contention that "[u]nhealthy bodies often cause unhealthy minds." While Pernick argues that Haiselden's physical and aesthetic judgments, aimed toward a mass audience, were at odds with eugenics' "professional leadership" and its focus on mental and intellectual health, the bodily rhetoric of eugenicists noted above suggests that Haiselden's film simply used visual media to press this logic (Pernick 72, 73).

But the public did not respond as Haiselden might have hoped. As Pernick shows, the film's melodramatic stories made space for interpretations that exceeded or undermined the eugenic narrative. While "Anne's horrifying vision of her future grandchildren and the prologue's assortment of social deviants portray a repulsive and menacing army of subhumans," during the representation of "individual real patients, their brave hopes and shy smiles at the camera convey an immediately appealing humanity." In addition, the adult version of Anne and Claude's child, played by Henry Bergman, is a "noble" and "appealingly human" figure, suffering in the face of social prejudice. The representation of abstract degeneracy in particular individuals thus interfered with the eugenic message: the New York State Motion Picture division disparaged the film in part for its "'inhuman' attitude towards infants" (122). Pernick finds that eugenic films' use of "individual heroes and villains" to personalize "the impersonal laws of science" "reinforced key ambiguities in the progressive health message," notably "the internal contradiction in the progressives' faith that science could be both impersonally objective and a source of moral imperatives" (146). The film also provided mixed messages about the role of economic structures and social attitudes in shaping disability. In its class politics, it both traced disease and deformity back to "the poor" and implied that class structures were at fault. In its disability narrative, it both presented the "defective" child's impairment as determinative and showed that "it's only after he leaves his mother's loving home for a hostile, rejecting world that his physical handicaps lead to crime and insanity" (145–46, 149).

Such contradictory readings reflected popular eugenic views that diffused or deviated from the official eugenic message, often mitigating its biological focus with reference to environmental and social influences. For instance, a 1913 newspaper notice about a Harlem Baptist church's eugenic classes listed topics including "the meaning of eugenics, the origin of species, influences of heredity, the business of marriage, sex hygiene, the social evil, and the rearing of a family."[59] Some eugenics-themed articles often offered "advice on marriage, divorce, and most importantly, how to deal with race poisons" such as alcohol or tobacco, intuiting eugenicists' own uncertainties about the congenital status of alcoholism and addiction.[60] Others construed eugenics as encompassing a responsible approach to child-rearing, "scientifically protecting children against getting anything bad from their parents, and assuring that parents gave their children nothing but the best."[61] Moreover, 1920s and 1930s newspaper articles often critiqued eugenic interventions. In 1927 a columnist in Portland's *News* asserted, "Eugenics is all right—if you wish to breed a fine race of animals—but if you wish to breed a race of brainy people—the best way is to leave it to old Dame Nature . . . who loves the poor—and makes great men and women of their children." In 1928 the San Francisco *Call* declared, "The humblest, least impressive human may be the father or mother of genius and of power. . . . The important thing is real affection between husband and wife." In the same year, the Minneapolis *Evening Tribune* contested eugenic conflation of class status and biological worth, concluding that some of the nation's good germ plasm "may be blacking boots today on a Staten Island ferry boat or running a short order restaurant in El Reno."[62] Accordingly, *The Black Stork*'s perhaps inadvertent representation of disabled characters as sympathetic individuals damaged largely by social prejudice spoke to popular discomfort with eugenic dramatization of particular "types" as biologically doomed to misery, criminality, and deviance.

*The Black Stork*'s intended propagandistic effects were also thwarted by the very disgust and repulsion toward deformed bodies that it wanted to elicit. Writes Pernick, "while many critics praised its educational and social value, they found it aesthetically unacceptable," variously describing it as "grim," "unpleasant," "repulsive," and "repellent." The *Chicago Tribune* declared it "as pleasant to look at as a running sore," and *Photoplay* considered the screenplay "so slimy that it reminds us of nothing save the residue of a capital operation." In late 1916 the National Board of Review of Motion Pictures polled community leaders, several of whom concluded that anyone who wanted to see such films "must be sick, suffering from a 'morbid' perversion of the aesthetic senses." Pernick asserts, "These film regulators and censors shared the eugenic desire to pathologize ugliness, but they feared that displaying ugly diseases would only create diseased audiences." Like Joy, who conflated horror films with their gruesome characters to suggest both as deviant, critics of *The Black Stork* projected onto the film the disgust they were supposed to feel in response to its deformed bodies. Consequently, the National Board concluded that *The Black Stork* was suited only for medical audiences.[63]

The censorship of a eugenic film might appear to be an anti-eugenic act. But the National Board's decision construed impaired bodies and their visual representation as naturally disturbing to normal Americans, reflected concerns that the circulation of such bodies and images could damage national health, and worked to segregate such bodies and images within the medical sphere. It thus confirmed both eugenic films and disabled bodies as entities that belonged under expert scrutiny and control. The decision also circumvented the discomforting possibility that viewers were most unsettled not by the naturally repulsive forms of disabled figures but rather, thanks to the sympathy these figures elicited, by the horrific ugliness of eugenics itself. This possibility suggests a certain potency in the cinematic rendition of the eugenic vision, an illumination of cultural prejudice that attaches to the eugenic image and narrative, threatening its coherence and legitimacy by mingling sympathy with disgust and nurture with nature.[64]

The containment of *The Black Stork* in the medical realm effectively consolidated, rather than diminished, eugenic powers. Pernick argues that the film's censorship led to a firmer distinction between educational, medical, and social films, on the one hand, and entertainment films, on the other. Reflecting this shift, new film standards designed in 1918 by the Pennsylvania State Board of Censors "barred virtually all unpleasant aspects of medicine from the commercial screen. . . . Medical films were targeted not just for their possible sexual content but for their aesthetic and emotional effects. The new standards banned any 'gruesome and unduly distressing scenes,' including 'surgical operations,' 'men dying,' or depictions of the 'insane.'" These censorial developments reflected a feeling in the American media that such topics were best left in the professional sphere: Pernick reports that the "*New York Times* strongly urged that nontreatment decisions [that is, the decision to withhold necessary treatment from sick infants] should be 'kept strictly within professional circles,' 'without the horrified exclamations of unenlightened sentimentality.'" Accordingly, he argues, overt eugenic and euthanasia themes virtually disappeared from mainstream films during the 1920s and 1930s, even as professional powers to intervene in the bodies and lives of the "unfit" continued to expand.[65] In 1927, the same year as an edited version of *The Black Stork* was rereleased under censorial restrictions, the Supreme Court affirmed the right of Virginia, and thus other states, to compulsorily sterilize "feebleminded" persons.[66] The lawyer defending Carrie Buck, the woman whose sterilization was at stake, warned, "A reign of doctors will be inaugurated and in the name of science new classes will be added, even races may be brought within the scope of such regulation, and the worst form of tyranny practiced."[67] While the public averted its gaze from eugenic cinema, then, its production and punishment of "monsters" flourished.

But while overtly eugenic films may have become less acceptable in the entertainment arena, eugenic themes and imagery continued to surface in other literary and cultural forms, including self-help texts, modernist literature, plays, and popular art.[68] *Hideous Progeny* contends that eugenic concepts are also evident in and, indeed, central to the classic horror genre that emerged a few years after the *Buck v. Bell* decision. The very images from medical films that concerned the Pennsylvania censors—scenes of men dying, surgical operations, and depictions of insanity—featured prominently in early 1930s films such as *Dracula*, *Frankenstein*, and *Dr. Jekyll and Mr. Hyde*. As we will see, horror films exhibited many of the same traits as the eugenic film: they displayed visibly aberrant bodies and monstrous behaviors; they did so in order to wreak aesthetic and emotional effects upon their viewers; and, as a result, they were often criticized and censored: the 1932 horror movie *Freaks* generated the same effort to police the line between medicine and entertainment, with the *New York Times* reviewer questioning whether the film "should be shown at the Rialto . . . or in, say, the Medical Centre."[69] Indeed, Pernick argues, some of the state censorship guidelines developed in response to eugenic films significantly shaped the Production Code that guided frequent censorship of horror films during the 1930s. These commonalities suggest that classic horrors catered to continuing voyeuristic desires to see disabled and unusual bodies while making the subject matter "safer," encasing it in overtly fictional and sometimes supernatural narratives. Joy's desire to censor such films out of existence echoed public discomfort with silent eugenic films, using a moralizing discourse to validate "natural" reactions of disgust to disability and to conceal not only images of disabled people and other marginalized groups but also eugenic constraints and violations of such people. In inscribing eugenics within the conventions of horror, then, classic horror films kept eugenic dramas in the public eye and encouraged viewers to look at both disabled bodies and the ugliness of eugenic rhetoric and practice.

## CLASSIC HORROR CINEMA

In her introduction to the 1831 edition of *Frankenstein*, Mary Shelley famously responded to her publishers' request for "some account of the origin of the story" by constructing a birth metaphor, in which she apparently conceived her story after reading scientific theories and absorbing scientific discussions between her husband, Percy, and Lord Byron.[70] At the moment of literary conception, Shelley experiences a waking dream in which she sees "the hideous phantasm of a man stretched out, and then, on the working of some powerful engine, show signs of life, and stir with an uneasy, half vital motion."[71] "[P]ossessed" and "haunted" by this image, Shelley eventually produces her story, and, in 1831, reproduces it: "And now, once again, I bid my hideous progeny go forth and prosper. I have an affection for it, for it was the offspring of happy days."[72] In construing her monster and her book as "hideous progeny," Shelley appears to minimize her own intellectual and creative powers, representing her authorship as the passive bearing of male ideas, while implying that to the extent that the book *is* her "progeny" it is also "hideous." Yet the introduction does not obediently confirm the powers of male creativity so much as it asserts the impossibility of recuperating a singular and authoritative source for either monster or text.[73] Shelley's words thus thwart desires for fixed origins and clear lines of descent, suggesting instead a collaborative and discursive inception. Her command that the text "go forth and prosper" also counters eugenic impulses, echoing the injunction to "go forth and multiply" and unleashing on the world her "hideous" and potent creature.[74]

Scholars, too, have developed an affection for the hideous monsters of Gothic fictions, suggesting that texts such as Shelley's *Frankenstein*, Bram Stoker's *Dracula*, Oscar Wilde's *The Picture of Dorian Gray*, and Robert Louis Stevenson's *The Strange Case of Dr. Jekyll and Mr. Hyde* powerfully and valuably explore complex cultural, psychological, and sexual dynamics. For example, Judith Halberstam argues that monstrosity in these texts is powerfully ambiguous because the monster's form, visualized only in the reader's imagination, conflates anxieties and pleasures related to multiple categories, including class, race, ethnicity, gender, sexuality, and nationality.

Gothic texts thus shed light on the cultural and political effort to contain and demonize difference in particular—raced, classed, or sexualized—bodies. These novels can also enable subversive affiliations with the monstrous Other ("We are disposed as readers to sympathize with [*Frankenstein*'s] monster because, unlike the characters in the novel, we cannot see him") and thus interrogate processes by which cultures construct others as monstrous.[75]

Such a reading might suggest that the classic horror genre, to the extent that it makes visual and visceral these Gothic fictions, would also be credited with embodying productive and potentially subversive cultural politics. Certainly, Colonel Joy seemed alarmed by the unsettling implications of the genre, and, if he hoped that some kind of intervention could forestall the flourishing of a new and "gruesome" genre, he was out of luck. By the time he wrote his memo, Gothic adaptations of *Dracula* and *Frankenstein* had already succeeded beyond all expectations at the box office, impelling the flurry of Universal movies that would make the studio the undisputed champion of horror-film production. Critics had listed *Frankenstein* as one of the top ten films of 1931, and in 1932, Paramount's *Dr. Jekyll and Mr. Hyde*, another Gothic-inspired film and one of the objects of Joy's concern, won Fredric March the Academy Award for Best Actor and earned nominations for its screenplay and cinematography.[76] The same year saw the arrival of the other films listed by Joy, *Freaks* and *Island of Lost Souls*, along with movies such as *The Mummy*, *Doctor X*, *Murders in the Rue Morgue*, *The Most Dangerous Game*, *White Zombie*, and *The Old Dark House*. The next four years welcomed many of the horror genre's most enduring classics, including *King Kong*, *The Mystery of the Wax Museum*, *Murders in the Zoo*, *The Invisible Man*, *The Black Cat*, *Mark of the Vampire*, *Mad Love*, *The Raven*, *Werewolf of London*, *Bride of Frankenstein*, *The Devil-Doll*, *Dracula's Daughter*, and *The Invisible Ray*. The horror film, like Shelley's monster, had gone forth and prospered.

But scholars have suggested that these movies do not, like Gothic texts, use monstrosity to interrogate cultural norms. Once the monster is visually depicted, Halberstam contends, it encounters a "limit of visibility," failing to accommodate ambiguous and multiple interpretations and undermining audience sympathy.[77] Thus, Chris Baldick writes of 1931's *Frankenstein* that "the story's several possibilities have been narrowed and reduced by the sheer visual impact of Karloff's performance."[78] Moreover, Halberstam asserts, the fact that the visualized monster "must always fail to be monstrous enough" requires the horror film to conjoin it with "the explicit violation of female bodies," thus construing the monster only in terms of savage or aberrant sexuality and failing to question social demonization of a *range* of identity categories.[79] Accordingly, the classic horror film is seen to restrain potential for social disruption in the visibly deformed body of a singular monster, to play out a titillating but temporary sexual threat to female bodies, and to conclude safely with the monster's expulsion and a return to social norms. Writes Isabel Pinedo, "The classical paradigm draws relatively clear boundaries between the contending camps of good and evil, normal and abnormal, and the outcome of the struggle almost invariably entails the destruction of the monster. Although boundary violations are at issue in classical horror, repairs can be effected. Good triumphs over evil; the social order is restored."[80]

This narrative conservatism has long been used in categorizing the "classic" horror genre in opposition to later "modern" or "postmodern" developments. Some believe that the horror genre's truly classic era concluded by 1936 due to the effects of increased censorship, diminished budgets, and a change in ownership at Universal.[81] Others extend this period to 1938's popular double-bill rerelease of *Dracula* and *Frankenstein* or to the 1939 debut of *Son of Frankenstein* (dir. Rowland V. Lee, Universal), events that helped secure the vampire and Frankenstein's monster an enduring place in the American imagination.[82] Still others mark the classic era's conclusion in the mid-1940s, incorporating the many horror sequels and B movies of the first part of that decade.[83] But many critics are most concerned with distinguishing what Andrew Tudor calls the "secure" horror film, in which normalcy is restored, from the "paranoid" or postmodern horror film, where monstrosity comes to permeate and define "normalcy."[84] Such a distinction extends the classic period into the 1960s, with postmodern horror films typically dated from *Psycho* (1960) or *Night of the Living Dead* (1968).

Later "postmodern" horror films are often validated as complex, progressive, and less reassuringly conservative than their classic precursors. Robin Wood argues that "apocalyptic" movies such as *The Texas Chain Saw Massacre* (1974) locate horror less in singular and deformed bodies and more in dominant social structures, including the family and American culture. They also, he states, contest social norms through conclusions that no longer destroy the monster and safely reunite the family unit but instead intimate "that the monster cannot be destroyed, that the repressed can never be annihilated."[85] Similarly, for Pinedo, "the postmodern paradigm blurs the boundary between good and evil, normal and abnormal, and the outcome of the struggle is at best ambiguous."[86] And for Halberstam, postmodern horrors such as *The Silence of the Lambs* (1991) show that monstrosity cannot be contained within the body of the scapegoated Other: "[M]eaning refuses to coalesce within one hideous body" and "monstrosity" becomes "almost a queer category that defines the subject as at least partially monstrous." No longer singular and impaired bodies that reduce and impoverish cultural meaning, the monsters of postmodern horror emerge from within self and society, warning us against dominant "discourses invested in purity and innocence."[87]

Within this schema, classic horror film monsters are perceived as too-visible, too-material, and inadequately "cultural" in their forms. Because these material and impaired bodies engender apparently natural responses of fear and disgust in viewers, they supposedly force viewers to sympathize with the hegemonic order and against the monster, and they can only satisfy audiences with the reinstatement of social norms. Disability is again apprehended as a "'real' stigma" imposed, through prejudiced metaphor, on minority bodies.[88] Accordingly, a horror text can only be salvaged for intellectual and subversive interpretations by "reading" impairment as a placeholder for multiple (nondisabled) social identities and abstract "otherness."

The interpretation of impairment as metaphor for social otherness permeates critical understandings of horror film. For instance, Stephen Neale notes that each film genre has a narrative structure built on the disruption and restoration of order and that, in horror, the order/disorder conflict manifests as a battle between law and violence, conjoined "with images and definitions of the monstrous." He contends that the monster violates order, for instance by confusing animal and human characteristics or by challenging normative "spatio-temporal scales." But for Neale, these transgressions primarily symbolize more abstract, *meta*physical disruptions to clear distinctions between categories such as "'the empirical' ('the real') and 'the supernatural' ('the unnatural')."[89]

Scholarship has thus often focused on identifying the metaphysical significance of horror monsters and the fears assuaged by their containment or elimination. In psychoanalytic readings, the monster's material form has been translated as repressed, disavowed, and/or fetishized elements of individual psyches or of society at large.[90] Such analyses imitate Freudianism itself in interpreting disability or physical difference in sexual terms: Freud's "The Uncanny" explains the effects of horror texts by linking fear of disabilities such as blindness and the horror of mythic scenes such as the decapitated Medusa to the fear of castration.[91] Accordingly, Walter Evans interprets horror-film themes "of horrible and mysterious psychological and physical change" as commentaries on adolescent sexual development.[92] Similarly, just as Freud suggests that epilepsy and madness recall humanity's animistic and primitive beliefs, many horror-film readings interpret monsters as figures for the savage and bestial sexual passions normally sublimated in the service of civilization: they are "monsters from the id."[93]

In more recent decades, horror-film analysis has complicated these psychoanalytic studies while continuing to read the deviant body as symbolic. Robin Wood's influential 1979 essay "An Introduction to the American Horror Film" links psychological repression to social and political oppression and associates horror monsters with the return of the repressed Other: other people, women, the proletariat, other cultures, "ethnic groups within the culture," "alternative ideologies or political systems," "deviations from ideological sexual norms," and/or children.[94] Subsequent scholarship has continued to see the monster in primarily gendered or sexual terms: as a figure for patriarchal constructs of women or for women victimized by patriarchy; as an abject entity who indexes the undifferentiated infantile relationship with the mother's body; as the hystericized male; as the queer individual.[95] However, as mandated by Wood, aspects of racial, national, and class ideologies have also received some attention: for instance, zombies in *Dawn of the Dead* (1978) are seen to model capitalist consumers, while monsters in *The Texas Chain Saw Massacre* and *The Hills Have Eyes* (1977) embody the demonized "redneck," and the pod-people of *Invasion of the Body Snatchers* (1956) connote either/both soul-destroying Communists or McCarthyist conformists and sinister Mexican immigrants.[96]

Some horror critics have sought to recuperate classic horror as a genre worthy of study through intriguing and politically attuned readings. In *Frankenstein* and its sequel, for instance, scholars have found traces of class politics in the monster's working garb; have discovered eminently queer narratives traversed by non-normative relations between men; and have traced powerfully intertwined narratives of race and gender.[97] But these efforts to recover classic horror as a valuable genre require the translation of the genre's excessively, problematically corporeal forms into gender, racial, or class terms.

Such interpretations create the odd situation in which analysis of a genre identified by its representations of aberrant bodies and by its embodied effect on viewers—and populated by Frankenstein's oversized and "slow" monster, the diseased and degenerate Dracula, the convulsing Jekyll/Hyde, and a slew of mad doctors and assistants with deformed or scarred faces, hunchbacks, paralysis, missing eyes or arms—has rarely considered the disabled individual as one of the Others connoted by the monstrous body. Identifying the disabled figure so apparent in the monster's form is understood as acquiescence to the insistent and limiting reality of the material body, a refusal of the acts of interpretation through which inferior bodies must be recuperated as something else in order to unsettle hegemonic visual and cultural orders. The substitution of repressed/oppressed groups for the monster's body accomplishes its own repression of the monster's material form and of the culturally and historically specific notions of disability that make horror's metaphors possible.

For example, while it may be true that, as Elizabeth Young contends, the specter of interracial rape was already so overdetermined in the American imagination that the monster leering over the white woman in *Bride of Frankenstein* clearly evoked the mythical black rapist, the decision to code that figure through physical rather than racial deviance is nonetheless underwritten by particular assumptions about disability, disease, and biological inheritance.[98] A disability reading does not insist that *Bride of Frankenstein* is *not* about race: as *Hideous Progeny* makes clear, eugenics was a racist, classist, ethnocentric, sexist, and ableist discourse, and all of these elements find expression in classic horror films. Rather, a disability analysis of the genre illuminates the ways in which the film's racial iconography depends on an ableist and eugenic framework in which visible disability is a powerful sign of physiological and moral defect. Halberstam declares that "the Gothic form is precisely designed for the purposes of multiple interpretations. . . . What we should resist at all costs, therefore, is the impulse to make the monster stabilize otherness."[99] But disability remains the invisible term, the monstrous vehicle, through which this multivalence is secured, and the person with impairments remains representative of an utterly material and threatening deviance that cannot be recuperated for a progressive, or at least destabilizing, politics, unless impairment is elided altogether. The result is pernicious: bodily or mental difference is frequently seen to encode other kinds of difference but is rarely examined on its own terms.[100]

Not surprisingly, then, the few extant disability approaches to horror film have foregrounded the disability usually seen as a transparent marker of monstrous Otherness. However, such readings have also depicted all horror films as irrevocably ableist in their caricatured and negative view of disabled characters. The authors of "The Disabled: Media's Monster" declare that "from the first horror films to modern-day renderings, physical and mental disabilities have been shown to connote murder, violence, and danger."[101] Martin Norden singles out *Frankenstein* and its sequels for offering "a veritable sideshow of disability-related stereotypes," especially in "ascribing villainous or obsessive attributes to characters with twisted spines."[102] Mitchell and Snyder argue that horror films are "central in the recirculation, unveiling, and display of anomalies that would return us to an explanatory origin of psychic wounding"—that is, that they simplistically explain and understand external disabilities as evidence of inner trauma and defect—while Davis contends that horror films are, from a disability perspective, the equivalent of racist films.[103] Like the horror-film critics who view classic horrors as facilitating conservative responses through depicting their monsters in visual and material terms, disability scholars condemn horror films as racist and eugenic in demonizing those with unusual bodies or behaviors.[104]

In response to such interpretations, *Hideous Progeny* argues that classic horror films, while certainly rendering disability monstrous, also question the eugenic logic that visible impairment must either mean something other than itself or remain a reductive and material "fact" used to consolidate conservative and eugenic narratives. In so doing, *Hideous Progeny* insists on a material specificity often lacking in horror-film scholarship, even in those texts that attend closely to the genre's body politics. For example, Noël Carroll has valuably focused on horror monsters' physical appearance, arguing that these creatures elicit fear through their dangerousness and evoke disgust through their impurity: their incompleteness, formlessness, or obfuscation of oppositions such as living and dead.[105] He contends that monsters exploit two modes of representation: "fusion," in which categories are transgressed within the monster's body, as with zombies, which are at once living and dead; and "fission," in which the monster is different entities at different times, like werewolves or Jekyll and Hyde. However, despite explicitly referring to markers of impairment ("ghosts and zombies frequently come without eyes, arms, legs, or skin"), Carroll's discussion slides around disability matters. In particular, his definition of the monster as "any being not believed to exist now according to contemporary science" diminishes the significance of real-life "monsters"—sexual hybrids, "freaks" such as giants and little people, those lacking limbs—as actual beings who both legitimate and confound science's categorizing activities and whose material experiences are informed by constructions of disability in popular texts like horror films.[106]

Still, such interpretations provide important clues as to how quotidian and eugenic practices on the dysfunctional body dictate the form of horror monsters and the horror genre. In discussing types of monsters, Carroll invokes the eugenic history of the composite portrait. He first suggests that the "fusion figure" "may find its prototype in the sort of symbolic structure that Freud called the *collective figure* or *condensation* with respect to dreams."[107] He then notes that Freud—in *Interpretation of Dreams*, where he discusses dreams of individuals whose features conflate two real-life acquaintances—credits the father of eugenics for his insight, writing, "What I did was to adopt the procedure by means of which Galton produced family portraits: namely by projecting two images onto a single plate, so that certain features common to both are emphasized, while those which fail to fit in with one another cancel one another out and are indistinct in the picture."[108] Galton used the composite portrait to "obtain with mechanical precision a generalised picture; one that represents no man in particular, but portrays an imaginary figure possessing the average features of any given group of men." He went on to employ it in generating an image of potential criminals or ethnic or racial "types," a usage adopted by Lombroso in his criminal studies.[109] Thus, when Carroll notes that "the fusion figure of art-horror is a composite figure, conflating distinct *types* of beings," we see the commonalities between horror's symbolic politics and pseudosciences that condemned certain individuals and groups as criminal and degenerate types.[110] If the monster can be seen as the product of a technology of "typing," its links to the "real" bodies targeted by eugenic projects become more evident. But despite invoking terms such as "genus," "species," and "type," Carroll never acknowledges the eugenic politics that often attach to such rhetoric and that haunt the cinematic monster.

A similar erasure of body politics occurs in Wood's essay. Having articulated the horror-film formula as "normality is threatened by the Monster," Wood continues, "I use 'normality' here in a strictly non-evaluative sense, to mean simply 'conformity to the dominant social norms'; one must firmly resist the common tendency to treat the word as if it were more or less synonymous with 'health.'"[111] While Wood seeks to broaden "normality" to incorporate cultural prescriptions and thus open the term to critique, his comment shuts down an important aspect of that very normality. It is precisely by investigating how the discursive struggle over health and deviance plays out in the monstrous bodies of the horror film that we can also glimpse how eugenic discourse mapped biological health onto conceptions of national and racial health.

*Hideous Progeny* thus insists that we re-view the classic horror-film genre, attending closely to its story of impairment in a particular culture and moment, but also coming to understand the genre itself as one defined by its grappling with the politics and aesthetics of disability representation. Quayson's work asks us to attend to the many textual levels at which the "aesthetic nervousness" generated by disability representation operates; it occurs, certainly, "in the interaction between a disabled and nondisabled character" but is also "augmented by tensions refracted across other levels of the text such as the disposition of symbols and motifs, the overall narrative or dramatic perspective, the constitution and reversals of plot structure, and so on." Quayson concludes, "The final dimension of aesthetic nervousness is that between the reader and the text," residing in elements such as the reader's identifications or alignments with characters or narrators, the "reformulations of . . . perspective" required by the plot, and "the short-circuiting of the dominant protocols governing the text" produced by disability representation.[112] *Hideous Progeny* traces this movement, the proliferation of disability in and through narrative, aesthetic, generic, and spectatorial structures, its illumination or undoing of representational conventions in ways that cannot help but implicate and affect viewers—even as it also insists that the "nervousness" that structures disability representations and inhabits their spectators is not only a matter of anxiety or fear but also of horror, thrill, and excitement.

*Hideous Progeny* concentrates on several key films from the early to mid-1930s but also glances at influential films from the 1920s and salient films from the late 1930s and early 1940s. It begins in 1931, as chapter 1 traces the eugenic structure of the classic horror narrative set in place by *Dracula* and *Frankenstein*, noting these films' construction of monsters in terms of ethnic immigrants and feebleminded criminals. While the films appeal to visible manifestations of genetic defect, however, they also map both the erasure of such "proof" of dysgenic status and the proliferation of disability that marks the ostensibly eugenic couple as an impossible entity, a chimera. Chapter 2 also considers eugenic narrative structure, turning to *Freaks*, a film that inverts the horror narrative and replaces supernatural monsters with "real" disabled people. These changes draw viewer attention to the persistent cultural and generic framing required to make atypical figures eugenically revolting. To the extent that audience expectations are central to the horror codes that turn unusual bodies into monstrous freaks, *Freaks* foregrounds viewer complicity in constructing and consuming dysgenic and disability spectacles.

While continuing to consider classic horror's narrative politics, subsequent chapters increasingly address the genre's visual disability dynamics and their solicitation and positioning of spectators. Chapter 3 focuses on classic horror films' dramatic and horrific revelations of visible impairment, finding less the unmediated display of naturally repulsive and genetic defect than the self-conscious performance and projection of the cultural myths and politics that attach to impairment. Chapter 4 moves us from the impaired subject of the medical/cinematic gaze to the "mad doctor" who uses aberrant bodies to validate his social and medical authority. Mad-doctor films contest eugenic readings of aberrant bodies and minds, instead inscribing doctors and scientists as monstrous, disabled, and "mad." At the same time, they interrogate viewers' eagerness to shift blame for ableism to medical authorities, reminding them that movie spectators, too, enjoy and engineer spectacles of madness. Chapter 5 pursues this proliferation of disability outward to the viewer, juxtaposing the eugenic concerns of censors and critics that horror films might damage viewers with the tendency of movie marketers and the films themselves to embrace visceral spectatorship—and even temporary debilitation—as part of a pleasurable cinematic experience.

In its conclusion, *Hideous Progeny* returns again to the discourse of eugenics to mark its ostensible decline in the 1930s, in association with the dire events in Nazi Germany, and its rebirth in a more moderate and publicly palatable form. The conclusion raises questions about the persistence of ableist and implicitly eugenic perspectives that see impairment as naturally horrific and undesirable. Like the book as a whole, it suggests that looking away from classic horror out of distaste for its degraded and impaired bodies might mimic early-twentieth-century popular disgust toward eugenic films, which performed a sentimental concern for the welfare of disabled people while acquiescing to eugenic practices conducted out of the public's sight. While questions remain about the social and political efficacy of horror films, and while the films examined in this book cannot clearly be categorized as either eugenic or radically destabilizing in their effects, *Hideous Progeny* asserts their enduring value as testaments to eugenics' protean potency as well as the ways in which eugenics falters and fails in the face of its own perverse disability spectacle.[113]

# 1

# EUGENIC REPRODUCTION

## CHIMERAS IN *DRACULA* AND *FRANKENSTEIN*

I n 2005 an article in the *New York Times* appealed to horror film to contextualize the "weirdnesses" of genetic science. Nicholas Wade's "Chimeras on the Horizon, but Don't Expect Centaurs" defines the "original chimera" as "a tripartite medley of lion, goat, and snake." The reference is to the *Iliad*, in which Homer describes the Chimaera as a "raging monster, divine, inhuman— / A lion in the front, a serpent in the rear, / In the middle a goat— and breathing fire." The *Times* article lists other classical and fantastical chimeras: "centaurs, sphinxes, werewolves, minotaurs and mermaids, and the gorgon Medusa." In contrast to such fabulous entities, Wade avers, biologists' experimental chimeras are "generally bland," consisting, for instance, of the "patchwork mouse" produced by mixing the embryonic cells of a black and a white mouse. Still, Wade admits, more disturbing chimeras loom: humans with pig-valve hearts and anticipated entities such as human organs molded from stem cells and grown in animals or the "seeding" of human cells throughout an animal's system, perhaps even enabling an animal to reproduce with human eggs and sperm.[1]

The article refers twice to horror cinema. First, Dr. William Hansen, an expert in mythology at Indiana University, attributes human fascination and repulsion with chimeras to their "defiance of natural order," commenting, "They promote a sense of wonder and awe and for many of us that is an enjoyable feeling; they are a safe form of danger as in watching a scary movie." The article's second allusion to films also mitigates the "danger" of biological chimeras, noting, "Contrary to the plot of every good horror movie, the biologists' chimera cookbook contains only recipes of medical interest." The "scary" or horror film thus domesticates the unsettling implications of genetic experimentation. It offers a "safe," fictional engagement with a transgressive body, and it reassures by contrast, its fantastical plot throwing into relief the mundanity of biologists' chimeras.

The article thus marks off the ostensibly "bland" realm of genetic scientific inquiry as the purview of experts, while confirming popular preference for—and distraction by—the reassuringly unbelievable excesses of horror film. As a figure at once mythic, genetic, and horrific, however, the chimera points to the inextricability of horror-film monsters, biological hybrids, and real individuals exhibiting physiological aberrance. First, the chimera illuminates the supernatural status of classic horror monsters such as *Dracula*'s undead vampire and *Frankenstein*'s reanimated creature. It reminds us that these entities are in some sense very much *unreal*. Second, in keeping with these mythic beginnings, the figure of the chimera connotes an utter fabrication or illusion, as in John Donne's sentiment about distraction: "an any thing, a nothing, a fancy, a chimera in my braine troubles me in my prayer."[2] Here the chimera is an imaginary construct lacking material substance or transcendent significance. In *Dracula* and *Frankenstein*, then, the monstrous chimerical bodies may also be read as "any things," "nothings," "fancies" made up to serve particular cultural, social, or political purposes.

Third, the chimera is also a real phenomenon. The combination of genetic material from two zygotes, as when two fertilized eggs conjoin or when one fertilized egg absorbs another egg or sperm-cell, produces a single individual composed—like the mouse, in a rather "patchwork way"—of two sets of distinct genetic material. The chimera's odd genetic identity may be visibly "marked" in some way, for instance in admixed eye coloring or ambiguous genitalia, but, more often, chimerical humans are "normal" in appearance and never realize their genetic condition. Some researchers also point to evidence of what they call "microchimerism" to suggest that, due to the retention of fetal cells in mothers' bloodstreams, "our bodies are cellular mongrels, teeming with cells from our mothers, maybe even from grandparents and siblings."[3] While such phenomena occur naturally, chimerism may also be the product of scientific experimentation in laboratories, of artificial reproductive technologies, or of procedures such as transplants or blood transfusion.

It is this latter artificial and nonetheless biological form of chimerism that seems most relevant to *Dracula* and *Frankenstein*. *Dracula*'s thematics of blood mixing suggests a process by which the vampire's victims take on his "blood" or essence, remaining to some extent themselves, but nonetheless coming to exhibit vampiric traits. The vampire's prey is thus re-produced as chimeric. In *Frankenstein*, the scientist brings together organs, body parts, and a brain from diverse sources to fashion a creature that combines different genetic imprints in the same body. Even as the films foreground deliberate and artificial chimeras, rather than "natural" combinations of genetic material *in utero*, we shall see that the horror plot makes it difficult to maintain a distinction between the constructed and the natural chimera. Indeed, the horror film seems to reveal that it is, aptly, impossible for the chimera to be exclusively either one or the other, a discovery that in turn debunks as chimerical the possibility of a completely pure and natural act of reproduction.

The chimera is thus at once a mythic beast; a mental construct or whim; and an actual human, animal, or plant constituted from diverse genetic materials—through natural circumstance, biological experimentation, or medical transplantation. Similarly, monstrous bodies in horror films are at once fantastical entities descended from myth and legend, intellectual and artistic mirages, and material instances of hybridity or impairment. In contradistinction to the *New York Times* article, then, the horror-film chimera is not a mere distraction from or reassuring exaggeration of the politics of genetic science, but a body on which we may trace the scientific and cultural metamorphosis of mundane biological accident into grotesque monstrosity—and back again. The effectiveness of horror film depends on our willingness to perceive physiological anomalies as symbols through which we may manage social and cultural fears and desires. To that extent, it collaborates closely with American eugenic discourse of the early twentieth century. If, however, horror films are to be more than a grotesque imitation of and thus distraction from the politics of science, we must both attend to and trouble the processes by which such facile translations are accomplished. We must build interpretations that interrogate the monster's makeup and refuse to understand its physical form as merely a vehicle for something more important.

## MONSTERS IN THE BED: EUGENICS AND CLASSIC HORROR FILM

The iconic bodies of the eugenic drama were eminently familiar to horror-film audiences in 1931. The two genres even seemed to share the narrative formula, later ascribed by Robin Wood to horror texts, in which "normality is threatened by the Monster." Embodying "normality" in eugenic thought was the young, healthy, white woman, whose body had to be protected to secure the reproduction of the normal order. Opined eugenicist Harry H. Laughlin, "The perpetuity of the American race and consequently of American institutions depends upon the virtue and fecundity of American women."[4] Embodying the threat to such virtue and fecundity was the monster, in eugenic terms the product of "inferior" racial, class, or national groups, whose innate genetic defect and danger to normative reproduction was manifest as visible deformation. When author H. P. Lovecraft wrote condemning the "organic things—Italo-Semitico-Mongoloid" of Manhattan's Lower East Side in the 1920s, he contended, "The individually grotesque was lost in the collectively devastating; which left on the eye . . . a yellow and leering mask with sour, sticky, acid ichors oozing at eyes, ears, nose, and mouth, and abnormally bubbling from monstrous and unbelievable sores at every point."[5] The assertion of nativist Madison Grant that "The stature [of 'the dark Mediterranean or Iberian subspecies'] is stunted in comparison to that of the Nordic race and the musculature and bony framework weak," underwrote his view that "New York is becoming a *cloaca gentium* which will produce many amazing racial hybrids and some ethnic horrors that will be beyond the powers of future anthropologists to unravel."[6]

Impairments and deformities in eugenic texts thus naturalized the undesirability and aberrance of particular groups, as eugenicists exploited both a positivist belief in the visible and a presumably natural response of disgust toward certain anomalies. Discussing those deemed "feebleminded," one attendee of the 1923 Southern Minnesota Medical Association meeting declared, "the majority are such stunted, misshapen, hideous specimens, that they arouse feelings of repulsion."[7] Obvious defect was seen to transparently reflect intellectual and other kinds of interior degeneracy, generating a "repulsion" that validated exclusive politics. The antipathy directed here toward the "feebleminded" reminds us that "the disabled" were also counted amongst those groups whose reproduction was to be contained or forestalled. Disability, then, occupies an overdetermined position in eugenic discourse, at once the "privileged" metaphorical vehicle for an array of cultural, social, and racial deficiencies *and* a specific embodied identity targeted for sterilization, institutionalization, and immigration restriction. The disabled figure in eugenic thought is itself chimeric, at once a mythic and metaphoric construct and a real individual perceived as a physiological—and pathological—problem.

Eugenicists represented dysgenic individuals in terms of disability to persuade Americans of the need for eugenic measures. As noted in the introduction, literalizations of genetic deficiencies sought to convince audiences of the existence of processes of heredity that were, at the time, largely unexplained and invisible. But the representation of inner aberrance in visible terms was not in itself adequate to making the case for genetic inheritance. As well, eugenicists needed to assert genetic determination via the sexually reproductive act. They were convinced that all kinds of traits—both positive and negative, and encompassing the biological, moral, psychological, intellectual, and characterological—were passed along through reproduction and that the context of the procreative act and the health of its participants fixed in genetic form the offspring's eugenic or dysgenic future. Grant, for instance, dismissed the "widespread and fatuous belief in the power of environment, as well as of education and opportunity to alter heredity," insisting instead on sexual reproduction as the locus for eugenic progress or dysgenic degeneration: "Man has the choice of two methods of race improvement. He can breed from the best, or he can eliminate the worst by segregation or sterilization."[8] This pithy pronouncement invokes by prohibition the unspeakable union between the breeding female of the "best" and the evidently defective monster who represents the "worst." It is this relationship, between the reproductive female and the physiologically dysgenic figure, that haunts eugenic texts: an implicit, titillating, and frightening spectacle eugenicists hoped would galvanize individuals to eugenic action.

It is through the same relationship, between woman and monster, that classic horror films mobilize their narratives. In James Whale's *Frankenstein* (Universal, 1931), after his monster has assaulted his bride-to-be, a panicked Henry Frankenstein declares rather petulantly, "There can *be* no wedding while this horrible creation of mine is still alive!" The realization encapsulates the soon-to-be formulaic heart of classic horror movies: the transgressive entrance of a monster into an ordered society and its particular threat to a normative couple. Set in motion by this danger, horror-film narratives trace the pursuit and eventual destruction or expulsion of the monster, an act that recuperates the couple's union and reproductive future. As suggested by Henry's dictum that no wedding can occur while the monster lives, this plot also stands in for a racial, social, and national dilemma in which dysgenic monsters inhibit or overwhelm the normative reproduction of an entire society.

*Dracula* and *Frankenstein* thus employ narrative and representational practices that seem to confirm eugenic doctrine. Physically deviant monsters constellate the traits of several dysgenic groups—the immigrant, the diseased, the poor, the criminal, the non-white, the disabled—and hinder the proper union and reproduction of attractive representatives of the middle and upper classes. As David J. Skal comments, the monsters in early classic horror films "all revolved around fantasies of 'alternative' forms of reproduction."[9] The recurrence in the films of scenes depicting the monster's incursion into the bedrooms of young, marriageable women intimates the sexual nature of his threat, while the use of bodily signifiers—notably blood in Dracula and brains in Frankenstein—associates this disruption of normative procreation with physical degeneracy. When the films demonstrate that normal reproduction may only be secured through the monster's destruction, it seems that Dracula and Frankenstein model eugenic warnings against tampering with normative and "healthy" reproductive practices. Moreover, the dominance of physical impairment as a signifier of essential and genetic monstrosity consolidates an ableist discourse wherein disability is read as a fixed, congenital, and pathological condition, and disabled people are seen as monsters properly excluded from reproduction.

But it is also in the persistent representation of impairment and the harnessing of impairment to the procreative scene that the films rethink eugenic reproductive politics, for the scene of "natural" and "healthy" reproduction increasingly appears as a phantasmatic construction that cannot be realized either within the filmic narrative or beyond. The ideal eugenic union required a particularly high standard of physiological health, as described in a 1914 text entitled Science of Eugenics:

> The eugenic marriage, when it comes, WILL BE BASED UPON THE PRINCIPLES AND KNOWLEDGE OF HEREDITY. When a young man and a young woman, offering themselves for marriage, can produce certified records of their ancestry back for three or four generations, showing that their progenitors have been entirely, or largely, free from nervous prostration, sick headaches, neurasthenia, hysteria, melancholia, St. Vitus' dance, epilepsy, syphilis, alcoholism, pauperism, criminality, prostitution and insanity—when they can further show that their ancestors have been free from all other inheritable forms of nervous disorders, including certain forms of deafness, color blindness and other indications of defectiveness and degeneracy, then it may truly be said that such a union may be correctly styled a EUGENIC MARRIAGE.[10]

In its exhaustive list of conditions that must be barred from a eugenic marriage and in its inclusion of chapters with titles such as "How to Have

Perfect Children," this text illustrates two key aspects of eugenic discourse: first, that in order to imagine the ideal eugenic body or union, eugenicists must repeatedly iterate all of the ills and defects whose exclusion defines that body or union; second, that the more eugenic propaganda lists and invokes debility and impairment, the more it "produces" vital and potent images of disability that obscure and invalidate the perfectly eugenic reproductive act.

Thus, while at first glance the classic horror monster seems to constitute a singular, aberrant body generated by improper or artificial reproduction that reinforces eugenic ideas of "normal" or natural reproduction, the effect of this monstrosity is, in fact, a different kind of propagation, glimpsed in monstrosity's proliferation across several of the films' characters. In particular, the young, reproductive couple touted by eugenicists as the salvation of the superior class and race is, as the films progress, increasingly traversed by the couple's own perversities and impairments, compromised by the woman's attraction or vulnerability to the monster or the man's instability and impotence. By endlessly deferring the imminent honeymoon, and by revealing the engaged man and woman as themselves physiologically flawed, the films suggest that the real chimera at stake here is that of "normal" reproduction, at once fantastical and, in reality, inevitably genetically compromised. As a result, apparently cautionary eugenic tales morph into musings on the mutability, vulnerability, and obstinate materiality of the body. Disability appears not as something fixed and pathological, but rather as a generative, reproductive, and unstable encounter between textual and social constructs, on the one hand, and the embodied self, on the other.

Each of the films considered in this chapter plays out, in its own way, the slippery and contradictory logics of eugenic discourse. *Dracula*, in articulating blood as the problem, invokes eugenicists' frequent reliance on outmoded, inconsistent, and scientifically inaccurate metaphors. Such metaphors take on a metonymic life of their own, suggesting exchanges of bodily fluids not reducible to the act of sexual intercourse. At the same time, the film's constant elision of blood, the evasiveness of that bodily sign on which eugenics rests its case, indicates the holes in the eugenic narrative and the easy metamorphosis of genetically determinist rhetoric into specters of infection and disease that transform and rewrite biological destiny. *Frankenstein*, in its representation of the monster's abnormal brain, sets in motion eugenic concepts of "feeblemindedness" and its conflation with criminality. But it also—particularly when considered in concert with its sequel, *Bride of Frankenstein*—plays out a popular revision of eugenics by juxtaposing doctrines of nurture against those of nature and emphasizing environmental influence over biological destiny. In the very process of enacting eugenic narratives that reassert normalcy through the expulsion or destruction of the monster, these films suggest the continuity between, the reversibility of, monstrous and ordinary bodies. Eugenics is revealed in classic horror as a discourse that can reproduce anyone as a monster.

## BLEEDING OUT: *DRACULA*

That the 1931 film version of *Dracula* might adopt and adapt the eugenic rhetoric of its cultural moment is not surprising if we know a little about the history of vampire tales. Nineteenth-century folklorist Emily Gerard, whose essay on "Transylvanian Superstitions" influenced Stoker's novel, noted that Romanian stories had long connected the "nosferatu" to problematic births. The creature is said to emerge as the "illegitimate offspring of two illegitimate persons," a description repeated by folklorist Heinrich von Wlislocki, who adds that the multiply illegitimate "nosferatu" is also "still-born."[11] In turn, von Wlislocki continues, the vampire troubles normative sex and procreation:

> It often happens that women are made pregnant by the Nosferat and give birth to children who are very ugly, thickly covered with hair all over, and who very soon become *Moroiu* [a kind of vampire]. . . . Maidens made pregnant outside marriage frequently invoke the Nosferat as an excuse. Often, during bridal nights, a Nosferat appears to the bride, another to the bridegroom, and only when the embrace is consummated . . . do the newlyweds realize their error. In most cases, however, there is no embrace; instead the torturing spirits turn the maiden barren or the man impotent.[12]

Popular belief thus summoned the vampire to account for extramarital liaisons, impotence, infertility, illegitimacy, deformity, and stillbirths.

Eugenicists sought to displace such folklore with their own narratives of genetic determination. In *Heredity in Relation to Eugenics* (1911), for instance, Charles Davenport foregrounded congenital destiny over both supernatural forces and acquired conditions such as infectious disease, commenting, "[E]ugenics has to do with traits that are in the blood, the protoplasm. The superstition of prenatal influence and the real effects of venereal disease, dire as they are, lie outside the pale of eugenics in its strictest sense."[13]

Nonetheless, Davenport insisted, "the eugenic teachings that we think of as new are very old" and often conflict with contemporary medical science: "Modern medicine is responsible for the loss of appreciation of the power of heredity. It has had its attention too exclusively focussed on germs and conditions of life. It has neglected the personal element that helps determine the course of every disease. . . . It has forgotten the fundamental fact that all men are created *bound* by their protoplasmic makeup and *unequal* in their powers and responsibilities."[14] In myth, vampires thus function in a way that eugenicists might approve: they provide an embodied figure for the mysterious forces at work at conception, especially corrupt or dysgenic forces, "bad genes," whose effects will only become apparent later, in bodily impairment or deformities. Accordingly, both vampire tales and eugenic texts summon monstrous bodies to persuade audiences of (to "de-monstrate") the reality of biological processes that operate through the reproductive act to determine health and character.

Directed by Tod Browning, starring Bela Lugosi, and released in February 1931, Universal's *Dracula* articulates a straddling of old and new discourses—a collision of superstition and modern medicine—that corresponds to Davenport's portrait of eugenics. Folklore and feudalism attend the opening sequence where, ignoring the warnings of superstitious villagers, British realtor Renfield (Dwight Frye) takes a wild coach-ride to a Transylvanian castle complete with creaking doors, sweeping staircases, and giant cobwebs. There he meets the assured, gentlemanly Count Dracula (Bela Lugosi) and completes a transaction enabling Dracula to lease Carfax Abbey in London. Drugged by the vampire, Renfield falls unconscious. Dracula's three brides, who approach the realtor's insensible body, are waved away by the Count, who himself moves in on Renfield's exposed neck. Made insane by the vampire's attack, and lusting for the blood of small creatures, Renfield accompanies Dracula to England on a boat, guarding his master who hides by day in his coffin.

When the boat arrives in England, Dracula disembarks unseen, leaving behind the dead crew members and the raving Renfield, who is taken to Dr. Seward's lunatic asylum. Making himself at home in London, Dracula meets his neighbors Dr. Seward (Herbert Bunston), Seward's daughter Mina (Helen Chandler), Mina's fiancé John Harker (David Manners), and Mina's friend Lucy Western (Frances Dade), who later expresses an attraction to Dracula. That night, Lucy is visited and bitten by the vampire, and soon dies, eventually returning as a vampire herself.

Dutch scientist Professor Van Helsing (Edward Van Sloan) faces skepticism when he asserts that vampirism is at work and that Dracula can transform himself into a wolf or a bat. When Dr. Seward scoffs at the idea of vampires because they do not reconcile with "modern medical science," the sage Van Helsing muses, "I may be able to bring you proof that the superstition of yesterday can become the scientific reality of today." His statement sets in place a eugenic narrative propelled by the effort to "bring . . . proof" to the film's audience: to render visible and literal the deviant figure of superstitious tales who is responsible for his victims' bodily transformations and to explain scientifically the methods by which he inflicts debility. Unbeknownst to her father and fiancé, Mina is also bitten by Dracula and grows ill, at one point trying to bite Harker. She is hypnotized and eventually kidnapped by Dracula who takes her to his abbey, but Renfield, escaping from the asylum, unwittingly leads Van Helsing and Harker to the vampire's lair. Despite his pleading, Renfield is killed by Dracula. Finding Dracula asleep in his coffin, Van Helsing drives a stake through the vampire's heart, and thus saves Mina, who is led off in Harker's arms.

*Dracula*'s narrative depicts the threat of the vampire-monster to a normality understood in terms of marital, eugenic, and sexual reproduction and figured particularly in the anticipated union of the engaged couple, Mina Seward and John Harker. Harker's exemplification of normality is clearly established: while Lucy declares Dracula "fascinating," Mina demurs that she prefers someone "a little more normal." "Like John?" Lucy asks, laughingly. "Yes, dear, like John," Mina confirms.[15] Insofar as Dracula endangers the happy, eminently normal marriage of Mina and Harker, he embodies a sexual and reproductive danger. The film is structured around several scenes that portray his threat to normality as a sexual incursion into the bedrooms of young, marriageable women. Lucy becomes the vampire's target when, clad in a white nightgown, she opens her windows to the night, where Dracula lurks below. She slips off her lace shawl, baring her arms, before retiring to bed with a book. As she reads, a bat floats at her open window. Lucy becomes distracted, her eyes lift up to the ceiling, and she appears mesmerized. Slowly, her eyes close, and she seems to sleep. The bat enters through the window. The camera cuts again to the slumbering Lucy, and then pans right to reveal the Count, standing at the edge of Lucy's bed. He moves slowly forward, hunching over, his eyes piercingly fixed upon Lucy, his right hand extended toward her. He bends over her, his face nearing her own, his mouth closing in upon her exposed neck, before the scene fades to black (fig. 1.1). Later in the film, the vampire similarly assaults Mina, who sleeps in her bed while Dracula, in bat form, hovers outside the open window. Suddenly, Dracula is standing in the room, gazing intently at Mina. He assumes a predatory posture, shoulders hunched and arms raised, as he

**1.1** Monster in the bedroom: Dracula (Bela Lugosi) looms over Lucy (Frances Dade) in *Dracula* (1931).

moves toward her. The film cuts to an extreme close-up of Dracula's face, squinting and leering into the camera, before darkness blots him out.

The bedroom settings illuminate the monster's usurpation of normative sexual reproduction, a reading encouraged by the scenes' elision of the actual assault. As Rhona Berenstein notes, the "indirect representation" required by early 1930s censorial guidelines shaped conventions in which "a narrative ellipsis following a scene of a man and woman entering a bedroom . . . meant an out-of-sight sexual encounter." Accordingly, *Dracula's* timely cutting away from the vampire's approach "heightens the sexual connotations of their encounter for spectators."[16] Interpretations of the scenes as perverse sexual interactions were reinforced by advertising materials acclaiming the film as "The Story of the Strangest Passion Ever Known" and "The Strangest Love Story of All."[17]

In conjunction with these sexualized assaults, the film uses bodily signifiers to portray the vampire's attacks as actions that spread degeneracy by disrupting normative procreation or reproducing in aberrant ways. In contrast to the physically deformed monsters of subsequent horror films, Dracula's essential deviance is disguised by an apparently normal body and revealed only in marks of debility on the bodies he re-produces and, particularly, in the narrative's rhetoric of blood. Immediately after Dracula closes in on Lucy, a dissolve takes us to an operating theater where doctors

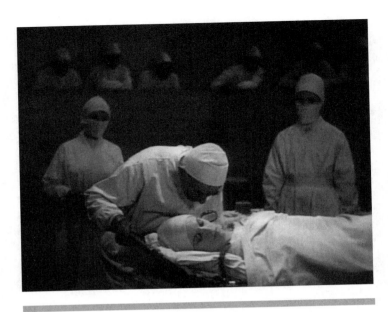

**1.2** The body of Lucy (Frances Dade) becomes the purview of doctors in *Dracula* (1931).

in white surgical gowns, masks, and caps surround a female figure lying on a table and covered by a white sheet. More surgeons occupy the room's tiered seats. As the camera moves slowly down toward the woman, we hear her declared dead. One doctor asks Dr. Seward how long ago "Miss Western" received her last blood transfusion, revealing the deceased as Lucy. "Four hours ago," Seward replies. The camera brings us closer to Lucy, as a doctor muses, "An unnatural loss of blood, which we've been powerless to check." Wielding a magnifying glass, he focuses on her neck, which *Dracula*'s viewers do not see, remarking as the scene fades, "On the throat of each victim, the same two marks" (fig. 1.2).

Similarly, after Dracula's first attack on Mina, dialogue confirms the debilitating nature of her encounter with the vampire. Mina relates a dream: "Just as I was commencing to get drowsy, I heard dogs howling. And when the dream came, it seemed the whole room was filled with mist. It was so thick, I could just see the lamp by the bed, a tiny spark in the fog. And then I saw two red eyes staring at me and a white livid face came down out of the mist. It came closer and closer. I felt breath on my face . . . and then, its lips!" Harker reassures her that she was only dreaming, but she continues: "And then in the morning, I felt so weak. It seemed as if all the life had been drained out of me."[18] Van Helsing removes her scarf and asks how long she has had the "little marks" on her neck.

Subsequent encounters between Mina and the vampire confirm the deviant nature of their relationship, again through the imagery of blood. When Dracula hypnotically summons Mina from her room, she glides toward him through the garden in the dark, her pale form swallowed by the darkness of his cape. Later, she confesses that the blood exchange is complete: "He opened a vein in his arm, and he made me drink." Dracula announces triumphantly to Van Helsing: "My blood now flows through her veins." These scenes thus link a deviant sexual act with signs of blood that index debility and jeopardize the women's capacity for healthy reproduction.

The sexual deviance of Dracula is also confirmed in the very first "bedroom scene" of the movie, in which the object of his desire is not a woman. Our eugenic interpretation suggests that if the narrative presents Dracula's threat as primarily sexual, the bedroom interaction between Dracula and a prone Renfield implies a homosexual encounter. Renfield is somewhat "queered" even prior to his meeting with Dracula: Michael Brunas, John Brunas, and Tom Weaver describe him as "a bit of a queen . . . with his effeminate look and prissy manner."[19] His interaction with Dracula compounds his sexual ambiguity: Dracula's dismissal of the vampire brides and his closing in on the young man foreground the transgressive and homoerotic sexuality long a part of the vampire image.[20] The scene's implications upset Universal producer Carl Laemmle, who wrote of the final screenplay, "Dracula should only go for women and not men!"[21] Harry M. Benshoff lists Dracula and Renfield as one of the "queer couples" prominent in early classic horror movies, and Skal argues that the film's "real 'story' is Renfield's tragic, unrequited love for the Count."[22]

To some extent, the reading of Dracula and Renfield's interaction as queer actually operates in keeping with a generalized eugenic narrative in which Dracula's deviance is tied to his perversion of the "normal" sexual and reproductive act. The elided but apparently sexual encounters the vampire shares with Lucy and Mina accomplish a transference and mixing of blood that, we are meant to understand, *stands in for* and *displaces* normative reproduction; the scene with Renfield prepares us for the notion that the vampire's reproductive activities are not "normal." Nonetheless, they are, perversely, reproductive. Dracula's bedroom visitations both sap the lifeblood of the upper classes and lead to an exchange of fluids that gives birth to more degeneracy. Dracula re-produces his victims as monstrous offspring; his blood flows through their veins. In turn, his victims generate their own perverse children: the vampiric Lucy stalks young girls in the night and, according to a newspaper report, bites their throats.[23] Mina struggles against the impulse to propagate monstrosity, telling Harker,

"You mustn't touch me, and you mustn't kiss me ever again. . . . It's all over, John, our love, our life together." In these admonishments, Mina mimics the self-sacrifice enacted by characters in early pro-eugenic films, as they abjure marriage or sexual congress rather than risk passing on hereditary conditions.[24] But the struggle against monstrosity's proliferation is difficult, eugenics tells us, for the superior but weakened elite must confront a genetically inferior but strong and fertile population. Mina's inner deviance eventually overpowers her eugenic impulses, and she tries to bite Harker and pass along her defect.

As already noted, eugenicists required signifiers of debility, linked to aberrant procreative acts, to demonstrate an invisible genetic truth. Like eugenicists facing a sometimes skeptical public or medical community, Van Helsing must point out and interpret such signs to persuade others of the existence and power of something they cannot really see or understand, in order to destroy the monster and secure the eugenic union of the young couple. In Stephen Neale's eyes, it is this imperative that characterizes "the narrative process in . . . horror films" which "tends to be marked by a search for that discourse, that specialised form of knowledge which will enable the human characters to comprehend and to control that which simultaneously embodies and causes its 'trouble.'"[25] Dracula's narrative musters material traces to prove the inherent defect—the "bad gene"—hidden in the vampire but re-produced and made manifest in his victims' bodies. The professor's interpretation of these clues leads him eventually to the vampire's lair. Forced by daybreak to retire to his coffin, Dracula is destroyed by Van Helsing's offscreen staking, and Mina, standing by in a trance, is released from his spell. Harker and Mina embrace and, leaving Van Helsing behind, ascend the sweeping cellar staircase, Mina's nightgown trailing behind her like a wedding dress, as the faint sound of church bells heralds the film's end. The professor has protected the reproductive couple against dysgenic forces and "proven" the existence of the elusive monster. The narrative thus functions as analogy for the eugenic expert's use of bodily signs and rhetoric to assert both the existence of genetic determinism and the necessity of protecting the eugenic and procreative couple.

However, the prominence of blood in the film's rhetoric illuminates eugenic predilection for bodily tropes that are meant to prove genetic heredity but that often, in their sensationalistic connotations, exceed a reproductive narrative. Eugenic invocations of blood suggest that the "real story" of Dracula is less the queer relationship between the vampire and Renfield and more the tale of blood that traverses the film's perverse relationships. In enlisting blood as "proof" for a dysgenic reproductive narrative, *Dracula* mimics American eugenicists' own usage of tropes of blood. But there is a certain dissonance between exchanges of blood and the procreative, genetic process of heredity they are meant to represent. Indeed, it is impossible that Dracula should impregnate Renfield, and there is no indication that he impregnates Lucy or Mina. Rather, he re-produces each of his victims in his own image through a transfer of blood that is *not* reducible to the sexually procreative act. When we trace in the text the marks of blood via which Van Helsing intends to substantiate Dracula as a "real" figure of debility, we find ultimately only the disappearance of blood, indexed to the chimera, the "nothing," at the heart of the eugenic enterprise: the unrealizable act of "healthy" and pure reproduction.

## Blood in the Gene Pool: Eugenic Rhetoric in *Dracula*

In the decades leading up to the 1930s, American eugenicists frequently relied on sanguinary metaphors to make the eugenic case. Even as the mechanisms of chromosomes and cells were perceived and understood more clearly, the older rhetoric of blood and protoplasm retained emotive value. David Starr Jordan's eugenic tract *The Blood of the Nation: A Study of the Decay of Races* (1902) maintained, "The blood of a nation determines its history. . . . The history of a nation determines its blood." He asserted the relevance of the rhetoric of blood even within a Mendelian understanding: "[T]he old word well serves our purposes. The blood which is 'thicker than water' is the symbol of race unity. In this sense the blood of the people concerned is at once the cause and the result of the deeds recorded in their history."[26] In a 1913 letter, Theodore Roosevelt, concerned about "race suicide," opined, "Some day we will realize that the prime duty[,] the inescapable duty of the good citizen of the right type[,] is to leave his or her blood behind him in the world."[27] And a 1927 document from the Eugenics Record Office included, in its list of the "principle [*sic*] business of eugenics," the responsibility "[t]o educate organized society . . . to a point, where it will act with an eye to racial progress, encouraging the reproduction of the 'best blood,' and discouraging or preventing the reproduction of its worst strains."[28] In these texts, blood becomes a figure for the reproductive act; to "leave one's blood behind" is to reproduce it in the form of children and thus perpetuate the nation's "best blood" while delimiting the "bad."

This rhetoric of blood also supports a slippage between, on the one hand, eugenicists' purported focus on impersonal processes of the inheritance of traits, and, on the other, their persistent demonization of particular economic, foreign, and non-white groups in possession of "inferior" blood. Imagery of blood often, for instance, denotes social and economic status, which is assumed to manifest the biological merit dictated by parental genetics or "blood." In *Dracula*, then, the "unnatural loss of blood" Lucy's doctors are "powerless to stop" encapsulates a class-based fear in which Lucy's death diminishes the strength of the nation's "best blood." Indeed, although there have been other victims, including a young flower peddler, the effort to identify and destroy the vampire only coheres once the middle and upper classes are threatened.[29] Like the doctors called on in the film, Francis Galton was particularly concerned to preserve the professional classes to which Dr. Seward, Mina, and Jonathan Harker belong.[30] The class-specific threats Galton articulated derived not only from those lower on the social scale, as we might expect, but also from the aristocracy. Sons of titled men, Galton contended, often inherited status but not wealth and were thus forced to marry "heiresses" whose frequent status as children without siblings marked their ostensible "sterility." Galton condemned what he called "the race destroying influence of heiress-blood" and criticized the peerage as imposing "destructive effects on our valuable races."[31] In turn, American eugenicists linked reproductive defects to the aristocracy's consanguineous marriages, its "pride of blood," which encouraged sterility and concentration of negative traits.[32]

In *Dracula*'s class narrative, then, the Count's threat lies in his representation of a degenerating and foreign aristocracy. Certainly, some scholars have interpreted Dracula as a "sanguinary capitalist," and Marxists have found vampire imagery valuable for their depictions of capitalism.[33] However, as a feudal figure fresh from terrorizing the peasants of Transylvania, Count Dracula more clearly embodies the incestuous aristocracy and system of primogeniture that bourgeois capitalism and meritocracy purport to have overthrown and that eugenics disavows, incarnating "the decadent feudalism of Continental Europe" condemned by eugenicist William Starr Myers in 1930.[34] The demonization of precapitalist forms of inheritance evident in Gothic literature is adapted in this film to eugenic visions of decaying aristocracies and the dangers of race suicide by the more desirable classes. Dracula's erotic appeal for Lucy, and later Mina, dramatizes Davenport's fear that dysgenic aristocratic practices might be both attractive to and dangerous for "America's grand families."[35]

Class is not the only dysgenic identity category invoked by the rhetoric of blood. Such imagery is also often called on to indict the "inferior" ethnic immigrant. The film's opening words are read from a travel guide by a young woman (producer's daughter Carla Laemmle) sharing Renfield's jolting carriage: "Among the rugged peaks that frown down on the Borgo Pass are found crumbling castles of a bygone age." This commentary not only confirms Dracula's figuration of degenerate aristocracy but also positions the viewer with the English tourist admiring exotic ruins, indicating that the Count's monstrous appeal resides at least partially in his foreignness, a trait marked most saliently by the vampire's—and Lugosi's—Eastern European accent. Lugosi, a Hungarian immigrant, was, prior to his success playing Dracula on Broadway, merely "an obscure political refugee scratching for work in a new country," and he brought to both the play and the film a slow, thickly accented dialogue.[36] In suggesting that Dracula's degeneracy derives from his status as a non-Nordic immigrant, then, the film also draws on the ethnic and national threads of eugenic discourse.

As southeastern Europeans, both Dracula and Lugosi represented the "new" kind of immigrant that deeply concerned American eugenicists. Eugenic lore held that, in the colonial period, the predominantly western European origins of immigrants to the United States formed the basis for a specifically American nationality, grounded in homogeneity of racial origin and cultural beliefs. Within this narrative, Van Helsing's Dutch origins and accent denote him as a desirable Nordic immigrant, capable of successful assimilation to the dominant society. However, from the Civil War onwards, immigration began to constitute what Henry Pratt Fairchild, American Eugenics Society president from 1929 to 1931, called "A New Menace," in the form of immigrants from Italy, Austria-Hungary, and Russia. The racial purity of immigrants from eastern and southeastern Europe was suspect, due to that region's history of invasion by "Mongoloid stock" via "the Avars, the Bulgars, Magyars, and Turks."[37] The ostensible resistance of such individuals to America's civilizing influences seems borne out by Dracula's importation of boxes of "his native soil" in which he must rest each night. Eugenic activism against such ethnic "inferiors" helped produce the 1921 Emergency Quota Act and the 1924 Immigration Act, which severely restricted immigration from Asia and eastern and southern Europe.[38]

Eugenic rhetoric presented such immigration in terms of the mixing and tainting of American blood, as in Davenport's condemnation of "the great influx of blood from South-eastern Europe."[39] In 1930, Lothrop Stoddard combined reproductive and sanguinary metaphors to assert, "The 'Slavic' peoples who occupy most of Eastern Europe are all impregnated with Asiatic Mongol and Turki blood."[40] John E. Edgerton's contribution to the 1930 volume *The Alien in Our Midst* represented Americanness as a matter of blood and avowed that "the obligation and the right of leadership in all corrective or forward movements involving interpretations of American ideals belong inseparably to those [white] natives of our country . . . having in their very blood an appreciative understanding of our institutions."[41] The "fusion" of Mina's blood with Dracula's becomes an image of the ethnic immigrant's impregnation of the white woman—and thus the national body—with inferior and mixed blood.

As these examples suggest, eugenic confusion of national and racial identity meant that the rhetoric of blood in anti-immigration diatribes also served anti-miscegenation discourse. The result of racial interaction between Americans and non-assimilable immigrants, Henry Pratt Fairchild believed, was inevitably dysgenic mating and reproduction, for "the sexual impulse knows no racial boundaries."[42] Harry H. Laughlin's warning that the mating of white women and "men with a small fraction of colored blood" could accomplish "a final radical race mixture" conflated tropes of blood and reproduction with little regard for either the nonbiological status of national identity or the mechanics of genetic transmission: writes Donald Pickens, "Despite scientific knowledge to the contrary, Laughlin wrote as if blood were the transmitting agent in heredity and nationality were race."[43] Moreover, with reference to both immigrants and African Americans, eugenic blood imagery often connoted animalistic devolution. Eastern and southeastern Europeans had the potential, Fairchild believed, to "introduc[e] into the American population considerable strains of Mongoloid germ plasm," to inhibit the continuation of the specialized "English" and "American type," and to contribute to a general "mongrelization" and a backward evolutionary step: "The result to be looked for in the offspring is . . . a primitive, generalized type—often spoken of as a 'reversion', 'atavism', or 'throwback.'"[44] Dracula, in giving visual form to the novel's use of atavistic imagery, picks up on these rhetorical strands. The vampire appears in the form of a bat and is linked to wolves. Harker likens Dracula to "a wild animal," and Renfield relates a vision of rats summoned for him by the vampire: "And I thought he seemed to be saying, 'Rats. Rats. Rats! Thousands, millions of them. All red blood, all these will I give you, if you obey me.'" Renfield's words suggest a connection between the language of blood and the racialized, animalistic Other.

In eugenic discourse, then, blood figures the invisible gene, blood-fusion stands in for dysgenic sexual reproduction between inferior and superior groups, and blood-loss encodes the diminishing of good genetic stock as the nation is overwhelmed by defective groups. The vitality of the dysgenic classes is evident in the film: having drunk Dracula's blood, Mina declares that she "feel[s] wonderful," while Renfield warns that "madmen have great strength" and bends the bars of his asylum cell, in the words of his keeper, "as if they was cheese." These developments confirm a eugenic narrative in which decadent and decaying classes, intransigent foreigners, and racialized atavists, all possessors of "bad blood," threaten to overcome the underreproductive elite. Blood thus becomes a central bodily sign through which both eugenic texts and *Dracula* cohere disparate national, ethnic, and social categories, and mark them as embodiments and perpetuators of physical and mental debility, all under the guise of providing proof for the invisible process of genetic determination at the moment of sexual reproduction.

## Blood Products: Disease and Disappearance in *Dracula*

Like the chimera, however, blood in the film of *Dracula* serves both scientific and phantasmatic purposes. Insofar as the movie's signifiers of blood actively work against the evocation of some locus of natural, pure, sexual reproduction, they can shed light on the dynamics of eugenic (il)logic and indicate eugenicists' failure to reduce inchoate bodily complexities to the procreative act. There remain a number of gaps or elisions in *Dracula*'s narrative, which correspond remarkably to the film's self-stated impetus to "bring . . . proof"—in bloody form—of invisible essences and dysgenic forces. The film conjures blood only to erase it repeatedly, asserting and then removing the possibility of positivist proof, tracing in the air the prospect of a normative sexual relation and reproduction that, the film's own narrative suggests, has never existed.

The story of blood in *Dracula* begins again with Renfield, who learns in the film's opening minutes, from Transylvania's frightened villagers, that vampires "feed on the blood of the living." In Castle Dracula, after confirming the Count's lease of the Abbey, Renfield shuffles his documents, cutting himself on a paper-clip. A close-up shows blood oozing from the end of his finger. Dracula, from the other side of the room, gazes intently at the blood and moves slowly toward Renfield but draws back sharply and covers his face when Renfield's crucifix falls in front of the wounded hand. Renfield assures Dracula "it's just a scratch" and sucks his own blood, while Dracula stares greedily. The Count then invites Renfield to drink his "very old wine," intoning, "I never drink . . . wine." The drugged wine causes Renfield to faint, and after shooing away the vampire brides, Dracula closes in on his hapless victim. Dracula's cravings are transferred to the realtor: on the storm-wracked ship, Renfield begs Dracula to ensure that, once they reach England, he will get "lives," "not human lives, but small ones—with blood in them." When the ship with its dead crew arrives in the harbor, a laughing Renfield is pronounced "mad" by the men who find him and "a raving maniac" by a newspaper report, which comments that his "craving to devour ants, flies and other small living things to obtain their blood, puzzles scientists." The newspaper also notes that Renfield has been consigned to Seward's sanitarium.

This sequence sets in motion a subplot that shadows Dracula's later encounters with Lucy, Mina, and Van Helsing. In several scenes where Renfield escapes his cell to find Seward and Van Helsing and advise them to take Mina away, his degeneracy is manifested in erratic behavior: not only his sudden changes of mood, his deranged laughter, and his hysterical wailing, but also his quest to absorb the blood of insects and spiders. His debility—that is, his insanity—is, like Mina's faintness and fatigue, indexed to blood. In the first scene in which we see Van Helsing, he mixes Renfield's blood with another liquid and investigates the result through a microscope; we are led to believe that in the blood lies confirmation and explanation of Renfield's condition.

But in its function as "proof"—of vampires or, in our eugenic terms, of genetic determination via the sexual act—blood proves rather evasive. The blood on Renfield's finger constitutes the only actual view of the substance provided in the entire film. When Renfield absorbs his own blood, the film foreshadows Dracula's *modus operandi*, the consumptive act that will exacerbate the blood-loss of the elite classes (fig. 1.3). But as the blood disappears into Renfield's mouth, so the film begins its process of bodily erasure; moments later, when Dracula closes in on Renfield, a fade to black obscures the penetration of Renfield's neck and vitiation of his blood, an elision repeated in subsequent attacks on the flower peddler, Lucy, and Mina.

The same elimination of signs of blood occurs in the scene that first presents Van Helsing as the character who can both see and successfully "read" the signifiers of debility. The professor, surrounded by beakers, microscope at hand, and wearing thick, magnifying glasses, first adds a transparent liquid to a test tube of Renfield's blood, which turns clear. He asks one of the men seated around the table to "read where I have marked," and the man reads aloud in Latin. Van Helsing then announces to Seward and the other men that they are dealing with "the undead," noting that the vampire attacks the throat and leaves "two little wounds, white with red centers," a reference to the marks on Lucy's neck. He continues: "Dr. Seward, your patient, Renfield, whose blood I have just analyzed, is obsessed with the idea that he must devour living things in order to sustain

**1.3** Renfield (Dwight Frye) consumes his own blood in *Dracula* (1931).

his own life." It is when Seward dismisses the idea as myth and superstition that Van Helsing declares his plan to prove that the superstition of yesterday may become the science of today. The scene affirms the wisdom of Van Helsing through his ability to interpret signs that are indecipherable to others: the Latin, the marks on the vampire's victims, the blood of Renfield. Like eugenicists seeking to convince a sometimes skeptical public, Van Helsing seeks to demonstrate the effects of an invisible force—he later admonishes Seward and Harker, "The strength of the vampire is that people will not believe in him"—and to do so he must reveal these bloody traces as material truths.

Within the mise-en-scène, however, each of these traces stages a kind of disappearing act. We are never shown the marks on Lucy's or Mina's necks, we see the blood in the test tube become transparent but do not learn the significance of this transformation, and we are never told the meaning of the Latin reading, which presumably confirms a connection between Renfield's blood and the practices of the vampire. The slipperiness of the film's dominant corporeal signifier undermines the bodily truth on which eugenic discourse is ostensibly based. The film's obscuring of the sight of blood suggests a logic at work other than that of genetic predestination at the moment of conception.

Most obviously, this alternative logic is one of contagion, wherein the exchange of blood—and by extension, other bodily fluids such as saliva—

exceeds a reproductive narrative and insists on the formative and nonge-netically determined effects of infection. The logic of contagion has long accompanied the vampire myth, which, Fred Botting argues, emerges from "fears of the Plague, thought, since the Middle Ages, to have emanated from the East."[45] The word *nosferatu* has been etymologically linked to the Greek *nosophoros*, meaning "plague-carrier," and both Stoker's *Dracula* and F. W. Murnau's *Nosferatu* emphasize the image of a disease-bearing for-eigner.[46] The presence in eugenic discourse of the rhetoric of disease sug-gests that such imagery can easily support biologically and racially deter-ministic understandings. As Judith Halberstam comments, referencing Max Nordau's *Degeneration* (1893), "predisposition to diseases like syphilis or the possibility of degeneration were ascribed to certain races (such as the Jews), to their genealogy and their lifestyles, in order to give moral structure to the seemingly random process of infection."[47]

But as the word "predisposition" suggests, disease could only function effectively within eugenic schemas as long as it could be contained within a genetically deterministic doctrine, a containment eugenicists did not always achieve. In discussing immigration, for example, eugenic writers frequently represented the foreign threat in penetrative, and thus implicitly sexual, terms, as in Madison Grant's statement that "[i]nstead of a popula-tion homogenous in race, religion, traditions and aspirations, as was the American nation down to 1840, we have—inserted into the body politic—an immense mass of foreigners, congregated for the most part in the large cities and in the industrial centers." But such concerns also shaded into a notion of disease revealed at skin level, as in Kenneth L. Roberts' represen-tation of Mexican immigrants, "sizzling with disease," as an "acute plague sore on the body politic." The image of disease in turn invoked that of infec-tion, as in the words of Albert Johnson, chairman of the Immigration Com-mittee of the House of Representatives in 1931: "How shall the Republic endure if there be steady deterioration of standards by ever-recurring new foci of infection, arriving in the land?"[48]

The mixed success with which eugenically inclined Americans sought to align the rhetoric of disease with the certainty of reproduc-tive determination is apparent in a circa 1910 article in *Pearson's Maga-zine*, in which Robert Wickliffe Woolley attributed the spread of syphi-lis to the miscegenation of white men with black women and to the subsequent importation by white men of the disease into the bodies of their wives. Woolley combined images of vampirism, blood, disease, and aberrant reproduction in consolidating the threat in the bodies of African Americans:

Stalking through the Southland, hand in hand with the negro and the mulatto, is the "Great Black Plague." Ten times as contagious as leprosy and more productive of morbidity and death, eventually, than tuberculosis, it works in secret because of the shame which overwhelms its victims, and it is to-day seriously imperiling the very existence of the Anglo-Saxon blood. The social body is being defiled, sapped and weakened, and a proud race is all too close to the verge of committing involuntary suicide. It is rendering sterile many of the fairest and noblest women in Dixie, and is either killing outright or making hopeless invalids of many more; it is destroying unborn babies by the thousand and is causing thousands more to come into this world degenerated, physically and mentally. And yet the land abounds with good, well-meaning persons who earnestly protest that this loathsome vampire must not be mentioned except to a physician and that the young must be kept absolutely in the dark as to its existence or its terrible effects.[49]

Woolley's diatribe seeks to make visible the plague-vampire whose existence is enabled by the silence and ignorance of "good, well-meaning persons." This effort is aligned with the containment of disease as a matter of inappropriate—that is, interracial and extramarital—sexual activity. But even as Woolley's focus on *sexually* transmitted disease enables him to subordinate matters of infection to a reproductive narrative, his comments also concede that even the most genetically sound ("the fairest and noblest women in Dixie") are vulnerable to the predations of disease. Eugenicists trod similarly unsteady terrain in their discussions of disease. Davenport was forced to admit that "usually specific diseases are not inherited," although he maintained that "a condition of liability or non-resistance to a particular class of disease" might be hereditary.[50] Anti-eugenicists pushed the point: African-American reformists responded to eugenic ideas of racial inferiority by invoking disease, one writer observing that "germs of disease have no race prejudice."[51]

Just as eugenicists sought to present the vagaries of infection as a biologically predictable phenomenon, manageable through proper sexual practices, so *Dracula* recasts *Nosferatu*'s proliferation of disease as a limited outbreak of vampirism, tied intimately to aberrant sexual reproductive acts, and brought under control by the scientific deductions and violent act of Van Helsing. Peter Hutchings suggests that the shift from the novel's infection-invasion narrative to the film's "perverse romantic" story is a matter of narrative expedience: "it focuses the narrative and makes it more linear and manageable for film-makers, as opposed to the sprawling and disjointed narrative structure provided by Stoker." For Hutchings, the alteration also indicates that "anxieties about alien incursions from the East would not have especially concerned American and British audiences and film-makers from the 1930s onwards," a contention that the history of anti-immigration sentiment in the United States belies.[52] Rather, it seems, the adaptation of the vampire narrative in romantic terms speaks to a eugenic context in which foreignness, degeneracy, and disease were consistently presented as players in a *reproductive* drama, in which disease, contagion, and all manner of bodily dysfunctions were almost always understood as innate and genetic, predetermined, and thus able to be contained and excluded from the normative, white, national body.

However, Hutchings' association of a "sprawling narrative" with themes of infection and invasion, in contrast to the more cohesive, "linear," romantic narrative, is suggestive. For while *Dracula*'s eugenic narrative reaches its predetermined conclusion with the vampire's destruction and the couple's reunion, several of the film's narrative loose ends thwart the containment of the vampire's threat in reproductive terms. As many commentators have noted, *Dracula*'s narrative progression is muddied and several issues left unresolved due to apparent directorial neglect, script and editing cuts, and the staging of dramatic, violent, or potentially offensive events offscreen.[53] For instance, while the staking and beheading of vampire Lucy forms one of the novel's most vivid scenes, it does not occur in the film. Van Helsing promises Mina that "after tonight [Lucy] will remain at rest, her soul released from this horror," but this action is never again referenced or confirmed, leaving Lucy, in viewers' minds at least, wandering the night in search of children's blood. Similarly, Dracula's three brides are introduced early in the film, rising from their coffins alongside him, and closing in on the fainted Renfield before Dracula chases them away. But they are not mentioned nor seen thereafter. Questions Roy Huss, "Does Dracula take them with him to England? If so, does Van Helsing stay behind in the crypt at Carfax Abbey in order to destroy them? If they remained in Transylvania (as shown in the novel), wouldn't they continue to be a menace, thus implicitly marring the happy ending?" For Huss, these unresolved puzzles constitute "a disfigurement of the plot."[54]

This narrative "disfigurement" relies, then, on implications of disease and infection that are not reducible to a sexually reproductive origin nor resolved by eugenic measures. The continued existence of the vampire brides and Lucy as narrative "disfigurements" also intimates that vampirism has not been contained by Van Helsing but persists, not only in the vampire women but in Mina herself. As Berenstein comments, Mina's anguished cry of pain as Dracula is staked suggests that "threats of monstrosity endure in women who survive narrative closure."[55] Consequently, the eugenic compulsion to manifest Dracula's inner degeneracy, which leads to reliance on tropes of blood and animality, ultimately undercuts the delimitation of his threat in terms of sexual reproduction and confounds racist and ableist efforts to restrict dysfunction to bodies other than those of the dominant "race."

But another logic is at work here, as well, one tied to the film's rhetoric of blood and particularly to Renfield, around whom so many of *Dracula*'s narrative gaps seem to form. As already noted, the disappearance of the blood from Renfield's finger precipitates an erasure of blood from the remainder of the film, even when it is *said* to be present: in Van Helsing's test tube, in the "red centers" of the marks on the vampire's victims, and in the blood exchanges between the vampire and his victims, which occur offscreen and are only narrated to us. This vanishing bodily signifier suggests that where eugenic narrative posits an all-determining point of origin in the sexual act, "proved" by somatic signs that can be read by experts, the film's operations point constantly to that point of origin as an impossible and invisible space and to the signs of defect as mere props. Such signs appear only long enough to point toward eugenicists' failures to "de-monstrate" genetic predestination and toward bodily dynamics that refute a purely genetic explanation. Narratives of disease and infection are not innocent of eugenic or racist tendencies, but their very existence, even in eugenic texts, indicates the inevitable and proliferating production of monstrosity at the heart of the eugenic enterprise and the textual (rather than sexual) origins and status of the dysgenic monsters, the chimeras, constructed by eugenicists.

In keeping with the film's early scenes, many of *Dracula*'s narrative inconsistencies attach to Renfield's character and take the form of puzzling gaps and absences in the plot's logic. Why does Dracula attack Renfield when "the script called for the vampire women to do the deed"?[56] Once he is incarcerated, why does Renfield repeatedly urge Seward to take Mina away, and what does he promise to do for Dracula? Indeed, why does Dracula need Renfield after the latter secures the lease of the Abbey for the Count? And what does Renfield do to the Sewards' maid? The original script and the Spanish film version, *Drácula*, reveal that when the young woman faints and Renfield crawls menacingly toward her, he is in fact pursuing a nearby fly.[57] But the scene's abrupt conclusion in Browning's film, with Renfield still advancing on the maid, leaves viewers confused, especially when she is later seen in apparently normal health. Finally, why does Van Helsing stay behind in the Abbey at the film's end? The original screenplay has him remain to "'fulfill [his] promise to Renfield,'" but the nature of that promise remains opaque.[58] Even if we assume that Van Helsing intends to stake Renfield and prevent his vampiric resurrection, the film does not make this clear, leaving spectators confused as to the professor's motivations and the final status of Renfield's soul.

Several critiques of *Dracula* dwell on these plot holes and on the film's frustrating tendency to have its most dramatic moments take place off camera, as with Mina's "dream" of Dracula, Renfield's vision of rats, and the appearance of Dracula as a wolf, the latter described to the other characters by Harker. In each instance, viewers' desire to see the "proof" Van Helsing promises, the manifestation of the monster and his degeneracy, is thwarted—not, perhaps, by artistic design, but rather by the quotidian realities of filmmaking: the gaps point to elements of the novel and the play that were cut or incompletely adapted and to scripted scenes never filmed or edited out. But precisely because the film's "failings" suggest the resistances of textual material to its reshaping in new forms, they also indicate the failure of a strict eugenic reading to gain purchase within the narrative. Instead, the "old" explanations of somatic difference—mythic, popular, racist, and religious—traverse the film: Van Helsing triumphs with crosses and wolfsbane and stakes, not with his test tubes and microscopes. And the signs summoned as evidence for the new, medicalized narrative, with its genetically deterministic explanation of the mysteries of reproduction and heredity, repeatedly shift, infect, and disappear.[59]

In sum, then, the monster's existence, "proven" in *Dracula* and in some eugenic texts by signs and invocations of blood, constitutes the evidence eugenicists require to sell their genetic narratives. But signifiers of impairment as some kind of bedrock for eugenic positivism become, in the film, remarkably elusive, suggesting that somatic materials and experiences disappear from the eugenic narrative to the extent that they refuse the meaning with which they are invested. In *Dracula*, the rhetoric of blood generates imagery of infection and disease that corresponds to understandings of disability as mutable and environmentally determined, rather than directly produced by procreative acts. At the same time, the discursive invocation of a "real" substance, blood, that repeatedly disappears or fails to appear, illustrates how bodily materials can thwart eugenic efforts to prove genetic determination. It is precisely the film's figures of deviance—mixed and lost blood, animals presumed to carry disease, the madman—that draw our gaze to the narrative's gaps and elisions and to the many unseen events that determine what happens in front of our eyes. We become aware of the incompleteness of the linear story of sexual reproduction and genetic determinism and are attuned to the reality of what lurks beyond the eugenic frame: the accidents, infections, and mutabilities of bodies and minds that remain irreducible to eugenicists' "germ plasm" or "protoplasm."[60] *Dracula*'s example suggests that if the horror film appeals through its capacity to literalize the monster's body, it also resists that literalization, insisting that as bodily traits and substances are made to "mean" within a narrative, they are also textualized, interpreted, displaced.

## BRAIN DAMAGE: *FRANKENSTEIN*

Although the dysgenic figures and signs of impairment invoked by *Frankenstein* differ from those of *Dracula*, the film also sets in motion a specifically eugenic narrative only to contest both genetic determination of character and the possibility of the ideal eugenic couple. The question of procreative origins has always been central to Mary Shelley's *Frankenstein* tale, a story in which a man eschews marriage in order to make a monster and in which the monster insists on his father's responsibility for his creation.[61] Such a plot seemingly lends itself to eugenic readings, presenting Frankenstein as a dysgenic figure whose failure to reproduce normally generates a monster destructive to the ideal family unit. Yet, at least in retrospect, the desires of the novel's "mad scientist" are also recognizably eugenic. Frankenstein's vision of the wonders his science will achieve ("A new species would bless me as its creator and source; many happy and excellent natures would owe their being to me") seems to anticipate "positive" eugenics, the belief that "the fit [must be] encouraged to increase their numbers, an objective achieved through a scientific knowledge and social application of heredity."[62] Shelley's text also divines the misogynistic and violent underpinnings of eugenics' happy dream, the correlative "negative" eugenic belief "that the unfit must be eliminated or at least limited in number," when Frankenstein contemplates the half-completed form of his monster's bride, and, imagining the horrific consequences of their coupling, fears that "a race of devils would be propagated upon the earth"; he consequently "[tears] to pieces the thing on which [he] was engaged."[63]

Whether Shelley's Frankenstein is a figure whose anti-eugenic actions and their terrible results reinforce notions of proper procreation or a eugenic figure whose horrific actions suggest the monstrosity of eugenics itself, the novel both makes central the (pro)creative act and unsettles the idea that identity forms biologically at conception, contesting Frankenstein's imagination of himself as "creator and source." The text ultimately looks unfavorably on Frankenstein's effort to arrogate creative powers to individual men and on the implicitly eugenic belief in the determinative powers of the (pro) creative act. Indeed, the novel suggests that the conditions of the monster's conception and birth are less important than formative events such as his abandonment, his observation of the de Lacey family, his education in literature and history, and his repeated rejections by prejudiced individuals.

Dramatic adaptations of the novel reduced its components to a more simplistically eugenic narrative, an effort extended in the 1931 film.[64] James Whale's Universal movie, starring Boris Karloff as the Monster, helps consolidate the classic horror-film formula: the imminent marital union of a more-or-less normative couple is threatened by a monstrous figure who seemingly embodies aberrant reproductive practices. *Frankenstein* associates its monster with a somewhat different set of signifiers than those of *Dracula*, using an "abnormal brain" to represent the monster's debility in terms reminiscent of the eugenic category of "feeblemindedness." As in *Dracula*, however, the introduction of a material signifier of defect ultimately displaces the determinative act of sexual reproduction; in *Frankenstein* and its sequel, the significations of the brain invoke familial nurture over neurological nature. Also as in *Dracula*, the somatic symptoms called on to prove innate degeneracy become shifting markers that traverse the plot and its characters in chaotic and decidedly nongenetic ways, again displacing and rendering impossible the chimera of idealized natural reproduction.

## Abnormal Brains: Feeblemindedness and Eugenics in *Frankenstein*

In *Frankenstein*, released in November 1931, the obsessive work of Henry Frankenstein (Colin Clive) toward the monster's creation keeps him from his fiancée Elizabeth (Mae Clarke). We first encounter Henry and his hunchbacked assistant Fritz (Dwight Frye) lurking around a fresh gravesite, from which they disinter a body. They also cut down a man who has been hung but whose broken neck necessitates further searching for a suitable brain. Soon thereafter, Fritz eavesdrops on a lecture by Professor Waldman (Edward Van Sloan, *Dracula*'s Van Helsing), Henry's former mentor, at Goldstadt Medical College. After the audience files out, Fritz steals the "normal" brain that Waldman was discussing, but when the jar slips and breaks, Fritz grabs the brain labeled "abnormal" and flees.

Meanwhile, Elizabeth, concerned by Henry's obsession, accompanies her friend Victor (John Bowles) on a visit to Professor Waldman. They discover Henry is no longer with the university, because his research was becoming too advanced and dangerous and because the university refused to provide him with cadavers. All three proceed to Henry's laboratory, a watchtower in the Tyrolean Mountains, and find him on the verge of realizing his creation. The pieced-together body is winched skywards where a bolt of lightning brings it to life. Once the Monster is animated, Henry and Waldman are alarmed by his appearance and by his aggressive response when Fritz taunts him with a flaming torch. They chain the creature, but when Fritz goads him further and pays with his life, the Monster's deviance seems confirmed. Henry agrees to allow Waldman to kill the sedated monster and accompanies Elizabeth back to the village to organize their wedding.

As Waldman prepares for dissection, however, the Monster awakens, kills Waldman, and gains his freedom. He encounters and plays with a little girl, Maria (Marilyn Harris), as they both throw flowers onto the water. Not realizing that she cannot float like the flowers, he throws her into the water, and she drowns. Soon after, the Monster enters Elizabeth's room as she awaits her wedding and prepares to attack her. Interrupted, he flees, pursued by villagers. He captures Henry and arrives at an old mill, where he is cornered. As the mob sets the mill ablaze, the Monster hurls Henry toward the ground from the top of the structure, before it collapses in flames around him. At this point, the script penned by the film's initial director, Robert Florey, called for Henry to die. However, while Whale originally envisaged a similar demise, he eventually appended a conclusion in which we glimpse Henry recovering in bed, with Elizabeth at his side, while the Baron makes a toast with his servants: "Here's to a son, to the House of Frankenstein!"[65]

The film thus counterposes Henry's dark act of creation to the conventional rituals of wedding and reproduction, marking the aberrance of the former through various signs of defect. The act that births the monster takes dead bodies as its materials and is enabled by the unnatural collaboration of two men—a hubristic, and apparently unstable, scientist and his "deformed" male assistant. Their deficiencies as (artificial) procreators are conveyed in terms of visible disability: Henry repeatedly exhibits hysterical behavior and physical weakness, while Fritz's aberrance is conveyed in his hunched back, lopsided gait, and eager, crazed expressions. But the film's clearest indication of the Monster's physical deviance is supplied via the disabled Fritz's theft of a brain labeled "ABNORMAL." (fig. 1.4). The organ's defectiveness confirms the degeneracy of any product of a non-heterosexual, non-natural, and thus non-eugenic act of procreation, initiating an explicitly eugenic narrative of biologically determined character.[66]

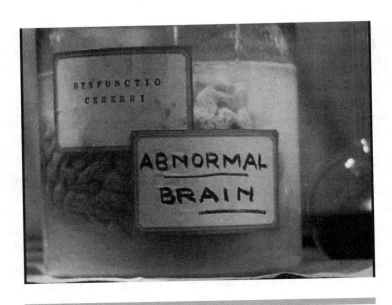

**1.4** A brain for the monster in *Frankenstein* (1931).

The narrative proceeds by interspersing scenes of the Monster's murder of Waldman, his escape, and his drowning of Maria with scenes at the Frankenstein house, where guests, servants, and villagers in the street celebrate Henry and Elizabeth's impending nuptials. These episodes emphasize the wedding as a ritual that marks and enables the normative conjoining of biological and socioeconomic inheritance. Earlier, the town burgomaster eagerly anticipates the union, declaring, "Such a lovely bride. Such a fine young man, the very image of his father." During the wedding preparations, Baron Frankenstein extends this sense of heredity as he presents Henry with a corsage: "For three generations, these orange blossoms have been worn at our weddings. Your great-grandfather wore this, Henry." Picking up a flower tiara, the Baron continues, "Thirty years ago, I placed this on your mother's head, Henry. Today, you'll make me very happy by doing the same for Elizabeth. And I hope, I hope in thirty years' time, a youngster of yours will be carrying on the tradition." The Baron then leads the toast for "a son, to the House of Frankenstein." The servants' participation in the toast and the Baron's subsequent address to the partying villagers remind us of the Frankenstein family's social importance and eugenic status: the family is wealthy, socially respected, and built on the consistent reproduction of healthy (male) children.

Within this eugenic narrative, *Frankenstein* mobilizes tropes of bodily and mental debility to affirm, through disability, the degeneracy of "inferior" classes. The film's rhetoric of abnormal and criminal brains references a eugenic discourse of "feeblemindedness," in which inferior intelligence, lower-class status, and criminality are consolidated in and confirmed by the monster's aberrant bodily appearance and behavior. As we have seen, the monster's abnormal brain constitutes proof of the aberrance of the reproductive method that brings him into being. The device of the deficient brain has been roundly condemned. Martin Tropp finds it *Frankenstein*'s "most absurd and unnecessary sequence," and Skal presents it as "a major subversion of Shelley's intended moral; it is not Henry's divine presumption that sets in motion the catastrophe, but a deception and cover-up by a handicapped employee."[67] Chris Baldick disparages the determinism implied by the scene, asserting that "the pickled brain . . . offers a crudely simple 'explanation' for the monster's motives" and thus contributes to the film's reduction of the novel's complexity.[68] Certainly, in linking an irregular act of reproduction with a physically determined degeneracy, *Frankenstein* posits a reductive explanation for the monster's behavior. But, in so doing, the film also updates the novel's concerns with monstrous creation, overtly referencing eugenic ideas and putting in motion a biologically deterministic narrative in which defect is traceable to a moment of organic origin. The invention of this sequence within the film—particularly insofar as it seemingly fails to "fit" and reduces complex and philosophical notions about identity to biological predestination—requires that we again attend to the apparently natural and bodily fact of impairment as something textually constituted to specific—and in this case, eugenic—ends.[69]

Fritz's theft of the brain is preceded by an anatomical lecture that reads the abnormal organ in eugenic terms. Professor Waldman interprets two sample brains for his university class:

> Here we have one of the most perfect specimens of the human brain that has ever come to my attention at the university. And here, the abnormal brain of the typical criminal. Observe, ladies and gentlemen, the scarcity of convolutions on the frontal lobe as compared to that of the normal brain. And a distinct degeneration of the middle frontal lobe. All of these degenerate characteristics check amazingly with the history of the dead man before us, whose life was one of brutality, of violence and murder.

In presenting a biological and measurable explanation of criminality, Waldman's speech draws on nineteenth-century scientific figures such as Cesare Lombroso, who viewed criminality as an inherited and atavistic trait deducible from facial and skull characteristics; Alphonse Bertillon, who developed criminal anthropometry, a practice of measurement of criminals' physical features; and Adolphe Quetelet, whose statistical studies examined correlations between crime and factors such as poverty. Waldman's words also invoke the twentieth-century eugenic discourse of feeblemindedness, which brought together notions of mental defect and criminal behavior via efforts to visualize and quantify the defective brain.

In the early twentieth century, the term *feeblemindedness* had displaced earlier labels for mental "inferiority"—such as "idiot" or "imbecile"—and would, after the heyday of eugenics, transmute into terms such as "mentally retarded" and more recent designations such as "developmentally delayed" or "intellectually disabled." Laughlin defined someone labeled "feebleminded" as "so deficient mentally that he is unable to cope with the complexities of the social organization in which he finds himself, without custodial care."[70] With the introduction of Alfred Binet's IQ tests to the United States by American psychologist Henry Goddard, American eugenicists sought to quantify feeblemindedness, categorizing individuals according to the particular age at which their intellectual and moral growth had, allegedly, prematurely halted: "*idiots* were those who tested under one or two years, *imbeciles* tested at ages three to seven, and the *feebleminded* [or 'morons'] tested between years eight and twelve."[71]

Feeblemindedness linked intelligence testing to nineteenth-century discourses of evolution and criminality. Goddard, who held that criminality was both heritable and a matter of mental inferiority, believed that the mental growth of "moral imbeciles" halted just as their primitive instincts were developing, dooming them to pursue forever primordial impulses toward deceit, theft, and sexual perversion.[72] Declared Dr. Walter E. Fernald in 1912, "Every feeble-minded person, especially the high-grade imbecile, is a potential criminal, needing only the proper environment and opportunity for the development and expression of his criminal tendencies."[73] Feeblemindedness and criminality were interrelated by a circular logic: the impropriety of those deemed feebleminded was read as criminality, while socially wayward or illegal actions, such as extramarital sexual behavior or prostitution, were read as evidence of mental defect.[74]

"Feeblemindedness" fixed and explained a host of social phenomena and individual characteristics in biological terms, becoming "a catchall for those found to display an unacceptable degree of deviancy."[75] Complex and potentially cultural phenomena were interpreted as physiological facts: C. F. Dight, president of the Minnesota Eugenics Society, described "the mind" and "morals" as matters of "the intellectual brain" and "the moral brain," declaring, "Eliminate, and free the world of people who have unevenly developed, unbalanced and defective brains, then sin and evil will disappear."[76] Social problems became a simple matter of genetics: in 1919, V. V. Anderson declared, "Scientific researchers have demonstrated the possible and close relationship of feeblemindedness to many of society's most serious social problems, and have pointed the way to a possible solution of, or at least a scientific and intelligent approach to, the problems of crime and pauperism, juvenile vice, prostitution, venereal disease, etc."[77] Concomitantly, eugenicists challenged views that social or cultural environment could significantly alter an individual's mental capacity. Wrote Goddard, "[N]o amount of education or good environment can change a feeble-minded individual into a normal one."[78]

In particular, feeblemindedness enabled the reinterpretation of social structures of class hierarchy as biological destiny. The characteristics of mental disability and criminality central to diagnoses of feeblemindedness were most often ascribed to the lower classes, as widely publicized in "family studies" such as Goddard's *The Kallikak Family* (1912), Arthur H. Estabrook's *The Jukes in 1915* (1916), Estabrook and Ivan E. McDougle's *Mongrel Virginians* (1926), and several other books on pseudonymous families such as the Nams, the Hill Folk, and the Pineys.[79] Such texts asserted an insidious class revolution: declared Goddard, "There are Kallikak families all about us. They are multiplying at twice the rate of the general population, and not until we recognize this fact, and work on this basis, will we begin to solve these social problems."[80] These eugenic genealogies presented poor families as "degenerate" and criminal burdens on state and taxpayer and validated social status as a matter of biological merit. They also helped develop a system of social control that extended "regulatory mechanisms" over the poor into rural areas.[81]

As discussed in the introduction, eugenicists' answer to the proliferating hordes of the criminal feebleminded involved subjecting the ostensibly "unfit" to marital restrictions, institutionalization, and/or sterilization. To make the case for such measures, eugenicists again sought to assert visual and physical "proof" of feeblemindedness as a genetic threat, as when the American Eugenics Society used flashing lights at State Fair exhibits to delineate differential birthrates between the desirables and the mentally unfit.[82] Eugenicists agreed with the Lombrosian idea that the brain could visually convey innate mental defect, atavism, and criminality: a display at the 1923 Second International Exhibition of Eugenics in New York, entitled "Massachusetts Department of Mental Diseases Exhibits Pictures of 59

Criminal Brains," depicted numbered, captioned photographs of two "normal" and six "criminal" brains.[83]

*Frankenstein*'s "abnormal brain" participates in a comparable visualization of intellectual defect in order to confirm the monster's criminality, as his facial appearance delineates the abnormal brain beneath. Makeup artist Jack Pierce asserted the pseudoscientific veracity of Karloff's visage: "If the monster looks like something I dreamt after something I ate, don't blame me. . . . Blame science! I made him the way textbooks said he should look. I didn't depend on imagination. In 1931, before I did a bit of designing I spent three months of research in anatomy, surgery, medicine, criminal history, criminology, ancient and modern burial customs and electrodynamics."[84] Criminology and medicine undoubtedly provided Pierce with phrenological and evolutionary understandings of the brain: to that end, he "exaggerat[ed] the bony ridges of Karloff's head" and achieved "a primitive, Neanderthal appearance that would stress [the Monster's] low intellect" by "slop[ing] the brow of the eyes in a pronounced ape-like ridge of bone."[85] Pierce also notes that his anatomical studies suggested the crude method Frankenstein might use to cut open the creature's skull in order to replace its brain, thus giving him a "square and flat" head, while his electrodynamic studies inspired the use of "metal studs" in the monster's neck as "inlets for electricity" (fig. 1.5). As well, Pierce drew on readings in Egyptian history, where he learnt that "the Egyptians used to bind some criminals hand and foot and bury them alive. When their blood turned to water after death, it flowed into their extremities, stretched their arms to gorilla length and swelled their hands, feet and faces to abnormal proportions. I thought this might make a nice touch for the monster, since he was supposed to be made from the corpses of executed felons." From this inspiration emerged the monster's long arms, oversized legs and feet, and gray-green face.[86] The monster's feeblemindedness and criminality were thus carefully inscribed onto his face and form in ways meant to elicit a sense of innate monstrosity, confirming the declaration of the eugenicist noted above, in which feeblemindedness expresses itself in the "stunted, misshapen, hideous" forms of its "specimens."[87]

*Frankenstein* mimics the eugenic tendency to visualize "feeblemindedness" in relation to lower-class status, primitivism, and criminality. Karloff's Monster shares salient traits with those poor and working classes most often subjected to eugenics' institutionalizing, objectifying, and medicalizing tendencies. In the nineteenth century, Shelley's monster had operated in political cartoons as a figure for "mob rule and violence" and an embodiment of "[t]he working class, the uneducated, and the Irish."[88] Continuing

**1.5** The face of a monster: Boris Karloff in *Frankenstein* (1931).

this association, Whale's film garbs the Monster in "laborer's clothes."[89] In the film, the Monster's size and strength also remind us of the eugenic narrative in which the intellectually deficient and bodily impoverished were, in fact, resisting and rising up against their biological superiors: in the words of Lothrop Stoddard, "[Feeblemindedness] is highly hereditary, and unfortunately it is frequently associated with great physical strength and vitality, so that feeble-minded persons usually breed rapidly, with no regard for consequences."[90] Thus, in *Frankenstein*, when Waldman describes the Monster's "increased resistance" to medical and surgical efforts to "fix" him, the professor suggests the creature's association with these biologically proliferating underclasses. Moreover, when Waldman advises Henry to kill the Monster "as you would any savage animal," he characterizes the creature in the evolutionary terms of eugenic discourse, presenting him as primitive, as less sentient than a "normal" person, and thus, as an animal deserving of euthanasia. Waldman's efforts to sedate and dissect the Monster also recall the practices of sterilization enacted on the bodies of those classified as feebleminded in order to forestall their reproductive threat.[91]

*Frankenstein*'s display of brains and physical representation of the Monster thus set in play a biologically deterministic narrative in which the Monster is doomed to be mentally and morally defective. Whereas the novel's monster is merely hideous and abnormally large, while also being articulate, rational, and learned, the filmic Monster embodies the "manifestly unfit" decried by eugenic proponents.[92] His "imbecility" is revealed by his abnormal brain, physical ugliness, halting gait, and simpleminded behavior.[93] These characteristics constitute evidence for readings of Karloff's Monster that accept the determinism of the "madman's brain" and describe him as "a murderous fiend, devoid . . . of reason and barely glimpsed as human during the episode of the child who befriends him and whom he gratuitously drowns in a lake."[94] Since the Monster's physical and intellectual traits purportedly express his mental and moral deficiency, his primitive and animalistic behavior, and his threat to society, the thwarting of Waldman's surgical intervention enables the dysgenic drama to play out in the Monster's implied rape of Elizabeth and his destruction of a young child.

## Brains: Nature or Nurture?

But *Frankenstein*'s emphasis on the primitive nature of the Monster, recalling as it does eugenic ideas that the feebleminded were individuals whose intellectual development arrested at childish levels, opens new interpretive possibilities. First, eugenicists' reductive mapping of age-levels onto intellectual disability made available an understanding of "feeblemindedness" that, in characterizing the "feebleminded" as childlike, engendered sympathy rather than antipathy. Karloff contended that he and Whale strove to depict the Monster as innocent rather than neurologically criminal. He noted that there were "fantastic numbers of ordinary people that got this general air of sympathy. I found all my letters heavy with it. Many also wanted to offer help and friendship. It was one of the most moving experiences of my life."[95] The sympathy elicited by the Monster thus undermines Lennard Davis's contention that horror films "remove the element of pity in the visual transaction between 'normal' viewer and disabled object."[96] Second, eugenic associations of cognitive disability with arrested development also draw attention to the monster's identity as Henry's child—albeit an artificially reproduced child—and to the possibility that he is not, as the "abnormal brain" might indicate, innately criminal but acts as he does because he is improperly nurtured from birth.

Like the rhetoric of disease invoked by *Dracula*'s blood imagery, discourses of pity and nurture are not necessarily innocent of ableist and discriminatory sentiment. Nonetheless, their mobilization points to a more charitable response to disability and invokes populist interpretations of eugenics that rejected strict biological determinism. As noted in the introduction, public interpretations of eugenics in the early decades of the twentieth century often defined it in relation to both biological heredity *and* parental upbringing, such that "'eugenics' meant not just having good genes, but being a good parent."[97]

The monster's childlike behavior thus calls attention to the neglect and abuse that he experiences. While the monster cannot articulately accuse his creator of abandonment, as he does in the novel, the film nevertheless makes clear his need for nurture and guidance. Trying to assuage Waldman's concerns soon after bringing the creature to life, Henry reassures him: "He's only a few days old, remember. So far he's been in complete darkness. Wait until I bring him into the light." Soon after, when the Monster enters awkwardly, slowly but obediently sitting where Henry directs him, Henry opens a shaft allowing daylight to stream into the room and onto the monster. Entranced, the Monster stands, walking toward the light, craning his neck upward, and raising his arms as if to touch the light. When Henry closes the shaft, the Monster grunts, bereft and confused. Moments later, he responds with hurt and aggression when Fritz flails a whip at him and attacks him with a burning torch. His murder of Fritz thus emerges as an act of self-defense, as does his killing of Waldman, which comes as the doctor prepares to dissect and destroy him. The film thus implies that the Monster acts like a "savage animal" because he is treated like one, denied the light by his creator.

The Monster's childlike behavior is evident again in his encounter with Maria. The Monster is both softened by the little girl's friendliness and excited by the concept of play. When he runs out of flowers to throw into the lake, he reaches happily for the little girl and tosses her in, apparently ignorant of his strength and the consequences of his actions. In the full scene, much of which was later censored, the Monster is clearly devastated by the girl's drowning: he starts to his feet, moaning sadly and anxiously, looks around wildly, and stumbles off into the woods. Later, when he confronts Elizabeth in her room, his mimicry of her scream confirms a childish eagerness and an ability to learn as well as the nature of the lesson: there is no welcome for him within the family or community. Thus, while Karloff's Monster lacks the eloquence of his novelistic predecessor, several moments in the film underscore his helplessness and vulnerability and indict Henry for seeking to dispose of him. From this perspective, the Monster's attack on Elizabeth enacts both vengeance on the maker who created and abandoned him and rage at the normative "eugenic" family from which he is excluded.

The idea that the Monster, as confused child, connotes populist views of eugenics as a matter of parental and environmental nurture becomes even more evident in *Frankenstein*'s sequel, *Bride of Frankenstein*, also directed by

Whale for Universal and released in 1935. Again, we witness the Monster's efforts to connect with others, including a shepherdess, whom he saves from drowning, and a gypsy family, whom he approaches for companionship and sustenance. Repeatedly, his approaches are misinterpreted and met with horrified and violent reactions. The exception lies in his interactions with the blind hermit (O. P. Heggie), where we find an extended examination of the Monster's more sympathetic personality. Attracted by the hermit's violin-playing, the Monster initially hides from the cottage's inhabitant. Unable to resist the music, however, he swings open the door. The hermit hears the Monster's grunts and invites him in, intuiting a connection to his injured visitor: "Perhaps you're afflicted too. I cannot see and you cannot speak. Is that it?" He tends to the Monster's wounds, provides him with food and drink, prays with him, and teaches him the rudiments of speech. At times, they are poised in a momentary embrace, and at one point the hermit puts the Monster to bed and then, kneeling alongside him, clasps his hand in a tearful prayer: "I have prayed many times for God to send me a friend. . . . I shall look after you and you shall comfort me. . . . Our Father, I thank Thee that in Thy great mercy, Thou hast taken pity on my great loneliness and now, out of the silence of the night, hast brought two of Thy lonely children together, and sent me a friend to be a light to mine eyes, and a comfort in time of trouble." The Monster, too, sheds a tear, and the scene fades to only the glow of the crucifix on the wall above the bed. The next day, the hermit and the Monster share a meal of bread and wine, and smoke cigars, as the hermit teaches him basic words. The monster learns that "Bread," "Drink," and "Friend" are good and that "Alone" is bad. To drive home the moral lesson, the hermit concludes: "There is good and there is bad." But the pastoral friendship is disrupted by the arrival of the hunters; in the following struggle, the hut is set on fire and the blind man hurried away by the intruders.

The scene models a condensed process of nurture and learning: the hermit gives the monster food, drink, prayer, and lessons in religion and language. The monster becomes a childlike creature in need of guidance rather than a deviant predestined to violent behavior. Sympathy for *Bride*'s monster pervaded reviews: one *New York Times* writer commented, "In more ways than one, this is a changed Monster. At first, one must recall, he was pretty much of a thorough-going brute, a killer for the killing's sake. Now . . . he is slightly moonstruck, hungry for kindness and, even—oh, perish the thought—for love."[98] Another *New York Times* piece elaborated: "'The Bride of Frankenstein' became the pitiful record of the monster's spiritual progress among human emotions. He heard music and wept. He won a friend and was glad. He wanted to be a man, but his neighbors hated and feared him because he was not like them."[99] The increased sympathy afforded the monster emerges, then, out of the film's emphasis on the larger community's failure to nurture him in the manner of the hermit (fig. 1.6).

The scene also clearly invokes a religious and sentimental worldview, and although this tendency has laid the hermit-monster relationship open to later parody, most notably in Mel Brooks's *Young Frankenstein* (1974), it also intervenes in eugenic discourse by invoking debates over the relationship of religion and spirituality to eugenic values. A certain opposition between spiritual and eugenic leaders was inevitable, given the view of Galton and many eugenicists thereafter that eugenics "must be introduced into the national conscience, like a new religion."[100] But many religious leaders in the United States, especially Protestants, were drawn to eugenics' potential for reforming and improving humankind. Religious eugenic discourse often addressed the danger of charitable efforts to protect and nurture the feebleminded, with one entry in the 1926 American Eugenics Society's sermon contest musing, "Surely the Kingdom can never come in all its fullness among a people descended from the Jukes."[101] Eugenicists, too, challenged the principles of religious charity: Los Angeles City Club president Hugh Pomeroy railed against "'Slobbery sentimentality' over

**1.6** Nurture: the monster (Boris Karloff) makes a friend (O. P. Heggie) in *Bride of Frankenstein* (1935).

criminals convicted of atrocious crimes," and AES executive secretary Leon Whitney avowed that it was "A Charity to Lessen Charity."[102]

But the Catholic Church, in particular, offered increasing resistance to such proposals. As Christine Rosen comments, "Catholics argued that natural, divine law—not the laws of biology—governed human behavior and protected, among other things, the indissolubility of marriage, the sanctity of procreation and human life (born and unborn), and the family. By interfering with these things, eugenicists violated natural law, and thus earned the censure of most Catholics."[103] At the 1939 Conference on the Relation of Eugenics and the Church, Father Francis J. Connell declared, "the soul of man is immeasurably more important than his body."[104] Consequently, as Daniel J. Kevles points out, "What to the eugenicist were biologically unfit people were, to the Church, children of God, blessed with immortal souls and entitled to the respect due every human being."[105] The Church's position was not by any means progressive, condemning eugenics along with other aspects of "the modern permissiveness" and constructing disabled people as objects of pity and charity. Nevertheless, its opposition to eugenics placed the Church and its representatives on the same side of the issue as other anti-eugenicists. In place of hereditary and biological determinism, religious figures proffered a program of instruction to inculcate morality in the criminal, and charity, to uplift the poor and succor the disabled and feebleminded.

*Bride* employs several religious elements in its implicit critique of eugenic notions. When Henry manically claims that he "know[s] what it feels like to be God," the film indicates, as many religious critics of eugenics believed, that "To practice eugenics was, in some sense, to play God."[106] When the monster is strung up on a pole in a manner akin to the crucified Christ and then instructed in morality by the hermit, the film employs a religious rhetoric of charity and love to counter popular perceptions that the monster lacks a soul and to suggest that generous and moral upbringing can nurture a soul in the disfigured, feebleminded, and even criminal of the modern world. In foregrounding sentimentality, the scenes between the Monster and the hermit oppose Pomeroy's condemnation of "slobbery sentimentality" for criminals, encouraging sympathy for the monster and delineating his monstrosity and criminality as environmentally created traits. Moreover, in presenting a poor and disabled man as a better parent and moral guide than the wealthy, socially significant, and educated scientist, *Bride* contests eugenic efforts to prevent poor and disabled people, including blind and "feebleminded" individuals, from marrying and procreating.

Of course, the interaction between the Monster and the hermit also mobilizes religious rhetoric to ends the Church would not approve, contributing to the film's extended disruption of—or depiction of the impossibility of—normative marriage. The monster and hermit's frequent touching and clasping, the Monster's long gazes into the unseeing eyes of the hermit, and the impassioned talk of friendship, care, and comfort significantly augment the film's much discussed queer or camp sensibility. Whale, an openly gay director, elicited from Ernest Thesiger a deliciously perverse and effeminate performance as the devious Dr. Pretorius and thus set in play queer readings of his interruptions of Henry and Elizabeth's marriage and his "procreative" activities with Henry. But if Pretorius' machinations confirm homophobic views of deviance, the hermit scene recasts concepts of normative familial relations and sexuality. Gary Morris refers to the hermit as "the monster's *first* mate" and avers, "No mistake—this is a marriage, and a viable one."[107] The sentimentality and wholesomeness of the scene position the two figures as outsiders establishing a fleeting utopia. Thus, when the hunters break in, terrorize the monster, and leave him in the burning hut, it is such normative figures, rather than the monster, that we associate with unwonted violence.

Accordingly, the film questions the heterosexual imperative itself. Gerald Gardner's comment that the only significant sexual aspect of the film likely to draw censors' ire was "the perverse chemical attraction of a monster for its mate" suggests that, following the film's elucidation of the monster and the hermit's sincere relationship, it is heterosexual and marital desires that come to seem aberrant.[108] The monster's pursuit of a Bride leads only to further violence when, rejected, the Monster brings the laboratory tower crashing down upon himself, his Bride, and the deviant Pretorius, intoning the lesson he has learned from a vicious society: "We belong dead." The bridal couple of Henry and Elizabeth is recuperated but seen very much as a product of the poignant and violent deaths of non-normative others.

In *Bride of Frankenstein*, then, we see the development of *Frankenstein*'s tendencies to refashion perceived biological deviance as a matter of nurture rather than nature. *Bride* employs religious iconography and charitable sentimentality to contest eugenic principles, representing two characters associated with monstrosity, disability, queerness, and poverty as the most Christian figures within the film. The interrogation of the heterosexual imperative undertaken by *Bride* also builds on a similar thematic in *Frankenstein*, one we can discern by tracing, in the earlier film, the proliferation across the "eugenic" couple of the movie's dominant signifier of impairment, "brain damage."

## "A Chimera in My Braine": The Eugenic Couple

It is not only the Monster whose symptoms of debility invoke some kind of "brain damage" in ways that coincide with eugenic discourse and that reveal the messy entwinement of nature and nurture in that discourse. Henry, too, is represented bodily and behaviorally in eugenic terms. Certainly, his psychological instability, physical weakness, and persistent nervousness fit into the kind of eugenic class narrative proffered by *Dracula*, in which the insular aristocracy that produced Henry has burdened him with a debilitating heritage. But Henry's symptoms also coincide with those attributed, in the late nineteenth and early twentieth centuries, to a condition called "neurasthenia." Diagnosed by George Beard in his *American Nervousness: Its Causes and Consequences* (1881), and defined as "deficiency or lack of nerve force," a draining of energy and vitality, neurasthenia was a modern condition that Beard attributed to the stresses of civilization.[109] As Gail Bederman has noted, those vulnerable to neurasthenia were those deemed most civilized: white men and women of the upper and middle classes with, in Beard's words, "fine, soft hair, delicate skin, nicely chiselled features" and "superior intellect."[110] Excessive intellectual activity was cited as a cause of neurasthenia: William Thomas Councilman, a Harvard professor of pathology, observed in 1913 that neurasthenia was "rife in the scholastic professions and among those who earn their living by brain work."[111]

Neurasthenia also figured in eugenic discourse. Davenport identified it as a manifestation of "nervous disease" to which individuals might inherit a susceptibility, using as evidence health records of over 200 families, "largely representatives of professional circles."[112] In eugenic texts, neurasthenia operated as a medical diagnosis confirming that the ravages of modern life had undermined, or even reversed, natural processes of the survival of the "fittest." Albert Wiggam, in his 1922 text *The New Decalogue of Science*, urged statesmen to attend to the lessons offered by biology. He noted signs "that the advanced races of mankind are going backward; that they are biologically plunging downward" and "that civilization always destroys the man that builds it." Such signs included increases in "the great physiological diseases of man's body"; in "the functional neuroses, the diseases that affect man's mind and behavior—neurasthenia, hysteria, epilepsy, insanity and the multiform minor mental and nervous derangements of function"; and in the numbers of "weaklings, wastrels, paupers, hoboes and imbeciles." Such increases, Wiggam argued, diminished "leadership and genius."[113] Neurasthenia thus affirmed the need for eugenic intervention and more careful reproductive practices to mitigate such damage. But in combining biological and environmental heredity, it also complicated genetically determinative edicts and pointed to the gendered and racial anxieties impelling eugenic thought, illuminating eugenic efforts to legitimate cultural fears through medical diagnosis.

In *Frankenstein*, Henry repeatedly exhibits neurasthenic exhaustion and nervousness. His mental health is in constant doubt, with Elizabeth lamenting, "Oh, if he should be ill!," while Dr. Waldman tells Elizabeth and Victor that Henry is "erratic," "has greatly changed," and exhibits an "insane ambition" and "mad dream." One of the elements of modernity to which Beard attributed American nervousness was "the sciences," and Waldman confirms that, indeed, Henry has changed as a result of his scientific and intellectual work.[114] Indeed, if the Monster's feeblemindedness is a matter of his abnormal brain, Henry's neurasthenia throws into doubt his own neurological health, for "[o]ne of the most characteristic features of cerebral neurasthenia is a weary brain."[115] Elizabeth begs Waldman to accompany them to see Henry with the language of someone about to have a patient committed: "Won't you help us to take him away?" And when the three arrive at Henry's tower, it is Victor's exclamation of "You're crazy!" that goads Henry to allow the visitors to witness the creation of the monster. Henry foregrounds his own role as a spectacle of dysfunction, leering scornfully at his audience: "Quite a good scene, isn't it?! One man crazy, three very sane spectators!" Then, with the act accomplished, and the monster's hand twitching, Henry manically and repeatedly cries, "It's alive! It's alive!" before having some kind of nervous fit, twitching and moaning as Victor and Waldman support him, his eyes raised to the skies. Thereafter, in the face of Waldman's warning ("You will ruin your health if you proceed in this madness"), Henry frequently exhibits nervous instability, staggering and breathing heavily after the monster's murder of Fritz and fainting when Elizabeth and his father come to the tower. When his friends carry him to a divan, and his father brings him around with brandy, Henry mumbles, "My work," but Elizabeth tells him firmly, "You must come home until you feel well again." Later, after the Monster's attack on Elizabeth, Henry wrings his hands a great deal, and while he manfully sets off after the culprit, the Monster easily knocks him out, eventually throwing him from the top of the windmill. In our final glimpse of Henry, he convalesces in bed, tended to by Elizabeth, while his father optimistically toasts to future generations.[116]

The signifiers of neurasthenia that attend Henry in *Frankenstein*, then, manifest the stresses of modern and intellectual life, which inhibit normative reproduction with his bride. Henry's neurasthenia thus indicates the condition's intermixing of the genetic and the environmental, affirming

the formative and physiological effects of cultural milieu and modern existence. Concepts of neurasthenia combined assertions of biological heredity with belief in the impact of technological and industrial life on bodily
and mental traits. In his book *Degeneration* (1893), Max Nordau described
neurasthenia as the "minor stages" of degeneration and hysteria, triggered
by the rapidly changing conditions of modern life—railways, marine travel,
commerce, publishing—and passed along to offspring, for "this fatigue and
exhaustion showed themselves in the first generation, under the form of
acquired hysteria; in the second, as hereditary hysteria."[117] Neurasthenia
thus recalled Lamarckian notions about the heritability of characteristics
acquired in the course of one's life, notions that conflicted with the biological determinism of mainline eugenics. Moreover, just as the Monster's
apparent feeblemindedness draws attention to efforts to explain social
problems in genetic terms, so Henry's hysteria, fainting, weakness, and
poor health point out neurasthenia's feminizing implications and suggest
the gendered and sexual motivations of such a diagnosis, thus undermining
the genetic determinism evident elsewhere in the film's narrative. These
overlapping connotations indicate the overdetermination of metaphors
of disability. But they also testify to a metonymic logic that works through
figures of impairment, proliferating disability across filmic narratives and
characters and resisting efforts to contain it in—or even to trace its origins
to—bodies safely marked as Other, as monstrous.

Like its neurological rhetoric, *Frankenstein*'s criminological discourse is
slippery, tainting characters other than the Monster with moral deficiency
and criminality. Fritz and Henry's thefts of bodies and criminal brains mark
them as equally, if not more, unlawful and unethical than the monster they
create. The film cinematically links and criminalizes all three characters
through frequent close-ups of their faces through bars and frames: Fritz's
face pops up on the other side of a window frame at the Medical College; a
framed photo of Henry's face dominates the foreground of an early scene
between Victor and Elizabeth; Fritz's face peers out from behind a barred
grate in the tower door as he tells the visitors to leave; the Monster freezes
momentarily outside the frames of the windows into Elizabeth's room; and,
in the climactic confrontation at the windmill, close-ups show first Henry
and then the Monster staring directly into the camera, their faces crossed
by the moving spindles of a cog in the windmill. Such moments "frame" the
characters as criminal, suggesting embodied deviance as something that is
constructed and projected rather than innate.

At the very least, these instances refuse to contain monstrosity and
criminality in the body of the Monster. The naming of Fritz in some scripts

and reviews as "The Dwarf" suggests that his character is defined by his impairment, while the fact that, although he is small and stooped, the actor is not *actually* a "Dwarf" indicates that specific defect is less relevant than manifestation of generalized and physically evident abnormality.[118] Inevitably, too, only months after his turn as *Dracula*'s Renfield, the casting of Dwight Frye in the role of Fritz exploited his association with mental imbalance and deranged behavior. From this point, the actor was "typecast as morons, ghouls, and hunchbacks," despite his 1933 plea for comic roles "before I go screwy playing idiots, halfwits and lunatics on the talking screen!"[119] The terms called on here to describe Frye's typical roles affirm the consonance between eugenic categories of mental defect and many of classic horror's stock characters: disability never inheres only in the monster's mind or body but frequently "touches" several more minor characters.

In *Frankenstein*, however, the disabling of characters extends also, clearly, to the supposedly eugenic couple, impinging on the film's faith in the viability of a properly eugenic and reproductive union. After her encounter with the monster, Elizabeth performs a horror heroine's conventional response: screaming, fainting, and, when roused, murmuring hysterically, "Don't let it come here. Don't let it come here. Don't let it come here." Upon exiting the room, Henry reports that he's not sure of her recovery: "She's still in a daze. Just looks at me and says nothing. It's maddening." Henry's odd and unsympathetic choice of adjective for Elizabeth's behavior—"maddening"—hints at the mental damage or derangement Elizabeth may have suffered, a cue that is picked up in the sequel, *Bride of Frankenstein*, when Elizabeth, now played by Valerie Hobson, matches Henry's ravings of what she calls his "insane desires" with her own visions of "a strange apparition . . . like death." Growing increasingly hysterical, she declares to Henry, "There it is! Look! There! There! There! It's coming for you! Nearer! Henry! Henry! Henry! Henry!," eventually collapsing in hysterical laughter onto Henry's sickbed. As the woman who embodies the all-important gateway into the race's eugenic health, Elizabeth comes to seem as mentally fragile and sickly as the monster is feebleminded and savage.

The film's closing scenes more fully bring to light *Frankenstein*'s disabling and criminalizing of "eugenic" characters, particularly with regard to Henry. The original script intended Henry to die, a conclusion conforming to Production Code demands that persons partaking in criminal and monstrous acts should be appropriately disciplined. But, after filming, the more upbeat epilogue was added, in which Henry survives to be tended by his wife and servants. The film still bears traces of its earlier denouement, however, indicting Henry as criminal and monstrous in ways that anticipate his punishment and death. Immediately after the scene inside the windmill, a villager shouts, "There he is, the murderer!" as first Henry and then the Monster appear at the top of the structure: the exclamation conflates the two as killers and illuminates their shared physiognomic characterization. Thereafter, in an earlier version of the script, Henry was to be accidentally shot and killed by Maria's father.[120] Such a conclusion would have punished Henry for neglecting his procreative duties with Elizabeth and, consequently, the monster's creation and Maria's death, enacting eugenic justice through the actions of a proper father. Henry's death is not successfully erased from the film for, as Tony Williams points out, when Henry tumbles from the mill onto the windmill blade and the ground below, "Realistically he could not have survived his fall."[121] The initial representation of Henry as monstrous and deserving of punishment lingers in *Frankenstein* and influences the meanings of the film's conclusion.[122]

That conclusion, as "weak coda," also seems marked by its status as an afterthought in which the eugenic family is ostensibly reasserted. Williams notes, "As the Baron toasts the future heir to the house of Frankenstein, we see no expected close-up of Henry and Elizabeth. Instead we view two background figures who could be substitutes (and possibly are)."[123] In a film so interested in correspondences between outer appearance and inner character, such substitution renders the happily reunited eugenic couple little more than a cipher, appended as a sop to normative and eugenic narrative conventions. Indeed, the use of stand-ins draws attention to the nature of the final scene as itself a substitute for an ending in which Henry's monstrosity is affirmed and his destruction assured (fig. 1.7).

Given the enduring traces of this representation of Henry as a mentally defective, queer, and criminal figure, the final scene's supposed restoration of the eugenic family unit and the Baron's anticipation of that family's reproduction actually runs counter to a more normative and eugenic narrative set up in earlier scenes. That is, while in *Dracula* the narrative of disease shadows—and rends holes in—a tidier romantic narrative, *Frankenstein*'s narrative of criminological neurology appears to triumph in the film with this concluding recuperation of a visibly debilitated and morally compromised couple. But remnants of the eugenic narrative persist: we perceive shreds of a romantic plot that sets up a post-Henry romance between Elizabeth and Victor. In the scene where Henry's photo looms between them, Victor tells Elizabeth, "You know, I'd go to the ends of the earth for you." When Elizabeth responds, smilingly, "I shouldn't like that. I'm far too fond of you," Victor murmurs, "I wish you were." Elizabeth looks down,

**1.7** The chimeric couple framed by class and familial structures: the concluding scene of *Frankenstein* (1931).

and walks away, admonishing gently, "Victor," and Victor briskly apologizes. Later, after the Monster has attacked Elizabeth and Henry prepares to go after him, Henry pointedly encourages Victor's relationship with Elizabeth: "You stay here and look after Elizabeth. I leave her in your care, whatever happens. You understand? In your care." The film thus paves the way for the death of the insane and hubristic Henry and for a subsequent, more normative relationship between Elizabeth and Victor; the latter is evidently more stable and more attentive to Elizabeth. Henry's emphasis on the "care" Victor can give Elizabeth points, too, to a eugenic conflation of romance and health.

In the added conclusion, then, Elizabeth and Henry's reunion offers a far less comforting and eugenic resolution than might first appear, running counter to the hinted-at "normal" relationship between Victor and Elizabeth and reuniting Elizabeth with a man who is hysterical, weak, and, in his own word, "crazy."[124] For Walter Evans, this conclusion actually questions the healthiness of the normative marital relationship: "Henry is only ready for marriage when his own body is horribly battered and weakened, when he is transformed from the vigorous, courageous, inspired hero he represented early in the film to an enervated figure approaching the impotent fatuity of his father and grandfather."[125] The imposition of a eugenic finale, fitting awkwardly as it does alongside the signifiers of deviance and dysfunction attached to Henry, thus recasts the eugenic union as a coupling of two individuals touched by monstrosity, sexual deviance, hysteria, and fainting spells. At this point, the premise of "a son, to the House of Frankenstein" seems, like the pompous Baron himself, rather laughable.

Indeed, this bedroom scene, in which the "normal" couple is finally united in the vicinity of a marital bed, renders dubious the ideal vision of healthy procreative coupling. The Baron's toast recalls his almost identical words earlier in the film and reminds us of the conventionalized rituals of Henry's aborted wedding: the passing down from male to male of symbolic corsages, of titles, of family names. In this light, socially sanctioned marriage and reproduction seem as "queer," artificial, and potentially monstrous as Henry's dark laboratory collaborations with his deformed assistant. Any kind of normative or "natural" reproduction is displaced entirely from the film and, perhaps, the realm of representation: the reunited couple is chimerical, revealed as at once an impossible phantom of purely healthy procreation and, in reality, genetically compromised.

The added final scene forms a filmic "frame" with *Frankenstein*'s prologue in ways that augment the representation of normative reproduction as chimerical. In the film's prologue, Edward van Sloan, the film's Professor Waldman, steps out from behind a stage curtain, and addresses the camera/audience directly:

> How do you do? Mr. Carl Laemmle [the producer] feels that it would be a little unkind to present this picture without just a word of friendly warning. We are about to unfold the story of Frankenstein, a man of science who sought to create a man after his own image without reckoning upon God. It is one of the strangest tales ever told. It deals with the two great mysteries of creation—life and death. I think it will thrill you. It may shock you. It might even—horrify you. So if any of you feel that you do not care to subject your nerves to such a strain, now's your chance to—uh, well, we've warned you.

*Frankenstein* thus anticipates the tendency of many other classic horrors to foreground their intentions to shock and even temporarily debilitate—perhaps render neurasthenic—their spectators. More importantly, however, the prologue commences the movie by drawing attention to the processes of artificial reproduction with which the film is inscribed: the producer, using the "lightning" of the silver screen, artificially produces a man who warns his audience about the horrors of artificially producing a man using lightning.[126] The film thus sets in motion a recursive logic in which each implicit invocation of natural procreation only brings us to yet another instance of perverse and monstrous re-production. It is such aberrant acts of generation that are, in fact, the norm, while the construct of healthy, eugenic reproduction is revealed not merely as an exception but rather a mirage, a chimera, whose conjuring holds powerful sway but whose true potency inheres in its shape-shifting capacity. The eugenic figure or couple, if we look long enough, transforms into a hybrid: neurasthenic, criminal, reproduced again and again, by signifiers of impairment, at once both monstrous and "merely" impaired, and thus, undeniably, human.

# ENFREAKING THE
# CLASSIC HORROR GENRE

## *FREAKS*

**E**arly in *Freaks* (dir. Tod Browning, MGM, 1932), horrified French caretaker Jean (Michael Visaroff) leads the estate owner (Albert Conti)
toward a troubling spectacle: a group of sideshow freaks gamboling in
a sunny, wooded clearing. Disgusted and fearful, Jean describes these unsettling bodies to his employer: "The most horrible, twisted things, crawling,
whining, laughing!" "Oh, monsieur!" he declares. "There must be a law
in France to smother such things at birth. Or lock 'em up!" Jean's effort to
oust the freaks (fig. 2.1) and his conviction that they should be imprisoned
or destroyed at birth echo both eugenic imperatives and the inclination of
censorial gatekeeper Jason S. Joy, discussed in the introduction, to "retard
or kill" the gruesome generic body of the horror film.

    *Freaks* was directed by Tod Browning, who had also helmed the first
classic American horror film, *Dracula*. At least one early review of *Dracula*
categorized it as an aberration: wrote Norbert Lusk, "the story of human
vampires who feast on the blood of living victims is too extreme to provide entertainment that causes word-of-mouth advertising. Plainly a
freak picture, it must be accepted as a curiosity devoid of the important
element of sympathy that causes the widest appeal."[1] Despite Lusk's conviction, *Dracula* became Universal's biggest earner of 1931, and producers hoping to repeat its profitable box office tentatively began exploring
similar projects.[2] Noted a *Variety* reporter in April, "[O]ther studios are

**2.1** Jean (Michael Visaroff) tries to eject Madame Tetrallini (Rose Dione) and her circus charges from his employer's estate in *Freaks* (1932).

looking for horror tales—but very squeamishly. Producers are not certain whether nightmare pictures have a box office pull, or whether *Dracula* is just a freak."[3] Both comments understand *Dracula* as potentially representative of a nascent genre that generates "squeamish" effects through a "nightmare" narrative. But they also anticipate the possibility that such a genre might not coalesce, leaving *Dracula* stranded, singular, and "freakish." With the success later the same year of *Frankenstein*, the critical acclaim bestowed the following year on *Dr. Jekyll and Mr. Hyde*, and the arrival of comparable 1932 films such as *White Zombie, Doctor X*, and *The Mummy*, *Dracula* was absolved of its freakishness, becoming instead a generic forerunner.

Paradoxically, the key factor enabling *Dracula* to cast off the "freak" label was the use in subsequent films of some of its "freakish" elements, for even if *Dracula* was not a freak, Dracula most certainly was. All the films that would be categorized with *Dracula* and *Frankenstein* and considered part of the classic horror genre exhibited a common trait: the sensationalizing of physical and psychological deviance with an eye to exciting and repulsing audiences. In the next few years, horror storylines and visual conventions consolidated around representations of somatic aberration, wresting such difference into the bounds of increasingly familiar—and eugenically inflected—forms and plots.

In that light, a 1932 film listed in Joy's memo, described appropriately as "half-complete," featuring several freakish bodies, and apparently designed to unsettle viewers, would clearly seem to belong within classic horror's generic bounds. But *Freaks* has frequently been perceived as not "really" a horror film. This chapter examines the argument for incorporating *Freaks* into the horror genre, an inclusive act comparable to the movie's central scene where the freaks invite a "normal" character to become "one of us." Understanding *Freaks* as a classic horror film renders it less freakish, suggesting that its complex and conflicted disability politics were not idiosyncratic but participated in a larger cultural impulse. It also renders horror films more freakish, pointing out their relevance not just to mythic understandings of monstrosity but also to "real" processes by which people with disabilities are made freakish. Indeed, this inclusion counters sentiments that representations of impaired bodies, like those central to both *Freaks* and the classic horror film, preclude progressive or subversive readings. *Freaks'* body politics, which strategically familiarize and defamiliarize freakish forms, speak back to scholarly dismissals of the classic horror cycle and point out the cultural work—in horror and beyond—that produces monstrous bodies.

## HORROR OUT OF PLACE: *FREAKS'* FREAKISH NARRATIVE

Why do unusual bodies so unsettle Jean the caretaker and Joy the censor? Freud raises a similar question in his essay on the "uncanny," wondering about the feelings of "dread and horror" and "repulsion and distress" elicited by encounters with or representations of dead bodies, injury to the eyes, bodily fragmentation, madness, and epilepsy. Such feelings, he argues, derive from the links of these physical or mental manifestations to repressed infantile or primitive thoughts and fears. Freud illustrates his claim that "the uncanny is that class of the frightening which leads back to what is known of old and long familiar" with reference to the German term *heimlich*. The word describes both what is related to the home and family, intimate, friendly, and familiar, *and* that which is concealed or secret, thus shading into its opposite, *unheimlich*, meaning something that is hidden, dangerous, eerie, fearful, or gruesome. Instances of bodily aberrance thus recall, for instance, the castration complex or animistic beliefs, fears that are at once intimate and deeply buried.[4]

Freud's uncanny usefully suggests that dismayed responses to freakish bodies do not derive merely from their unfamiliarity and valuably points to psychological processes that work to hide and disavow deformity. But Freud also reads corporeal disability as a symptom of innate identity and takes for granted that uncanniness is a natural and subconscious effect of physical difference. Lennard Davis points out that Freud, in presenting disabled bodies as privileged examples of uncanniness ("the familiar gone wrong"), also incorrectly assumes that the body most familiar and "homey" to us is a "whole body." However, Davis contends, our "original body *imago*" is, in fact, "inherently fragmentary," as glimpsed in Jacques Lacan's theory of the mirror-stage, where we experience our body as inchoate and out of control. For Davis, disability analyses reposition that fragmentary body at the heart of our cultural narratives: "In this process, the *heimisch* body becomes the *unheimlich* body, and the fragment, the disabled parts, can be seen as the originary, familiar body made unfamiliar by repression." Davis continues, "Dominant culture has an investment in seeing the disabled, therefore, as uncanny, as something found outside the home, unfamiliar, while in fact where is the disabled body found if not at home?"[5]

Together, Freud's uncanny and Davis's revision of the homey body ask us to see negative responses to freaks less as natural reactions to something utterly unfamiliar and more as psychological and cultural discomfort with what is at once eminently familiar and constantly disavowed: the fact of bodily variety, mutability, and contingency. In *Freaks*, we find what we might call a particularly uncanny horror film, one whose impaired bodies and other generic parts seem out of their conventional places. Such disordering should not exclude *Freaks* from horror-film membership, however, since it helps us recognize the disavowed and familiar freakish body that resides at home, in the heart of our cultural texts.

*Freaks* was conceived when MGM vice president Irving Thalberg, hoping to replicate *Dracula*'s success, engaged Browning to make a horror film for his studio. Browning, a veteran of sideshow employment and director of a litany of circus- and sideshow-themed movies, the latter often starring the protean Lon Chaney, amassed a cast of "real" freak performers, including little persons and brother and sister Harry and Daisy Earles; conjoined twins Violet and Daisy Hilton; the "half-boy" Johnny Eck; Austrian hermaphrodite Josephine/Joseph; "pinheads" Jenny Lee Snow, Elvira Snow, and "Schlitze"/Simon Metz; "Prince Randian," a limbless black man from British Guiana; and dwarf Angelo Rossitto.[6] It is oft-reported that when scriptwriter Wallis Goldbeck showed Thalberg his treatment of the Tod Robbins short story, "Spurs," on which the film is based, Thalberg clasped his head in his hands and sighed: "I asked for something horrifying . . . and I got it."[7]

*Freaks'* dominant plot focuses on little person Hans (Harry Earles), who, despite being engaged to fellow little person Frieda (Daisy Earles), falls in love with trapeze artist Cleopatra (Olga Baclanova), "the most beautiful big woman [he has] ever seen." Cleo, with the help of her strongman lover Hercules (Henry Victor), pretends to return Hans' affections and marries him in order to murder him and gain his considerable inheritance. At the wedding banquet, the freaks invite Cleo to become one of them, but, horrified, she screams her disgust at them and completes her humiliation of Hans by picking him up on her shoulder and galloping around the now empty banquet table. Cleo has already begun to poison Hans, who collapses and becomes ill. She continues to administer the poison, but every shot of her activity is intercut with watching eyes, as freaks peer through windows and lurk under wagons. Hans confronts her in front of his friends, who produce knives and guns to force her to surrender the poison. Cleo runs from them and, in the film's climactic scene, as the circus wagons travel at night in a torrential storm, the freaks, armed with their weapons, slither and crawl through the mud. A dwarf flings a knife into Hercules' side as he tries to kill one of the good-hearted "normals," Phroso the clown (Wallace Ford). Several freaks then advance on the injured but struggling Hercules, just as others chase a screaming Cleopatra to accomplish their revenge.

*Freaks* clearly includes narrative elements consistent to *Dracula, Frankenstein,* and other classic horrors—notably monstrous bodies, acts of violence, and the jeopardizing of the female body. But it reverses the classic horror narrative in which the monster disrupts equilibrium through acts of violence before its expulsion or destruction enables the reassertion of the normative body and family. As we have seen, the film presents near its *beginning* the eugenic effort to eject or eradicate the monstrous and disabled body, with Jean's desire to remove the freaks from his employer's estate. That eugenic impulse is undercut when circus owner Madame Tetrallini (Rose Dione) maternally protects the freaks, introducing them as "children from my circus," and reassuring her charges: "Have I not told you that God looks after *all* His children?" Having begun with the groundskeeper's eugenic readings of, and solutions for, the freaks' bodies, the film sets out to challenge such reactions.

The narrative proceeds as an effort to domesticate, to render in familiar, homey terms, the freaks and their anomalous bodies, rewriting the eugenic representative strategy in which physical appearance connotes inner health, morality, and character. Our sympathy lies increasingly with the freaks, the targets of the prejudice, greed, and criminal actions of the physically attractive but morally monstrous Cleo and Hercules. If classic horror film narratives typically dramatize the monster's threats to "healthy" marriage and reproduction, *Freaks* portrays the freaks as *representatives* of such normative practices. As commentators have noted, scenes of the freaks doing laundry and conversing with neighbors "normalize" them and deconstruct their eugenic representation as monsters.[8] Several scenes foreground courtship, marriage, sex, and birth, as when the freaks visit the Bearded Lady (Olga Roderick) to admire her newborn bearded daughter (fig. 2.2) while the proud father, the Human Skeleton (Peter Robinson), hands out cigars. In a subplot, conjoined twin Daisy (Daisy Hilton) marries stuttering clown Roscoe (Roscoe Ates), while her sister, Violet (Violet Hilton), also becomes engaged; Violet's fiancé and Daisy's husband each politely invite the other couple to come visit sometime. The unusual-looking "Bird Girl" (Elizabeth Green) tells the "Armless Girl" (Frances O'Connor) that an admirer has followed her from another town and is bound to make her "Eddie" jealous.

Despite the non-normative aspects of these couplings, then, the film works to assert that the freaks are really just like "us" and to refashion notions of family and community. The line between the freaks' romantic affairs and that of "normals" is obscured even in the romantic subplot of Phroso and Venus the seal-trainer (Leila Hyams), when Phroso mysteriously tells Venus, "You should have caught me before my operation!" The effort to "normalize" the freaks is also assisted by what Méira Cook calls the "systematic monstering . . . of the so-called normal characters."[9] Despite Cleo's and Hercules' attractive appearances, the narrative methodically casts them as immoral, murderous criminals; this dysgenic couple conspires to pervert the proper course of inheritance, marriage, and reproduction and to attack the circus's formerly happy and healthy family.[10]

After beginning, rather than ending, with the eugenic effort to expel the monstrous body, and proceeding to represent the ostensible monsters as normal participants in customs of marriage, procreation, and communal activity and the attractive "normal" people as criminal deviants, the film unsettles its characterizations at the wedding banquet. Here, Angeleno the dwarf (Angelo Rossitto) cries, "We'll make her one of us!" and carries a loving cup from mouth to freakish mouth, before offering it to Cleo as the guests chant: "We accept her, we accept her. Gooble, gobble, gooble, gobble. One of us, one of us." Cleo draws herself to her full height, and flings the wine back at them, shouting, "Dirty . . . slimy . . . freaks! Freaks! Freaks! Freaks! Get out of here!" As the freaks slink out, she spits, "Make me one of you, will you?" The scene counterposes a gesture of inclusion, an invitation to Cleo to belong, with an aggressive gesture of exclusion, in which Cleo ejects the freaks from the banquet space (fig. 2.3). The politics of inclusion

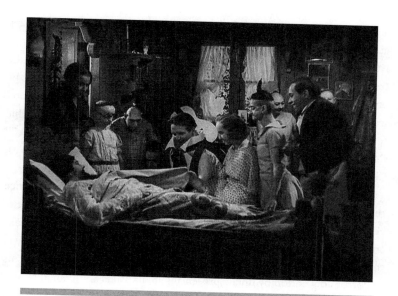

**2.2** Normalcy: the freaks celebrate the birth of the Bearded Lady's baby in *Freaks* (1932).

**2.3** Uncomfortable identifications: the freaks rejected at the wedding feast in *Freaks* (1932).

and exclusion here affect viewers, too, who are alternately positioned gazing at Cleo from the perspective of the freaks and at the freaks from the perspective of Cleo. While spectators may have accepted the domestication of the freaks, perhaps few will be willing to be inducted into their community, to be one of them. It is a moment that fractures affiliation with these unusual bodies, likely contributing to the belief of a *Variety* reviewer that "it is impossible for the normal man or woman to sympathize with the aspiring midget."[11] Consequently, spectators are uncomfortably "physically aligned" with Cleo's ableist response and murderous monstrosity.[12]

Where classic horrors typically *begin* with a monstrous act of violence that upsets hegemonic equilibrium, *Freaks* saves its most enduring act of violence until its end, with the climactic assault in which some of the freaks crawl through the mud toward Hercules (fig. 2.4) while others run through the thunder and lightning toward the screaming Cleo. *Freaks* thus conforms to horror convention by finally presenting its unusually embodied figures as primitive, animalistic, and violent. Indeed, several analyses have criticized the way the scene undermines the film's earlier challenges to ableist or prejudiced views and reinscribes notions of the freaks as monsters.[13] Yet by presenting this act of violence at the end of the narrative arc, as a logical, if not justified, action resulting from the monstrous violences of "normal" people, the film demands that its viewers rethink monstrosity as something created rather than inborn.[14]

**2.4** The crawling attack of the freaks on Hercules in *Freaks* (1932).

*Freaks* frames this plot with two scenes that augment its discomforting reversal of horror-film narrative conventions. Prior to the opening of the story proper, a sideshow barker (Murray Kinnell) gathers a crowd of spectators with his spiel: "We didn't lie to you, folks! We told you we had living, breathing monstrosities. You laugh at them, shudder at them, and yet, but for the accident of birth, you might be even as they are. They did not ask to be brought into the world, but into the world they came. Their code is a law unto themselves. Offend one, and you offend them all." The barker leads the spectators to the side of a pit, into which the film audience cannot see. He announces: "And now, folks, if you'll just step this way, you are about to witness the *most* amazing, the most astounding, living monstrosity of all time. [*One of the female spectators screams.*] Friends, she was once a beautiful woman. A royal prince shot himself for love of her. She was known as the peacock of the air . . . " At this point, without the object of the barker's narrative being revealed, the film fades into the story proper and a shot of Cleopatra being watched adoringly by Hans. But at the end of the film, we return to the barker and his fascinated audience, to observe what has become of Cleo after the freaks' nighttime attack. The shot shows her mutilated almost beyond recognition, her face scarred, her body severed above the waist and feathered, and her hands covered with gloves resembling webbed feet. The "peacock of the air" is now a squawking chicken-woman (fig.2.5).[15] The film's ending thus resists the expulsion and punishment of monstrosity we expect

**2.5** Cleo (Olga Baclanova): the chicken-woman at the end of *Freaks* (1932).

of classic horror, leaving the vengeful freaks at large and adding to, rather than destroying, their membership, with the creation of chicken-Cleo.

Nonetheless, *Freaks'* conclusion also calls on eugenic and physiognomic beliefs in ways that emulate other classic horror films. As Joan Hawkins has noted, like the presentation of the freaks as vengeful monsters, Cleo's transformation seems to use physical deformation as belated "proof" of her innate immorality.[16] *Freaks* thus reasserts notions of morality as biologically encoded and borrows from eugenics' most prurient elements in suggesting that failure to excise monstrosity leads always to a salacious, violent attack on the body of a woman, even as it legitimates the attack as punishment for Cleo's degenerate ways. We are reminded that, however it disorders them, the film also on some level exploits key horror elements, using aberrant bodies to gruesome effect, conjoining monstrosity with a vulnerable female body, and ultimately confirming the monstrosity of the physically different.

This conclusion's eugenic implications were, however, not considered evident enough. The unsettling effects of *Freaks'* image of persisting monstrosity registered at a preview screening where patrons responded negatively.[17] The studio thus appended a more conventional and overtly eugenic finale.[18] In this scene, an isolated and desolate Hans, in his large, luxurious study, tells his butler he will not see visitors. But his former friends from the circus, Venus and Phroso, barge in with Frieda and then tiptoe out to allow the little couple to reconcile. Frieda tells Hans that Cleo's mutilation was not his plan, nor his fault ("You tried to stop them. It was only the poison you wanted"), and he collapses sorrowfully in her arms as she comforts him: "Don't cry, Hans. Come to me, my *liebchen*. Don't cry. Oh, Hans. Don't cry. *I* love you. *I* love you." Frieda thus explains Hans's inclusion in the brief shot of four freaks running after Cleo, absolves Hans from an act of monstrous violence, and helps recuperate a more or less "normal," if miniature, heterosexual couple—although, as in *Frankenstein*, the male partner emerges from his encounter with monstrosity rather battered and enervated. The ending also further domesticates the film's disruption of categories of monstrosity and normalcy; as David J. Skal suggests, it creates a "hierarchy of freaks" in which those who most closely approximate normative bodies are pardoned of monstrosity, while those more freakish freaks who crawled their way toward Hercules confirm the groundskeeper's initial eugenic reaction: to him, the freaks were always "crawling," "laughing," and implicitly criminal.[19]

Like *Dracula*, *Frankenstein*, and subsequent classic horror films, then, *Freaks'* use of typical horror conventions presents seemingly confused eugenic messages, both mustering sympathy for and demonizing its monsters. But *Freaks'* unusual narrative ordering of horror elements and its attachment of them to the bodies of "real" freaks generated a more outraged reaction than any other American horror film of the period, leading to the film's ejection from theaters and, in subsequent critical analyses, from the classic horror genre. A closer look at the film and its reception reveals how discomfort with the film's disability politics underwrote audience distaste for the movie and how ableist assumptions continue to haunt debates about its generic classification.

## HORRIFIED: RESPONSES TO *FREAKS*

*Freaks* began generating disgusted reactions even before its theatrical debut. During filming, complaints from others on the MGM lot led to the freaks' confinement to a separate mess hall so that, in the words of story editor Samuel Marx, "people could get to eat in the commissary without throwing up."[20] As already noted, a California preview screening fared poorly: a *Los Angeles Times* article claimed that "some horrified spectators got up from their seats and ran—did not walk—to the nearest exit," while the film's production manager reported that "a woman . . . tried to sue the studio, claiming the film had induced a miscarriage."[21] Such objections saw the film's New York premiere delayed until July, while the studio wavered on how to promote the film. Its advertisements juxtaposed sensationalism ("Do the Siamese Twins make love? Can a full-grown woman truly love a midget? Do the Pin-Heads think? What sex is the Half-Man, Half-Woman? THE BIG EXPLOITATION NOVELTY SENSATION OF THE YEAR!") with appeals to pity: "What about the Siamese twins—have they no right to love? The pinheads, the half-man half-woman, the dwarfs! They have the same passions, joys, sorrows, laughter as normal human beings."[22]

Similar confusion attended *Freaks'* popular and critical reception. The film flourished in locations such as Cincinnati, Buffalo, Boston, and St. Paul but flopped at the box office in major centers such as Los Angeles and Chicago. Wrote *Variety*, "In spots, it has been a clean-up. In others it was merely misery."[23] Some reviews registered this ambivalence: the first *New York Times* review called *Freaks* "excellent at times and horrible, in the street meaning of the word, at others," while the second concurred, deeming it "very good in spots and very bad in others."[24]

Others were more positive: J. C. M. of the *New Yorker* commended the film as "a little gem," Charles E. Lewis of the *Motion Picture Herald* found it "interesting and entertaining," and Louella Parsons enjoyed its "sensationalism."[25] However, many reviews were overt in their disgust. *Freaks* was dubbed "an unhealthy and generally disagreeable work," "revolting to the extent of turning one's stomach," and so "loathsome" that it was "not fit to be shown anywhere."[26] Displeasure mounted: the Atlanta Board of Review pulled *Freaks* from its Fox Theater, with board secretary Mrs. Alonzo Richardson describing it as "loathsome, obscene, grotesque, and bizarre," while John C. Moffitt of the *Kansas City Star* chided, "In *Freaks* the movies make their great step toward national censorship. If they get it, they will have no one to blame but themselves."[27] After a dismal New York premiere, the film was pulled from U.S. circulation, having made barely half its production cost.[28] The film was banned from Britain, and its bleak reception severely damaged Browning's career.[29]

It appears that *Freaks'* "problem," the reason for its uncomfortable reception, was its use of "real" freaks. In arraying for audiences several freak-show performers, many of whom sported actual deformities, Browning had reached back past Lon Chaney's performed disabilities in the silent era. Instead, he had drawn directly from the kinds of "corporeal wonders" populating Barnum's circus, dime museums, and sideshows, "from wild men of Borneo to fat ladies, living skeletons, Fiji princes, albinos, bearded women, Siamese twins, tattooed Circassians, spotted boys, and much more."[30] Such shows had flourished in America in the nineteenth and early twentieth centuries but were waning in popularity by the early 1930s. Mythic understandings of freaks were being displaced by medical and eugenic imperatives deeming such persons pitiable and pathologically flawed and transferring such bodies from public view to institutions under expert surveillance. The American freak show thus increasingly encountered an "explicitly moral rejection" premised on the "medicalization of human differences."[31] In confronting moviegoers with an outmoded disability discourse, *Freaks* was accorded the same moralizing disdain that marginalized the freak show. The *New York Times* reviewer worried whether the film "should be shown at the Rialto . . . or in, say, the Medical Center," and many critics condemned the film as unethical and exploitative, as when the *Motion Picture Daily* called it "unkind and brutal" and Frances Diehl of the National Organization of Women lamented "the disgrace of making money out of hurt, disfigured, and suffering humanity."[32]

The powerful cultural notion that people with disabilities should not be seen and did not belong in public was thus mapped on to *Freaks* itself, in suggestions that it was "not fit to be shown" and more appropriate for "the Medical Center." Others wondered whether *Freaks* belonged in the horror genre—or, indeed, in any recognizable class. Wrote Harold Heffernan in the *Detroit News*, "No such film has ever been produced before. It is reasonably certain that nothing like it will ever be attempted again."[33] The *New Yorker* reviewer explicitly segregated it from other films, declaring it "a very special case" that "stands in a class by itself." The factor determining *Freaks*' special status was, again, its reality: "Considered as a strict horror picture, 'Freaks' differs from others of the kind, like 'Dr. Jekyll' or 'Frankenstein,' in its strict realism."[34] Other reviewers marked *Freaks* as horrific in a special way: the *Boston Herald* declared, "Tod Browning can retire in peace, satisfied that he has directed the ultimate in horrors"; the *Boston Evening Transcript* acknowledged the presence of a "catalog of horrors" but a lack of "artistry"; and a *New York Times* review confirmed, "There is a good deal of horror—in the strict sense of the term."[35] The notion that *Freaks* was excessively, unartistically, and "strictly" horrific, along with the contention noted above that it was "horrible, in the street meaning of the word," affirmed this sense that the film distilled horror in a more intense, unsettling, and *real* form than the horror films that preceded and followed it.

*Freaks*' freakish status, then, is inextricably tied to its foregrounding of freakish bodies that are more real than the monsters of *Dracula* and *Frankenstein*. Leslie Fiedler has identified the "Freak" as a figure positioned between "monsters," on the one hand ("creations of artistic fantasy like Dracula, Mr. Hyde, the Wolf Man, King Kong, and the nameless metahuman of Mary Shelley's *Frankenstein*") and people with disabilities, on the other ("the category of unfortunates whom early French teratologists called *mutilés*: the blind, deaf, dumb, lame, crippled, perhaps even hunchbacks and harelips . . . along with amputees, paraplegics, and other victims of natural or manmade disasters"), who are "objects not of awe but of pity." Paying homage to Browning's film, Fiedler declares that the "Freak" straddles the worlds of the merely disabled and the mythically monstrous, appearing as "one of us, the human child of human parents, however altered by forces we do not quite understand into something mythic and monstrous, as no mere cripple ever is."[36] To some extent, then, *Freaks* mediates between the "real" people often targeted by eugenic discourse, on the one hand, and horror-film monsters, on the other, pointing out to its viewers the cultural process by which, counter to Fiedler's assertion, an ordinarily impaired person can, in fact, become "something mythic and monstrous."[37] *Freaks* both enacts and points to the enfreakment of disability on which our cultural texts rely, indicating the reliance of all classic horror films not just on mythic monsters but also on culturally shaped views about more quotidian impairments and their bearers.[38] As both a product of and a commentary on the horror genre, *Freaks* also works to contest critical disparagement of classic horror's cultural value because of its visualization of the monstrous body.

## THE DEFECTIVE BODY OF THE CLASSIC HORROR GENRE

In showcasing a repulsed response to shudder-inducing bodies, Jean the caretaker and the critics of *Freaks* also anticipated attitudes toward the monstrously visual bodies of horror film exhibited by scholars late in the twentieth century. As discussed in the introduction, academic studies have characterized the monstrosity of Gothic novels as powerfully ambiguous, open to multiple interpretations and thus capable of uncovering textual, cultural, and political constructions of Otherness. But the visualized monster of early horror films has been seen as reductive and too-corporeal, generating naturally disgusted responses, and thus underwriting the pathologization of Otherness as monstrous. For instance, as discussed in chapter 1, scholars have condemned Whale's *Frankenstein*'s invention of the monster's abnormal brain as a visual and narrative depreciation of the novel's multivalent and universal themes, confirming the monster as biological aberration rather than a product of a flawed culture, and legitimating his violent expulsion from a conservative world order.

From this perspective, a film like *Bride of Frankenstein* fits into the classic horror genre because, having paraded the Monster's ugliness, violence, and sexual threat, it concludes by having him save the heterosexual couple, Henry and Elizabeth, before pulling the lever that brings down the laboratory tower on himself, his monstrous bride, and the effete Dr. Pretorius. The Monster's intonation, "We belong dead," affirms the restoration of normalcy through the destruction of aberrant bodies. By displaying and then excluding freakish bodies that do not belong, *Bride* denotes its own belonging to the freakish body of the classic horror genre, but also manifests the classic horror's alleged inferiority and social conservatism.

As noted in the introduction, some films can be recuperated through readings that interpret the monster's body in relation to race or class or ethnicity, readings that understand disability as a pathologizing disguise, imposed on minority figures, which must be stripped away in order to critique and complicate the films' racism, classism, or ethnocentrism. Paradoxically, however, this distaste for the too-visible body of classic horrors reenacts the kind of conservative expulsion of monstrosity for which these films are disparaged; just as Frankenstein's monster does not belong in normative society, so classic horror films allegedly *do not belong* in the effort to recuperate horror for a progressive, or at least a destabilizing, politics. In eliding disability through metaphoric interpretations and in suggesting that the horror genre can only be rescued for progressive readings through repudiating the body of "classic" horror films, critics mimic the conservative exclusions of aberrant bodies by which the classic cycle is supposedly debased.

This implicit deprecation of classic horror calls to our attention the politics at stake in genre definition. It risks invoking a biological model of genre as an organic entity that evolves toward its proper and superior form, as in Robin Wood's presentation of 1980s "apocalyptic" horror films as the "final emergence of the genre's real significance," or it risks presenting genre membership in suspiciously eugenic terms, as in what John Swales calls the "definitional" approach, which "asserts that, in theory at least, it is possible to produce a small set of simple properties that are individually necessary and cumulatively sufficient to identify all the members and only the members of a particular category from everything else in the world."[39] According to such a model, membership in the defective classic horror genre requires the expression of specific traits, including the display of and eventual expulsion of monstrosity; lacking this trait, *Freaks* cannot be a classic horror film. A more forgiving construction of genre is the "family resemblance" model, which draws on Wittgenstein's assertion that members of a capacious category do not all exhibit all of the same traits but rather participate in "a complicated network of similarities overlapping and criss-crossing" like "the various resemblances between members of a family."[40] This model provides for a "looser" set of relationships amongst genre members but comes with its own problems, like the genealogies generated by biased eugenic field workers: Swales quotes David Lodge's statement that "'no choice of a text for illustrative purposes is innocent'" and also points out that "it can be objected that a family resemblance theory can make anything resemble anything."[41]

*Freaks* itself appears to raise questions about both generic approaches and their dependence on visible traits, especially to the extent that the bodies of the freaks are—or are not—presented as members of a genre. While the audience is presumed to apprehend immediately the sameness of the freaks to one another in their shared "abnormality," the consistency of the "genre" of abnormality is repeatedly placed in doubt. The group cannot be seen as homogeneous in type of disability, as it includes individuals with intellectual impairments, growth disorders, missing limbs, and hirsuteness. The freaks' radical differences in size, shape, movement, form, mannerisms, and speech patterns disintegrate any coherent notion of "freakishness." Moreover, the category of "natural" or congenital impairment is contested by freaks whose aberrance seems constructed: the "Bird Girl" is merely a woman of unusual appearance; Josephine/Joseph's intersexed status is conveyed primarily through clothing, makeup, and hairstyle; and while Olga Roderick, the "Bearded Lady," may well have been the genuine article, many such performers were in fact men impersonating women. To that extent, an indistinct line separates the freaks from those whose role in the sideshow seems performative, such as Roscoe, the stuttering man who dresses as a Roman lady. These examples also point to the refusal of some of the freaks to inhabit clear gender categories, while the frequency of animalistic personae assigned to or claimed by the freaks—as with the "Turtle Girl," the "Bird Girl" (Green, who was often billed as "The Stork Woman"), and "Koo Koo" (Minnie Woolsey, who performed under titles such as "the Bird Girl from Mars")—frustrates categorizations in terms of the animal or the human.[42] In its cast of performers, then, *Freaks* contests a genre politics grounded in the identification of a fixed set of traits.

Familial resemblance is equally unstable as a category of generic definition in *Freaks*. Such resemblance is apparently confirmed when Phroso reports that the Bearded Lady's daughter will have a beard, but while the film presents the Human Skeleton as a proud father, no evidence is provided that the child has also inherited her father's skeletal physiology. Not only does the film thus suggest physical resemblance as an inadequate indicator of genetic heritage, but it also pushes to uncomfortable extremes the notion that like belongs with like. The scenes in which conjoined twins Daisy and Violet navigate the former's marriage to Roscoe and the latter's engagement to Valdez rely for comic effect on cultural uneasiness about the incestuous, homosexual, and polygamous implications of the men's affiliations with the sisters' united and apparently identical bodies.[43] And the ostensibly normative ending that reestablishes the little heterosexual couple and confirms that little people/freaks belong with one another reads rather differently once we know that Harry and Daisy Earles are brother and sister and notice their familial resemblance. The film thus not only questions a eugenic politics based on groupings according to physical appearance but also uncovers the incestuous and perverse implications of eugenic classifications that privilege sameness and biological kinship.

However, in the barker's speech at the start of the film, we glimpse another view of genre that explains both the freaks' group identity and makes space for *Freaks* within the classic horror category. The barker accentuates the reactions of viewers to the freaks ("You laugh at them, shudder at them") before asserting, "Their code is a law unto themselves." In emphasizing audience response and in presenting terms such as "code" and "law," words that imply a *constructed* set of norms or rules, the barker's spiel channels genre theories focused on the constructed, dynamic, and ideological status of genre categories. Thomas Schatz presents genre as "a sort of tacit 'contract' between filmmakers and audience" and the genre film as "an actual event that honors such a contract." Schatz notes, "As we repeatedly undergo the same type of experience we develop expectations which, as they are continually reinforced, tend to harden into 'rules.'" Engaging with a generic film text becomes "a kind of secular, contemporary cultural ritual," a working-through of social problems or conflicts.[44] Familiar codes and trajectories produce enjoyment—writes Edward Buscombe, "The conventions are known and recognized by the audience, and such recognition is in itself a pleasure"—and social commonalities: declares Schatz, "It is this system of conventions—familiar characters performing familiar actions which celebrate familiar values—that represents the genre's narrative context, its meaningful cultural community."[45] At the same time, as Stephen Neale points out, "if each text within a genre were, literally, the same, there would simply not be enough difference to generate either meaning or pleasure."[46] Thus, "a genre film depends on a combination of novelty and familiarity" or, in Neale's words, a process of "difference *in* repetition" governed by a set of generic "rules" that shape the way in which generic elements are both repeated and transformed.[47]

These approaches to genre allow for greater flexibility in the combination of familiar codes and generic difference, making possible an understanding of *Freaks* as a horror text that "repeats" certain generic elements—the iconography of aberrant bodies, a narrative in which monsters threaten a beautiful woman—but also "transforms" them, reversing the order of narrative events and inverting the logic by which deformity corresponds to inner deviance. These generic views also define genre as an interaction between the text, encoded with certain cues, and audience members, who respond with pleasure to the interplay of the familiar and the different. In this sense, *Freaks* not only emerges as a classic horror film but also makes more apparent the generic workings of classic horror films: by functioning both to make the freakish body more homey and then to render it uncanny, *Freaks* draws our attention to the ways horror codes manipulate disability, calling into question the assumption that the visibly impaired body consistently and naturally disturbs spectators without significant cultural framing and audience cooperation. Such defamiliarizing of generic codes perhaps explains viewers' displeasure with the film, insofar as its differences exceed expectations and disrupt, by exploring the political implications of, the generic "contract." But like the barker's speech, the film draws attention to the possibility that the freaks' code, their final act as a homogeneous group bent on revenge, emerges as a direct response to the cultural and generic codes that have made monsters of them, indicting viewers for the very generic expectations that the film appears to violate.[48]

## DE/FAMILIARIZING

As we have already suggested, *Freaks'* early depictions of its freaks as "normal" work within the dialectic of *heimlich* and *unheimlich*, achieving both defamiliarizing and familiarizing effects. The film defamiliarizes by familiarizing the freaks, dissipating their purportedly natural ability to elicit awe and fear, to be uncanny. This process of de/familiarization is at work in many of the "homey" scenes where the narrative grinds to a halt to display the bodies of the freaks. Mundane conversations provide a pretext for the camera to linger on, for example, Prince Randian, "the Human Torso," as he takes out a cigarette and lights it with his mouth or on Frances O'Connor and Martha Morris as they hold utensils or wine glasses between their toes. The fascination of these scenes inheres in the unfamiliar ways in which anomalous bodies perform familiar activities. On the one hand, the scenes' separation from narrative flow emphasizes their status as disability spectacle; we are conscious that our attention would not hold if "normal" bodies were carrying out these daily tasks. On the other, the lack of sensationalism and the very "normal" and quotidian nature of the scenes remind us, by contrast, of the excessive framing that usually surrounds extraordinary bodies. The monsters of freak shows and horror films are defamiliarized and made again familiar as the contingent, fragmented, and perfectly ordinary bodies we all inhabit.

As we have also already noted, however, the film's processes of de/familiarization change direction at the wedding banquet, whose dynamics of inclusion and exclusion indicate the political and constructed nature of the freaks' degraded status. For if the banquet scene denotes the film's failure to sustain a reversal of normative identifications, returning us to a stereotypical view of the freaks as monsters, it also constitutes its most poignant dramatization of the pervasiveness of monstrous and violent eugenic dictates. The freaks' inclusive invitation seems to upturn eugenic laws that exclude otherness as they seek to include someone different from themselves. But the invitation is presented more as an imperative than a request ("We'll make her one of us!"), and its realization eventually takes the form of the freaks' monstrous punishment of Cleopatra, which indeed makes her one of them. To include Cleo in their community, the freaks know that they must make her a freak and thus effectively *exclude* her from the human community; the ritual's "gooble gobble" chant already anticipates her transformation into a chicken-woman. The horror of the freaks' act relies on the eugenic logic that physical aberration defines generic belonging and that the physically aberrant *do not belong* in normal society. Accordingly, even as Cleo's transformation undermines the film's overt efforts to normalize the freaks, even as it reaffirms the physiognomic code that marginalizes them, it may also be read as the film's strongest anti-eugenic statement, for the worst punishment the freaks can conjure is to make someone one of them, to include someone in the dehumanizing and monstrous exclusions violently imposed on atypical bodies.

*Freaks* thus inverts society's exclusion of the horror-film monster, instead offering the viewer the chance to be included within the sphere of the monstrous. Or, at the more quotidian level of disability, rather than only putting forth ableist views of a disabled minority, *Freaks* also asks viewers to consider themselves vulnerable to bodily transformation and to the social and scientific opprobrium directed at unusual forms. It was not impossible that *Freaks*' original audiences might have understood and even embraced such a radical invitation. The strategic inclusion carried out by the freaks reflects the increasing likelihood, in the 1920s and 1930s, that "average" Americans might find themselves included by eugenic texts in an ever-increasing circle of undesirables and thus might find themselves excluded from the ideal national body. Eugenic lectures and articles often implied the degeneracy of all but a small, elite percentage. For instance, a 1928 headline declared, "91.1 Per Cent of Kindergarten and First Grade Pupils Found with Physical Imperfections," while the American Eugenics Society's State Fair display claimed that only "[a]bout 4% of all Americans" are "high grade" with "ability to do creative work and be fit for leadership."[49] Such assertions indicated the artificiality of the increasingly elusive norm against which individuals were measured, as well as eugenics' creation of a powerful elite on the backs of a growing class of Americans deemed inferior or deviant.

Economic disempowerment, too, led "average" Americans in the Depression to feel oppressed and to contemplate rebellion. Like the freaks set on avenging their wrongs, for instance, farmers protested mortgage foreclosure sales by declaring, "The time has come when we farmers must take the law into our own hands."[50] Such activism blurred lines between middle Americans and marginalized groups, including those with disabilities. A few months after *Freaks'* premiere, the nation was shocked by the brutality with which Gen. Douglas MacArthur's federal soldiers routed the Bonus Expeditionary Force, a veteran group of several thousand that had camped out on Pennsylvania Avenue, demanding early payment of their war service bonus. *Time* quoted MacArthur's description of the B. E. F. as "a bad looking mob animated by the essence of revolution" but proffered a more sympathetic image of the revolutionaries: "A legless veteran inside the Government building loudly challenged the police to remove him. He was ignored."[51]

Together, the farmers' and the veterans' protests assert both the susceptibility of anyone to the vagaries of impairment—economic or physical—and the injustice of social and political attitudes that transform such impairment into disempowerment and disability. As J. Hoberman notes, "*Freaks* is asking a Depression audience to identify not with the Beautiful People who were going to make it in Hollywood, but with sideshow mutations, a total underclass. As a reflection of the time, it's almost revolutionary."[52] Indeed, eugenics' own biological meritocracy, in conflating the poor and working classes, the disabled, and the criminal, connected them in ways that might have fostered revolution. By encouraging "ordinary" Americans to recognize themselves as dysgenic, eugenic discourse risked revealing its own experts—like the nation's economic and political powermongers—as privileged men advancing a selfish agenda as if it were natural and immutable. These social shifts made all the more pertinent *Freaks'* positioning of the vengeful anger of the freaks at the *end* of a narrative, representing their actions as an understandable response to an outrageous assault. The instant in which we are invited to belong to the freak community, then, channels the productive *frisson* of a historical moment in which theories of biological determinism are revealed as acts of violence wielded against individuals whose actual traits are less significant than their deviation from a constructed and unattainable norm.

Still, if the ways in which *Freaks* was pilloried, censored, and withdrawn are any indication, the transgressive implications of its politics of inclusion were either lost on or too threatening for the viewers of 1932. Hoberman concludes, "Depression audiences were not prepared for this kind of thing."[53] Viewers were apparently not comfortable facing up to their commonalities with the freaks, suggesting the difficulty of severing entrenched assumptions about disability from people with impaired or unusual bodies. And to the extent that generic texts constitute a negotiation between filmmakers and audiences, with pleasure provided by the recognition of familiar elements and the meeting of certain expectations, *Freaks'* viewers likely felt that a tacit agreement had been betrayed. The conventions they expected had been irretrievably disordered, their sympathies had been apparently misdirected, and the conclusions they looked for had failed to appear. At the same time, the film's insistent re-presentation of the monstrous Other in its concluding moments both asserts *Freaks'* horror identity and uncovers the genre's "code" of freakishness as a cultural prop. The power of *Freaks* thus resides in its capacity to draw attention to the politics of generic expectations, undercutting the notion of "natural" responses to atypical bodies by highlighting the classic horror film as a ritualized and often contradictory engagement with and construction of bodily aberrance.

## FRAMING FREAKS/*FREAKS*

*Freaks'* poor reception is, as we have seen, often associated with the "realness" of the freaks' bodies and the related belief that such bodies are innately disgusting and horrifying. Robin Larsen and Beth A. Haller, drawing on an unpublished work by Bret Wood, suggest that *Freaks'* preview, in particular, horrified its viewers because they were not properly prepared:

> The tradition of previewing without any framing at all exacerbated its reputation with exhibitors. Wood, for example, argues that the preview version of *Freaks* failed largely because the audience needed prior knowledge of title, phrases, and images describing the film, advertising messages, and a brief scenario, so that they could better prepare themselves for "the candid and unflinching depiction of physical abnormality."[54]

The implication is that viewers could not bear to see a "candid" representation of "physical abnormality" without the kind of framing that could distance them from and help them explain or make sense of such bodies. In particular, audiences needed to know the generic frame that would contain such bodies, relying on "title, phrases, and images describing the film, advertising messages, and a brief scenario" to tell them how to position themselves in relation to the freaks.

But the history of people with disabilities is one of continuous cultural and social framing: the projection of meaning onto troublesome bodies in ways that legitimate public fear, elicit horror, and underwrite practices of marginalization or exclusion. And, as we have seen, *Freaks'* de/familiarization works not by *not* framing its freakish bodies but by reframing them in ways that conflict with acceptable and conventional modes of framing disability and that thus draw attention to such framing's politics and consequences. Like the literary uses of disability that, according to David T. Mitchell and Sharon L. Snyder, fail to reassure readers of their own wholeness and autonomy, that "flaunt" the illusory status of the invulnerable self, *Freaks* repeatedly draws our attention to the frame. It thus not only refuses to present a seamless illusion designed to reassure able-bodied viewers about the otherness of disability but also engenders Ato Quayson's "aesthetic nervousness." The anxiety the film provokes points to the "ethical core" it touches upon, as it reveals—in both horror film and ableist discourses such as eugenics—"a series of structural devices that betray themselves when the disability representation is seen predominantly from the perspective of the disabled rather than from the normative position of the nondisabled."[55]

*Freaks'* constant uncovering of the prosthetic illusions based on freakish bodies begins with the last frame of its opening credits. As we look at the title card, a hand suddenly tears through the word FREAKS. This act brings us to the barker with his promise to reveal something unspeakably horrific, a scene that frames the freaks/*Freaks* in familiar, if outmoded, sideshow terms. Like the tearing of the title frame, the barker's appearance titillates with the premise of going behind the scenes of a circus. However, subsequent scenes reveal not the illicit and deviant acts of monstrous creatures, but instead the freaks' familiar daily and domestic rituals. It is not that there are no frames in these scenes, it is just that the frames in place—eminently familiar melodramatic conventions of family life and conflicts—contrast dramatically with the freak-show frame we were led to expect. These frames position viewers not as shrieking and gasping spectators in the face of otherness but as allies with the good-hearted, if unusually shaped, victims of moral corruption. This switch-and-bait occurs in compressed form in the early pastoral scene: cued by Jean's disgusted response, we see the freaks as anomalous, trespassing creatures that ought to be targeted by eugenic solutions, until, as the estate owner smiles kindly upon them, they gather in apparent childlike fear around Mme Tetrallini, and we must reposition ourselves in relation to them. Similar conflicting frames become evident in moments of ordinary spectacle, such as Prince Randian's lighting of the cigarette. Such scenes elicit a kind of voyeurism but, lacking the staging and spiel of the sideshow act, and enacted in front of able-bodied characters who do not view the moment as extraordinary, also suggest that the freakishness of the freaks would soon dissipate if consistently framed in such homey terms.

*Freaks'* inconsistent spectatorial address insists on the viewer's cooperation in cultural constructions of monstrosity. In discussing classical Hollywood film, David Bordwell has presented film-viewing as a participatory act. Bordwell discusses the compositional, cinematographic, editing, and narrative means by which viewers are encouraged to develop certain expectations or subscribe to certain illusions:

> Gombrich has . . . shown that visual illusion demands that the spectator propose, test, and discard perceptual hypotheses based on expectation and probability. For illusion to work, the spectator must meet the work of art halfway.
>
> If perceptual illusion requires some spectatorial activity, even more is required for that imaginative involvement solicited by narrative. . . . [W]e form hypotheses, make inferences, erect expectations, and draw conclusions about the film's characters and actors. Again, the spectator must cooperate in filling the film's form.[56]

Typically, classical cinema enables illusion by only including elements that forward a causal narrative, achieve a certain "verisimilitude," and fulfill generic requirements. Nonetheless, Bordwell argues, even classical cinema uses instances of "artistic motivation," or what Russian formalists called "baring the device": "a component may be justified by its power to call attention to the system within which it operates." Artistic motivation appears in classical films in moments of "spectacle and technical virtuosity," parody, and self-referentiality, but because such instances are not used "repeatedly and systematically," "story causality remains dominant" and the film remains classical. Nonetheless, Hollywood's use of artistic motivation "imputes a considerable alertness to the viewer: in order to appreciate certain moments, one must know and remember another film's story, or a star's habitual role, or a standard technique. To some extent, artistic motivation develops a connoisseurship in the classical spectator."[57] Instances of artistic motivation thus remind viewers of their participation in the film experience, their willingness to "complete the illusion."

Oliver Gaycken draws on Bordwell in discussing Tod Browning's *oeuvre*, noting that while Browning's work is eminently classical, it has a "recurring tendency to 'bare the device.'" For Gaycken, "What makes Browning remarkable . . . is his integration of this 'disruptive' element into the fabric of his narrative system, his elevation, in other words, of deception to the level of form and his display of the trickery that is the cornerstone of cinematic storytelling."[58] In *Freaks*, as in his other films, Browning looks behind the illusion and reveals the labor that generates freakishness. Several scenes feature sideshow personnel rehearsing their acts, repeatedly revealing circus tricks and bodily surfaces as a matter of props and prosthetics, their effectiveness dependent on the audience's willingness to be fooled. In revealing the mechanics of illusion, then, Browning's films enact "a critique of voyeurism" enabling "a different, more skeptical spectator."[59] *Freaks'* viewers are from its opening moments encouraged to be conscious of the generic and cultural codes at work.[60]

In particular, the banquet scene foregrounds the prosthetic cinematic operations typically used to frame dysfunctional bodies in order to reassure or horrify spectators. The scene opens with an intertitle more at home in a silent film, heralding "The Wedding Feast," indicating that it was in fact filmed silently, with sound added later.[61] For Skal, the success of this scene—its enduring effect on viewers—marks the failure of the film as a whole; he argues that *Freaks* would have been more successful and aesthetically pleasing *as* a silent film:

> The freaks' glaring deficiencies in reading dialogue would have been obviated, and the heightened stylization of the silents, with the formality of intertitles and continual musical accompaniment, could have done much to cushion viewer response. . . . The uneasy line readings of the freaks served only to break the narrative illusion, and by extension the whole unspoken contract between the audience and Hollywood.[62]

Again, the film's excessive realism, especially its too-real cast, is summoned to explain the film's failure and anomalousness, and the silent scene, in which the freaks' articulations become an asynchronous gabbling chant, is deemed more palatable, perhaps insofar as it repositions its freaks in a more illusory and fantastical realm.

This view recalls the assumptions of some critics of early sound cinema who felt that talking films' increased realism—understood as an increased "bodiliness"—impaired imaginative and creative viewing experiences and fostered a passive acceptance of the film's view of reality. For instance, in 1928, Rudolf Arnheim criticized sound film for rendering its images too like daily embodied experiences and thus foreclosing on silent cinema's fantastical possibilities. The beauty of silent movies, he contended, was lost when "the visual picture suddenly [became] three-dimensional and tangible," regressing "film art . . . back to the good old peepshow."[63] In the same year, Harry Potamkin asserted that the talking film, particularly in its focus on embodied effect, revealed cinema as little more than a "physical attack" on passive spectators. And film critic Ernest Betts declared there to be "something monstrous about a speaking film," maintaining, "The soul of the film—its eloquent and vital silence—is destroyed. The film now returns to the circus from whence it came, among the freaks and the fat ladies."[64] Tim Armstrong suggests that sound film's supposedly too-real mimicry of embodied and material reality generates a repressed and monstrous degraded body that appears in such rhetoric: "the body reappears traumatically in sound cinema, as a maimed or aggressive object: a ventriloquist's dummy, a statue throwing stones, freaks and fat ladies; as a physical 'attack.'"[65]

Thus, just as some critics believe that classic horror's depiction of embodied form narrows the monster's signifying capacity, these critics understood an apparent increase in cinematic reality and audience affect as a reductive return to a degraded and freakish bodily experience. But their dissatisfaction with the extreme realism of early sound film coexisted with the discomfited perception of many filmgoers that early talkies manifested a certain unnaturalness, a *lack* of realism. As discussed by Robert Spadoni, just as late-nineteenth-century viewers of early film were disturbed by the "graphic ugliness and gigantism" of faces in close-up and unsettled by moving cameras, so viewers of early sound film found themselves once again unused to filmic conventions that would soon come to seem natural. Early sound films' synchronization problems, dialogue errors, and apparent dissociation of voice from body meant that viewers, rather than being absorbed in movies' narratives and illusion, experienced "renewed awareness of the mechanical nature of the cinema" and "of films as manufactured objects."[66]

Frustrations thus emerged not necessarily because sound films proffered crude realism in place of transcendent fantasy but because "viewers were responding to a cinema that, as it took what was widely perceived to be a major step toward a fuller representation of reality, simultaneously became *more* unreal."[67] Sound was often perceived as "something extratextual pieced onto the whole for effect," a supplement in the Derridean sense as described by Jonathan Culler: "an inessential extra, added to something complete in itself, but . . . added in order to complete, to compensate for a lack in what was supposed to be complete in itself."[68] The addition of sound, then, did not necessarily supply the complete, embodied experience derided by some of its critics but instead drew attention to the artificiality and incompleteness of the cinematic product. Such contradictory perspectives point to a sudden, disconcerting revelation of cinema's prosthetic practices. And, in each case, the degraded body forms the rhetorical and visual grounds on which battles over cinema's essence and status occur, just as it has constituted evidence for disparaging interpretations of the essential identity and value of classic horror.

It did not take long for audiences to become familiar with sound film conventions and, with the improvement of sound technology, movies once again produced convincing illusions for filmgoers. But *Freaks* juxtaposes the two modes of spectatorship, highlighting the prosthetic practices that underwrite the "unspoken contract" of cinematic illusion. As Skal notes, the characters' speech in earlier scenes is often stilted and unconvincing, while, in some instances, heavy accents or mumbled speech frustrate viewer immersion in the filmic illusion. Similarly, the dissonant lip-synching and recycled dialogue of the wedding banquet perhaps gratingly recall a moment when "viewers . . . lacked the cognitive training to process this new constitutive element of cinema as routinely and transparently as they had the silent film intertitle."[69] The collision of silent and sound conventions in *Freaks* uncovers the workings of cinema's body politics: we glimpse the cheap tricks of the freak show and the figure behind the "ventriloquist's dummy"; we perceive the institutional and formal processes that construe bodies, particularly unusual bodies, as degraded, too-real, and monstrous; and we glimpse the cues that typically prompt our participation in such constructions.

The film thus moves from presenting the freaks as somewhat sympathetic characters—a presentation always marked, however, by our perception of them as "deficient," and "uneasy" speakers—to unsettling our view of them through the dissonant chanting of the wedding feast, to an eventual silencing. In the mute and menacing attack on Cleo and Hercules, the freaks finally conform to generic requirements by becoming dumb and violent monsters. Rather than violating the generic expectations of the horror-film viewing community, the film fulfills them, apparently confirming that physical monstrosity is aligned with inner corruption. But coming after the more sympathetic and "normalizing" representations, the attack scene draws attention to its own excessive and artificial status *as* a horror-film convention, to the artificiality of the act of reinstalling the freaks in the familiar guise of aggressive monsters (see fig. 2.4).

The film's de/familiarizing strategies thus make more evident the nature of the generic contract between the horror film and its audience, confronting spectators with the violent implications of the ableist narratives and conclusions they demand from the genre. Writing from 1964, John Thomas aptly summarizes the powerful and alienating effect of the revenge scenes:

Certainly the final sequence in which the freaks hunt down and mutilate Cleopatra and Hercules is as ghoulish as anyone could wish. . . . [T]he darkness swarms with crawling, hopping shapes, lit grotesquely by momentary flashes, all humanity seemingly erased.

This is our last image of the freaks and perhaps it may be counted as an artistic mistake. If the picture is really an attempt to evoke sympathy, can it end with the freaks transformed into monsters?

It can, and does, because the ground has been so carefully prepared that the audience must, at the end of the film, react against its own revulsion. We are horrified, but we are simultaneously ashamed of our horror; for we remember that these are not monsters at all but people like us, and we know that we have again been betrayed by our own primal fears. . . . [W]e are plunged back into the abyss of our own sick selves, to recall once again that the most fearful inhumanity we can know is our own.[70]

As Thomas indicates, the de/familiarizing part of the film has made it difficult for us to consume the attack scene unself-consciously, to immerse ourselves in its gruesome and thrilling premise without some misgivings about its reversion to the freaks-as-monsters conceit that underpins most horror, without some attention to the cinematic means by which the freaks are made into monsters: their menacing expressions, their sinister silence, their clutching of penetrating weapons, their animalistic and irrational crawling through the mud directly toward ground-level cameras, their framing by darkness and lightning and rain. From such a perspective, we must question the very concept of "primal fears" that override human sympathy and instead begin to interrogate our investments in a continued and deliberate estrangement from unusual physical forms.

It is the image of Cleopatra that brings home to viewers their awkward complicity in the construction of freaks. In one last, unsettling move, the film refuses to deliver the generic punishment and destruction of its monsters, while flaunting what remains only implicit in the usual iconography of the horror film: our desire to see the beautiful woman deformed by the monster's violent assault. As a "made" freak, Cleo clearly shifts focus from congenital deformity—the barker's reassuring and sinister claim that "but for the accident of birth, you might be even as they are"—to the ways in which accident, injury, and violent attack may refashion the body, refusing eugenic narratives that contain aberrance in terms of genetic destiny. But Cleo's evident makeup, clothing, feathers, and gloves also remind us of the ways disability operates as a coerced performance, its bearers costumed according to the meanings foisted on them. To that extent, the freaks' inclusion of Cleo in their ranks imposes on her the obligation to signify also imposed on them; they send a message born out of their own silencing. The obviously artificial, prosthetic status of Cleo's disabled body uncovers cultural and textual uses of disability as a "crutch," while her outraged squawks both capture and protest against the debasement of the speechless but signifying monster (see fig. 2.5). In this way, *Freaks* displays the prosthetic uses to which disability is put by cultural narratives, including classic horror narratives, embodying the ways cultural texts force impaired bodies to signify but prefer them not to speak.

Cleo's status as a freak reminds us that when critics have seen early sound film as a degradation of silent cinema's ethereal fantasies, horror film as a reductive corporealization of literary ambiguity, classic horror film as a conservative and unevolved generic form, or *Freaks* as an improperly realistic horror film, in each case the disabled or deformed body has been summoned as a transparent marker of inferiority. Cleo's hybridic body and crude vocalizations, made freakish so as to expose the enfreakment of every unusual body, thus also represent the problematic and multiply degraded forms of *Freaks* and the talking classic horror picture. Her discordant shrieks resonate with disparagements of early sound cinema, as in critic Clifford Howard's 1929 censure of the new medium as it "squawked forth into speech and song."[71] Her confused physique also realizes the mixed and unnatural genre so despised by classical critics, imagined by Horace as a monstrous body: "Suppose some painter had the bright idea / Of sticking a human head on a horse's neck / And covering human nether limbs up with / Assorted feathers so that a beautiful / Woman uptop was an ugly fish below, / And you were invited in to look, / How could you possibly keep a straight face?"[72] As the beautiful woman become feathered and ugly chicken, Cleo calls attention to the mixed nature of both *Freaks* and the classic horror genre, their conjoining of melodrama and horror and "real" and mythic monstrosity.

In "making" Cleo, *Freaks* thus makes itself freakish, embracing formal incongruity to draw attention to its multiply aberrant status and to unveil the dependence of aesthetic pleasure and narrative illusion on the simultaneous exploitation and elision—the constant "framing"—of disabled bodies. Gaycken argues that the tearing of *Freaks*' title card shapes all of the film's subsequent unveilings, including that of Cleo the chicken-woman, asking us to see not the freaks' innate monstrosity but "the mise-en-scène of [Cleo's] mutilation that allows her to be claimed for the side show community as 'one of us.'"[73] Indeed, what the film reveals throughout is not the deviant monster promised by its framing but the mise-en-scène that puts monstrosity in (its) place: the barker's spiel that encourages our horror; the costumes and rehearsals that refashion the sideshow performers as spectacle; the revenge sequence that makes monsters of freaks; the epilogue that puts the littlest freaks back in place, that reorders the heterosexual couple, that redresses perceived immorality, that puts the audience back in place and yet, in its evident artificiality, reminds the audience that it is being put back in place. *Freaks'* viewer address thus combines with its attention to artifice and staging in ways that make difficult an unself-conscious reading or experience of the final sequence.

## *FREAKS* REFRAMED

Subsequent to the disastrous preview, various efforts were made to provide more familiar conventions and framings for *Freaks'* spectators, efforts that in their inconsistent effects often again merely drew viewers' attention to fact that they were being positioned, thus disrupting the expected generic experience. Studio advertisements, as we have seen, mimicked the film itself in combining appeals to prurience, pity, and horror, but thus only highlighted their own exploitative qualities, prompting the *Motion Picture Daily* to complain that the film "could not simultaneously capitalize on human misfits and pretend to pity them."[74] The appended epilogue meant to restore order was awkwardly positioned outside the sideshow narrative, emphasizing its own status as an artificial convention designed to reassure. Wrote the *New York Times* reviewer: "The real end of the picture comes when the woman is changed into a freak herself. . . . But, apparently under the belief that the picture as it stood was a little too horrible, the producers have tacked a happy ending on it. . . . As the real climax had formed the most powerful part of the picture, the addition is doubly unwelcome."[75]

And in 1947, when MGM relicensed *Freaks* to exploitation-film entrepreneur Dwain Esper, he added a long, scrolling prologue that remains attached to many circulating prints and VHS/DVD copies today and that constitutes the most blatant framing of all. The prologue, entitled "Special Message," touts the film as a "HIGHLY UNUSUAL VISUAL ATTRACTION," declaiming, in the rhetoric of the sideshow barker, "BELIEVE IT OR NOT——STRANGE AS IT SEEMS."[76] The text then glosses a cultural history of atypical bodies, moving from "ancient times" when "anything that deviated from the normal was considered an omen of ill luck or representative of evil" to the attribution of "deeds of injustice and hardship" to "the many crippled and deformed tyrants of Europe and Asia."

It lists historical and folkloric figures "who have altered the world's course" including "CALIBAN, FRANKENSTEIN," and "KAISER WIL-HELM," before forwarding a sympathetic view of the constructedness of responses to disability: "The revulsion with which we view the abnormal, the malformed, and the mutilated is the result of long conditioning by our forefathers. The majority of freaks, themselves, are endowed with normal thoughts and emotions. Their lot is truly a heartbreaking one." Esper's text then builds on the "code" mentioned by the barker in the opening scene: "They are forced into the most unnatural of lives. Therefore, they have built up among themselves a code of ethics to protect them from the barbs of normal people. Their rules are rigidly adhered to and the hurt of one is the hurt of all; the joy of one is the joy of all. The story about to be revealed is a story based on the effect of this code upon their lives." Finally, the preamble reassures viewers of scientific progress toward bodily perfection ("Never again will such a story be filmed, as modern science and teratology is rapidly eliminating such blunders of nature from the world") before returning to its simultaneously pitying and sensationalistic tone: "With humility for the many injustices done to such people (they have no power to control their lot) we present the most startling horror story of the ABNORMAL and the UNWANTED."

In arousing viewers' desires for a particularly "startling horror story," moralizing about the plight of "the ABNORMAL and the UNWANTED," and on occasion entitling the film *Forbidden Love*, Esper cued savvy readers to expect an exploitation film: Skal and Savada describe it as "a distributor's cynical attempt to position the picture with a moralistic, 'educational' defense—just like the pictures about sex and drugs."[77] Esper's framing, however, valuably presents the freaks' "code" not as a result of innate monstrosity but as a response to a hostile society. In turn, his assertion that *Freaks* is "a story based on the effect of this code upon their lives" construed the film as a response to conventional and hostile framings of freaks, one that enacts the horror code in order to convey its effects on the bodies it frames. Esper's commentary illuminates *Freaks*' legitimate claim to exploitation status, insofar as it carries several of the traits Eric Schaefer assigns to such films: it clearly deals with "a 'forbidden' topic" and was presented with "carnivalesque ballyhoo." And while its disruptions of classical Hollywood style were not due to cheap independent production, *Freaks* certainly "centered on some form of forbidden spectacle that served as [its] organizing sensibility."[78] But *Freaks*' forbidden spectacle—foregrounding constructed disability rather than exposing sexual acts—proved inadequately exploitative: viewers at a North Carolina drive-in threatened to riot because "they hadn't seen any skin."[79] Esper's framing had contributed to, rather than minimized, the ways in which *Freaks'* displaced generic clues predisposed audiences to revolt.

Since audiences ran from *Freaks* in 1932 and rejected it in 1949, however, the film has gone through a slow process of recuperation, one marked by frequent efforts to remove it from the horror category and reframe it as a countercultural or avant-garde text. In the 1950s, *Freaks* developed a cult following in France, playing to the small and "elite audience" of "the tiny moviehouses of the Latin quarter" and receiving praise in Paul Gilson's *Ciné Magic* (1951).[80] The film's art-house status was cemented with a well-received screening at the Venice Film Festival in September 1962, just a month before Tod Browning's death.[81] Soon after, *Freaks* was screened for the first time in Great Britain and reentered the American cinema scene, where it made the rounds of midnight movies and was embraced as "part of the canon of the counterculture, the mythology of the dissident young."[82] Since the sixties, the film has made regular appearances at film festivals and cult movie screenings, has received a great deal of scholarly and critical attention, and has been issued on VHS and DVD.

Central to *Freaks'* changed reputation was its audiences' willingness to identify with the freaks. Embracing marginality and opposition to bourgeois social norms, midnight moviegoers—especially the "dissident young people" whom Fiedler notes were proud to claim the name of "Freak"—saw *Freaks* as "a movie about a persecuted class of people . . . who eventually pool their resources and join forces in order to defeat the cruel oppressors who mock and exploit them."[83] The struggle against tyranny humanized the freaks: Tom Milne in *Sight and Sound* insisted that "fascinated revulsion turns into tender comprehension" and that "the revelation of the film is its warmth and humanity," while Andrew Sarris wrote, "As much documentary as low-grade revenge fiction, *Freaks* stared unblinkingly and compassionately" at its unusually shaped characters, to the extent that he felt it to be "one of the most compassionate movies ever made."[84] Such readings gave preeminence to *Freaks'* realistic elements, not condemning them as alienating or disruptive of fantasy, but finding in them a powerful social message.

Along with the valorization of *Freaks'* realist elements and social commentary, reframings of *Freaks* often praised the avant-garde nature of its fusion of realistic and sympathetic portraits of the freaks with the more horrific depiction of them in the concluding sequence. In a 1963 article, Raymond Durgnat acclaimed the "shock" effects of *Freaks'* combination of "guignol" and "matter-of-fact" elements, likening the "blackness" of its moral to the works of Luis Buñuel, while French critic Christian Oddos noted res-onances with Fellini's monsters and clowns and, like Thomas, commended the self-examination prompted in viewers by the film's de/familiarizing of the freaks: "For . . . the closer the monster comes to our human condition, the more its deformity touches us and the more the average viewer is ill at ease before the projected image."[85]

For such critics, however, recognition of *Freaks'* social relevance and avant-garde elements required its elevation above the purported conser-vatism and inferiority of horror film. For Thomas, the film's emphasis on the freaks' humanity precisely precluded it from horror-film membership: the "conventional horror film," he wrote, concerns "our responses to the nonhuman element in the world . . . the irrational, the inexplicable," requir-ing our identification with the monster's victims and receiving "release in the monster's ultimate death." In contrast, he contends, *Freaks* locates "in the humanity of the freaks a moral center for the universe."[86] This sense persists in recent criticism: for Peter Hutchings, the realism and humanity of the freaks "undermin[es] the special effects–generated body horror on display in the likes of *Doctor X* and *Mystery of the Wax Museum*," rendering *Freaks* "a kind of anti-horror film" labeled horror only "because no one could think of any other generic category where it might belong."[87] *Freaks* is thus deemed too complex and radical to be a horror film: writes Thomas, "*Freaks* will disappoint no one but the mindless children who consume most horror films."[88]

Other recent critics dispute such elevation. Returning to the film's revenge sequence, they insist that *Freaks* ultimately exploits conservative depictions of "monsters" and thus conforms to the regressive nature of the classic horror film. For instance, the Pacific Film Archive's (PFA) 1990 pro-gram note on *Freaks* suggests that contemporary audiences easily "digest" the film's supposedly revolutionary thesis: "that 'freakishness' is only skin deep, and that differently formed people have all the feelings, intelligence and humor of 'normal' folks." But, the note argues, the film itself finally undercuts this view:

> What keeps *Freaks* "freakish" is rather the duality of Browning's own inten-tion. Despite being one of the few films that, *mutatis mutandis*, treats the Other as "one of us"; and despite purporting in the original prologue to be an exposé of the exploitation of "nature's mutants," *Freaks* is guilty of the crime it denounces. By virtue of its bizarre revenge plot, the film traps its charac-ters (and thus its actors) in a horror mode. More disruptive yet is Brown-ing's style, which interrupts the crude melodrama for dreamlike sequences

whose lyricism voyeuristically peers into, as it celebrates, the "other world" of these carnival performers.[89]

The film, this commentary suggests, is hypocritical in juxtaposing its sympathetic prologue and melodramatic story with voyeuristic spectacle and a revenge plot that "traps its characters . . . in a horror mode." In this view, author-generated generic codes and cues, particularly the admixture of realistic and horrific conventions shaped by Browning's "dual intention" and "disruptive style," confuse and mislead viewers, ultimately imposing on them a reactionary and prejudiced spectacle that forces a horrified and ableist response.[90] Hawkins similarly suggests that the film's realism encourages "the audience to read the freaks' story as a semidocumentary of circus life," thus rendering more potent and "plausible" the otherwise clearly artificial horror-film conventions of the freaks' vengeful code and their violent attack. Thus, the conclusion "plays on the very audience prejudices and fears that the early part of the film attempts to challenge."[91] From a disability perspective, Martin Norden refers to a purported 1962 Cannes screening of *Freaks* in the horror category as "unfortunate," presumably because this act of generic categorization, as stated by Cook, "traps [*Freaks'*] carnival subjects securely within the horror mode, thus reinscribing physical difference as a terrifying spectacle."[92]

To appreciate fully the anomalousness *and* conventionality of *Freaks*, it is necessary to take from the critics of the 1960s and 1970s an insistence on the value and radical effects of the film's use of real and eminently human forms, while heeding the cautions of recent critics as to the viscerally horrifying effects of the film's concluding scenes. At the same time, it is necessary to contest the reductive view of horror that both sets of criticisms maintain. To the extent that *Freaks* was imagined and marketed as a horror film, relies on recognizable horror elements, constructs itself as an inverted horror film, and presents its most enduring scenes within the horror mode, we cannot ignore its claim to membership in the classic horror genre. In particular, we cannot overlook the ways in which the revenge scenes work to elicit horrified and fearful responses, using familiar and effective cinematic techniques. But we must also attend to the film's avant-garde signaling of its audience manipulation, which undercuts any easy explanation of our response to the freaks as "primal." We thus experience the revenge scenes in a divided way: we "react against [our] revulsion"; "[w]e are horrified, but we are simultaneously ashamed of our horror." Notes French critic Claude Beylie, "Horror, if there is horror, boomerangs; it does not reside in the spectacle itself . . . but in the perfect naturalness which governs cruel games, condemning us to pass 'to the other side.' . . . We do better than 'understand' the monsters, we discover through their piercing eyes a quite worse monstrosity, that of men." And Oddos suggests that the monstrosity we discover inheres in our spectatorship: "*Freaks* constrains us to watch a spectacle that we have always refused to see, insists on our status as voyeur vis-à-vis fantasy film and denounces our hypocrisy. . . . We have agreed to witness this spectacle, this reality underscored by a circus ringmaster's two extreme interventions: our innocence is not proven!"[93] Thus, the "duality" and implicit hypocrisy for which the PFA indicts Browning are our own, insofar as we accept the cues that frame the freaks as both sympathetic and monstrous. And even if we resist, it is because we become conscious of our own framing, *conscious of ourselves as horror viewers*. By the film's later stages, it is difficult to maintain the pretense that only Browning is to blame for "trapping" his characters in "the horror mode," and thus difficult to experience the revenge sequence without some discomfort at its monstrous depiction of the freaks, some culpability for the outrageous de-formation of the female body, and some complicity in the satisfying nature of the revenge. We realize that Browning's subject is not the freaks so much as what Thomas calls "our own sick selves."

*Freaks'* powerful combination of the real and the horrific requires us to revisit our assumptions about both the function of "real" impaired bodies in horror-film formulae and the subsequently inferior and conservative status of classic horror films. Exclusions of classic horror films from the larger horror genre accept at face value the Monster's declaration, in *Bride of Frankenstein*, that he and his Bride do not belong, taking it as biological truth rather than the tragic mouthing of a learned cultural prejudice and reenacting his destruction by excluding disability as a political status. They also underwrite Joy's desire to forestall the genre, rather than viewing both the monsters' bodies and the movies themselves as potent incarnations of the fraught relationship between particular bodies and social, cultural, and aesthetic systems. When Wood advanced the horror-film formula as "Normality is threatened by the monster," he insisted that the "normality" at stake should not be defined too literally in terms of "health."[94] But for Sally Chivers, *Freaks* can *only* fit into this definition of horror if "normality" encompasses assumptions about "what comprises a healthy [or moral] body."[95] Discussing the mutability of genres, Ralph Cohen noted: "Each member alters the genre by adding, contradicting, or changing constituents, especially those of members most closely related to it."[96] It is my argument that including *Freaks* within the generic body reveals the assumptions about healthy and unhealthy bodies on which all classic horror films are based.

Just as *Freaks'* inclusion of Cleo in the genre of "freaks" forces our reconsideration of what it means to belong to a particular and disenfranchised class, the inclusion of *Freaks* in the horror genre forces our reconsideration of the genre's status. Reading *Freaks* as a horror film thus does not necessarily mark it with the derogatory and ableist body politics attributed to classic horror, as Norden implies, but instead maps the realism and "homeyness" of *Freaks'* freaks onto the monsters of *other* classic horror movies. As a classic horror film that has been judged an exciting and complex social text, *Freaks* contests views of classic horrors as more conservative than and inferior to literary Gothic or postmodern horror. As a film that foregrounds cultural and generic framings of bodies, it requires us to reject the notion of the impaired body as a self-evidently degraded form and to trace in other classic horrors the complex and laborious processes of de/familiarization required to render impairment uncanny, gruesome, and strange. Further, as a film that inconsistently frames its characters, *Freaks* also challenges readings in which all horror movies are seen to use monstrous bodies to the same effects, illuminating instead the inconsistencies, transformations, and de/familiarizations that traverse the genre's texts, and insisting, *contra* Norbert Lusk's disparagement of *Dracula*, that classic horrors may arouse sympathy as well as horror for their monstrous characters.

Moreover, seeing *Freaks* as a classic horror film complicates overly teleological models of genre. Schatz valuably emphasizes the ideological ambivalence of genre films, which are "not blindly supportive of the status quo" but often "both criticize and reinforce the values, beliefs, and ideals of our culture." The insight makes space for competing readings of *Freaks'* and other classic horror films' conflicting attitudes to and understandings of debility and deformity. But Schatz also argues that genre films typically evolve toward greater complexity and self-consciousness: "As a genre's classic conventions are refined and eventually parodied and subverted, its transparency gradually gives way to *opacity*: we no longer look *through* the form (or perhaps 'into the mirror') to glimpse an idealized self-image, rather we look *at* the *form itself* to examine and appreciate its structure and its cultural appeal."[97] Schatz points to the role of changing cultural attitudes in shaping such generic revisions, and *Freaks'* shifting reception history certainly affirms that alterations in social context made possible a broader appreciation of its attributes. But the very fact that some 1932 viewers responded not only to the freaks but to the film's manner of framing them indicates that the horror genre, from its earliest days, has incorporated reflexive considerations of its conventional elements and audience positioning.

To this extent, classic horror films are not innately regressive, just as they are not innately progressive. As Kent Brintnall points out:

> Understanding *Freaks* as a progressive text is not an experience that Browning imposes on his audience; instead, the film presents clearly and precisely the abject body, as well as the cruelty and inhumanity of the mechanism of abjection, alongside culturally normative beautiful characters who are terrorized and attacked and disgusted by these abnormal physiognomies. The film merely provides its audience an opportunity to resolve their own subjective positioning with respect to each. . . . *Freaks* bears repeated viewings for the way in which it compels an active engagement, a choice, a *decision* from its spectators on questions related to voyeurism, exploitation, community and vengeance.[98]

*Freaks*—like, I argue, other classic horrors—encodes and foregrounds the genre's *raison d'être*, our desire to both see and experience bodily debilitation and aberration. The pleasurable display of the monstrous body is framed in familiar terms, a framing that in turn insists on our own collaboration in forgetting the familiar and homey freakish body so that we can again and again be frightened and repulsed and excited by its (re)appearance.

To see differently the figure of disability in classic horror films is thus to defamiliarize what has seemed natural about our readings of it—to contest the assumption that visibly impaired bodies are naturally and materially objectionable and can have no cultural meanings of their own—and to refamiliarize ourselves with the disabled bodies that are at once culturally ubiquitous and constantly disavowed. *Freaks*' visions of disability as cultural prosthesis underlie the remainder of *Hideous Progeny*, which continues to address the formulaic plots, characters, and themes of classic horror films but also increasingly turns to the cinematic conventions and politics of reception crucial to the genre's representation of disability. The films under consideration, so often apparently premised on simplistic eugenic paradigms, often gesture outwards, through processes of identification and audience positioning, toward the spectator, in ways that exceed and undo the limited eugenic paradigm and invoke other kinds of investments in, desires for, and cultural framings of disability.

# REVELATIONS AND CONVULSIONS

## SPECTACLES OF IMPAIRMENT IN CLASSIC HORROR FILM

The narrative and metaphoric construction of disability in classical myth, folklore, and literature has invested certain impairments with particular symbolic meanings. Blindness, for instance, often figures an absolute helplessness or dependency, accompanied by the sentiment summarized in *Oedipus the King*: "Better to be dead than live blind."[1] Alternatively, blindness indicates, or is compensated with, inner sight and wisdom, as in Sophocles' prophet Tiresias. Eugenicists also interpreted blindness according to their purposes, associating hereditary blindness with insanity and degeneracy and translating earlier discourses of blind people's helplessness into economic terms, emphasizing the "cost" of blindness to the nation and, consequently, seeking to prevent blind people's marriage and procreation.[2] Classic horror films picked up on these various meanings of blindness, featuring insightful and virtuous blind characters such as *Bride of Frankenstein*'s hermit, *The Invisible Ray*'s Mother Rukh, and *The Devil-Doll*'s Madame Levond; helpless and passive blind victims such as the men of Dearborn's Institute for the Destitute Blind in *The Dark Eyes of London* (aka *The Human Monster*); and blind "deviants" such as *The Dark Eyes of London*'s hulking and murderous Jake, described by the *Motion Picture Herald*, in eugenic terms, as "Jake, an imbecile monster."[3]

The degeneracy of Dracula, the "visual disruption" offered by Frankenstein's monster, the deformities and cripplings of mad doctors, and the "imbecilic" blindness of Jake, while conveying the visible "unfitness" and monstrosity on which eugenic narratives relied, do not simplistically embody specific "real" disabilities.[4] In considering these characters "disabled," we should be careful not to assume a purely reflective relationship between "reality" and art, like some disability approaches that castigate texts for unrealistic or negative portraits of disability, or like "the medical diagnostic school of criticism" which "sought to accomplish corrective surgery upon misbegotten disabled characters."[5] Nevertheless, to assume that any visual marker of disability or deformity—a limp, a misshapen face, a missing arm—functions in the same way as any other marker is to elide the textually specific manner in which it operates. Attending to the specific meanings attached to particular forms contests their absorption into a generic "degeneracy" and helps illuminate the complex visual disability vocabulary that underwrites horror films and other cultural texts.

As we have seen, eugenicists consistently arrogated particular impairments to abstract defect. When the Eugenics Record Office sent out fieldworkers and solicited family histories, it did so in order to document all kinds of physical, mental, and behavioral traits. The files resulting from ERO studies included characteristics as varied as skin conditions, hirsuteness, tuberculosis, body build, feeblemindedness, paranoia, quick temper, wanderlust, larceny, "taste for singing," social leadership, sympathy, needlework, cleft palate, hemophilia, and "monstrosities."[6] These records of diverse traits, it was believed, would prove and explain the operations of genetic heredity. And such studies did contribute valuable information about hereditary conditions that, along with Mendelian genetic theory, helped establish the operation of recessive, dominant, and sex-linked genes in conditions such as albinism, congenital cataracts, and hemophilia. But, as suggested by the trait-file categories, eugenicists frequently failed to distinguish between disorders that "have easily definable symptoms (phenotypes) and are caused by single genes," and "complex disorders and traits, whose phenotypes are difficult to define and which are now known to involve multiple genes or are influenced by the environment."[7] Moreover, eugenicists also persistently and unscientifically linked any given physical disability to other "defects" and conflated physical or mental impairment with moral failing, as in studies of blindness that connected it to "degeneracy" or "deviance."[8] Eugenicists thus adapted historical and mythic views of impairment to their own ends, presenting cultural interpretations of certain conditions as medical and biological truth.

This chapter seeks to invert that interpretive move, examining classic horror visions of particular impairments, specifically facial deformity and seizures, and drawing out the ways in which such apparent "facts" actually encode and perpetuate impairment-specific mythic, cultural, and pseudo-scientific meanings. At stake here is the notion of "impairment" as something "real," purely material, genetically determined, and empirically evident to the expert eye. The Foucauldian work of Shelley Tremain contests this view of impairment, contending that it cannot be a neutral description of a somatic or mental condition, but is always already invested with ideological significance. In Tremain's view, regulatory discourses produce an *illusion* of impairment as "natural" and "antecedent" to, and a justification for, governing mechanisms.[9] Thus did eugenicists present visible traits as indisputable evidence of genetic heredity in order to legitimate their management of "inferior" populations.

In considering selected classic-horror moments that display specific impairments—deformed faces and convulsive seizures—this chapter argues that such spectacles work counter to the truth claims of eugenics' visual politics. In classic horror films' disability "revelations," impairment is framed in ways that uncover the subjective, contradictory, and dynamic nature of cultural narratives about disability. While the revelations work to excite shock and horror in viewers, they also confuse genetically determinist narratives: they foreground impairments that may be acquired rather than congenital; they illuminate cultural and mythic interpretations of impairment that continued to attach to and undercut the scientific claims of eugenic discourse; and they bring to light the spectacular, manipulated, and performative—that is, the culturally and textually generated—elements of disability. In doing so, they do not present disability as purely textual or socially constructed; rather, they insist that, disabled or not, humans are profoundly, and even physically, shaped by stereotypes and myths of, and prejudices toward, physical, mental, and behavioral differences. Horror's disability spectacles present impairment as a dynamic aspect of human experience that is constantly culturally produced through powerful imaginary constructs. At the same time, horror's visions of impairment also have recourse to material and "real" bodily experiences that are not absorbed without trace in a constructionist worldview but instead resurface in both the actors' production and the audience's consumption of horror spectacle.[10]

## ON THE FACE OF IT: FACIAL POLITICS IN EUGENICS AND CLASSIC HORROR

It is a paradigmatic moment in the history of the horror spectacle: Mary Philbin, as Christine Daae, sidles up behind Lon Chaney's Phantom as he plays the organ in his quarters beneath the Paris Opera House during

*The Phantom of the Opera* (dir. Rupert Julian, Universal, 1925). Despite the fact he has promised her safety if she does not touch his mask, Christine is intent on revealing his face. Her hands creep over his shoulders as he plays but start back as he straightens and turns slightly. When he resumes his playing she moves closer once more. As her right hand reaches his mask and pulls it away, the camera cuts suddenly to a frontal view of the Phantom, with Christine behind him (fig. 3.1). The Phantom's disfigured face—with its sunken cheeks, receded nose and flared nostrils, darkly ringed wide eyes, and gaping mouth—contorts in shock and surprise, staring into the camera; Christine's face mirrors his shock for the camera although she cannot yet gaze fully on the Phantom's visage. Only when the Phantom turns does she reel backwards, her face registering horror as she shields her eyes with her hands and collapses to the floor, while the Phantom harangues her in an intertitle: "Feast your eyes—glut your soul, on my accursed ugliness!"

The moment of monstrosity's revelation, the shocking sight on which horror film depends, is often performed as the disclosure of a deformed or ugly face. The affective dominance of this moment over the film's narrative structure is suggested in Mordaunt Hall's review of *Phantom of the Opera*: "The most dramatic touch is where Christine in the cellar abode is listening to the masked Phantom . . . as he plays the organ. Then she steals up behind him . . . and . . . suddenly snatches the mask from the Phantom's face. . . . In the theatre last night a woman behind us stifled a scream when this happened, as this is the first glimpse of the Phantom's physiognomy."[11] The use of a lie detector to measure spectators' physiological responses to a preview of *Frankenstein* similarly indicates the powerful affect of a suddenly appearing and aesthetically jarring face: reports *Time*, "A live spot in *Frankenstein* as revealed by the 'Lie-Detector' [is] one in which the ugly face of Frankenstein's dwarfish assistant pops up from behind a graveyard fence."[12] In a different construction of facial revelation, *Frankenstein* itself seeks to attenuate the monster's first confrontation with the camera as he backs into the room and then slowly turns to face both the camera and the waiting Henry and Waldman. The camera then effects three quick zooms, the last of which brings a close-up of the monster's head and neck: its square skull and jaw, sunken cheeks, heavily lidded eyes, and the electrode bolts in its neck.

Audience response to the skull-like form of the monster's head and face is shaped not only by these performative and cinematic elements but also by viewers' familiarity with scientific and social discourses around the cranium. In the late eighteenth and early nineteenth centuries, German anthropologist Johann Blumenbach analyzed skulls in order to establish five racial

**3.1** Facial revelation: the Phantom (Lon Chaney) is unmasked by Christine (Mary Philbin) in *The Phantom of the Opera* (1925).

categories—Caucasian, Mongolian, Ethiopian, Malay, and American—and to assert Caucasian skulls as superior in beauty.[13] In the nineteenth century, phrenologists such as Franz Joseph Gall and Johann Spurzheim held "that the brain was the 'organ of the mind,' containing the different tempera-ments and emotions within defined areas whose shape lay imprinted in the form of the skull."[14] Their belief that "like produces like," that moral attri-butes were hereditary, and that some organization of propagation would benefit humanity "helped to circulate many of the rhetorical common-places, metaphors, and clichés that would become standard arguments in eugenical tales."[15] The value of the cranium to such studies was its value as a material and discernable feature that signified its bearer's innate identity. As discussed in the introduction, criminal anthropologist Cesare Lombroso legitimated his studies of criminal skulls by describing the "revelation" he experienced before the skull of a famous brigand:

> At the sight of that skull, I seemed to see all of a sudden, lighted up as a vast plain under a flaming sky, the problem of the nature of the criminal—an ata-vistic being who reproduces in his person the ferocious instincts of primitive humanity and the inferior animals. Thus were explained anatomically the enormous jaws, high cheek bones, prominent superciliary arches, solitary lines in the palms, extreme size of the orbits, handle-shaped ears found in

criminals, savages and apes, insensibility to pain, extremely acute sight, tattooing, excessive idleness, love of orgies, and the irresponsible craving of evil for its own sake, the desire not only to extinguish life in the victim, but to mutilate the corpse, tear its flesh and drink its blood.[16]

Lombroso's comments present the skull as the most naked and truthful indicator of criminality and evolutionary regression, a blazingly obvious sign of deviance to expert eyes. However, in spiraling outward from that skull to more external features such as eyes and ears and on to antisocial behavior, Lombroso also reads the imprint of the skull in outward appearances. Thus, his works feature not only images of "criminal skulls" but also photographs of criminals' faces. This leap made possible imaginings such as those of an 1872 manual entitled *Physiognomy Illustrated*, which envisaged the day when any criminal would fear to walk the streets, as his features would be "a sign-board denoting the rottenness within."[17] These ideas were still current in 1930, when the *New York Times* reported that analysis of the skull of an Australian multiple-murderer, executed in 1892, had "revealed striking resemblances to the skull of the anthropoid ape," in a discovery deemed "of first importance to medical science and jurisprudence."[18] Particular types of faces and skulls were thus imagined as transparent signs of atavism and violent criminality.

American social policy reflected this effort to read innate menace on faces and bodies in so-called "ugly laws," originating in the 1880s, which anticipated eugenic overinvestment in surface analyses. Causing others aesthetic displeasure became adequate cause for social exclusion: the laws held that "[a]ny person who is diseased, maimed, mutilated, or in any way deformed, so as to be an unsightly or disgusting object, or an improper person to be allowed in or on the streets, highways, thoroughfares, or public places in this city, shall not therein or thereon expose himself to public view." As Susan Schweik notes, "The language of the ordinance, its framing of a person who is self-evidently, before the law, 'diseased, maimed, and deformed,' and so on, may have bolstered . . . later legal justifications for eugenic sterilization."[19] Sharon L. Snyder and David T. Mitchell similarly situate "ugly laws" in a eugenic trajectory toward the removal of people with atypical or "unsightly" bodies or behaviors from public view.[20] Martin Pernick, too, insists that despite pretensions to scientific and genetic truth, eugenics retained "a powerful aesthetic dimension," particularly in the work of popularizers such as Albert Wiggam, who declared, "If men and women should select mates solely for beauty, it would increase all the other good qualities of the race." Such assumptions were also reflected in the views of Harry Haiselden, the Chicago doctor who wrote of a disabled infant whom he allowed to die, "It was terribly ugly. . . . To be hideous, utterly hideous, is a terrible curse."[21]

Even in more sober and ostensibly scientific eugenic research, bodily and facial surfaces were overdetermined as a locus for revelations of hereditary health or defect. Facial features were read as clear and empirical evidence of genetic transmission; between 1907 and 1910, as Jan Witkowski notes, Davenport and his wife, Gertrude, published four papers applying "Mendelian principles to the human inheritance of eye color, hair color, hair texture, and pigmentation."[22] In his book *Heredity in Relation to Eugenics*, Davenport called for detailed genealogies in which all physical traits—including "extra dentition, aquiline nose, [and] lobeless-ears"—were deemed significant: "there is hardly an organ or the smallest part of an organ that has not its peculiar condition that stamps a family." He also requested "abundant photographs of the persons whose biographies are given; especially, strictly full-face and profile, to facilitate comparisons," while his anthropometrical work gave detailed instructions on the measurement of cranial, facial, and body parts.[23] Following this lead, fieldworkers for the Eugenics Record Office were instructed in observation of the face and head, receiving lectures on "Features of the Skull," "The Living Head—Formulae for Measurement of Cranial Capacity and Brain Weight—The Face," and "Facial Features: Forehead—Nose—Mouth."[24] The workers produced family pedigree charts and analyses of individuals featuring photographs of research subjects and emphasizing facial and physical appearance, while mappings of the heredity of visible physical traits such as cleft palate, unusual skull shape, and red hair served to ground, by association, chartings of more diffuse characteristics such as "musical, literary, and inventive ability," "wanderlust," and "pauperism and criminality."[25]

But this fetishization of the body's surface has always raised questions about its reliability as a gauge for internal and genetic health. Nineteenth-century degeneration theorists such as Benedict Morel feared that degeneration "could just as well be concealed as revealed by the exterior of the body" and, even as they "earmarked the surface features of degeneracy[,] . . . also evoked a mysterious and hidden world of pathology."[26] The possibility that external and internal features did not neatly correspond was suggested in the variety and diversity of Lombroso's criminal faces; as Mary Gibson and Nicole Hahn Rafter point out, he justified his study of photos, skulls, and criminals' drawings with "explanations" that indicated "a need for creative interpretation," producing displays that "drench[ed] objects with symbolic meaning."[27] Such inevitably subjective interpretation affected even mundane eugenic analyses: Witkowski notes that while the Davenports' early facial studies were "respectable," they relied on data supplied by the Davenports' friends, whose "subjective assessment" generated ambiguous and inconsistent eye-color descriptions.[28] Even in genetically defensible eugenic studies, then, the vagaries of visual judgment "colored" the supposedly self-evident traits under examination.

Other eugenic documents continued to validate surface readings even as they cautioned against overemphasizing visible traits as clues to inner health. For instance, the Public Health Service's 1918 *Manual of the Mental Examination of Aliens*, in instructing examiners of prospective immigrants for "higher grades of mental defectiveness," declared,

> Most experienced examiners agree that very little dependence can be placed upon appearance alone, although idiots and many imbeciles generally present some physical signs which immediately attract attention to their mental condition. The low, narrow forehead, receding chin, closely set eyes, protruding and misshapen ears, and other facial irregularities so often referred to as the "signs of degeneracy" have not the importance formerly supposed. A great many feeble-minded persons on ordinary inspection present no physical signs whatever which would indicate real lack of intelligence. Nevertheless, the examiner should have made close observation of facial expressions, both in normal and abnormal persons, especially as to whether they may be said to be gloomy, sad, anxious, apprehensive, elated, hostile, confused, sleepy. . . . An examination of the photographs which appear herewith . . . may prove interesting and instructive in this connection.[29]

Despite efforts to emphasize the unseen processes of genetic determination, then, those working in eugenic research and policy found themselves repeatedly relying on subjective responses to superficial markers such as facial expressions.

The moment of revelation of the disfigured face in horror film picks up on these conflicted eugenic tendencies. It delights in the "tension between the image of the degenerate and the unseen essence of degeneration," toying with both the fear of hidden deformity and the relief of its disclosure, its affirmation of the monster's moral degeneracy.[30] But classic horror films also disrupt neat correlations of surface appearance and innate or genetically determined character. As well as emphasizing social and environmental causes and exacerbations of physical deviance, classic horrors repeatedly associate hideous facial features with illusion, performance, and cinematic trickery, suggesting the misleading and ableist conclusions drawn from surface traits.

For example, *Phantom of the Opera* presents its monster's disfigured face and head as sites that both reveal and conceal innate deviance. In its skull-like appearance, the Phantom's face invites criminological interpretation and apparently reveals his degeneracy to the world. Christine proves herself an apt Lombrosian scholar, declaiming, "He is a monster—a loathsome beast!" But the uncertainty that plagues physiognomic premises also appears in the Phantom's facial revelation. As Linda Williams has noted, the Phantom's disfigurement connotes lack: his "face lacks the flesh to cover its features," his nose "gives the effect of two large holes," and "the lips fail to cover a gaping mouth." He is monstrous either through deficiency or excess, as suggested in the dispute between two dancers over whether the Phantom had no nose or one that was huge: "Either the monster is symbolically castrated . . . or he is overly endowed and potent."[31] This interplay casts doubt on the "truth" represented by the uncovered face/skull. Although the Phantom's past exile to Devil's Island for the "criminal insane" apparently confirms his inner degeneracy, his playful and performative tendencies trouble surface readings. At the film's end, cornered by an angry mob, the Phantom pulls back his hand as if to throw a grenade, laughs at the suddenly still and fearful crowd, and opens his hand to reveal nothing: thus, "the Phantom's last act of the film is to restage the drama of lack he represents to others."[32] If we consider this scene a revelation like the uncovering of the Phantom's face, his gesture suggests the emptiness of physiognomic interpretations. Similarly, at the Bal Masque, the Phantom mocks the superficiality of Lombrosian science, covering his skull and skull-like face with a skull mask, layering lack upon lack as if to deride the logic of a depth-model of truth and essence. In this way, the Phantom exhibits a sideshow quality that exemplifies Chaney's performances: "Chaney's films suggest that in the star's cinematic sideshow, nothing on the 'platform' should be taken at face value."[33]

Indeed, in all three instances of facial revelation—that of the Phantom, of Frankenstein's monster, and of Fritz—the warning against taking things at "face value" appears in reflexive markings that, in differing ways, denote the staged nature of the disclosure. As we have already seen in relation to *Freaks*, disability and deformity require a certain narrative framing to render them consistently horrifying; when *Freaks* disorders the classic horror plot, it highlights the artificial narratives required to construe disability as monstrous. Similarly, even—or especially—in classic-horror moments where impairment or deformity seems at its most raw, shocking, and material, cinematic devices and techniques announce themselves, high-lighting the cultural and visual construction of the most apparently "real" physical aberration.

Thus, the initial revelation of the Phantom's face occurs directly into the camera with Christine peering over his shoulder, subverting, as Gay-lyn Studlar comments, the Hollywood convention that would either show Christine's shocked response and then the deformed face or vice versa.[34] Instead, Williams notes, "[t]he audience . . . receives the first shock of the horror even while it can still see the curiosity and desire to *see* on Chris-tine's part," the shot drawing attention to the dynamics of desire and fear caught up in such a spectacle and thus reminding cinemagoers of the construction of this moment for their viewing pleasure/horror.[35] In a com-parable way, the first revelation of Frankenstein's monster's face disrupts the suspension of disbelief as the monster must shamble in *backwards* to achieve the desired effect. Further, in its three quick zooms, the scene breaks the classical Hollywood illusion sustained by clearly motivating camera-movements according to character gaze or movement.

Reflexive framing also attends the several early and sudden appearances of Fritz's staring face. Christian Metz has argued that scenes with "screens in the screen, mirrors, windows, folding screens, and so on" proffer a filmic self-reflexivity; rather than promoting purely "objective" or "subjective" shots that naturalize the gaze of the camera, such reflexive moments draw attention to the constructedness of film and, I would argue, to cinema's dependence on constructions of unusual bodies.[36] In Fritz's first and second appearances, his face is framed by the bars of the cemetery fence, while a few scenes later his face pops up behind a barred window, which he subsequently raises and enters. The fact that horrified responses to deformity depend on persistent aesthetic defamiliarization is supported by the waning of shock value through repetition. The *Time* article on the lie detector notes that the reappearance of Fritz's face cannot regain its initial shocking effect: "Dead spots: the reappearance of the dwarf's face in subsequent scenes when famil-iarity has made it less frightening."[37] As noted earlier, this framing in *Fran-kenstein* also visually indicts the scientist himself, presenting Henry's face rising behind the barred fence next to Fritz's, and incorporating bars, win-dows, and photo frames in other shots of the scientist. Such shots suggest the deformed and shocking face as a product of cultural and scientific con-structions *and* testify to the subjective and erratic qualities of the "expert" meant to witness and diagnose defect. These "revelations" of impairment thus point to the cultural and visual fictions that uphold scientific framings of "degenerates."

Classic horror's facial revelations are also often allied with themes of epistemological uncertainty that counter appeals to the body's surface as a transparent sign. One of Gothic and horror fiction's uncanny conventions, as perceived by German psychiatrist Ernst Jentsch and discussed by Freud in "The Uncanny," is its mobilization of "doubts whether an apparently animate being is really alive; or conversely, whether a lifeless object might not be in fact animate." Freud, however, contends that the real uncanniness of E. T. A. Hoffmann's "The Sand-Man" lies not in the inanimate mechanical Olympia but in "the theme of the 'Sand-Man' who tears out children's eyes," an act Freud links to castration. Freud thus contends that uncanny instances that engage "intellectual uncertainty" are less striking and potent than those that refer to unconscious fears of castration.[38] I would argue, however, that horror often mobilizes both forms of the uncanny—that is, intellectual and epistemological uncertainty on the one hand, and supposedly more primal and deep-seated fears of disability on the other—in a manner that insists that our "natural" fears of physical and visible disability are, in fact, always products of cultural and intellectual compositions of unusual bodies.

This association of facial revelation and thematic uncertainty is prominent, appropriately, in a classic horror about the uncanniness of lifelike inanimate beings, *The Mystery of the Wax Museum* (dir. Michael Curtiz, Warner Bros., 1933). The movie opens in a London wax museum in 1921. Lionel Atwill plays Ivan Igor, a wax-sculptor who is intimately fond of his creations, figures such as Joan of Arc, Voltaire, and his favorite, Marie Antoinette. But Igor's business partner, Joe Worth (Edwin Maxwell), frustrated that Igor will not cater to the sensationalist whims of the public with sculptures of Jack the Ripper and the Mad Butcher, burns down the museum for the insurance, leaving Igor to perish in the flames. Igor survives, however, and reopens his wax museum in New York in 1933. Now in a wheelchair, and with his hands badly burned, Igor must rely on students such as Ralph Burton (Allen Vincent) to re-create the figures he lost, although only the suspicious Professor Darcy (Arthur Edmund Carewe) is able to provide perfect replicas of Voltaire and Joan of Arc. Ralph's girlfriend Charlotte (Fay Wray) visits the museum with her roommate, wise-cracking reporter Florence Dempsey (Glenda Farrell). Florence is suspicious about the resemblance between the wax Joan of Arc and an heiress whose body has gone missing and between the wax Voltaire and a murdered judge whose body has also vanished. When she follows Darcy into a building's cellar, she glimpses a shuffling, facially disfigured man. Captured by the police, the drug-addicted Darcy confesses that Igor is having people killed and embalmed in wax to replace his statues.

Meanwhile, the ingenue Charlotte, who reminds Igor of his lost Marie Antoinette, comes to the museum looking for Ralph. Igor corners her, raising himself from his wheelchair to reveal his paralysis as a sham. As he approaches and embraces Charlotte, promising her eternity as a wax statue, she screams and beats on his face with her hands. Igor's face cracks open, revealing his visage to be a waxen mask covering the burned and scarred face beneath (fig. 3.2). "You fiend," breathes Charlotte in horror, "You fiend!" Igor declares that the real fiend is Worth, who turned him into "this terrible living dead man with these burnt hands and face." He flings open a coffin lid to show Charlotte his vengeance: the dead Worth is bound like a mummy. Igor sets about transforming Charlotte into Marie Antoinette, but she is rescued at the last moment from a molten death, and Igor tumbles into his own vat of boiling wax.

This scene of facial revelation does not exploit any notable reflexive or defamiliarizing elements. The exchange between Igor and Charlotte deploys a conventional shot/reverse-shot sequence that alternates shots of Charlotte's frightened face with shots of Igor over her shoulder. We are watching over Charlotte's shoulder when Igor's face cracks open and Charlotte, with an inarticulate utterance, pushes away what remains of the wax head and hair to fully uncover his burned face. The camera cuts to a frontal shot of Charlotte's face as she looks in horror and then screams. This visual

**3.2** Facial revelation: Ivan (Lionel Atwill) is unmasked by Charlotte (Fay Wray) in *The Mystery of the Wax Museum* (1933).

orthodoxy reflects the film's similarly conventional narrative of disability, in which the aggrieved disabled man lives to avenge his disfigurement: Igor declares of himself, "For twelve years, twelve awful years, this terrible living dead man . . . has searched for the fiend." In this respect, Igor conforms to the ableist stereotype of the "Obsessive Avenger," whom Norden describes as "an egomaniacal sort . . . who does not rest until he has had his revenge on those he holds responsible for his disablement."[39]

Other scenes also affirm ableist understandings of facial and cranial form and conflate them with racist categories. For instance, Florence converses with a policeman soon after witnessing the disfigured man, whom we later recognize as an unmasked Igor. She reports:

FLORENCE: It wasn't like anything human. It . . . it hobbled, and swayed like a monkey. And the face! [*Gasps*] From the glimpse I got of it, it was like an African war mask.
OFFICER: You mean he was colored?
FLORENCE: I don't know what he was, but he made Frankenstein look like a lily.

The exchange recalls Blumenbach's racial categorization of skulls, Lombroso's equation of criminal skulls to evolutionary throwbacks, and Henry Fairchild's eugenic discussion of racial antipathy, in which he declared that most of "the characteristic differences between races are associated with the head."[40] Igor's burned face thus fits into a racialized narrative in which disfigurement of the face and head embodies and meshes primitivism, criminality, insanity, and racial otherness: the Phantom is a "loathsome beast" and "criminal[ly] insane," the Frankenstein monster is a "savage animal," Fritz is a lunatic, and Igor is a "fiend" who is not human but is possibly "colored," in that he makes "Frankenstein" look white.

At the same time, Florence's reference to "Frankenstein" somewhat denaturalizes such racist and ableist associations, indicating that horror-film monsters had already become cultural touchstones for the description of deformity and disability.[41] Despite its normative visual conventions, then, *The Mystery of the Wax Museum* uses its plot to generate uncertainty about the relationship between depth and surface, continually blurring the real and the unreal, the living and the dead, originals and imitations, the authentic and the performative. The movie begins with Igor's loving treatment of his "children" and "people," wax replicas of famous historical figures. Although they are clearly not real, their "deaths" in the fire, the only deaths in the film to occur on-screen, are horrific: faces silently melt and run, heads fall, and bodies collapse in liquid heaps. Introducing the New York crowd to his new statues, twelve years later, Igor presents them as replicas of his original figures; as imitations of original imitations they thus stand at two removes from "reality." And yet, as Florence discovers, these statues are more real than the originals on which they are modeled, for their simulated exteriors conceal flesh-and-blood dead bodies. Significantly, Florence confirms her discovery by scrutinizing the new statue of Voltaire and comparing it to a photograph of Judge Ramsey, associating visual representation with a kind of entrapment, not unlike encasement within a wax façade.

Florence's investigative activities emphasize the intellectual aspect of determining real from fake, and her detective success seems to confirm the validity of close interpretation of bodily surface and photographic evidence in order to gain access to the truth beneath. But her trajectory toward resolution unfolds in concert with Charlotte's very different experiences. As Charlotte moves through the museum's darkened rooms at night, watchful eyes follow her movements from behind the faces of wax statues, although we never find out who it is that thus surveils her. She is also menaced by Hugo (Matthew Betz), Igor's deaf and mute assistant, whose inarticulate vocalizations and wild gestures construe him as a potential killer for much of the film. Norden comments that the film's denial of sign language to Hugo and the lighting of his face from beneath have "the effect of reducing him to a strange and sinister beast whose sole purpose was to provide transient shock value."[42] But since Hugo is not to blame for any of the murders, I would contend that the deliberate misleading of the audience in this way somewhat undermines the facile equation of surface disability with inner depravity, while the artificial lighting perhaps draws attention to the manipulative framing of a disabled character. Charlotte's uncertainty and fear in this situation thus mimic those of the horror-film spectator, who feels deeply the uncanniness of the statues and who cannot determine the identity of the monster from surface appearance. Moreover, while Florence offers a more savvy perspective for the filmgoer already jaded by monster films, her confidence in her ability to read surfaces does not enable her to recognize the shuffling, disfigured man she sees as the wheelchair-using but handsome and distinguished Igor. Florence is also involved in moments of banal revelation, as when police open the coffin Florence has found, expecting a grisly corpse, only to find bootlegged whisky. While, at one level, such elements are obvious efforts to "play" the audience, to subject audiences to repeated shocks, they also highlight the epistemological politics of horror; the convergence of "intellectual uncertainty" and symbolic exploitation of embodiment question the correlation of outward features and inner essence.

It is precisely the uncertainty over whether what one sees is illusory or real, the "uncanny" as construed by Tzvetan Todorov in *The Fantastic*, that opens the spectator to the transience, permeability, and ambiguity of bodily "truth." Susan Stewart, in an analysis of the structures of horror fiction, discusses the genre's three levels of epistemological uncertainty: that of content (the liminality between man and beast, life and death); that of context ("the viewer rarely knows more than the victim" and must hesitate between different interpretations); and that of genre (is the story realistic or fantastic, true or false?). She suggests that such pervasive ambiguity undermines conventions of interpretation: "What is at risk in these stories is our good faith in our ability to know the world by means of a socially given system of interpretation. Our hierarchies of relevance, our assumptions of the social, and our faith in the reliability of the self and its potential for apprehending the real are all suspended, put into brackets." This experience positions the reader/listener/spectator on the side of disability and deformity: "It is not simply a matter of the listener sympathizing or identifying with the victim; rather, by means of a complex narrative process, the listener is transformed into the victim. It is as if in stripping the victim of his dramatic mask, the listener has uncovered, to his horror, his own face."[43] Epistemological uncertainty thus forces viewers to confront spectacles of impairment as projections of their own socially, scientifically, and cinematically shaped prejudices.

In *The Mystery of the Wax Museum*, such indeterminacy is also due to the performative agency of the disabled character. Igor "performs" one kind of debility (paralysis of the legs) while hiding a "real" impairment (his disfigured face), all the while leaving his impaired hands in plain view. While Igor's deception might seem to place him in the realm of another of Norden's stereotypes, that of beggars with fake disabilities in early cinematic shorts, the logic of dissimulation is more tangled here.[44] In "Simulacra and Simulations," Jean Baudrillard clarifies that "[t]o dissimulate is to feign not to have what one has. To simulate is to feign to have what one hasn't. One implies a presence, the other an absence."[45] In this sense, Igor at once dissimulates, pretending not to be facially scarred, and simulates, pretending to be paralyzed. Of course, the presence/absence opposition is even more confused, depending on whether we understand disability as something that one has—one *has* paralysis or a scarred face—or that one does *not* have—one *lacks* a normal face or functioning legs. Moreover, if "disability" is understood as a generalized condition of defect, rather than in terms of specific impairments, it is impossible for Igor to *pretend* to be disabled, since he "really" is disabled. Nonetheless, his performance exploits the different responses occasioned by different impairments:

Igor understands that a disfigured face will immediately be read as a sign of inner depravity, while wheelchair-use will instead signal helplessness or passivity. Igor thus exploits normative responses to bodily difference, blurring the lines between, on the one hand, material, visible impairment and, on the other, disability as a mediated product of the encounter between culture and body.

Igor's simulation of impairment also encourages us to look more closely at the cinematic disability performances central to so many classic horror films. As Baudrillard notes, the logic of simulation complicates matters still further, "since to simulate is not simply to feign. . . . Someone who simulates an illness produces in himself some of the symptoms." This blurring of true and false in the act of simulation, this emphasis on the possibility of producing biological symptoms through nonbiological means, challenges medical discourse: "Psychology and medicine stop at this point, before a thereafter undiscoverable truth of the illness. For if any symptom can be 'produced,' and can no longer be accepted as a fact of nature, then every illness may be considered as simulatable and simulated, and medicine loses its meaning since it only knows how to treat 'true' illnesses by their objective causes."[46] At a postmodern extreme, such a view risks denying the embodied and felt reality of pain, impairment, or illness. At the same time, it suggests that the "simulation" of disability conducted by actors in classic horror films both draws attention to the cultural and cinematic mediations of disability and "calls out" audiences for their role in demanding and consuming disability spectacle, a point to which we shall return.

In examining the representation of a specific disability experience, the seizure, the remainder of this chapter examines the interaction of horror films' disability themes and their formal presentations of impairment, including the embodied performances of their actors. This chapter thus operates in the realm of performance studies as conceived by Erving Goffman, with his attention to "the presentation of self in everyday life," and as elaborated by Judith Butler, whose term "performativity" describes the constrained acts or "doings" of gender and sexuality in which we are always engaged.[47] Butler presents normative gender as a phantasmatic and impossible ideal, against which actual gender performances are always imitative drag acts: "If gender is drag, and if it is an imitation that regularly produces the ideal that it attempts to approximate, then gender is a performance that produces the illusion of an inner sex or essence of psychic gender core; it produces on the skin, through the gesture, the move, the gait (that array of corporeal theatrics understood as gender presentation), the illusion of an inner depth."[48] Butler's theatrical language draws attention to gender as a performative process rather than a "natural" inner essence that is transparently reflected in bodily appearance and behavior. Such a theoretical model has significant implications for understandings of disability: Robert McRuer, for instance, suggests that able-bodiedness is not the transparent expression of inner health or moral goodness but, rather, a performative norm that we all, to a greater or lesser degree, fail to approximate.[49] Carrie Sandahl and Philip Auslander note that if, for Butler's subjects, identity "is performed unconsciously," disabled people are often more aware of being called on to perform certain roles for the public or of needing to "pass" by conducting "a performance of able-bodiedness."[50] Like the drag performers Butler studies, then, disabled people perhaps experience the theatrical elements of subjectivity more immediately than those who seem to "fit" more neatly into normative identities.[51]

These dramaturgical models enable us to consider the disability performances of horror cinema as instances where enactment of impairment fails to consolidate the phantasmatic and able-bodied norm. With drag performances, Butler notes, "what determines the effect of realness is the ability to compel belief, to produce the naturalized effect." A performance "works" to the extent that it cannot be "read," for reading is "exposing what fails to work at the level of appearance," while success "means that a reading . . . appears to be a kind of transparent seeing, where what appears and what it means coincide."[52] Like Lombroso before the brigand's skull, we may be tempted to view what we see as self-evident, biological truth. But when our visual text both invokes a series of overdetermined and unreconcilable meanings and marks its revelations with self-reflexive devices, we have entered into a disability performance that, in Petra Kuppers' words, exploits a "suspicion of visibility machines" and maps a trajectory "from knowing and fixing to unknowability and generative uncertainty."[53] For Sandahl and Auslander, the value of such theatrical constructions lies in their presentation of disability as "something one does rather than something one is" and in their understanding of the disabled performer or passer as someone seeking "to become an active maker of meaning, rather than a passive specimen on display."[54] Of course, like Butler's gender performativity, disability performance should not be seen as a freely chosen activity but rather a constrained set of actions and negotiations. Still, the performative premise enables us to "read" horror's disability spectacles as instances that foreground the production of disability at the point where the theatrical simulation of impairment and the "visibility machine" of cinema coincide.

## EPILEPSY: TROUBLING THE MEDICAL GAZE

If there is a single condition that most powerfully combines sudden and dramatic visible revelation with the possibilities of performance and simulation, it is epilepsy. The ancients often interpreted epilepsy as a "sacred" disease, that is, as an affliction sent by a higher power, a sign of demonic possession, or a manifestation of sin.[55] One of the earliest known texts on epilepsy, Hippocrates' "The Sacred Disease," works to demystify this "divine" explanation, asserting instead the disease's determinable and biological character:

> It is my opinion that those who first called this disease "sacred" were the sort of people we now call witch-doctors, faith-healers, quacks, and charlatans. These are exactly the people who pretend to be very pious and to be particularly wise. By invoking a divine element they were able to screen their own failure to give suitable treatment and so called this a "sacred" malady to conceal their ignorance of its nature.[56]

Hippocrates goes on to explain epilepsy as a hereditary disease in which the brain fails to adequately secrete phlegm both *in utero* and shortly after birth: "Should these routes for the passage of phlegm from the brain be blocked, the discharge enters the blood vessels which I have described. This causes aphonia, choking, foaming at the mouth, clenching of the teeth and convulsive movements of the hands; the eyes are fixed, the patient becomes unconscious and, in some cases, passes a stool."[57] Hippocrates' thesis at once disparages past explanations of epilepsy as disingenuous efforts to disguise expert ignorance and puts forth a notion of repressed forces that would continue to shape interpretations of the condition. Cultural and medicalized responses to epileptic seizures, including eugenic and psychoanalytic readings, have often characterized epileptic seizures as the revelation of some hidden, inner truth or reality. At the same time, interpretations of epilepsy repeatedly produce contradictory understandings of a disorder that, rather than manifesting an evident truth, is permeated with cultural and psychological fantasy. The truth uncovered by seizure in these discourses often has little to do with epilepsy as a fact or a material experience, pertaining instead to the cultural investments and prejudices that shape visual encounters with impairment.

Medical definitions of epilepsy indicate its varied and ambiguous nature. Lisa Cartwright notes that *Dorland's Illustrated Medical Dictionary* defines epilepsy as a set of "paroxysmal disturbances of brain function that may be manifested as episodic impairment, loss of consciousness, abnormal motor phenomena, psychic or sensory disturbances, or perturbation of the autonomic nervous system." The origin is described as either "idiopathic (cryptogenic, essential, genetic) or symptomatic (acquired, organic)." In other words, modern epilepsy is a heterogeneous and ambiguously genetic or acquired condition.[58]

Modern studies of epilepsy have pursued greater clarity by penetrating ever inwards: *Adams and Victor's Principles of Neurology* explains that the development of electroencephalography technology has enabled tracing of the brain's electrical activity during a seizure. This recent insight has led to the classification of two predominant epileptic forms. *Generalized* or *"grand mal"* seizures begin bilaterally in the brain and may produce major convulsions and loss of consciousness, although they also may be nonconvulsive and cause only a brief loss of consciousness or "absence." *Partial* seizures, sometimes referred to as "temporal lobe" seizures, have an initially localized onset in the brain; they may proceed to generalized seizures but also more often include hallucinatory experiences or an altered state of mind and do not necessarily result in loss of consciousness. As *Adams and Victor's Principles of Neurology* illustrates, however, there remain a number of variant forms of seizure housed within or exceeding the bounds of these two dominant types.

Generalized and partial seizures thus exhibit divergent, if occasionally overlapping, symptoms. A generalized tonic-clonic seizure may be foreshadowed by "one of several subjective phenomena (a *prodrome*)," including the jerking of limbs and feelings of apathy, depression, or irritability, or it may strike without warning, "beginning with a sudden loss of consciousness and a fall to the ground." In the tonic phase, "The initial motor signs are a brief flexion of the trunk, an opening of the mouth and eyelids, and upward deviation of the eyes. The arms are elevated and abducted, the elbows semiflexed, and the hands pronated. These are followed by a more protracted extension (*tonic*) phase, involving first the back and the neck, then the arms and legs." The seizure then transitions into the clonic phase, which begins with "a mild generalized tremor," proceeds to "brief, violent flexor spasms that come in rhythmic salvos and agitate the entire body," and concludes in "a deep coma," sometimes followed by a period of sleep.[59] A partial seizure's symptoms, however, vary widely depending on the location of the discharging lesion: patients might experience initial turning movements before progressing into a generalized seizure; they might move directly into a generalized seizure; they might experience sensory seizures; or they might experience vivid "hallucination or perceptual illusion":

> Hallucinations are most often visual or auditory, consisting of formed or unformed visual images, sounds, and voices. . . . Fragments of certain old memories or scenes may insert themselves into the patient's mind and recur with striking clarity. . . . Emotional experiences, while less common, may be dramatic—sadness, loneliness, anger, happiness, and sexual excitement have all been recorded. Fear and anxiety are the most common affective experiences, while occasionally the patient describes a feeling of rage or intense anger as part of a complex partial seizure.[60]

While these types of seizure have often been called "auras," physicians now hold that "they represent electrical seizures and have the same significance as a motor convulsion."[61] Epilepsy thus manifests in diverse and overlapping ways—often within the same body, since many patients experience both partial and generalized seizures—and brings together physical and psychological components.

Such dramatic and unusual movements and behaviors have long been understood in relation to their effect on viewers. In the United States, epileptics were included in many regions' "ugly laws" because, as Charles Henderson wrote in his 1906 book on the "dependent, defective, and delinquent classes," "[i]n sociable intercourse the epileptic is an object of dread, and no one who has witnessed the person in a convulsion can quite escape from the haunting memory of the spectacle and entirely free his mind from terror or disgust."[62] In "The Uncanny," Freud asserts that an epileptic seizure recalls for its witnesses primitive beliefs in animism and reminds them of an uncivilized animalistic force within themselves. Both responses again see seizures as manifesting something uncanny, that is, something that should remain hidden or repressed. Recalling Davis's assertion that uncanniness attaches to the chaotic body all humans first experience but eventually disavow, we might suggest that seizures kinetically enact a lack of bodily and neurological control that everyone shares but that some are able to disavow to a greater or lesser degree. That horror films might approximate the encounter with another's seizure is suggested in Philip Brophy's response to scenes of bodily metamorphosis in *Scanners* (dir. David Cronenberg, 1981) and *An American Werewolf in London* (dir. John Landis, 1981): "It's not unlike being on a tram and somebody has an epileptic fit—you're there right next to the person, you can't get away, and you can't do anything."[63]

Expert discourses seek to ameliorate these uncanny and upsetting effects by containing them in familiar narratives. For instance, Freud uses literary and psychoanalytic analysis to diagnose Fyodor Dostoyevsky with "hystero-epilepsy" and to explain his condition as a hysterical response of guilt to his father's death, an event Dostoyevsky had wished.[64] But Dennis Patrick Slattery speaks back to this and other "diagnoses" of Dostoyevsky, insisting that we consider his condition "not strictly in terms of how it is projected onto characters or in terms of the writer's medical and psychological history but also in terms of what we might learn about the multifaceted character of the illness as a biological phenomenon, a cultural construction, and a mythic structure that provided the writer with an epistemological paradigm."[65] Using Jungian philosophy, Slattery locates the fascination of Dostoyevsky's *The Idiot* with the condition's double and oppositional nature, its "extreme heights of euphoria and deep caverns of depression," which invoke both "the safe stasis of eternity and the rushing ambiguity of temporality."[66] For Slattery, readings of "actual" impairment are inevitably caught up in cultural and textual meanings.

A similar slippage informed eugenic uses of epilepsy. The condition was seen as a self-evident mark of defective genes and was one of the five most concerning conditions targeted by American Breeders' Association subcommittees.[67] Prospective immigrants were rejected if they were epileptic, and epileptics were vulnerable to sterilization legislation in many states, often facing institutionalization along with those deemed feebleminded or insane. Eugenics Record Office fieldworkers sought to establish a hereditary relationship between epilepsy and catchall "conditions" of feeblemindedness and insanity, often also linking them to diseases whose inherited status was questionable, including alcoholism and syphilis.[68] Indeed, epilepsy's indeterminacy may have functioned to the advantage of eugenicists who sought to assimilate it to—and use it as visible evidence of—more abstract conditions.

Such confusion is evident in medical and psychological reports about epilepsy, also kept on file at the Eugenics Record Office, which show increasing insistence that epilepsy is not a simple and hereditary trait in itself but, rather, an inherited predisposition shaped by environmental influence. A 1922 piece in the *American Journal of Psychiatry* declares that the authors "are quite convinced that epilepsy, as such, does not exist and is by no means entitled to the classification of a disease entity. The syndrome which goes to make up the condition which has borne the name of epilepsy is neither constant nor characteristic." Further, the authors felt that individuals inherited not epilepsy itself but a tendency to nervous or mental deficiency that might or might not become manifest.[69] In the *Archives of Neurology and Psychiatry*, C. W. Burr reached a similar conclusion, stating that "a predisposition to nervous or mental disease is inherited [but] the resulting specific disease depends on external causes—it is environmental in the broadest meaning of the word."[70] Medical conference attendees "emphasized that only 20 per cent of epileptic cases were of hereditary origin" and that "less than 5 per cent of epileptics were institutional cases"; surgeons touted successful surgical treatment of epilepsy caused by head injury; and newspapers reported that the "ketogenic diet" had been shown to ameliorate the condition.[71] Eugenic equations of epilepsy to innate criminality and feeblemindedness were thus contested by arguments emphasizing its production and amelioration by environmental forces.

Epilepsy's confounding of experts suggested an epistemological crisis that threw into doubt the value of the bodily surface for medical and moral interpretation. Lisa Cartwright's discussion of the "epilepsy biographs," films made in 1905 of patients' seizures at the Craig Colony for Epileptics in upstate New York, argues that while the films extended a comprehensive surveillant practice, they ultimately only provided for William Spratling, the colony's medical superintendent, "a metaphor for [his] own anxiety about neurology's inability to control epilepsy," indicating the inadequacies of "the [neurological] discipline's traditional techniques of observation, recording, and classification." In the face of such uncertainty, Spratling sought clarity in a gendered division of epileptic traits: he "associated epilepsy in men with social factors" such as "alcohol, illness, or brain injury," but he viewed "the condition of epilepsy in women"—and in the single black man at the colony—"as both degenerate and innate." Such gendered distinctions appeared in the films' different presentation of men's and women's seizures: while the men underwent naked convulsions with a definite beginning and end, the women were filmed fully clothed and standing in a state of "athetosis—that is, slow, continual, and involuntary writhing, particularly of the hands and arms." While the men's films coincide with Spratling's view of their convulsions as a moment of "release" from "systemic poisoning," the women's films provide no clear narrative or explanation and thus "signify a methodological lack," the failure of medicine and film to diagnose seizures.[72]

These medical films thus both tried to impose a specific meaning on epilepsy and bore the traces of epilepsy's resistance to such projects. Indeed, as instances of visual technology called on to transparently represent impairment, the films instead foregrounded the doctor or scientist's framing role and the performative elements of the patients' movements. Cartwright notes that neurologist Francis X. Dercum, who collaborated with Eadweard Muybridge in the latter's cinematic motion studies, "mechanically induced seizures in his experimental subject," by having a nude woman model hold a "restrictive position" until "she experienced violent, spasmodic muscular contractions resembling seizure," at which point her movements were filmed. Dercum's assertion that "[t]he convulsions introduced artificially were as genuine as any form of convulsive movement and there was no simulation on the part of the subject" further troubles claims that the condition manifests organic and internal traits; the experiments suggested both that "self-control" was subject to "mechanical forces" and "not guaranteed even among 'healthy' subjects" and that "the healthy body could be made to mimic pathological expression."[73] The confusion between "real" and performed debility played out in worker compensation cases where neurologists scrutinized motion pictures of victims of "train mishaps and farm and factory machinery accidents" to determine if their neurological damage was genuine or faked.[74] Thus, expert scrutiny of photos and movies was deemed an acceptable form of analysis, despite mounting evidence that the medical gaze not only could not successfully or accurately diagnose in this fashion but also often produced—or simulated—deviance where it had not previously existed. These, then, are the competing visual, medical, and cultural politics that suffuse dramatic horror-film representations of impairment, specifically, the epileptic-like seizures of the protagonist-monster in three *Dr. Jekyll and Mr. Hyde* films.

### Seizing Up: Convulsive Performances in the Jekyll/Hyde Films

A consideration of epilepsy's "cultural performance" in three filmic versions of *Dr. Jekyll and Mr. Hyde* more fully illuminates the complexities of cinematic impairment, as it accentuates the psychological and cultural meanings that produce and make sense of convulsions, foregrounds the cinematic strategies by which visual media represents impairment, highlights the medical figure's role in producing impairment as something monstrous, and reminds audiences of their complicity in the disability spectacle.[75]

Robert Louis Stevenson's novel *The Strange Case of Dr. Jekyll and Mr. Hyde* takes up the cultural connection between epilepsy and doubleness or dividedness, presenting Jekyll's metamorphoses into Hyde in ways evocative of epileptic seizure. Jekyll describes his first transformation: "The most racking pangs succeeded: a grinding in the bones, deadly nausea, and a horror of the spirit that cannot be exceeded at the hour of birth or death." Later, when Jekyll no longer has control over the episodes, he writes: "At all hours of the day and night, I would be taken with the premonitory shudder. . . . I became, in my own person a creature eaten up and emptied by fever, languidly weak in both body and mind, and solely occupied by one thought: the horror of my other self."[76] As Leonard Wolf comments, "These shudders strongly resemble the aura some epilepsy sufferers experience just before the onset of a seizure. Indeed, the violence with which the personality changes are accompanied has much in common with *grand mal* epilepsy structures."[77]

Readings of the novel often parallel discursive interpretations of epilepsy. Certainly, ancient views of epilepsy as the manifestation of inner sin seem apt for interpretations that emphasize Hyde as an evil monster, while the novel also obviously takes up cultural themes of doubleness or dividedness that have also been associated with epilepsy. Also relevant are Freud's view of epilepsy as the apparent return of primitive beliefs and eugenic views of epilepsy as a symptom of degeneracy which, since social Darwinist times, had been linked to evolutionary regression: the novel's frequent reference to Hyde in animalistic terms suggests him as an atavistic monster, a savage and primordial man. At the same time, the notion that Jekyll's transformations represent the unleashing of uncivilized drives, particularly repressed sexuality, calls on psychoanalytic understandings of disability as something tied to repressed impulses and trauma. In turn, however, interpretations that focus on Jekyll's hidden desires in terms of homosexuality suggest less an individual psychosexual drama than a cultural critique, in which Jekyll's seizures index resistance to Victorian repression and sexual hypocrisy. Thus, the "doubleness" of epilepsy maps onto debates about the novel's conflicting meanings: the emergence of Hyde might seem to affirm the dangers of sexual indulgence or it might assert that extreme sexual repression is to blame for his monstrosity.

These cultural interpretations of epilepsy are also on display in the three *Dr. Jekyll and Mr. Hyde* films of 1920, 1931, and 1941. The earliest of these, the silent *Dr. Jekyll and Mr. Hyde* (dir. John S. Robertson, Famous Players–Lasky Corporation, 1920), featuring John Barrymore as Jekyll, presents the most physically obvious manifestation of seizure but also clearly embeds the convulsions in a cultural and psychological context. Early in the film, Jekyll is mocked by Sir George Carew (Brandon Hurst), the debauched father of his fiancée, who lures him into temptation by taking him to see an exotic Italian dancer, Gina (Nita Naldi). Awakened "to a sense of his baser nature," intertitles inform us, Jekyll ponders whether "the two natures in man could be separated—housed in different bodies," enabling him to "yield to every evil impulse, yet leave the soul untouched." Prior to his first transformation, Jekyll hesitates over the potion, but the leering face of Carew appears superimposed over the laboratory scene; Jekyll stares wildly at this mental image before determinedly taking up the serum. Upon drinking, Jekyll clutches at his throat. His body and head arch backward before he repeatedly doubles over, rubbing his hands on his face, his arms twitching and convulsing. As Skal comments, these activities had a pragmatic purpose: "Barrymore . . . contrived to apply the paint [with his hands] without stopping the camera, making efficient use of each doubling over and convulsion, of which there were many."[78] The camera then focuses on Jekyll's hand as, in a single dissolve, its fingers lengthen and its nails become clawlike. The completed Hyde sports long, stringy hair, pointed head, lumpy face, and beaked nose, with dark makeup around his wide, staring eyes. As he shambles into the next room to find a mirror, we see that he has somewhat of a hump back and walks in a hunched and scuttling manner. Satisfied with his first transformation, Hyde takes the antidote and repeats his convulsions, this time falling violently to the ground, his arms rigid and thrashing (fig. 3.3). He stiffly staggers to his feet soon after, restored as Jekyll.

The performance mimics some epileptic symptoms. In the transformation to Hyde, the apparition of Carew works either as a metaphor for the prodrome stage of a generalized seizure, manifesting Jekyll's depression or

**3.3** Convulsion: Hyde (John Barrymore) in the throes of transforming back into Jekyll in *Dr. Jekyll and Mr. Hyde* (1920).

anxiety, or as evidence of visual hallucination in a partial seizure. The rest of this first seizure is suggestive of a partial or focal seizure originating in the sensorimotor cortex, since Jekyll also undergoes spasms of his face and arms, but does not lose consciousness. The metamorphosis back to his typical form is more imitative of a generalized convulsive seizure, although, again, it does not seem that the character loses consciousness.

Jekyll is not labeled as having epilepsy, and it is evident that Jekyll-Hyde transformations are not particularly accurate reflections of epileptic seizures. In this, they call attention to factual flaws in many cinematic depictions that *do* purport to represent epileptic experiences. As the work of the Kerson family has shown, film "portrayals have not reflected medicine's understanding of epilepsy," using "fictive and often incorrect images" that exaggerate the uncontrolled and violent nature of seizures and almost always construe epileptics as violent, abnormal, or victimized.[79] Driven by the "enthralling" visual experience seizures can provide, the films studied by the Kersons substitute fictive images for actual knowledge or understanding of the condition: "the image particularly of a tonic-clonic seizure is so cheap to execute, easy to insert and consistently enthralling and terrifying that it works like Baudrillard's concept of a simulation. . . . That is, long after one has lost knowledge of the real, the copy remains as a kind of replacement reality." For the Kersons, this tendency perpetuates "negative, obsolete and just plain wrong" views of epilepsy and stigmatization of people with the disorder; they call for more accurate and positive portraits of epileptic characters and experiences.[80] As we have seen, though, the elusiveness of a singular or "real" epilepsy experience has preoccupied medical as well as cultural representations of the condition. Thus, the sensational and theatrical nature of movies' epileptic depictions precisely direct attention away from the "real" experience of seizure and toward the simulative processes that turn epilepsy into a fictionalized, but nonetheless powerful, cultural narrative and horrific spectacle.

The 1920 film's epileptic motions thus point toward pervasive eugenic and cultural understandings of the condition. First, in representing Hyde as a figure for Jekyll's repressed sexual desires, the film draws on eugenic efforts—as in pedigree charts entitled "Syphilis and Epilepsy" and "Epilepsy and Feeblemindedness: A Forced Marriage"—to amalgamate epilepsy, feeblemindedness, and sexually transmitted diseases as interrelated symptoms of an amorphous degeneracy.[81] The commentary on the Kino Video DVD of the 1920 *Dr. Jekyll and Mr. Hyde* suggests that Hyde's visual form following the transformations marks his condition as a disfiguring disease, connoted particularly by the dark rings around his eyes. An early scene supports this interpretation as Jekyll and his colleague Dr. Lanyon (Charles Lane) look through a microscope at moving organisms, with the "tiny organisms resembling the swimming spirochaete that scientists had pinpointed as the minuscule agents of syphilis." Gina's appearance further reinforces the idea that the debilitating force is a sexually transmitted disease. By the time Hyde has ravished her, installed her in his apartment, and then abandoned her, she exhibits the same dark rings around her eyes.[82] The deviant body produced by Jekyll's epileptic convulsion, then, is coded as degenerate by virtue of its deformity and its disease and the connection of both to sinful and transgressive sexuality.

Second, the film codes this degenerate and epileptic body racially. Freudian associations of epilepsy with primitivism and eugenic rhetoric of epilepsy as an index to racial degeneracy lend themselves to a racist iconography around the convulsing body. Halberstam notes Victorian ideology ascribed "predisposition to diseases like syphilis or to the possibility of degeneration . . . to certain races (such as the Jews), to their genealogy and their lifestyles, in order to give moral structure to the seemingly random process of infection."[83] The form taken by the post-seizure Hyde conforms to the physiognomy iconically and racistly attributed to Jews: the hooked nose, piercing or shifty eyes, and dirty and unkempt hair.[84] Moreover, the camera in this film persistently exposes and lingers on an array of racially or class-coded degenerates: poor and ragged children playing in the street, a fat and unkempt female bartender, the Chinese man who delivers a prostitute to Hyde. The link between these members of the underclasses and the disabled is foregrounded in one scene in a seedy bar where Hyde sees a man writhing and hitting at himself with his hands, in a manner reminiscent of Jekyll's transformative contortions. "He thinks he's covered with red ants!" the bartender laughingly tells Hyde. The hallucinating madman, the prostitute, the immigrant, and the syphilitic Hyde are conjoined in a narrative of degeneracy that uses the iconography of impairment to render deviance visible and controllable. A later transformation scene has a similar effect: Jekyll, sleeping, wakes in horror to see a huge, ghostly spider, with the tiny head of Hyde, mount his bed. Jekyll faints, and the spider mounts his body, disappearing as it is apparently absorbed into Jekyll—who wakes as Hyde. In having Jekyll hallucinate a spider, it links him to the madman who hallucinates ants, while also underwriting racial associations of Hyde with the parasitic, crabbed Jew.

The film thus sediments political, sexual, and racial discourses in particular, impaired bodies. Like other classic horrors, though, the movie resists strictly genetic and congenital interpretations of impairment or other marginalized bodies. As already noted, Jekyll's repressive and hypocritical social environment, personified in the corrupt Carew, may also bear responsibility for rendering him monstrous. As well, the premise of the story, in which Jekyll's transformations are initially precipitated by a potion, asserts the shaping power of ingested substances, not only reminding us of efforts to ameliorate epilepsy through diet but also invoking the conflicted status of alcohol and drugs in eugenic doctrine. Some eugenic figures argued that substance addiction was just another indicator of defective stock: just as Davenport insisted that "nature protects most of her best blood from [sexual] diseases; for the acts that lead to them are repugnant to strictly normal persons," so he felt that alcoholism and "the selection of associates" that might exacerbate it were "determined by innate tastes which are doubtless hereditary."[85] G. Frank Lydston, whom Davenport cites, declared damningly, "It is a noteworthy fact that the family histories of dypsomaniacs are largely tinctured with nerve disorders. Hysteria, epilepsy, migraine, and even insanity are found all along the line. In such cases inebriety is but one of the varying manifestations of bad heredity."[86]

But many others with eugenic interests, such as early-twentieth-century temperance advocate Carrie Nation, countered that such "race poisons" contributed to the deterioration of otherwise valuable racial stock and "were responsible for transmitting nervous diseases, epilepsy, weakened constitutions, depraved appetites, and deformities of all kinds."[87] David Starr Jordan contended that alcoholism constituted a danger to even the best and strongest of the race:

> It is drink which causes appetite, and not appetite which seeks for drink. In a given number of drunkards but a very few become such through inborn appetite. It is influence of bad example, lack of courage, false idea of manliness, or some defect in character or misfortune in environment which leads to the first steps in drunkenness. . . . [W]e must admit that it is the strong and vigorous, not the weak and perverted, that are destroyed by [the influence of alcohol]."[88]

Accordingly, the scenes in which Jekyll "imbibes" do not necessarily dramatize the release of the degenerate inner character of a singular and defective individual; they instead suggest that similar substance abuse might produce anyone as bestial and primitive. The man who hallucinates ants is perhaps not insane but drunk, given his residence in a bar, or drugged, given his proximity to an opium den. The significance in the film of such substances emphasizes the significance of "race poisons" in challenging purely genetic and deterministic eugenic narratives and acknowledges influential factors beyond biological inheritance.

Thus, the transformation scene, while using the visual dynamics of epileptic seizure to proffer visual revelation of eugenic degeneracy—the mad hallucinations, convulsive actions, and monstrous appearance of a defective individual—also illuminates the environmental causes of certain symptoms and the cultural interpretations that color epilepsy's visualization. As Pick argues of Gothic texts, tropes of degeneration work to explain otherness, "securing the identity of, variously, the scientist, (white) man, bourgeoisie against superstition, fiction, darkness, femininity, the masses, effete aristocracy" and guaranteeing that "the degenerate has a definite physiognomy." But, as Pick also notes, Gothic texts also implicate everyone in their "scenario of racial decline" and proffer their readers "a world of entropy or some future dissolution of stable positions."[89] In this transformation scene, we not only glimpse the reassurance of innate debility revealed in a man's aberrant motions but also confront the possibility of acquired debility to which even this privileged, white, and apparently nondisabled man is vulnerable. Ultimately, Jekyll's metamorphosis into Hyde visualizes a degenerative process triggered by a synthetic substance, indicating the transformative influences of external phenomena and thus the instability of individual health and social standing.

Like Robertson's *Dr. Jekyll and Mr. Hyde*, Rouben Mamoulian's 1931 film indexes seizures to environmental and cultural factors, while intensifying the earlier film's use of surrealistic elements to insist on the subjective and fantastical construction of epileptic performance. The film opens with an extended sequence in which the camera and the viewer occupy the visual perspective of Jekyll (Fredric March) himself. Later, this subjective viewpoint is again taken up when Jekyll first consumes his potion. Jekyll raises the beaker to his eyes, the camera adopts his perspective, and the glass blurs; Jekyll lowers it to reveal himself/us in the mirror. As Jekyll approaches the mirror, the camera zooms in, confronting us with his reflected image. With his head and shoulders framed in the mirror, Jekyll drinks the potion. His throat seems to constrict: he clutches at it with one, and then two hands, wheezing. As we watch him in the mirror, his face begins to change: his lips thicken, his mouth widens, his face seems darker and more heavily lined. The use of trickery and makeup in this scene is widely heralded:

The transformation scenes were ingeniously filmed, and relied on the manipulation of color filters that would be undetectable in the black-and-white film. The first signs of Hyde's distorted features—wrinkle lines, enlarged nostrils, etc.—were painted directly on March's face in red makeup. Photographed through a compensating red filter, the makeup was invisible to the camera. As the filter gradually changed from red to blue, monstrous details seemed to erupt from the actor's face.[90]

But, at this point, the transformation is far from complete. Jekyll, still seen to us only in the first-person reflection, staggers suddenly away from the mirror, as the camera tracks rapidly along with him/us. Jekyll collapses onto the floor, and the scene moves into a surrealistic dream sequence. First, the camera enacts a 360-degree pan at increasing speed to a loud, ringing, discordant sound; everything blurs and becomes smoky.[91] Voices fill the soundtrack as flashes of recent events occupy the camera: among them, Jekyll declaring "Marry me, Muriel! I can't wait!"; Lanyon's (Holmes Herbert's) disapproving "Positively indecent!"; and Ivy's leg-swinging flirtation, as she whispers, "Come back soon, won't you? Come back! Come back!" As the dream sequence ends, we return to the spinning camera, which slows and refocuses. Panting fills the soundtrack, and we resume Jekyll's point of view as he rises and moves toward the mirror. We are now confronted with Hyde's reflection: liquid rubber applied directly to March's face has broadened his cheeks and nose; false, protruding teeth fill his gaping mouth; his hair is thick and unruly and his eyebrows bushy. Only now does the camera cut to a more conventional shot, in which we see Hyde's reflection over his shoulder and are once more outside of his perspective, as he crows into the mirror: "Free! Free at last!"

This transformation scene again recalls traits of epileptic seizure. The facial contortions in the first stages of the transformation are even more evident in the second metamorphosis, wherein extreme close-ups of Jekyll's face reveal the clenching of his teeth and the rigidity of his lips (fig. 3.4), while the camera focuses on first his right and then his left hand as each grasps the chair arm and is compulsively raised and lowered. These actions might serve to represent the generalized seizure's body rigidity in the tonic phase and convulsion in the clonic phase or, again, might suggest partial or focal seizures. In the first transformation, this stage of contortion is followed by a collapse: whether Jekyll loses consciousness or simply experiences an altered state remains unclear. But the surrealistic sequence that follows, with its superimposed images and overlapping voices—consistent with descriptions of epileptic hallucinations that have

**3.4** Seizing: Jekyll (Fredric March) begins his second transformation into Hyde in *Dr. Jekyll and Mr. Hyde* (1931).

visual and auditory components and draw on specific memories—insists on the complex cultural and psychosexual elements of Jekyll's condition.

Mamoulian's *Dr. Jekyll* also forwards an association of epilepsy and a degeneration visualized in racial terms. As noted by Virginia Wright Wexman, "Hyde's dark skin, thick lips, and broad, flat nose" conflate bestiality with racist physiognomics. Like *Bride of Frankenstein* as discussed by Elizabeth Young, Mamoulian's film exploits the myth of the black rapist, concluding with what Wexman describes as "a sequence that bears a sinister resemblance to a lynching, complete with an angry mob and the shooting of a monstrous criminal who is suspended in the air, as though hanging from a tree."[92] Mamoulian himself claimed to be most preoccupied with Hyde's animalism:

> I thought that a more interesting dilemma would be not that of good versus evil or moral versus immoral but that of the spiritual versus the animalistic which are present in all of us. . . . Therefore, as a prototype for Hyde, I didn't take a monster but our common ancestor, the Neanderthal man. Mr. Hyde is a replica of the Neanderthal man. He is not a monster or animal of another species but primeval man—closest to the earth, the soil."[93]

But while Mamoulian insists on Hyde's initial, animalistic innocence and holds that his perversion is purely a result of his human elements, Hyde's animalism cannot help but be read racially: Jekyll's facial deformation conforms to Lombrosian narratives of skulls and faces and points to a racialized vision of evolutionary regression.[94] Such bestial iconography also confirms cultural and mythic perceptions of epilepsy as revealing primeval forces at work within the body. As in the 1920 film, then, this iconography projects the disabled body onto (and interprets it in terms of) racial and class deviance: Hyde seeks out those who apparently lack the civilized tastes and self-control of the upper-class individuals with whom Jekyll normally socializes.

Eugenic understandings of Jekyll's condition are, however, troubled by environmental and cultural interpretations: like Barrymore's Jekyll, March's doctor exhibits addictive behavior in relation to his potion and also battles repressive Victorian propriety, when his fiancée's father repeatedly delays their marriage. Very clearly, the potion provides a release, supporting one of Spratling's notions about men's epilepsy: that the seizure was in fact a moment of healthy discharge of poisons. Moments after his creation, Hyde stretches repeatedly as if to emphasize his liberation from a long, restrictive confinement. This reading undercuts simplistic notions of Hyde as Jekyll's repressed id, suggesting that it is Jekyll himself, in his untransformed state, who is "crippled" by hypocritical cultural standards. The duality of epileptic experience is projected onto a duplicitous society that "hides" its fleshy desires. In turn, the film uncovers the function of disability as a metaphoric construction enabling social criticism, a deviant reflection of normative society rather than a pathological fact.

As a film preoccupied with aesthetics and cinematic virtuosity, Mamoulian's *Dr. Jekyll* telegraphs this cultural tendency to exploit impairment in constructing of social ideals. Indeed, Mamoulian's use of experimental cinematic techniques, including montage, diagonal wipes, and split screens, repeatedly draws attention to the multiple lenses through which we can view Jekyll's transformation. The film's formalist images clearly construct an image of the idealized white body that opposes the film's degenerate and dark underclasses. Wexman contends that Mamoulian uses an Eisensteinian experimental aesthetics to espouse an individualist, rather than a collective, utopia, based on "an ideal of physical beauty represented by the body and its sexuality."[95] The images of white statuary that preoccupy the film affirm, for Wexman, the association of idealized beauty with whiteness and youth, while depictions of the later Hyde associate deformity with darkness and old age. Thus, Jekyll's idealistic aim of self-perfection is confounded by the eruption of difference and death. But the film also intertwines the idealized bodily form—realized in the handsome Dr. Jekyll, the white flowers and statuary of his elegant home, and frequent shots of tall, white candles—with the degraded and decayed bodily form—figured in the hirsute, darkened, and wizened Mr. Hyde, the statue of the black demon beside the mirror during Jekyll's first transformation, and shrunken and used-up candles that feature in several scenes.[96] Accordingly, the film's formal operations, repeatedly moving back and forth between ideal and degenerate figures, mock and thwart Jekyll's desire to separate the idealized human form from markers of defect and age. It is, the film suggests, the effort to deny impairment as necessarily part of the human condition and the effort to interpret it as "other" than the self that reproduces impairment as deviant monstrosity.

The continuity between the ideal and impaired self suggested by Mamoulian's aesthetic politics is even more evident in MGM's *Dr. Jekyll and Mr. Hyde* (1941), directed by Victor Fleming and starring Spencer Tracy. More than the earlier versions, this film insists on the impact of modern life as an epileptic factor while also emphasizing the conflicted and subjective status of the ostensibly authoritative field of medicine. The film opens in a church, but as the priest declaims on good's triumph over evil, a man in the congregation, ignoring the hushing of his wife, leaps to his feet and begins to cackle, shouting out against the priest and the church's ability to abolish evil. Outside, the man's distraught wife tells Jekyll that her husband has been this way since a recent explosion. Jekyll reveals his diagnosis to a skeptical dinner party that evening:

> JEKYLL: The man had been spiritually distorted, through shock. That explosion in the gas main last month. Before that, he was a fine, solid citizen. A gentleman, kind with his children and deeply in love with his wife. Since then, he had undergone a complete change, until this afternoon I found him completely reverted to the animal.
> LANYON (Ian Hunter): But look here, Harry, we can clearly understand a shock to the nervous system but . . . but what's that got to do with the soul?
> JEKYLL: I think the man had been shocked from normal good into complete evil.

Jekyll's subsequent experiments, building on his beliefs about the duality of man's nature and the accessibility of the soul through environmental and chemical means, are thus constituted as an effort to cure the man, who has, in his madness, already intuited a connection between himself and Jekyll: "You're a fun-blooded young fella, you'll tell him! *We* know, don't we!?" But when the man dies before Jekyll can administer the concoction, the doctor takes his place as subject of his own experiment.

We are cinematically prepared for the transformation scene by a series of quick dissolves and superimpositions featuring the apparatus of Jekyll's lab as he works with his chemicals. Sitting at a table, Jekyll confronts the full beaker. Shots alternate between the beaker and extreme close-ups of Jekyll's face. Swiftly, he makes his decision and drinks. A close-up of Jekyll's hands shows him taking his own pulse; he writes down the result. Then his right hand reaches to his chest. Suddenly, he is convulsed with pain. His body stiffens and stretches out across the table, knocking over the empty beaker, before he falls from the chair onto the floor. A surrealistic dream sequence clearly inspired by the Mamoulian film follows: lilies float in water, while a superimposed closed eye fades from sight. We see the smiling faces of Jekyll's fiancée Beatrice (Lana Turner) and bar-girl Ivy (Ingrid Bergman) in the water and then we watch them sink in an oozing mud. Next, in a piece of blatant pseudosexual imagery, Jekyll stands on a coach, whipping on a pair of horses, which, when we cut to them again, are revealed as the two women (fig. 3.5). During the entire sequence, orchestral music builds to a crescendo. The dream sequence for Jekyll's second transformation also generates vivid images. The faces of Beatrice and Ivy appear in a glass bottle. Jekyll is shown turning a corkscrew to open the bottle, against the background of a flaming explosion. The corkscrew resembles a detonator device, and as Jekyll uncorks the bottle, a huge explosion occurs, generating fire, clouds of smoke, and lava.

After the first transformation, the camera follows Hyde, initially glimpsing him only distortedly through a glass jar as he stumbles toward the mirror. We are conscious of his shoulder in the corner of the shot, but the shot focuses on his reflection. Hyde wipes his arm repeatedly across the mirror to clear it of steam, until his new visage is clearly revealed. Director Fleming here eschewed the extreme makeup of earlier versions: Hyde is conveyed through Tracy's disheveled hair, slightly bushier eyebrows, and fuller face, although his appearance grows more rumpled and hairy with each transformation. And only in the third transformation, the first to happen without the trigger of the chemical, does the camera witness the facial change: a process accomplished through superimposing slight makeup changes and Tracy's dramatic expression alterations, until Hyde is revealed. A story goes that when Somerset Maugham visited the set of this film, he asked, "Which one is he now, Jekyll or Hyde?"

**3.5** Hallucination: Jekyll's vision of Ivy (Ingrid Bergman) and Beatrix (Lana Turner) as he transforms into Hyde in *Dr. Jekyll and Mr. Hyde* (1941).

The lack of major visible distinction between Tracy's Jekyll and his Hyde indicates the 1941 film's greater emphasis on the psychological and neurological elements of physical disorders and testifies to the unreliability of the bodily exterior as a sign of health or degeneracy. The hallucinatory images again conflate epileptic and sexual release, pointing to repressed sexual desires as the source of individual malaise, but the visual and verbal rhetoric of explosions and their shock effects also emphasizes the physical impact of modern phenomena on neurological and psychological health and thus on the vulnerability of anyone to the triggers of epilepsy or insanity. Rather than functioning in typical melodramatic fashion, by rendering the political in purely personal terms, this *Dr. Jekyll* suggests the complex network of physiology, neurology, psychology, sexuality, and environment that is shaped in the relationship between impairment and medicine.

The tracing of seizure symptoms—both as medical and mythic productions—in these scenes should, again, not work to "diagnose" our cinematic Jekylls, fixing their problems in terms of a specific disorder. Rather, these readings indicate that disability is one lens through which these scenes should be read in order to understand the way psychological, sexual, racial, and social concerns are oriented toward visual and bodily representations of impairment. The scenes show that despite the appeal to a dramatic and self-evident physical aberrance, visual depictions do not and cannot surrender a "truth" that explains the condition. Instead, the "revelation" of disability and degeneracy is represented as a performance of eugenic, medical, and cultural narratives. These scenes' use of surreal elements suggests the always constructed and mediated nature of impairment. Further, the formative movement of the drug from the bodily exterior inwards (from the outside in) undermines a eugenic perspective in which the inner self shapes and defines the somatic surface (from the inside out) and in which deviance can be safely contained in other bodies, predestined to impairment. The films' attention to surface appearances and the shifting appearance of Jekyll/Hyde—both within and across the films—destabilize assumptions that one's exterior faithfully manifests one's soul. The transformation scenes testify that Hyde's apparent class and racial otherness is a matter of chemical intervention and surface representation, contesting assumptions that his primitive appearance, evident debility, and racial categorization incarnate genetic destiny. Consequently, the films hint, race, devolution, and deformity may be artificially created rather than biologically determined. They are material certainly, but forged in and on the somatic exterior, a eugenic fiction sedimented at the level of bodily signifiers.

## THE REALITY IN CINEMATIC CORPOREALITY

We have seen that classic horror's revelation scenes resist eugenic efforts to consolidate pathology in the impaired body, spinning out from visible deformation and physical convulsion toward conflicting mythic and medical narratives of aberrance that are, in turn, projected back on to atypical faces and bodies. But this mediation should not override attention to the realities of pain and impairment, so far as we can glimpse them in cinematic horror. Tobin Siebers has noted that social constructionism, while valuable in opposing medical and pathological views of disabled people, risks erasing "the harsh realities of the body." Theoretical views of pain tend to present it as either a tool of the dominant, regulatory society or as "an unmanageable supplement of suffering that marks out the individual as a site of resistance to social regulation." Such theories often focus on psychic rather than physical pain and portray suffering, disability, and prostheses as resources for new, pleasurable, and subversive identities. But, Siebers asserts, "most people with a disability understand that physical pain is an enemy. . . . The great challenge every day is to manage the body's pain, to get out of bed in the morning, to overcome the well of pain that rises in the evening, to meet the hundred daily obstacles that are not merely inconveniences but occasions for physical suffering." He cautions that "[t]he disabled body is no more real than the able body—and no less real":

> I am not claiming . . . that the body exists apart from social forces or that it represents something more *real*, *natural*, or *authentic* than things of culture. I am claiming that the body has its own forces. . . . The body is, first and foremost, a biological agent teeming with vital and often chaotic forces. It is not inert matter subject to easy manipulation by social representations. The body is alive, which means that it is as capable of influencing and transforming social languages as they are capable of influencing and transforming it.

What we must consider, Siebers argues, are the ways in which "the disabled body changes the process of representation itself."[97]

Even as classic horror films make evident disability's production through environmental, cultural, and eugenic discourses, they rarely lose sight of the body as a material entity with its own forces. It is a concept hyperbolized in movies such as *The Beast with Five Fingers* (dir. Robert Florey, Warner Bros., 1946), where a disembodied hand takes on a life of its own, and *Mad Love* (dir. Karl Freund, MGM, 1935), where a pianist's transplanted hands, taken from the corpse of a criminal, carry out violent acts against his will. The *Dr. Jekyll* films, too, even as they portray the construction and production of Jekyll/Hyde's seizures, also move relentlessly toward the triumph and tragedy of the body's own "vital and often chaotic forces," as Jekyll discovers his "condition" has exceeded his control and become organic. Whatever mediations of disability classic horrors uncover—whatever revelations of the disablings produced by dominant discourses—they continue to depend heavily on the spectacular presentation of physical pain and unwanted bodily transformation.

Of course, as the films' own cinematic elements make clear, such presentations are performed acts. However, media and advertorial materials for classic horror films often appealed to corporeal reality by emphasizing the real pains and impairments endured by particular horror actors. Lon Chaney's protean persona as the Man of a Thousand Faces, for example, grew out of frequent coverage of the physical extremes he pursued in his roles. In *The Penalty* (1920), Chaney portrayed a double-leg amputee by using a "painful leg harness" that, worn for long periods, cut off his circulation and contributed to frequent collapses. In *The Hunchback of Notre*

*Dame* (1923), he labored under a 50-pound rubber cast, and for his facially deformed character in *The Phantom of the Opera*, he "used a contoured wire appliance to flare and pull back his nose," a device that reportedly caused significant pain and bleeding. As Skal notes, Chaney's suffering was likely exaggerated for press purposes, "but it would be a mistake to believe that Chaney did not willingly undergo a perverse amount of discomfort in pursuit of his art."[98]

Barrymore's performance as Jekyll/Hyde also merged disability performances and "real" impairment. In marking Hyde's degeneracy with a hunched back and awkward gait, Barrymore connected his daytime performances on the film-set with his nighttime theatrical performances of Richard III. This doubled disability act took its toll: soon after, Barrymore suffered a nervous collapse and was consigned for a period to a White Plains sanitarium.[99] Indeed, his life was dramatically shaped by alcoholism, memory problems, and frequent visits to sanitariums and hospitals.[100] Actor Claude Rains similarly experienced the exacerbation of impairment due to his performance in *The Invisible Man* (1933). His daughter reported that Rains "had been gassed in the war," was claustrophobic, and was virtually blind in one eye. When, in the making of a mask required to produce the illusion of invisibility, his face was "encased in plaster . . . with straws through the nose and mouth," Rains found the ordeal "frightening."[101] Thus, all three actors' simulations of bodily aberrance, even as they foreground the constructed nature of cinematic impairment, are connected in indeterminate ways to actual psychological or physical debility. Their stories indicate a certain reality constituted by the actor's body insofar as facial expressions and physical gestures belong both to actor and character: in the one image, we see both Chaney's pain etched on his face and the Phantom's pain etched on *his* face.

The real debilities associated with these actors' feigned impairments complicate condemnations by disability scholars and activists of movies' use of nondisabled actors to play disabled characters. For Norden, this tendency is "a type of fraudulence akin to white actors performing in blackface," part of the movie industry's consistent "misrepresentation" of people with disabilities.[102] For Tobin Siebers, it constitutes "disability drag," in which ablebodied actors perform disability as "a façade overlaying ablebodiedness," a mask that will reassuringly be removed in the actor's subsequent performances.[103] But a distinction between disabled and nondisabled actors and filmmakers is not always obvious. If we take into account just a few examples—along with the impairments of Chaney, Rains, and Barrymore, we might include the "[d]entofacial injuries" and other physical damage sustained in a car accident by director Tod Browning, the alcoholism of *Frankenstein*'s Colin Clive, the chronic appendicitis suffered by Helen Chandler while playing Mina in *Dracula*, and the weak heart and constitution of *Freaks* producer Irving Thalberg—we see that many of those involved in constructing horror films' disability performances were no strangers to impairment.[104]

Just how we might appreciate the presence of material impairment and pain in film scenes—and thus trace the disabled body's effects on "the process of representation"—remains unclear. For some early film theorists, cinema's power lay in its indexical connection to reality, its photographic capacity to record and project material life in ways often tied to the form and face of the actor. For some of these theorists, the value of the facial close-up was its revelation of hidden truths. Béla Balázs felt that "in the isolated close-up of the film we can see to the bottom of a soul by means of . . . tiny movements of facial muscles." This "microphysiognomy" "shows you your shadow on the wall with which you have lived all your life and which you scarcely knew," providing "dramatic revelations of what is really happening under the surface of appearances."[105] Here, the reality of physical expression, rendered in enormous detail, is again reified as the visible sign of ineffable and invisible truths. But for Siegfried Kracauer, the close-up works not only to reveal emotional or psychological truths but also as "an end in itself." Writing of a close-up in D. W. Griffith's *After Many Years* (1908), where Annie yearns for her shipwrecked husband, Kracauer suggests that "Griffith wanted us also to absorb the face for its own sake instead of just passing through and beyond it; the face appears before the desires and emotions to which it refers have been completely defined, thus tempting us to get lost in its puzzling indeterminacy." Similarly, a close-up in *Intolerance* of Mae Marsh's "huge hands with the convulsively moving fingers" not only illustrates her emotional condition but "reveals how her hands behave under the impact of utter despair."[106] Kracauer thus finds in "such huge images of small material phenomena . . . disclosures of new aspects of physical reality," arguing that Griffith's cinema "cannot adequately account for . . . inner developments unless it leads us through the thicket of material life from which they emerge and in which they are embedded" (48).

The physical gestures of horror monsters in the throes of impairment, then, the visible convergence of performed and experienced pain, may offer—alongside the metaphors, myths, and medical narratives—an "end in themselves," instances of material "indeterminacy" that cannot be reduced to intellectual, emotional, or eugenic "truths." Horror is not, of course, a particularly realistic genre; moreover, it has strong connections to the German expressionism that Kracauer condemned for distracting viewers from a chaotic and sinister political reality with abstract hallucination and psychological projections.[107] But Kracauer's theory nonetheless makes space for the kinds of visualizations evident in classic horror film.

First, Kracauer declares, cinema can reveal the overlooked realities of our daily lives, uncovering "the unfamiliar in the familiar" (55). The increasing familiarity of Fritz's face in *Frankenstein* suggests, like the domestic depiction of freaks in *Freaks*, the possibility that deformity might come to seem ordinary, rather than fantastically frightening; what is "familiar," then, the narrative of degeneracy and criminality that typically informs responses to facial disfigurement, is at least momentarily displaced by the unfamiliar experience of deformity as familiar and nonthreatening.

Second, Kracauer continues, cinema can usefully depict "phenomena overwhelming consciousness," such "[e]lemental catastrophes, the atrocities of war, acts of violence and terror, sexual debauchery, and death." Certainly, film may sensationalistically exploit such subjects, responding to long-standing human desires for violent or excessive spectacles that "shock the shuddering and delighted onlooker into unseeing participation." But, Kracauer insists, it also "adds something new and momentous: it insists on rendering visible what is commonly drowned in inner agitation . . . [,] transforming the agitated witness into a conscious observer" (57, 58). The increasing familiarity of Fritz's aberrant face transforms the viewer's initial shock into a more detached contemplation. The cinematography that reveals the Phantom's face allows the viewer time to absorb not only Christine's disgusted shock, which typically cues viewers' own response, but also the psychic pain experienced by the Phantom *as he is seen*, as he anticipates the horror and rejection his face will engender. The interplay in the *Jekyll and Hyde* films of mythic discourses, eugenic degeneracy narratives, and the monster's seizing body calls on spectators to trace the psychological and cultural origins of their repulsion and fear in the face of the epileptic convulsion. Thus, our growing awareness of the performative elements of horror's disability spectacles should not elide the reality of facial disfigurement, epileptic seizures, or other convulsive conditions and experiences. Instead, it should warn us to distrust any presentation of visible traits as transparent "proof" of the kinds of deviance on which eugenic, psychological, medical, and cultural discourses often depend, in turn asking us to re-view the moment of impairment's revelation in terms of bodily forces not reducible to cultural narrative.

Finally, Kracauer concludes, "films may expose physical reality as it appears to individuals in extreme states of mind generated by [disasters or shocking events], mental disturbances, or an other external or internal cause." Here, Kracauer—unlike realist film theorist André Bazin, who celebrated Italian neorealism's dearth of intrusive editing and surrealistic imagery—allows for nonclassical camera angles and movement, cinematic distortions, and frenetic editing to give access to non-normative modes of reality (58, 59). Thus, the hallucinations of the various Dr. Jekylls work to convey to viewers a dramatic physiological experience. Indeed, in rendering directly to the viewer the sights and sounds of such hallucinations, and of course in the first-person cinematography of Mamoulian's film, these movies work not only to show but also to *provide to and elicit in the viewer* a comparable physiological experience.

The spectacle of impairment in horror thus implicates both actors' and viewer's bodies. As Walter Benjamin has pointed out, cinema is a medium, unlike the theater, built on the physical *absence* of the actor's body.[108] Nonetheless, the production of the cinematic image may be inordinately physical: the whirling room of Jekyll's hallucination in the 1931 film is enabled by a spinning camera weighted down by a man's body, while the eerie pounding on the soundtrack derives from a reversed recording of Mamoulian's racing heart. These bodily techniques produce "distancing and alienation-effects," which, as discussed by Steven Shaviro, exploit cinema's freedom from "any illusion of naturalness or presence" that might adhere to theatrical performance, where the actors' bodies are present. Such effects work in order to more completely "captivate" the viewer. That is, while the actor's body is absent, its representation, especially through nonclassical cinematic devices, works on the *viewer's* body: "Images themselves are immaterial, but their *effect* is all the more physical and corporeal." Shaviro imagines a film-viewer subjected to assaultive imagery, whose "perception becomes a kind of physical affliction, an intensification and disarticulation of bodily sensation."[109] Thus does the revelation of impairment both derive from and project itself toward the body and its chaotic forces.

These tentative thoughts on the status of the material body in classic horror cinema lead us from the monster's body, revealed as impaired, toward those who gaze on that body and register its impairment in their physiological response. Siebers argues, rightly, that our society continues to disavow the likelihood of our own disablement: "Most people do not want to consider that life's passage will lead them from ability to disability. The prospect is too frightening, the disabled body, too disturbing."[110] But, as this chapter has shown, horror often depicts characters who not only seek out and produce spectacles of deformity but also consequently experience their own impairment. This characteristic particularly attaches to the genre's "mad" doctors, such as Frankenstein, who waits excitedly to witness the monster he has created and consequently experiences manic episodes, nervousness, and fainting fits, and Jekyll, who produces monstrosity on and in his own body before enthusiastically gazing on his handiwork in the nearest mirror. Having considered the impaired monster at the center of horror's disability spectacle, the remainder of *Hideous Progeny* traces the proliferation of disability outward toward those who solicit and summon it. Chapter 4 focuses on the medical figure as architect of the pathologizing gaze, considering how selected films from the mad-doctor subgenre present the act of gazing at the impaired monster—justified by a rhetoric of pathology and cure—as a covert and voyeuristic desire *for* disability that opens up mad doctors to their own experiences of debility and aberrance. In turn, chapter 5 argues, mad doctors become figures for the horror-film viewer, who also seeks out visions of aberrance that impair and debilitate. Like the cinema that Kracauer commends, which both uses sensational spectacle to agitate and excite viewers and reconstructs the viewer as a "conscious observer," these horror films both accommodate viewers' desires to expose their minds and bodies to—to be "captivated" by—cinematic debilitation and ask them to confront their complicity in constructing spectacles of disability.

# MAD MEDICINE

## DISABILITY IN THE MAD-DOCTOR FILMS

DR. RICHARD VOLLIN (Bela Lugosi): A doctor is fascinated by death and pain. How much pain a man can endure.

DR. JERRY HALDEN (Lester Matthews): I disagree with you, Dr. That's not why I'm a doctor.

DR. VOLLIN (*slightly mockingly*): You're a doctor because you want to do good.

DR. HALDEN: Yes!

. . . . . . . .

JEAN (Irene Ware): Dr. Vollin is a little mad.

—*The Raven* (dir. Louis Friedlander, Universal, 1935)

Released at the end of the 1930s, the British horror film *Dark Eyes of London* (dir. Walter Summers, John Argyle Productions, 1939) contains stock ingredients from earlier American classic horror films—for instance, starring *Dracula*'s Bela Lugosi and featuring an impaired monster who stalks the movie's heroine. Lugosi plays the dastardly Dr. Orloff, a former doctor who has his insurance clients murdered for their money. Orloff also masquerades as Dearborn, the congenial, blind director of a Home for the Destitute Blind, where he exploits the men under his "care." Orloff's henchman and assassin is Jake (Wilfred Walters), a hulking and facially scarred blind man who, at one point, menaces the film's leading lady, Diana (Greta Gynt), in the darkness of her apartment. But the film's most horrific and enduring scene precedes Jake's attack on Diana. Angered by suspicions of betrayal, Orloff ties one of his blind helpers, Lou (Arthur E. Owen), to a hospital bed and injects him with an unnamed substance. When that fails to produce the desired result, Orloff admonishes the frail man: "You have been very foolish, Lou. . . . You're blind and you can't speak, but you can hear. And that will never do." The doctor then charges up a generator and straps electrodes to Lou's head. As the scene cuts to the blind men laboring in a room below, Lou's scream fills the air. When a detective inspector arrives, he can get no answer from the still, silent, and now deafened man. But Orloff is not yet content and, when police make their move on the institution, he drowns Lou in a tub and dispatches him into the Thames.

Dark Eyes of London's presentation of a "mad" doctor who debilitates his patient was a significant factor in its reception by the British Board of Film Censors (BBFC). The movie was one of only five British films to receive the BBFC's "H" classification, which had been introduced in 1933 as a response to American horror films and which designated a film as "horrific," restricting its viewing by filmgoers younger than sixteen. Another British film slapped with the "H" classification was The Man Who Changed His Mind (aka The Man Who Lived Again; dir. Robert Stevenson, Gainsborough Pictures, 1936), in which Boris Karloff featured as an increasingly obsessive scientist seeking to transpose his mind into another body. This movie, too, was targeted for its themes of medical abuse.[1] Deviant doctors in American horror films also came in for criticism: Universal's The Raven, which presented Lugosi as a scheming surgeon bent on capture and torture, was described by one British reviewer as "quite the most unpleasant picture I have ever seen, exploiting cruelty for cruelty's sake."[2]

Indeed, The Raven was the last American horror film approved for release in Britain during the 1930s. In 1935 the BBFC announced that it would no longer accept horror-film imports. This decision had a profound effect in the United States, as indicated by a Variety article linking declining horror production directly to British sentiment: "Reason attributed by U[niversal] for abandonment of horror cycle is that European countries, especially England, are prejudiced against this type product [sic]. Despite heavy local consumption of its chillers, U[niversal] is taking heed to warning from abroad."[3] The British ban—along with increased censorship at home and, to some extent, the Laemmle family's loss of control at Universal—is often seen as contributing to the end of "A-budget devotion to horror"; scholars frequently designate 1936 as the end point of the first and most defining American horror cycle.[4]

Ironically, the downturn in horror production precipitated by the British ban also helped ensure that the "mad doctor" or "mad scientist" type of film that censors found so troubling would come to constitute a recognizable horror subgenre well in advance of others with which we are now familiar. Certainly, the 1930–1936 period encompasses many of the genre's significant classics, but by 1936 only *Dracula* and *Frankenstein* had each produced a (single) sequel, and the mummy, vampire, zombie, and werewolf subgenres had yet to take shape. It wasn't until the 1938 rerelease of *Dracula* and *Frankenstein* as a double bill and the success of *Son of Frankenstein* in 1939 that Universal committed itself to the film cycles that, along with the contributions of B movies from the "Poverty Row" companies, would shape these subgenres.[5]

By the mid-1930s, however, the mad-doctor film was already perceived as a specific type of horror movie. A 1936 London *Times* article despaired of films that seemed to delight in depicting medical torture:

> 'Now,' one fancies [the gentlemen who make films] exclaiming, 'now we shall see whether at last the fellow can be made to blench!' and they proceed to depict some surgical operation, complete with a formidable apparatus of high-powered lamps, pumps, dials and knives. Very rarely is the intention to save life or to effect a cure for some malignant disease. The favourite purpose of an operation on the screen is either disfigurement or the creation of a monster who will presently be employed to stalk the heroine, most likely in a graveyard. . . . The ghosts and goblins that used to lurk in dark corners to pounce upon the unwary pale into ineffectual shadows before the grim figure of the demon surgeon brandishing his scalpel.[6]

This perspective recognizes the central elements of the mad-doctor subgenre: medical interventions that produce monstrosity and the simultaneous mapping of monstrosity onto the body of the doctor, who displaces the "ghosts and goblins" of old.

The development of the mad-doctor subgenre reflected an important shift in the classic horror formula. In *Dracula*, the battle lines were clear: the aberrant monster, the vampire, brought blood-loss, madness, and disease to his victims, while beneficent medical science, in the form of Professor Van Helsing, diagnosed and explained the problem. While Van Helsing's efforts to prove Dracula's deviance and to treat his victims were somewhat compromised, the professor nonetheless clearly possessed great knowledge and capacity to mitigate physiological damage. Even Dracula admitted the professor's wisdom and strength of will. Van Helsing was gentle and protective toward his patients and staunch in the face of the monster, eventually securing the health of Mina and the reunion of the eugenic couple. If subsequent horror films had mimicked *Dracula* in this regard, the horror-film's typical doctor or scientist would have been a thoroughly decent man, ultimately successful in his efforts to ward off disease and debilitation.

But when Edward Van Sloan, the actor behind Van Helsing, reprised his benevolent doctor role as Waldman in *Frankenstein*, his character came into conflict with a different kind of doctor: the obsessive, nervous, crazy, criminal Henry Frankenstein. Where Waldman respects boundaries to scientific knowledge, Henry is indicted by his mentor for his "insane ambition to create life" and for producing, in his effort to advance the cause of medicine, a hideous and violent monster. Waldman meets an untimely demise at the hands of the Monster, enabling *Frankenstein* to set in place key mad-doctor conventions: a hubristic scientist or physician seeking knowledge beyond traditional bounds; a doctor whose mental dysfunction manifests itself in his own behavioral or other visible impairments as well as in the monster he creates; and a climax in which the monster turns on his creator, becoming the vehicle of punishment for the doctor's medical meddling.

In showing us the mad doctor at the other end of the decade, *Dark Eyes of London* presents him as even more sinister. Here, the monstrous body is no longer an unintentional product of well-meaning efforts to thwart death and decay; it is now the premeditated result of destructive medical intervention. In the distance between the ostensibly good-hearted Henry and the gleefully criminal Orloff, the later film perhaps differentiates between well-meaning medical practices and the more egregious eugenic excesses of both the United States and Nazi Germany. But the similarities between *Frankenstein*'s and *Dark Eyes*' portrait of the mad doctor suggest a critique of even the most apparently benign medical and curative practices. Like Henry, Orloff has challenged the boundaries of medicine, complaining that his efforts to heal were thwarted by "narrow-minded medical men." Like Henry, Orloff gives his deviant thoughts and intentions corporeal form, in his case by employing the blind brute Jake to carry out his murderous plans. And, like Henry, Orloff is eventually attacked by this monstrous manifestation of his own aberrance, when Jake is enraged by Orloff's murder of Lou and kills the doctor. These commonalities reduce the distance between well-meaning and deliberately destructive medical acts. As *Dark Eyes* reimagines the scene in which a scientific or medical figure administers electricity to an aberrant body strapped to a table or bed, it demonizes not only the most excessive acts carried out in the name of medicine but also more apparently genial practices. In both *Frankenstein* and *Dark Eyes*, medical and scientific efforts usually framed or perceived as protective, life-giving, or healing in fact prove perverse and disabling.

Thus, more than any other horror subgenre, mad-doctor and mad-scientist films provide potent evidence for a link between medical science and disability. Their formulaic tropes and plots focus on characters/monsters who are clearly bodily, cognitively, or psychologically deformed or impaired; they engage the ethical dilemmas of scientific and medical "advances"; they explicitly mobilize the power dynamics of the medical gaze; and they repeatedly trouble any easy distinction between health professionals and the problematic bodies that they survey, interpret, diagnose, and seek to fix. To that extent, they indicate a popular anxiety about the powers wielded by medical men, a concern that eschews faith in eugenic principles and their proponents and, using the visual rhetoric of disability, transfigures doctors into monsters and monster-makers. This chapter considers how films such as *Doctor X, Mad Love, The Invisible Man,* and *Dr. Jekyll and Mr. Hyde* refuse to validate the medical gaze as objective, disinterested, and disembodied, instead presenting the monstrous patient as a projection of the doctor's own mind and body and mapping that monstrosity back onto the medical man himself. In particular, the films' vexed dynamics of the medical gaze suggest that curative efforts to assert power and procure normality out of what Davis calls "the maw of disability" cast doubt on science as a disinterested enterprise designed to help mankind.[7] In fact, the films suggest, the act of medical visualization often only sediments the seer more deeply within the vulnerabilities and pleasures of the embodied, marked, and visible self.

## MEDICAL SPECTACLES

The clinical gaze, Michel Foucault asserts in *The Birth of the Clinic,* emerged in the late eighteenth century and developed throughout the nineteenth, bolstered by corpse dissections whose revelations were projected onto the symptoms of sick individuals. With this information, doctors could presume to interpret, from outer signs, the inner pathologies of a degenerate or diseased body. Visualization, Foucault notes, plays a central role in medical observation, epistemology, and exercise of power: "the absolute eye of knowledge" effects "a suzerainty of the visible, and one all the more imperious in that it associates with it power and death."[8] The medical gaze colludes with the disciplinary gaze of prisons, schools, and hospitals where eyes "see without being seen" in "an apparatus in which the techniques that make it possible to see induce effects of power."[9] The drama of medical vision proves central to mad-doctor films and is particularly evident in *Dark Eyes of London*, with its use of blindness as plot device and trope. In the film, Orloff lays claim to a position of power by "see[ing] without being seen"—or seeing without being seen *seeing*—concealing his gaze by masquerading as the blind Dearborn. Meanwhile, the blindness of Orloff's charges facilitates their subjugation. Orloff explicitly equates vision to knowledge when he scoffs, "The men downstairs know nothing; they are blind." Lou proves Orloff wrong when he uses Braille notes to tell police about Orloff's activities. But the power wielded by the seeing doctor over the blind and objectified patient is confirmed when, under pretense of ministering to Lou, Orloff further debilitates and eventually murders him.

What mad-doctor films thus offer is a literal rendition of the politics of visibility at play in any space where someone—usually a doctor or scientist—lays claim to power and knowledge by regarding and interpreting a disabled body. Rather than injecting dramatic elements into medicine, however, or transporting medical situations into the realm of drama, horror films simply exploit the dramatic potential that has always inhered in scenarios where a patient's visible symptoms supposedly reveal an innate defect. Such theatricality was particularly evident, for example, in the late-nineteenth-century practices of neurologist Jean-Martin Charcot at the Parisian clinic La Salpêtrière. Charcot presented his "cases," typically women diagnosed with hysteria, in weekly lectures to audiences of both medical professionals and the general public. He also sketched and photographed his patients, often during hysterical seizures, in order to render their illnesses visible for a larger audience: "Charcot saw the incongruities of the external manifestation of the patient and was able almost intuitively to extrapolate from them the nature of his illness," positing a "direct relationship . . . between physical characteristics and brain disorder."[10] However, visual depictions of Charcot's lectures—notably André Brouillet's *Charcot at the Salpêtrière* (1887)—suggest evidence of a certain staging, of "[a]n elaborate machinery . . . at work to bring the neurological, internal working of the hysteric condition into visibility, and to mark it on the body it 'possessed.'"[11] Brouillet's engraving hints at such staging, portraying not only the fainted hysteric, Blanche Wittman, her neck and throat bared by a low-cut dress, supported by Charcot's colleague Joseph Babinski, and surrounded by gazing men, but also, on the back wall of the room, a drawing of a woman on a bed in hysterical crisis, her back dramatically arched. From one perspective, the picture-within-the-picture provides a reflection and extension of the woman at the center of the medical and artistic gaze, whose body arcs slightly as she swoons into the hands of Babinski. From another, however, the patient mimics and responds to the medical-artistic construction at the back of the room: indeed, scholars suggest that Wittman was an apt pupil, "as she learned from the representations of the hysteric how to appear as a hysteric."[12] As Sander Gilman notes, the staged quality of the performance is further indicated by the inclusion in Brouillet's engraving of a man apparently sketching Wittman. The man is Paul Richer, the artist of the image on the rear wall, and his presence contributes to a circular relationship in which the expression of symptoms cannot be certainly positioned as preceding their artistic construction.

Charcot's efforts to prove the reality of hysterical disorders through manifestation had, as Petra Kuppers asserts, some empowering effects for his female patients, "establish[ing] the legitimacy of psychological conditions and their effects on the physical body." At the same time, Charcot's use of hypnosis, his collaboration with Duchenne de Boulogne in inducing seizures through shock applications, and his stage-managing of medical performance and photographic sessions suggest both the exploitation and objectification of his female subjects and the "theatrical labor" that produces their bodies as "visual evidence." Kuppers contends that this labor is even more evident in the photographs of one of Charcot's star patients, fifteen-year-old Augustine:

> Images of Augustine such as *Extase, Erotisme,* and *Supplication amoreuse* (all 1878) look like tableaux: held positions, rather than snapshots of a "fit." The subject is positioned in front of the spectator's gaze with full assurance. Nothing is incidental; everything seems planned (Augustine is displayed on a bed, with disarrayed, flowing hair, plunging neckline, frontally oriented to the camera) and captured in such a way as to coincide transparently with the caption.[13]

Such an analysis does not diminish the reality of Augustine's emotional, psychological, and/or physical conditions, but it does insist that Charcot's efforts to render visible an inner and unseen condition necessarily implicate doctor, patient, and audience in a performance constructed both by medical and artistic conventions and—as the titles appended to the photographs of Augustine suggest—by gendered and sexual desires.[14]

Charcot's medical displays resonate with typical scenes from classic horror films. For instance, the description of Augustine evokes horror-film visions of vulnerable, beautiful young women sleeping or fainted on their beds. Like Charcot's theatrical lectures, the horror tableaux ostensibly manifest the dangers of debility and impairment—literalized in the monster's advance upon the female body—but simultaneously operate as salacious spectacles staged by a male director. *Dracula*, for instance, links the cinematic positioning of Lucy in her silky white nightdress at her bedroom window to her subsequent presentation as a (dead) body beneath a white sheet on a table in an operating theater (see fig. 1.2). In the latter scene, the camera begins at an upper corner of the room, revealing an audience of male medical figures garbed in white surgical gowns and caps, occupying the theater's tiered seats. The camera moves slowly in and down to the object of the men's gaze, Lucy's recently deceased body. The juxtaposition of the two scenes imports a sexual frisson into the latter: the men's gazes upon Lucy carry some of the same implications as Dracula's sinister and apparently lustful gaze in the preceding scene. At the same time, the theater scene presents the damaged female body as the carefully displayed "evidence" of biological deviance that legitimates the male medico-scientific project of diagnosis and cure. In *Dracula*, this project is subsequently taken up by Van Helsing and drives the filmic narrative.

In mad-doctor films, the physician's dependence on stage-managed performances becomes even more explicit. Many such movies openly engage the relationship between the medical gaze and that of the theatrical spectator by presenting their doctors as consumers of artistic or dramatic performances. *The Raven* first draws attention to Dr. Vollin's (Lugosi's) medical gaze when he encounters the young, beautiful, injured, and unconscious Jean prior to her surgery. He stares at her intently, as an extreme close-up of his piercing eyes accentuates his objectification of his patient. Soon after he heals Jean's crippling neurological injury, Vollin's visual obsession becomes more apparent as he watches her dance before an audience to a reading of Poe's "The Raven." Occupying a second-floor box, the doctor leans enthusiastically toward the stage under the suspicious eyes of Jean's father (fig. 4.1). The incisive medical gaze of the earlier scene that enables Vollin's cure of Jean converges with the obsessive gaze the doctor exhibits at the performance. That gaze soon morphs into something even more malignant when, denied access to the object of his passions, Vollin concocts a plan to subject Jean, her fiancé, and her father to his Poe-inspired torture devices.

Similarly, in *Mad Love*, we meet Dr. Gogol (Peter Lorre) sitting in the audience of Paris's Le Theatre des Horreurs, watching the object of his desire, actress Yvonne Orlac (Frances Drake), performing as an adulterous woman being tortured by her vengeful husband. Gogol, also in an upper-level box and with his face half-hidden in deep shadow, directs his

**4.1** Dr. Vollin (Bela Lugosi) gazes intently at Jean's performance while her father (Samuel S. Hinds) looks on in concern in *The Raven* (1935).

rapt, heavy-lidded gaze at Yvonne as her character is stretched on a wheel and burned with a hot iron, greeting the end of the scene by closing his eyes in a look of pained fulfillment. Later, Gogol attends the execution of Rollo (Edward Brophy), an American circus knife-thrower who has killed his father; the doctor wishes to procure the corpse for medical analysis. As the prisoner is positioned, Gogol coolly appraises the guillotine and then, as the blade falls offscreen, allows himself a fleeting, satisfied smirk. The effect of both scenes is to render Gogol's "diagnostic gaze"—and, by extension, his professional, medical practice—indistinguishable from his baleful spectatorship at moments of theatrical and real bodily destruction. The fantasies and desires evident in Gogol's gaze at Yvonne become intertwined with his altruistic and curative activities, for instance coloring scenes that show him reassuring and caressing young, poor girls whose paralysis he charitably aims to cure.

*The Raven* and *Mad Love* thus present the medical gaze as inevitably compromised—and, moreover, *produced*—by theatrical convention. Certainly, the doctors wield a medical gaze that helps them diagnose and treat inner conditions that have physically disabled their patients. But, insofar as the same doctors are shown to enjoy or imagine spectacles of violence and torture, the films map one kind of visual activity onto another, suggesting that the aesthetic pleasures of such spectacles necessarily shape the physician's gaze upon the impaired body. Accordingly, curative and destructive acts become less distinct than they might initially appear. Indeed, in each film the audience sees the doctor "treat" a patient in a manner that intensifies and extends the latter's debilitation.

## BODY AND SOUL: DISCIPLINING PATIENTS IN
## *THE RAVEN* AND *MAD LOVE*

In associating spectacles of torture with medical practice, *The Raven* and *Mad Love* interrelate the clinical gaze and the disciplinary gaze elucidated by Foucault. Foucault begins *Discipline and Punish* by considering public spectacles of torture and execution that "revealed truth and showed the operation of power" as they "reproduce[d] the crime on the visible body of the criminal." In the eighteenth century, however, the increasing perception of such punishments as "Gothic" and barbaric facilitated the shift of punishment toward a surveillant model. In the Panopticon prison envisaged by Jeremy Bentham, a model that Foucault argues imbues all kinds of disciplinary spaces, including hospitals and schools, a supervisor in a central tower oversees captives arranged in surrounding, well-lit, segregated cells. Patterned on efforts to contain the spread of plague, the Panopticon is oriented toward the control and normalization of aberrant bodies through an organization of visual power: "in the peripheric ring, one is totally seen, without ever seeing; in the central tower, one sees everything without ever being seen." In this surveillant society, the prisoners' bodies are subject to the gaze of a range of professionals, including warders, prison supervisors, chaplains, doctors, and psychiatrists: "A whole set of assessing, diagnostic, prognostic, normative judgements concerning the criminal have become lodged in the framework of penal judgement." Notes Foucault, "the Panopticon was also a laboratory; it could be used as a machine to carry out experiments, to alter behaviour, to train or correct individuals."[15]

This distribution of power has two significant effects on those under surveillance. First, the disciplining of their bodies is understood not as an end in itself, as in the days of torture, but as an appeal to the noncorporeal soul, psyche, or moral character: "The expiation that once rained down upon the body must be replaced by a punishment that acts in depth on the heart, the will, the inclinations." Second, and relatedly, the subjects of the panoptic gaze, never knowing quite when they might be under surveillance, internalize their disciplinary subjection: "He who is subjected to a field of visibility, and who knows it, assumes responsibility for the constraints of power; he makes them play spontaneously upon himself; he inscribes in himself the power relation in which he simultaneously plays both roles; he becomes the principle of his own subjection." Together, disciplinary power's appeal to an inner self and its engendering of self-surveillance *produce* the subject's "soul" as an inner, ostensibly immaterial entity that constrains him/her: "A 'soul' inhabits him and brings him to existence, which is itself a factor in the mastery that power exercises over the body. The soul is the effect and instrument of a political anatomy; the soul is the prison of the body."[16]

The passion of the doctors in *The Raven* and *Mad Love* for spectacular physical torment aligns them with the punishments of old, wherein power and truth were visibly inscribed in the flesh of the convicted. But the doctors also exploit panoptical schemas, each carrying out on one of their patients the kind of laboratory experimentation Foucault invokes to describe the modern prison. For instance, Vollin offers to "fix" the "ugly" face of the criminal Edward Bateman, played by Boris Karloff, but instead further scars and disfigures his face. Dependent on Vollin to undo the facial damage, Bateman feels compelled to carry out the doctor's orders to imprison and torture Jean and her family. Similarly, Gogol enacts a "cure" that becomes a debilitation when Yvonne's husband, concert pianist Stephen Orlac (*Frankenstein*'s Colin Clive), has his hands damaged in a train accident. Gogol secretly amputates Stephen's hands and replaces them with the hands of the executed knife-thrower, Rollo. He hopes that the pianist, discovering his hands' affinity for knives, will be driven to insanity and murder, leaving Yvonne open to Gogol's advances.

While the doctors' actions seem oriented toward torture and the physical inscription of flesh, their proximity to modern medical and disciplinary gazes is suggested by their clear intent to produce in their patients a soul or inner "self." In *The Raven*, bank-robber Bateman confides to Vollin that his external ugliness seems to have affected his character: "Ever since I was born, everybody looks at me and says, 'You're ugly.' Makes me feel mean. . . . Maybe if a man looks ugly, he does ugly things." Bateman contends that people's perception of his appearance as the revelation of an "ugly" character has in fact *produced* that character in and upon him.[17] In refusing Vollin's effort to recruit him to further crime and in begging him, "Fix me so I look good," Bateman understands that he can lay claim to normalcy or "goodness" only by "looking good." The soul, he intuits, is a creation of social categorization based largely on visible traits. Vollin's further deformation of Bateman augments the effects of this disciplinary gaze on Bateman. In pretending to "cure" Bateman, Vollin merely intensifies his patient's demarcation as aberrant, suggesting that medical efforts to make people "normal" and "whole" can in fact assist disciplinary subjugations of individuals and groups already seen as impaired.[18]

In particular, by forcing Bateman back toward criminality, Vollin's operation literalizes the disciplinary production and constraint of those deemed "delinquent." Foucault argues that as social structures shifted from identifying and punishing criminal acts to diagnosing and treating the criminal, they also generated a category of delinquents whose abnormal "souls" differentiated them from normal individuals. The supposed failure of the prison system to prevent recidivism, Foucault argues, in fact indicates "that the prison, and no doubt punishment in general, is not intended to eliminate offences, but rather to distinguish them, to use them." In "producing the delinquent as a pathologized subject," disciplinary power *uses* delinquency, domesticating radical challenges to power and class structures by containing and directing violent crime.[19] Vollin's surgery on Bateman's face secures the doctor's ability to foster and direct his patient's criminality. The film thus conjoins the criminalization of impairment and the pathologization of criminality, recasting diagnosis and "cure" as acts underwriting a system that exploits marginal individuals.

The moment of revelation after Bateman's surgery emphasizes the alliance between the medical gaze and the power dynamics of the panoptic prison. After Vollin removes the bandages, Bateman asks to see himself. Vollin leaves him in the operating room where, moments later, a series of curtains pulls open, one after the other, each revealing a full-length mirror. Confused and horrified, Bateman whirls around to confront his new and hideous face in mirror after mirror (fig. 4.2), before using his gun to shoot and shatter his reflections, while Vollin mocks him from a trapdoor opening in the ceiling. The scene portrays Vollin as the all-seeing doctor/warder and Bateman as the prisoner compelled to regard his own reflection, the pathological and internalized self-image. The criminal's gesture of violent rage shatters the images but cannot fashion a new self, and Bateman is forced to become the deformed delinquent of Vollin's making.

*Mad Love* similarly depicts a doctor's deliberate disabling of a patient in an effort to produce a pathologized, criminal "soul." Gogol's "cure" for Stephen's damaged hands is also disabling, for the pianist not only fails to recapture his musical capabilities but seems unable to control his hands' tendency to throw pens and knives in moments of anger. The film thus apparently confirms bodily aberrance as a sign of inner deviance: Rollo's innately criminal, violent soul has left its mark on his hands. But the transference of that criminality to Stephen via Rollo's hands mobilizes a more complex logic. The source of Stephen's increasingly erratic behavior is

**4.2** Offscreen, Dr. Vollin orchestrates the mirrors' revelation of Bateman's (Boris Karloff's) disfigurement in *The Raven* (1935).

not, the film hints, physical or biological but rather lies with "the power of suggestion." Initially, Gogol deceives Stephen, telling him that his hands are his own and explaining their deviance with a pseudo-Freudian spiel about "arrested wish-fulfillment" linked to a childhood desire to throw knives. This suggestion holds that cure is facilitated by the expurgation of inner—in this case, psychological—defect, as Gogol instructs Stephen, "If you could bring that forgotten memory, whatever it is, into consciousness, you would be cured instantly." But such logic is undermined when Gogol describes his comments to his assistant as "a lot of nonsense I don't believe myself." He continues, "I didn't dare to tell him his hands are those of a murderer. That would probably drive him . . . to commit murder himself." In this moment, Gogol realizes the power of diagnosis to bring about the very condition it purports to describe. Soon after, stung by Yvonne's disgusted rejection of his advances, Gogol experiences a hallucination of his own image telling him to employ "the power of suggestion" to destroy Stephen and win Yvonne. Gogol murders Stephen's father and then, donning a disguise, presents himself to Stephen as the reincarnated Rollo, convincing the hapless pianist that his substitute hands have murdered his own father.

In invoking the powers of suggestion, *Mad Love* indicates that medical diagnoses and administrations can engender in patients the defects they supposedly discover. A montage sequence of Stephen's "rehabilitation," showing a repeated prodding, poking, rubbing, and X-raying of his hands, augments rather than diminishes their apparent monstrosity, indicating again the capacity of medical intervention to generate deviance. Accordingly, Stephen's violent behavior seems less a matter of innate defect embedded in the hands themselves and more the result of suggestive influence and "treatments" that produce monstrosity.[20] A *Daily Variety* review of the film demonstrates this reading. Beginning with incredulity, the review opined, "If an audience can accept this premise that an urge to kill resides in a man's digits instead of his soul, then the rest of the fabulous development becomes acceptable." However, the article concludes, "the story finally relies on murderous suggestion implanted in Clive by Peter Lorre."[21] Such a commentary both takes for granted a disciplinary model in which the "soul" dictates and explains bodily appearance and behavior and, seemingly contradictorily, suggests that such a "soul" may be "implanted."

The same kind of inconsistencies inform Gogol's plan. It certainly relies on Stephen's own belief that biology faithfully reflects abstract inner qualities—that Rollo's violent and criminal tendencies are replicated in the hands that are now Stephen's. But it also depends on Stephen's failure to question the process by which external actions and alterations to his body—such as the attachment of Rollo's hands—are nonetheless believed capable of investing *him* with a criminal and abnormal soul. No coherent narrative of bodily function is possible: the film simultaneously champions the body as a manifestation of the soul, the soul as the product of disciplining a body, body parts as material entities with independent drives, and the body as subject to mental impressions generated by both witnessed events and fictional narratives.

Mad-doctor films thus often refuse to explain or "fix" disability. Such films' doctors certainly present and exploit reductive narratives, relying on their patients' belief that physical disability originates in the mind or soul and, thus, that embodied defect signifies innate mental or moral disturbance. But the ability of Vollin and Gogol to project their fantasies onto others' bodies through material inscriptions that in turn create "criminal" selves or souls suggests the indistinct boundaries, the mutually informing relationships connecting bodies, minds, souls, and disciplinary systems. These films validate the apparently contradictory notions of, on the one hand, a self shaped and defined by bodily experiences and, on the other, a noncorporeal and transcendent "self" that is, or can be strategically viewed as, distinct from one's bodily impairments and pains.[22]

Vollin's and Gogol's powers reside in the fact that they understand these nuances while others do not; they willfully exploit others' beliefs in simplistic correlations between physical defect and internal abnormalities.

But the doctors also fail to recognize that, even as they occupy the position of vision and power, they, too, are subject to the material effects of their own reductive fictions. In Foucault's Panopticon, power is not securely possessed by select individuals but operates "in a certain concerted distribution of bodies, surfaces, lights, gazes, in an arrangement whose internal mechanisms produce the relation in which individuals are caught up." The gaze of the authority figure, while it may assist him in the exercise of power, also enmeshes him in the system's "internal mechanisms": "[E]nclosed as he is in the middle of this architectural mechanism, is not the director's own fate entirely bound up with it? The incompetent physician who has allowed contagion to spread, the incompetent prison governor or workshop manager will be the first victims of an epidemic or a revolt."[23] Both Vollin and Gogol are eventually subjected to "revolts" that confirm the disciplinary politics they have endorsed. In The Raven, Bateman struggles with Vollin until both men are trapped in one of the doctor's own torture devices, a room whose walls close in to crush its inhabitants. The room literalizes the entrapment of both seer and seen, doctor and patient, within the carceral effects of disciplinary power. In Mad Love, Gogol is duped by the kind of masquerade he himself has perpetrated when, unbeknownst to him, Yvonne is cornered in his drawing room and forced to act as her own wax statue. Distracted by the love object that has apparently come alive, and attempting to preserve her by strangling her, Gogol is killed by Stephen, who throws a knife in his back. The disciplining of Stephen's mind and body has certainly not been ineffective: just as Gogol predicts, Stephen finds himself driven to murder. But, enclosed with Stephen in the "architectural mechanism" of the medical gaze and the impaired body, Gogol, like the incompetent warden or physician imagined by Foucault, is the "first victim" of the disability masquerade he sets in motion.

The mad doctors of horror films thus not only wield the medical gaze but are also, eventually, subjected to its disciplinary measures. In the course of the film, they embody both the seer and the seen, the medical figure of authority and the monster whom the pathologizing gaze objectifies. This duality—the intimate relationship between the medical gazer who projects and directs the disability spectacle and the monster or patient whose body constitutes the star attraction—is nowhere more evident than in films where the doctor or scientist quite literally makes himself into a monster. In a film such as The Invisible Man, for instance, the scientist Jack Griffin erases his own body from sight to more effectively wield a disciplinary gaze, damage others' bodies, and claim a position of privilege and power. However, despite his aspirations to power through invisibility, Griffin finds himself hunted, objectified, perceived as monstrous, and, eventually, fatally impaired. In presenting Griffin's invisibility as a path not to transcendence but to debility, and in conflating power and disability within a single body, the film insists that invisible privilege is closely allied to the visualization and marking of "aberrant" or "inferior" bodies. Moreover, in emphasizing the corporeality of even the Invisible Man, the film presents able-bodiedness as a temporary and unstable identity under constant threat from the disability it demonizes.

## INVISIBLE PRIVILEGE: DISABILITY IN *THE INVISIBLE MAN*

H. G. Wells' 1897 novel *The Invisible Man* might seem to run precisely counter to the visualization of impairment, insofar as its aberrant figure goes unseen for almost the entire narrative. In the book, young scientist Griffin, having succeeded in experiments that have made him invisible, arrives in the village of Iping swaddled in a coat, hat, pair of glasses, and fake nose and settles in to discover an antidote that will return him to visibility. Goaded by the villagers' prying, he reveals his secret and goes on a violent rampage, eventually seeking refuge in a house that, coincidentally, belongs to a former university acquaintance, Professor Kemp. Griffin solicits Kemp to help him unleash a "reign of terror" but, when Kemp betrays him, tries to murder the professor.[24] He is eventually trapped and attacked by Kemp and a group of townspeople, becoming visible as he dies of his injuries.

Despite—or because of—the character's invisibility, however, corporeal aberrance plays a central role in the novel. Two particular moments indicate the plot's dependence on physical deformity. In the first instance, Griffin describes himself to Kemp as "a younger student, almost an albino, six feet high, and broad, with a pink and white face and red eyes" (89). It is his albinism, he explains, that makes his invisibility possible, for skin and hair pigmentation remain the only bodily elements he cannot render transparent. Griffin's physical disorder thus appears as evidence of an innate psychological defect also manifested in his mad experiments, his violent and erratic behavior, and his invisibility. In the second instance, at the end of the novel, Griffin's deformity is made apparent—both to other characters and the audience—when his dead body is revealed as "naked and pitiful" and "bruised and broken," his hair and beard uncovered as "white with the whiteness of albinism," and his exposed eyes likened to "garnets" (169).

The Invisible Man is refashioned as a pitiful spectacle whose physiological deviance testifies to his irredeemable madness and whose threat is contained only when everyone can *see* his aberrant body.

Nonetheless, the unreliability of the gaze that understands visible difference as inner defect is always foregrounded in the novel and, to an even greater extent, in James Whale's 1933 movie adaptation of *The Invisible Man* for Universal. The book suggests that Griffin is only impaired to the extent that curious onlookers view him as such, deducing from his bandages and coverings that he has "had an accident or an operation or something" or that he's a patchy "piebald" who might "show enself at fairs." The novel accentuates the compromised nature of the gaze that scans Griffin's disguised form for defect: his landlady's perception that he has "an enormous mouth wide open" arises at a time when "[e]verything was ruddy, shadowy, and indistinct to her, the more so since she had just been lighting the bar lamp, and her eyes were frazzled" (5, 22, 8). In dispensing with the device of albinism, James Whale's 1933 film more explicitly presents Griffin's condition as a matter of external influence and social construction. The swiftness and inaccuracy with which characters "diagnose" Griffin (Claude Rains) is again evident: the suspicious landlady Jenny Hall (Una O'Connor), like her counterpart in the novel, attributes the stranger's bandages to an "'orrible accident," a bystander describes him as "a raving lunatic," and, confronted by an uncovered Invisible Man, Constable Jaffers (E. E. Clive) declares him "all eaten away." Soon after, the constable gets things right, asserting "He's invisible, that's what's the matter with him!" although his presentation of invisibility as something that is "the matter" clearly understands it as a defect. The film soon turns such pathologizing judgments against the villagers, when a radio broadcast describes Iping's inhabitants as the victims of a "mysterious disease" that "takes the form of a delusion that an invisible man is living among them." Diagnoses of mental and physical debility thus appear as knee-jerk and often inaccurate reactions to unusual appearances.

If, in the novel, albinism might be seen as an exterior symptom that "proves" Griffin's character flaw, Whale's *The Invisible Man,* like the *Dr. Jekyll and Mr. Hyde* films, presents its protagonist's disability as something that operates from the exterior inwards. The film explains Griffin's invisibility and his madness as the result of his injection of the mysterious Indian drug "monocaine." When Griffin's employer, benevolent scientist Dr. Cranley (Henry Travers), discovers a list of chemicals left by Griffin, he tells Griffin's unlikable colleague Dr. Arthur Kemp (William Harrigan) that monocaine "is a terrible drug" that "draws color from everything it touches." He describes an experiment in which the drug turned a dog "dead white, like a marble statue" and "also sent it raving mad." Griffin's albinism and his madness are refashioned as artificially produced conditions, as the film presents the possibility that legitimate experimentation—which Griffin later explains was motivated by his poverty and his desire to become economically stable for his fiancée Flora (Gloria Stuart), Cranley's daughter—has transformed the scientist from the outside in.

Wells construed this alteration to his text, and particularly the representation of Griffin as "mad," as an unwelcome pathologization of his own eccentric but sane protagonist. He testily declared that he preferred a story about "the inherent monstrosity of an ordinary man in this extraordinary position" to one about "an Invisible Lunatic." Whale responded, "If a man said to you that he was about to make himself invisible, would you think he was crazy already?"[25] Whale's comment may imply that only a preexisting tendency to insanity could explain Griffin's experiments. But his phrasing actually emphasizes not innate degeneracy but the matter of its perception: the question is not whether a man aspiring to invisibility *is* insane but only whether *you think* he is. As both novel and film intimate, *believing* that the Invisible Man is impaired and insane is enough to make him so: the film's Griffin declares exasperatedly to the villagers, "You've left me near madness, with your peering through the keyholes and peeping through the curtains!" The film thus illuminates the compromised and subjective gazing that transforms impairment into a disabling experience.

It is the desire to escape such objectification—and, indeed, to become its agent rather than its victim—that motivates Griffin's desire for invisibility in the novel. To evade the disciplinary gazes of the prying public, as well as creditors and policemen, is, he presumes, to attain transcendent heights: "I beheld, unclouded by doubt, a magnificent vision of all that invisibility might mean to a man,—the mystery, the power, the freedom." He describes his initial experience of invisibility in the streets of London as one of able-bodiedness amongst the impaired: "I felt as a seeing man might do, with padded feet and noiseless clothes, in a city of the blind" (104, 116).[26] Griffin's experiments thus place him in the position of the "faceless gaze" described by Foucault that exercises power through surveillance.[27] In the movie, Griffin has the same aspirations, convinced that his invisibility will give him the power to discipline and punish. He exclaims to the astonished villagers, "An invisible man can rule the world! Nobody will see him come. Nobody will see him go. He can hear every secret. He can rob and wreck and kill!" To Kemp, he confides, "Suddenly I realized the power I held. The power to rule, to make the world grovel at my feet." And even to Flora, who begs her fiancé to abandon his plans, the Invisible Man gloats, "I shall offer my secret to the world, with all its terrible power. The nations of the world will bid for it—thousands, millions. The nation that wins my secret can sweep the world with invisible armies!" The power of Griffin's invisible gaze, accentuated in several scenes by the dark sunglasses or goggles that he wears, is evident even in his absence: on more than one occasion, anxious characters remind one another that the Invisible Man might be standing in their midst, an observation that unfailingly generates nervous glances and frightened movements.

The Invisible Man's pretensions to power via invisibility reveal the nature of privilege as an evasion of disciplinary gazes and objectification. Recent studies have argued that dominant groups are unmarked because their members do not consider themselves as, for instance, racialized or gendered. Whiteness, masculinity, and heterosexuality function as transparent norms, in contrast to identities "marked" as black, female, or homosexual. Writes Richard Dyer, "As long as race is something only applied to non-white peoples, as long as white people are not racially seen and named, they/we function as a human norm. . . . At the level of racial representation, in other words, whites are not of a certain race, they're just the human race."[28] But invisibility is predicated on others' visibility, and the erasure of whiteness as a racial category is dependent on the conscription of other bodies. This dynamic is aptly represented in a novel whose title suggests its shared themes with Wells' and Whale's texts: Ralph Ellison's *Invisible Man*. Ellison's narrator is instructed to stir ten drops of a black substance into "Optic White" paint to make it, in the words of his employer, "'as white as George Washington's Sunday-go-to-meetin' wig and as sound as the all-mighty dollar! . . . the purest white that can be found!'"[29] The paint's absorption of the mysterious liquid both utilizes and erases blackness in order to make white seem whiter. The scene illustrates the "use" of blackness to create an American-ness whose freedom and presumed whiteness is underwritten by black exploitation. In the same way, Toni Morrison has argued, canonical American literature employs an "Africanist persona" ("the image of reined-in, bound, suppressed, and repressed darkness") to perform "duties of exorcism and reification and mirroring" that enable the "construction of the American as a new white man."[30] Images of whiteness as norm thus depend heavily on representations of blackness as a specific racial identity associated with the qualities abjected from the (white) American national body.

Whale's *The Invisible Man*, despite its apparent distance from American racial frictions, invokes the aesthetic politics of race in its tropes of visibility and invisibility. Dr. Cranley's comment that monocaine "draws color from everything it touches" and thus turns a dog "dead white" reflects a common understanding of whiteness as a *lack* of color, transparency, rather than a specific racial identity. Griffin's invisibility takes this logic to an extreme: he is of no color, no apparent race. Moreover, his invisibility is immediately recognized, by all those who are *not* literally invisible, as an unjust and dangerous privilege that frees him to wreak violence and mayhem on the visible. Indeed, Griffin manifests whiteness as it often appears from the perspective of those lacking racial privilege: bell hooks argues that mythic associations of whiteness with goodness and blackness with evil or danger are disrupted by "the way whiteness makes its presence felt in black life, most often as a terrorising imposition, a power that wounds, hurts, tortures."[31] In becoming an unseen source of terror and violence for others, Griffin makes visible, and quite literal, the operations of invisible privilege.

The movie also demonstrates the dependence of whiteness—and its claims to invisibility—on rhetorical and visual tropes of blackness. Griffin himself first demonstrates the manner in which "marking" a body with blackness effectively subjugates it and confirms the power of the privileged. While invisible, he throws a jar of black ink at a police officer so that its contents drip down his face. The act, which associates blackness with visibility, presages the destruction of the policeman, who is immediately murdered by Griffin. Authorities seek to mark and destroy Griffin in the same manner, taking the advice of a caller who counsels, "You get your own back, and splash ink about with a hose pipe until you hit him. The ink'll stick on him, see? Then you can shoot him." The police plan a stakeout in which they will spray Griffin with a black liquid: "One splash of this on his skin and we've got something to follow at last!" The efficacy of the technique is demonstrated by extensively blackening a white sheet, but the only creature thus entrapped is a small white cat that, once painted, becomes virtually invisible against the night sky. To "blacken," then, is a technique that both renders visible, in order to capture and control, and erases, eliding the existence of the marked individual.

*The Invisible Man* illuminates a similar paradox at work in the experience and perception of disability. As we have seen, the construction of people with evident impairments as objects of surveillance often serves as a trap.[32] Bodily difference is deemed abnormal and used to justify disabled people's constant subjection to the pathologizing medical gaze, to pervasive stereotyping, and to the quotidian "stare" of the public eye. Yet this relentless visibility comes attached to and reproduces a certain social and political *in*visibility. Increasing medicalization, having segregated people with disabilities into institutions and out of public sight, renders them "invisible," insofar as their needs and desires are politically, economically, and socially overlooked.[33] This simultaneous objectification and erasure serves the production of an unmarked and purportedly universal norm, akin to whiteness: "Much in the same way that 'whiteness' is an invisible insignia of the norm, 'ablebodiedness' is also an unquestioned, unremarked upon state which only becomes notable in its absence."[34]

The interrelation of race and disability is suggested in the novel's figure of the albino, which combines visible physical aberrance with an exceptional form of racial privilege. In intensifying the visual appearance of whiteness, albinism corporealizes a typically unmarked racial identity. At the same time, given that albinos have been born into non-white families, such pigment disorders throw into doubt racial categories grounded in physical and epidermal features. Moreover, insofar as albinism is perceived as a bodily aberration, it reinvents whiteness as a marked and abject trope, suggesting the artificiality and instability of invisible norms.

Whale's *The Invisible Man*, while eschewing the device of albinism, enacts a similar strategy in its concluding scenes, where both invisibility and whiteness are associated with Griffin's corporeal debilitation. Although the scientist evades the efforts to "blacken" his body and remains invisible, authorities are able to track him by indexical signs of his physical presence, including his snoring in a hay barn and his footprints as he escapes the barn. The indentations of Griffin's feet in white, newly fallen snow enable police to shoot him, leading to the indentations of his invisible form on the white sheets and pillow of his hospital bed. The preeminence of whiteness in these concluding scenes, associated with the apparition of Griffin's pale visage as he expires, suggests the return of whiteness as a corporeal and deadly force: the Invisible Man's experiments have, as his employer worried, left him insane and "dead white."[35]

To an even greater extent than Vollin and Gogol, who only seek out debility vicariously and who are unwittingly trapped by their own experiments, Griffin deliberately imposes on himself the physiological and psychological debilitation often rendered by the medical gaze. Further, while in the novel the Invisible Man bemoans the fact that clothes or food consumption render him partially visible, "mak[ing] of [him]self a strange and terrible thing," in the movie he seems to embrace such liminal and shocking moments, gleefully dancing around in only a shirt or donning a pair of pants to chase a shrieking woman down a country road. Indeed, conscious of his power to horrify through his abnormal appearance, Griffin turns his unveiling into a theatrical moment, crying "There's a souvenir for you!" as he tosses his plastic nose to the floor, and reveling in the anticipation that his undressing will give "the country bumpkins" a shock and provide "[a] nice bedtime story for the kids." Griffin's enthusiasm for his monstrous role both indicates the performative aspects of medical displays of the disabled body and suggests that mad doctors at some level covet a direct experience of the debility and aberrance whose careful staging has underwritten their privilege and prestige. The film thus glimpses the possibility that the construction of disability as something that should not be seen in a public space gives it the quality of a forbidden and perverse pleasure for those commissioned to police normalcy and eradicate bodily and behavioral aberrance.

In mad-doctor films, it is this desire not only to cause but also to experience bodily impairment that becomes the quintessential symptom of the doctor's madness and the justification for his punishment. The apparent impossibility of at once wielding the gaze that produces its object as monstrous *and* inhabiting the place of that monstrous object is contested in a scenario that recurs within the subgenre: the mirror scene. In gazing at his reflection, the mad doctor renders himself both agent and object of his medicalizing and monster-making gaze. To the extent that the desire to occupy the place of the abjected and impaired individual is seen as deviant, these mirror scenes also serve to make visible—to produce—the inner psychological aberrance of the doctor figure. Just as the monster is produced out of the objectifying disciplinary-medical gaze, rendered pathological and criminal merely because it inhabits an anomalous body, so the mad doctor is produced—by the film itself—as a visibly pathological case. When the *Daily Variety* reviewer wrote of *Mad Love*, "Lorre's shaven head seems to expose a naked soul full of macabre lusts," he applied a physiognomist's (or phrenologist's) eye to Gogol's skull, from which he deduced the character's abnormal soul.[36] Similarly, when mad-doctor films present their crazed physicians and scientists as already visibly impaired—like, for instance, the variously scarred, wheelchair-using, and one-armed doctors of *Doctor X*—they impose on these characters the same hallmarks of delinquency and madness that the modern medical state—and certainly American eugenics—"discovers" in marginalized groups. If, then, the film's punishment of the doctor for his monstrous medical exploits inheres in his objectification as impaired, it seems to sit at odds with the filmic narrative's apparent criticism of exactly that objectifying process. But the virtuosity of the filmic staging and special effects required by these mirror scenes suggests a certain cinematic reflexivity, which points out to viewers their own fraught ethical position as they gaze both with and at the mad doctor.

## THROUGH THE LOOKING GLASS: HOW THE MOVIES MAKE DOCTORS MAD

Classic horror's mad doctors are a vain bunch. In the 1920 silent film *Dr. Jekyll and Mr. Hyde*, John Barrymore's Jekyll, having transformed into his crabbed alter ego Hyde for the first time, risks discovery to glimpse his own reflection, sneaking at night out of his laboratory, across the courtyard, and into his house to discover a wall mirror and admire his new form. Once restored to himself, Jekyll asks his butler to place a full-length mirror in his laboratory, to make future self-regard more convenient. The request indicates that his mutations will not seem real unless he can apprehend his body visually, as an object separate from his own corporeal and sensorial experience. But if Jekyll—and many of his mad-doctor colleagues— find confirmations of reality in the mirror image, the film spectator discovers that such mirror scenes question the visual strategies used to project degeneracy. The staging of such scenes often points to the artistry and trickery required to convince audiences that they are looking at a doctor who is patently, visibly, mad.

The image of the individual before the mirror often represents a crystallizing moment in the construction, perception, or projection of identity. In Lacan's schema of subjectivity, for example, the "mirror stage" constitutes the Imaginary phase in which the infant, still lacking control over his motor functions, views his reflection as an autonomous and controlled self, a fiction that facilitates his sense of identity.[37] As already noted, Lennard Davis valuably argues that this scenario depicts the chaotic body as primary in the subject's experience and the "normal" body as a secondary fabrication and disguise.[38] For mad doctors, then, the mirror reflects the idealized self they seek to inhabit or perform successfully. But it also reveals the obverse of that unified image, the visibly aberrant and chaotic self, whose dysfunction and monstrosity the mad doctor is compelled to embrace.[39]

Thus, *Mad Love*'s mirror scene both illustrates the normative and respectable identity Gogol seeks to inhabit and confirms his insanity by giving it visible and audible form. After Yvonne reviles him as a disgusting liar and a hypocrite, Gogol walks in a dejected trance to an operation. Mechanically taking up the scalpel, he prepares to cut into his young female patient but jumps when he "hears" Yvonne's voice again denouncing him. As he stares around the room, distorted point-of-view shots convey his unsteady vision. Looking faint, Gogol staggers into an adjoining room, shedding his surgical mask and gloves. He stands at a sink in front of a mirror, rubbing his face. When he opens his eyes, he sees in the mirror a version of himself, still wearing his mask and gloves, who tells him, "They are laughing at you in there!" and urges him to return to the operation. But the same voice quickly cries from another part of the room, "Let them laugh!" Gogol whirls around to see his reflection in an angled full-length mirror, standing in the room's corner (fig. 4.3). As he moves toward this mirror, his reflection is replaced by an image of himself in a dark suit, admonishing him that all that matters is Yvonne. As he stares, his voice emerges from yet another location, and he turns and crosses to a third mirror, positioned above his head and angled downward, where he appears in slightly different form, wearing a dark, fur-trimmed coat and black dress-hat. It is this mirror image that introduces the idea of the "power of suggestion," noting to the apparently hallucinatory Gogol, "See how easy it is? Already working . . . "

On the one hand, this scene illustrates a more or less "normative" process of subjective identity, as the mirror offers to Gogol idealized images of himself as a confident and expensively dressed gentleman. On the other, the scene manifests Gogol's insanity, conjuring the talking mirror images as evidence of his delusions. This apparent contradiction hints at the "madness" and mirage inherent even in normative identity, wherein the experience of the body as incomplete and uncontrolled is denied by the fiction of the normal self. But the scene goes further, implying the power of illusory and manipulated images to affect "real" bodily experience. Gogol adopts the suggestion of his mirror image by costuming himself as the dead Rollo, donning a hat, sunglasses, gleaming metal hands and forearms, and a neck brace. The outrageous ensemble, which convinces Stephen that Rollo has returned from the dead to indict him for murdering his own father, conveys the power of bodily fictions and surface aesthetics to influence the suggestible spectator. When Gogol's "reflection" says, "See how easy it is? Already working," it sets up a parallel between the mirror images, whose suggestions "work" on Gogol, and Gogol's masquerade as Rollo, which "works" on Stephen.

Thus, even as Gogol's changing reflections are presented as visible, external symptoms produced by internal madness—real "proof" of his dysfunction—they are also clearly marked as figments and deceptions. The illusory status of the images is indicated not only by their references to the "power of suggestion" but also by the scene's self-conscious composition. At one point, Gogol's "actual" body vanishes entirely, while his reflection appears fully in one mirror, is seen partially in a second mirror

**4.3** Dr. Gogol's (Peter Lorre's) body is absent from the shot but multiply mirrored in front, behind, and in the top-left of the screen in *Mad Love* (1935).

that reflects the first, and is barely glimpsed in an angled overhead mirror at the very upper-left edge of the shot. As noted in chapter 3, Christian Metz has suggested that scenes representing screens and mirrors engage a kind of reflexivity, foregrounding as they do the spectacle of film itself.[40] The disconcerting, doubling, and eliding effects of this mirror scene thus remind the audience of the framing techniques used to produce specters of deviance, which simultaneously mimic and erase the "actual" body of the impaired subject.

If the mirror images thus constitute a kind of deception, they are designed to mislead not only Gogol but, more importantly, the film audience for whom they are displayed. Insofar as the reflections are fabricated *by the film itself* for the sole purpose of convincing the audience of Gogol's insanity, that audience is aligned with both Gogol and Stephen as a gullible spectator. Accordingly, viewers are implicated, like Charcot, in the medicalized interpretation of manufactured body signs as pathological symptoms. At the same time, viewers are themselves pathologized, for if both Stephen and Gogol are mad to believe and act on these somatic spectacles, the audience is mad to believe that these cinematic phantoms prove Gogol's innate psychological dysfunction. The mirror scene thus works to reproduce the film audience *as* the simultaneously pathologizing and pathologized mad doctor.

*Mad Love*'s use of mirrors to point out the audience's complicity in bodily spectacles shares common ground with other visual texts that interrogate aesthetic politics through the use of reflecting surfaces. For example, the seventeenth-century painting *Las Meninas* (*The Maids of Honor*) by Diego Velázquez, analyzed at some length by Foucault, at first glance offers as its center-point the Infanta Margarita. The princess is flanked by her courtiers and ladies-in-waiting, while to her right stands the painter himself, having stepped away from a large canvas whose angled back faces the viewer. Several of these figures stare out at the viewer, whose attention is drawn to a second and more properly central point. On the rear wall of the depicted room, beneath and alongside several indistinct paintings, hangs a mirror, in which two figures are distantly reflected. The mirror, we are to understand, reflects the royal couple, King Philip IV and Queen Mariana, the presumed focus of the other figures' gaze and the likely subject of the unseen painting within the painting. The mirror thus proffers a glimpse of what most images cannot represent: the bodies and gazes of those for whom the image is organized. At the same time, as Foucault notes, it also withholds representation of those others who must also occupy that central location: the artist and the painting's viewer.[41]

Peggy Phelan expands on Foucault's reading, asserting that the mirror in the painting, according to the rules of Renaissance and theatrical perspective, constitutes the "vanishing point" where parallel lines converge to provide an illusion of reality and depth. The vanishing point, Phelan comments, "presuppose[s] a parallel point outside the frame called the viewing point" and thus uses "the composition inside the frame" to construct "spectatorial space outside the frame."[42] In *Las Meninas*, as in *Mad Love*, the reflection figures those who are physically absent from the image and yet thoroughly framed within it. The sovereign couple, like Gogol, both seems to orchestrate its own reflection—it is the couple's invisible gaze to which the scene is oriented—and to be subjected by it, captured at its central point. As well, the viewer, aligned with the King and Queen, is positioned as both sovereign gazer and multiply framed object, all the more disconcertingly given that the mirror's reflection diverges from his/her own perceived bodily appearance.

While, in the *Mad Love* scene, the movie spectator never occupies Gogol's perspective, the screen nonetheless employs the illusion of depth in ways that implicate the viewer. First, the proliferation of mirrors and their reflections reminds the viewer that just as gazing into a mirror provides an illusory sense of depth on what is in fact a flat surface, so film-watching requires a belief—or, at least, a suspension of disbelief—in the depth of the depictions projected onto a flat screen. Second, as Phelan notes, a major effect of perspectives organized around the vanishing point is "the construction of depth . . . [,] the 'invention' of physical interiority and psychic subjectivity."[43] Just as the mirror in *Las Meninas* provides a sense of depth that reaches beyond the painting to the spectator, so the mirror images of Gogol provide for the film viewer the perception of Gogol's psychic depths. But insofar as those depths are represented as delusional, the correspondence between bodily representation and the viewer's own interior subjectivity is uncovered as hallucinatory. In both texts, it is precisely the disjunction between the mirror image and the body it should reflect that points out for viewers their "mad" faith that these figures should neatly correspond.

The illusions procured by the vanishing point are even more evident in the mirror scene depicted in *The Invisible Man*. Having costumed himself to put Kemp more at ease, Griffin wears pajamas and slippers, a robe, gloves, a long surgical bandage wound around his face with holes for the eyes and mouth, and a pair of sunglasses. After sending Kemp to bed, Griffin begins to undress, shedding his robe before a wall mirror over a small table. Staring into the mirror, he unwinds the facial bandage with his gloved hands (fig. 4.4), revealing the nothingness beneath. In the next shot, a seemingly headless and handless Griffin drops the bandage onto the dressing table and, still wearing the pajamas, crosses on invisible feet to his bed. In earlier

**4.4** The spectacle of the mad doctor (Claude Rains) and his invisible image in *The Invisible Man* (1933).

scenes, as noted above, Griffin has unveiled his invisible self for a diegetic audience. Here, however, he is alone, which again suggests that the film's audience is being directly addressed by the scene's astonishing—and non-narrative—spectacle.[44]

Once more, the audience is encouraged to recognize its own visual deception. In the preceding scene, a bystander announces of reports about the Invisible Man, "It's a conjuring trick, that's what it is! I saw a man make a peanut disappear once." The mirror scene is the cinematic equivalent of a conjuring trick, one of several enacted by the film's director of special effects, John P. Fulton, and his team.[45] The movie's invisible spectacles were achieved in two different ways. In scenes where Griffin was entirely invisible, wires were used to transport objects supposedly moved by Griffin. But in scenes where Griffin was wearing clothes and thus partly visible, a separate shot was required. The "missing" body parts were covered in black velvet and Rains was filmed against a black velvet background. The resultant image was later combined with a shot of the set and the other actors, giving the illusion of a semi-invisible man.[46] The mirror scene required the greatest artistic effort. Because the glass doubled Rains's appearance, the scene entailed four different shots: the "real world" image constituted a shot of the back view of the Invisible Man as he unwrapped his head and another of the room in which he stood, while the reflected image required a shot of the Invisible Man's front and another of the room as reflected in the mirror. All four shots were later combined to create the overall illusion. To the extent that the scene presents itself as a spectacle for consumption— framing, reflecting, and doubling the object of our amazement—and to the extent that it constitutes one of the most virtuosic visual effects of the film, it clearly raises the specter of its own nature as a "conjuring trick."

The Invisible Man's reflection does not occupy the central "vanishing point" of the scene in the same way as the sovereign couple's reflection in *Las Meninas*. Nor does the "actual" body of Griffin vanish momentarily like Gogol's in the *Mad Love* mirror scene. The viewer sees at all times, and from the side, both Griffin's body and its mirror image. But the scene's staging of bodily revelation as in fact an erasure again registers the elision of "actual" bodily experience facilitated by medical reflections and projections and by the spectator's willingness to grant depth and reality to such manipulated performances. Like the King and Queen, whose sovereignty "cannot be rendered except as reflected in the gaze of their subjects" and is sustained by "theatrical props" such as "dogs, maids, courtiers, children, artists," the Invisible Man, at once the agent and impaired object of this spectacle, is shown as the product of props and sleight of hand.[47] Both his power and his debilitating aberrance are revealed as a matter of fabric and bandages, carefully staged—by a special effects director often called "The Doctor"—for an audience willing to be deluded.[48] Where there is, in fact, a body, we are tricked into seeing nothing; where there is, in fact, nothing except the vanishing point that is our own gaze, we believe we see manifested the interior aberrance of a mad doctor.

The persistence of medical processes of visualization in horror films' mirror scenes links the concept of the "vanishing point" to the normalizing and curative impetus that so often both demonizes and erases the disabled body. Johnson Cheu argues that the "vanishing point" has significance for disability performances:

> The vanishing point in painting and performance presumes an illusionary point of convergence between viewer and performer, and thus allows a viewer to add "depth" at the vanishing point. In disability performance, I suggest, medical cure serves as the "vanishing point" because it is the proverbial convergence where medicine and the disabled body appear to intersect. . . . In other words, medical cure, the possibility of a "normal" body, is a *perspective* that is assigned by the able-bodied viewer to the disabled body. . . . [I]t is the able-bodied viewer who assigns desire for normalcy, achievable through medical cure, to the disabled body. . . . [T]he moment of medical cure becomes the point at which the disabled body, as corporeal entity and as performative signifier, supposedly vanishes to become reconstructed as whole, cured, normal, and so forth.

Cheu focuses on the performances of disabled people whose impaired bodies refuse to "vanish" in the service of a normalizing cure, a resistance which means that "medi[c]al cure, as a dimension of how disability is constructed and represented, becomes more visible and more solid to the audience."[49] That is, such performances ensure that the "invisible norm" of cure, rather than the seemingly self-evident deviance of disability, becomes visible and is held up to the scrutiny of the audience whose perspective has, in the first place, helped to both produce and elide that norm.

Cure and normalcy become similarly visible in our final mirror scene, drawn from Rouben Mamoulian's *Dr. Jekyll and Mr. Hyde* (1931). As discussed in chapter 3, the mirror plays a central role in Jekyll's transformations into Hyde; like his silent predecessor, Fredric March's Hyde staggers immediately to a mirror to confirm his existence and outward appearance, celebrating his evident deviance. The momentary use in this scene of a first-person perspective, in which we, the audience members, *become* Hyde looking at his reflection, again aligns viewers with the doctor-monster and indicts them in the visual production of monstrosity. But it is an earlier mirror scene that first reaches out to spectators and insists on their participation in the production of a stultifying and curative norm. From the moment that the opening credits fade, a first-person camera gives us Jekyll's own point of view. We look, with the as-yet-unseen Jekyll, down at the pipe-organ keys where his hands play the tune that has carried over from the credit sequence.[50] As the scene proceeds, we, with Jekyll, turn to gaze at the butler, Poole (Edgar Norton), who deferentially urges his master to hurry to his lecture at the university. After conversing with Poole, Jekyll moves out into a hallway, turning left toward his front door. Here, we get our first glimpse of Jekyll, sharing his gaze at his (our) reflection as Poole brings him a cape, hat, and cane and Jekyll dons them. The doctor then departs into the world to give his lecture; en route, a series of uniformed or suited men gaze at him (us) with respect and admiration, repeatedly addressing him (us) as "Sir." Arriving at his destination, Jekyll enters an auditorium filled with an excitedly murmuring audience, whose members gaze down expectantly at him (us). It is not until the doctor begins his lecture that the camera dispenses with this perspective and we look on him from an external point of view.

As in *Mad Love*, the image proffered by the mirror confirms for Jekyll his wealth and social standing. Indeed, the mirror's reflection of Jekyll's prestige is mimicked by the subsequent series of respectful, admiring, and awed faces that, in gazing at the doctor, project for him his own status and power. But the mirror scene also relentlessly documents the many props required to make up this ideal self-image. First, Jekyll's gaze reveals to us the ornate decorations of his home. Muscular statues, aristocratic portraits, white flowers, and tall white candles invoke the impermeable and beautiful classical body and encourage us to see the attractive Jekyll as a surface construction.[51] Second, the ritual of outfitting Jekyll undertaken by Poole accentuates the doctor's social role as a theatrical performance. Throughout the film, Jekyll is repeatedly shown taking off coats, capes, and other accessories, handing them to servants, and then reclaiming and re-donning them. Halberstam has suggested, in reference to the Robert Louis Stevenson novel, that "the grotesque effect of Gothic is achieved through a kind of transvestism, a dressing up that reveals itself as costume." She argues that Stevenson's text relies on "tropes of doubling and disguise," insofar as Hyde is both Jekyll's "foundation," hidden beneath the form of Jekyll, and also "the costume that Jekyll assumes at times." Consequently, Jekyll and Hyde "are cross-dressing monsters slipping in and out of each other's clothes."[52] But the mirror scene demonstrates that even before the manifestation of Hyde, the normal or idealized Jekyll is a careful bodily production and thus, to some extent, an illusion.[53]

Moreover, as with the mirror scenes of both *Mad Love* and *The Invisible Man,* Jekyll's self-regard is the product of cinematic and theatrical trickery. Because the first-person perspective is provided by replacing March with the camera, if "Jekyll" were to actually look in a mirror the viewer would be confronted only with the reflection of the camera and cameraman. Thus, the "mirror" for the scene is in fact merely an opening in the wall, something perhaps glimpsed by the astute viewer who notices that, as Poole moves ahead of Jekyll and passes the "mirror," his reflection does not appear. When Poole opens a door next to the "mirror" and enters a "closet" to fetch Jekyll's hat and cloak, he in fact passes into a room on the other side of the wall's opening. Both Jekyll and then Poole subsequently "appear" as mirror reflections simply by presenting themselves through the opening to the camera. Jekyll's body is at once absent, insofar as we occupy its location and see only his (our) reflection, and present, in the guise of a reflection. The viewer is again aligned with the body of the doctor and duped by a bodily spectacle. Here, however, the spectacle is that of apparent normality. The deceptive image is not that of the abnormal monster but the normative self-image the audience is presumed to desire. The scene's reliance on trickery, then, testifies not (only) to the construction that makes monstrosity out of physical difference, something that becomes more apparent in later representations of Hyde, but, more radically, the performative, theatrical, and self-deluding elements of normative identity.

As Cheu asserts, such normative perspective is closely aligned with the medical gaze and the impetus toward cure. Jekyll's idealized self-image is clearly dependent on his professional activities, most notably in scenes where he ministers to his charity patients. The doctor assures young Mary that she can walk without her crutches, admonishing, "If you don't believe me, I can't do anything for you." Mary anxiously declares, "I believe you, sir," but isn't convinced until Jekyll removes her crutches and she takes her first, hesitant steps toward him. As she repeatedly and melodramatically exclaims, "I can walk, sir!" her joyful gaze at Jekyll becomes her gaze at us, relayed through another first-person camera shot that underscores the adulation evinced by the doctor's curative powers. The image of Mary's face then dissolves into that of another patient being comforted by Jekyll: Mrs. Lucas, a bed-ridden, middle-aged woman. As he touches her stomach, she moans, and Jekyll says, sympathetically, "It hurts, doesn't it? Sometimes, a doctor must hurt you a little to make you well. . . . I want you to know what's going to cure you." Echoing Mary in the previous scene, Mrs. Luca declares fervently, "Oh, I believe you, sir."

In both scenes, the women become mirrors onto whom Jekyll projects his medical gaze and healing powers, their bodies and gazes reconfigured as materials with which he shores up his ideal vision of himself. Indeed, for Gogol, Vollin, and Jekyll, each of whom cures a girl who cannot walk, their remedying of disabled bodies anchors their perspectives of themselves as superlative doctors and powerful healers. The action of curing, particularly in the scene with Mary, takes center stage: through his diagnostic gaze, Jekyll denies the girl's knowledge of her own body, when she declares that she cannot walk, and through the power of his pronouncement, directs her body to perform normally. Again, however, we witness cure's alliance with the production of disability: Mary reacts almost hysterically to her rehabilitation, uttering breathy, moaning laughs, and walking stiffly with her bent arms raised, her clenched fists parallel with her head. Mary's desire to please the doctor, reminiscent of Charcot's female patients, thus motivates a drama of debility that masquerades as cure.

The mirror, these scenes suggest, reveals, if nothing else, the susceptibility of the body to visual perceptions. "Real" bodily effects are constantly generated by still-unexplained responses of the brain to illusive representations. It is a lesson that medicine has drafted into its curative practices: today, phantom limb pain is treated by "mirror therapy," wherein the reflection of the remaining leg tricks the patient's brain into thinking that the missing leg in fact exists, enabling her to "adjust" that limb and thus reduce discomfort.[54] But the dominance of visual techniques in medical perceptions all too often evacuates other bodily experiences, an effect illustrated in the "vanishing" tendencies of mad doctors before their mirrors. In considering human body consciousness, Sobchack discusses the phenomenon of proprioception, "that sixth and grounding sense we have of ourselves as positioned and embodied in worldly space. . . . [S]uch an image emerges not from the objective sight of our bodies (or directly from vision) but from the invisible and subjective *lived feeling* of our material being." Sobchack refers to a case discussed by Oliver Sacks in which a woman, losing her proprioception, was forced to reclaim her body only through visualization, "learn[ing] to use her eyes to position or, more aptly, pose her body in the world, to operate it and move it about as an objective thing." As a result, her posture became "'statuesque,' artful, forced, willful, histrionic; her voice, too, emerge[d] as stagy and theatrical, the voice of a performer."[55] It is this obsessively visual experience of self that the mad doctors both impose on their patients and inhabit themselves: their musical performances, dramatic declamations before rapt audiences, and tendencies to melodrama all coincide with the "histrionic" performance of the cured Mary. In each instance, the self-representation is conducted as if seen in a mirror, visually posed, objectively experienced.

In contrast, Sobchack posits a more material, sensory, and cognitive experience of the body. She comments that her own rehabilitative experience, after having a leg amputated and gaining a prosthetic, required her to look away from the mirror:

> what helped me walk was not the sight of my body or the artificial limb given to me outside myself but rather my subjective imagination of the bodily arrangement or *comportment* informing my actions from "my side" of my body. . . . I learned my body—my substance, weight, and dimension; my balance, my gravity, my tension and motility—not as an objective and visible *thing* but as a subjective and synoptic *ensemble of material capacities* for being.[56]

Sobchack does not disavow the importance of the visualized self, nor does she present her own bodily experience as more valid or correct. Rather, she suggests that a purely or even predominantly visual approach to the body elides many aspects of our complex individual and cultural experiences of ourselves.

In mad-doctor films, then, the pervasive objectification and visualization of the body subtends both the production of disability as hidden, perverse, and illicit and the production of normality as the invisible site from which power is exercised. First, the films repeatedly mimic the disciplinary and objectifying gaze, using formal techniques to align the viewer with the physician's perspective and to illuminate the physical effectivity of medical paradigms. Second, they enable the spectator to turn that gaze on the doctor himself, to watch as the film expurgates visible, corporeal, and surface evidence of the doctor's supposedly innate psychological deviance. The viewer collaborates with the viewing apparatus to punish the doctor's "use" of others' bodies in the production and experience of perverse monstrosity; ironically, however, that punishment takes the form of "using" the body of the mad doctor, reproducing it as a symptom of perverse monstrosity. Finally, the film turns its own indicting gaze on the spectator, condemning his/her tendency to read staged performances of debility as evidence of pathology, and construing such a tendency as itself a pathology, a self-delusion, a kind of madness. The film becomes a monster-maker, (re)creating its ostensibly normal spectators as the mad bearers of the medical gaze. Accordingly, in the next chapter, horror films' production of disability in spectators is explored through the lens of 1930s critical and censorial reactions to the genre. The disability spectacles so central to horror films' elicitations of fear, disgust, and pleasure are seen to envelop characters, filmmakers, and audiences, until no one is innocent of the exploitation, the abjection, or the experience of embodied impairment.

# SHOCK HORROR AND DEATH RAYS

## DISABLING SPECTATORSHIP

*octor X* (dir. Michael Curtiz, First National/Warner Bros., 1932), a sensationalistic horror movie filmed in Technicolor, has a climactic scene that encapsulates the dynamics of horror-film spectatorship. A series of murders in New York, in which the bodies are mutilated and partially cannibalized at the time of the full moon, has been linked, through the use of a specific surgical instrument, to Dr. Xavier's medical academy. Xavier (Lionel Atwill) sequesters himself and the academy's four other doctors in his isolated mansion, in order to determine the murderer's identity. The suspects provide quintessential images of crazed doctors hunched over body parts in their laboratories late at night and marked with foreign accents, physiognomic defects, and visible disabilities: Dr. Wells (Preston Foster) is one-armed; Dr. Haines' (John Wray's) face, as described in one shooting script, "plainly shows traces of lust and sensuality"; Dr. Rowitz (Arthur Edmund Carewe) has a prosthetic eye and scarred face; and Dr. Duke (Harry Beresford) is in a wheelchair and plaintively describes himself as "a hopeless paralytic."[1] Because the victims were strangled with two hands, Xavier excludes Dr. Wells from suspicion. The others, including Xavier, are bound into chairs and attached to scientific equipment that measures their "increased heart-rate and nerve reactions" as they watch reenactments of the murders.

During the first performance, the house lights go out suddenly, and when they come back on, one of the doctors has been mysteriously murdered. The hysterical maid, Mamie (Leila Bennett), refuses to participate in further reenactments, so Xavier co-opts his daughter Joanne (Fay Wray). Handcuffed in chairs bolted to the floor, the doctors prepare to watch Joanne, lying on a bed in a nightgown, play one of the victims who was "murdered and horribly mutilated as she was lying weak and helpless in a hospital bed." The mansion's butler (George Rosener) has been drafted to play the murderer, but he is killed and replaced by Wells, the real murderer, now bearing a synthetic arm and crazed by the moon. Unable to move despite their struggles, the doctors are forced to watch as Wells menaces Joanne, who writhes and screams but cannot flee (fig. 5.1). With one hand at her throat and the other, synthetic hand hovering over her body, Wells utters a long explanation for his actions, describing his research with African cannibals and his appropriation of human flesh in order to create prostheses: "Their flesh taught me how to manufacture arms, legs, faces that are human, or make a crippled world whole again!" The trapped doctors struggle in vain as Wells moves in for the kill. Only the bumbling reporter Lee Taylor (Lee Tracy), who provides the film's comic relief, saves Joanne at the last minute by leaping from the wings and wrestling Wells out a window to his death.

The film self-consciously represents the horror-viewing scenario. This scene builds on others in the film that foreground characters' physiological responses to shocking or frightful events: Taylor faints; Joanne screams; the formerly paralyzed Duke is shocked into walking by what Xavier terms a "hysteria reaction"; and the Xaviers' superstitious maid suffers frequent hysterical fits. But it is in the scene in which the men are tied into their chairs that *Doctor X* most explicitly correlates scientific and horrific spectacle. The doctors are attached to a device that fulfills the scientific desire to penetrate to the inner truth of the body, as Dr. Xavier explains: "Shrewd and brilliant, [the killer] could conceal his madness from the human eye, even from himself. But he can't conceal it from the eyes of the radio-sensitivity. Every time his heart beats from mental excitement, the thermal tubes will betray him." Red liquid in the tubes, Xavier asserts, will rise according to the level of the spectators' excitement. The scene thus allies the scientific effort to visually expurgate bodily truth and the construction of horror spectacle for maximum effect on its viewers.

The effect of this analogy between medical experimentation and sensationalistic horror is to suggest that both share a fascination with the body beyond a mere desire for objective or scientific truth. The sexual sadism implicit in the medical spectacle is acknowledged in Duke's sardonic comment to Xavier: "If she were my daughter, she wouldn't be up there on a

**5.1** Doctors as spectators: Dr. Haines (John Wray), Dr. Duke (Harry Beresford), and Dr. Xavier (Lionel Atwill) (*foreground*) watch the monster (Preston Foster) menace Joanne (Fay Wray) in *Doctor X* (1932).

bed, in nothing but a nightgown, to satisfy some lunatic's experiment." But the scene also forwards a model of horror-film viewing like that posited by Carol Clover, in which male spectators derive thrills not, or not only, from sadistic identification with the monster persecuting a young woman but also from masochistic identification with the victim herself, thus accessing a bodily experience disavowed by masculine norms.[2] Similarly, in discussing *Doctor X*, Rhona Berenstein notes that the film is traversed with "female performances of fear" and "male passivity" and contends that Joanne's body is actually a vehicle for the paralysis and pains of the watching men.[3] The fact that the doctors here become the objects of their own bodily experimentation reveals their sadomasochistic investment in the visualization of somatic processes.

The doctors do not seem to be motivated only by sexual desire, however. The film takes literally the notion of male "paralysis" and "pains," both marking out the men as impaired prior to this viewing experience and suggesting that the show can cause their heart-rates to rise, generate "hysterical reactions," and even lead to death. The spectacle of Joanne's vulnerability at the hands of the deformed and disabled monster is, thus, not merely exciting because it threatens sexual violation but also because, in imaging the corporeal impairments and vulnerabilities of both monster and woman, it enables the men to experience and intensify their somatic "pains" and impairments (fig. 5.2). In this sense, *Doctor X* provides a valuable lens through which to consider the place of the body and disability in theories about film spectatorship and in the 1930s' rhetoric of horror-film reception. In these discourses, and in the films themselves, we find a complex understanding of the impact of cultural phenomena upon bodily health, wherein, ultimately, the "shocks" and impairments of modernity are embraced even as the spectacles of monstrosity constructed by medical professionals are indicted as destructive products of the medical gaze.

## WATCHING BODIES: DISABILITY AND HORROR-FILM SPECTATORSHIP IN THEORY

The immobilized, disabled male spectators of *Doctor X* literalize a vision of film-viewers that gained currency in 1970s psychoanalytic and ideological film theory. In the work of Jean-Louis Baudry, filmgoers are likened to the "prisoner-spectators" of Plato's cave, chained in front of shadowy images they mistake for reality, or to Lacan's infant in front of the mirror, who misrecognizes his chaotic and "fragmented body" as an autonomous and integrated self.[4] The cinema thus proffers, through illusory images of bodies, a kind of prosthetic experience. In identifying with cinema's freedom of movement and masterful vision, Baudry's spectator perceives her/himself as an autonomous and "transcendental self."[5] The work of Christian Metz and Laura Mulvey builds on these ideas, advancing an understanding of cinema in which processes of identification, whether with the apparatus or with characters on screen, facilitate an illusory but pleasurable sense of the spectating self as sovereign, self-controlled, and powerful.[6]

As we have seen, however, the hapless doctors of *Doctor X* are engaged in a dramatic performance of fearful writhing and shock response that belies the image of a transcendent and omnipotent spectator. Indeed, horror-film scholarship has had to confront a very different experience of spectatorship dictated by the genre's monstrous impaired bodies and depictions of bodily damage, especially given that horror is "the only genre named for its effect on the reader [or viewer]."[7] As noted in the introduction, the word *horror* derives from the Latin "horrēre," meaning "to bristle." As well as primarily meaning "[a] painful emotion compounded of loathing and fear; a shuddering with terror and repugnance . . . the feeling excited by something shocking or frightful," "horror" retains the meaning

**5.2** Doctors Xavier (Lionel Atwill), Duke (Harry Beresford), and Haines (John Wray): spectatorship intensifies pain and impairment in *Doctor X* (1932).

of "[a] shuddering or shivering, now *esp* (*Med.*) as a symptom of disease," a definition that anticipates 1930s' fears of horror film's dysgenic influence.[8] For Noël Carroll, such physical affect is central to the definition of the genre: horror texts seek, by portraying monsters that frighten and disgust, to elicit an emotional response that is necessarily physiological. Carroll's description of some of the sensations that may be evoked, including "muscular contractions . . . , tingling, frozenness, momentary arrests . . . , paralysis, trembling, [and] nausea" convey spectatorship as a potentially disabling experience.[9]

In this way, the physiological effects of horror film, themselves generated by the depiction of bodily deformity or violation, challenge "normal" or "healthy" bodily states and boundaries, an effect that has led to a certain distaste for or devaluation of the genre. Linda Williams' discussion of horror, melodrama, and pornography notes that these genres are marked as "low" not only because they "share a quality of uncontrollable convulsion or spasm—of the body 'beside itself' with sexual pleasure, fear and terror, or overwhelming sadness" but also because "the body of the spectator is caught up in an almost involuntary mimicry of the emotion or sensation of the body on the screen." These films are characterized by a lack of distance, a sense of excess and "over-involvement," and spectators can feel manipulated into uncomfortable bodily expression by these "tear-jerkers" and "fear-jerkers."[10]

Examinations of horror-film affect have nonetheless argued that the genre can fit into the kind of viewing model put forward by psychoanalytic theorists, insofar as the viewing of and interaction with images of bodily distress reinforce normative concepts of the embodied self, functioning to make the viewer feel "whole." Like the rituals of abjection discussed by Julia Kristeva in *Powers of Horror*, horror movies are seen to enable, by contrast and resolution, the reconstitution of the "proper" body: "the horror film attempts to bring about a confrontation with the abject (the corpse, bodily wastes, the monstrous-feminine) in order finally to eject the abject and redraw the boundaries between the human and nonhuman."[11] Writes Isabel Cristina Pinedo, "Much as the horror film is an exercise in terror, it is simultaneously an exercise in mastery, in which controlled loss substitutes for loss of control."[12] To that extent, watching a horror film is akin to attending a freak show or staring at a disabled person: "Normality has to protect itself by looking into the maw of disability and recovering from that glance."[13]

The assumption underwriting such views of the horror-film experience, as discussed in previous chapters, is that both the dysfunctional body on screen and the bodily response it engenders are inherently "natural," nondiscursive and, thus, reactionary, unavailable for cultural critique or politicized interpretation. For instance, in deriding attempts to render horror film "arty" and cerebral, Morris Dickstein contends that "horror, even at its most commercially exploitative, is genuinely subcultural, like the wild child that can never be tamed, or the half-human mutant who appeals to our secret fascination with deformity and the grotesque."[14] Again, the figure of the freak is seen to threaten temporarily our own secure boundaries but, through that very process, reassure us of our own normalcy: Stephen King likens horror to a freak show where "you look at the guy with three eyes, or . . . the fat lady, . . . or Mr. Electrical. . . . And when you come out . . . you say, 'Hey, I'm not so bad.' "[15]

But to understand horrified responses to visual spectacles of disability as purely natural—and thus, as conventional recuperations of illusions about bodily or psychological integrity—is a rather eugenic reaction. For instance, eugenicist Henry Pratt Fairchild, in *The Melting-Pot Mistake*, distinguishes "true racial repulsion" from "race prejudice," asserting that "the former is not a judgment, but a feeling, and it does not arise in advance of the evidence, but arises as a natural reaction on presentation of the evidence." He continues, "The evidence consists of the traits of a person recognized to be of another race. The feeling is a feeling of revulsion or withdrawal that arises spontaneously under these conditions."[16] Like the disabilities of horror monsters, racial otherness is presented as self-evidently ugly or aesthetically unpleasant, generating a "natural" response of "revulsion or withdrawal" that legitimates racist acts of exclusion or discrimination. But to argue that horror films function at a "subcultural" level because of their bodily images and effects is to ignore the ways in which depictions and experiences of impairment are pervasive *within* our cultural formations and, in particular, to elide the fascination with and desire for disability that impel us to sit down before a horrific spectacle.

In this light, the men of *Doctor X* testify to a pleasure offered by the potentially debilitating encounter with the monstrous body or the horrific scene but not reducible to the affirmation of the normative body. For Williams, the fantasies of body genres "are not, as is sometimes thought, wish-fulfilling linear narratives of mastery and control leading to closure and the attainment of desire. They are marked, rather, by the prolongation of desire and by the lack of fixed position with respect to the objects and events fantasized."[17] For Stephen Shaviro, the "masochism" on display is something that, following Leo Bersani and Gilles Deleuze, we can understand positively: "the violent stimulation of the body and loss of ego boundaries that are foregrounded in masochism, but that characterize sexual play in general, are at once desirable and threatening. . . . Fearfulness is itself a thrill and a powerful turn-on, as any devotee of horror films knows." Horror-film identifications, Shaviro contends, extend primarily to the victims of violence and dismemberment and only to the monster or killer insofar as it "is in its own right victimized and driven by a passive compulsion."[18] Accordingly, the men of *Doctor X* identify with the helpless Joanne, on the verge of violation, mutilation, or death, but also with poor Dr. Wells, a raving lunatic, slathered with synthetic flesh and made only more monstrous by his obsessive efforts to "fix" his disability and make himself whole. The doctors, by allowing themselves to be chained into their chairs, prolong their terror/desire and intensify their debilitating viewing experience.

*Doctor X* is thus instructive to the extent that it challenges theoretical squeamishness about embodied spectatorship. In the words of Vivian Sobchack, "carnal responses to the cinema have been regarded as too crude to invite extensive elaboration" and '[b]odily responses to [body genre films] are taken as an involuntary and self-evident reflexology."[19] Sobchack argues for a model that attends to the sensitization of the viewing body by the cinematic spectacle, neither dismissing the embodied experience of film as a "subcultural" reality nor exploiting it only as a metaphor for psychological or conscious cognitive processes. Images on-screen, Sobchack asserts, solicit our sensorial and bodily investment. But, given that

> I cannot literally touch, smell, or taste the particular figure on the screen that solicits my sensual desire, my body's intentional trajectory, seeking a sensible object to fulfill this sensual solicitation, will *reverse its direction* to locate its partially frustrated sensual grasp on something more literally accessible. That more literally accessible sensual object is *my own subjectively felt lived body*. Thus, "on the rebound" from the screen—and without a reflective thought—I will reflexively turn toward my own carnal, sensual, and sensible being to touch myself touching, smell myself smelling, taste myself tasting, and, in sum, sense my own sensuality.[20]

What the doctors in *Doctor X* enact, then, is a spectatorship in which the experience of entrapment, fear, bodily vulnerability, and impairment that they *see* "rebounds" onto their own bodies, here represented as equally immobilized, vulnerable, and disabled. Their willing subjection to the spectacle parallels the desire of horror-film spectators to similarly expose their own bodies. Rather than facilitating a recuperation of the normative body, horror-film viewing proffers a mediated and yet material physiological experience of disability, one evident as well in the rhetoric of film and horror-film reception.

## MEASURING FILM'S SHOCK EFFECTS

At the time of *Doctor X*'s release in 1932, the scene of spectators tethered to scientific equipment designed to assess the physiological impact of their viewing was not, as it might seem, a far-fetched fabrication specific to the horror film. Due to social concerns about the impact of film-viewing on audiences, and especially on children, doctors and scientists were called on to ascertain the nature and extent of that impact. From 1929 to 1933, the Motion Picture Research Council drew on the financial support of the Payne Fund, an organization devoted to the welfare of youth, for a series of studies on the health effects of film on young people. Several monographs were published as a result of the studies, and Henry James Forman's book *Our Movie Made Children* (1933) presents a summary of the studies and their general conclusions. Forman's title conveys the profound ways in which films were believed to be shaping children: a belief also indicated by the muddled sentiments in Forman's comment that "'A movie a week' is with us a national slogan, almost a physical trait absorbed by the children with their mother's milk."[21]

In discussing the potential physical effects of films on children, Forman draws on, among others, the Payne studies of Dr. Samuel Renshaw, psychologist at Ohio State University, and of Drs. Christian A. Ruckmick and Wendell Dysinger, psychologists at the University of Iowa. Renshaw and his aides examined the influence of moviegoing on children's sleep patterns. Taking a group of subjects from the Ohio State Bureau of Juvenile Research at Columbus—"a place established for the observation of children who are referred there by Juvenile Courts or Probate Courts"—the doctors used an "electrical hypnograph" to measure the children's movements while they slept, comparing the records for nights on which children had seen films to those for nights in which they had not. "Briefly," writes Forman, "they found that, though the variety of effect upon different individuals is considerable, *boys, after seeing a movie, showed an average increase of about twenty-six per cent, and girls of about fourteen per cent greater hourly motility than in normal sleep!*" Dr. Renshaw concluded that "[f]or certain highly sensitive or weak and unstable children . . . the best hygienic policy would be to recommend very infrequent attendance at carefully selected films." Ruckmick and Dysinger, in experiments reminiscent of those of Dr. Xavier, also used electrical equipment to measure the emotional effects of films on children and to ascertain their "specific influences upon the health and nervous systems of children." Forman explains the operation of the instrument in question, a "psycho-galvonometer":

> The degree of this resistance, owing to changes in the chemistry of the body, is raised or lowered under stress of various emotions. The electrical currents used are so faint they cannot be felt, but, in the presence of the varying degrees of emotion, the body's resistance causes the delicately poised needle of the galvonometer to oscillate and to give an index of the amount of that resistance. So, if you thrill at a feat of Douglas Fairbanks, or recoil from the horror of a Mr. Hyde or a Frankenstein monster, the deflection of the needle of the galvonometer promptly indicates the intensity of the emotion involved.

The children were installed in a local theater and prepared for the experiment:

> The subject of the experiment had the second and fourth fingers of his left hand washed with alcohol and wrapped above the first joint with adhesive

tape. The tips of these fingers were placed in liquid electrodes, (a normal salt solution), the arm on the arm-rest. . . . The heart apparatus was placed over the pulse of the right arm, and all that was asked of the young people was as little movement as possible.

Ruckmick and Dysinger noted that "the pulse rate of the children watching [the films] ran up from a normal of 75 or 80 to 125 and 140."[22]

Forman emphasizes that the movies chosen for these experiments were typically of the ordinary and unsensational kind; horror film remained an extreme whose effects on children one might only imagine. Of one film that heightened viewers' pulse rates, *The Yellow Ticket*, Forman comments, "Yet, it certainly did not compare for harrowing visions with such highly intense movies as 'The Phantom of the Opera,' 'Dr. Jekyll and Mr. Hyde,' 'The Lost World,' or 'Frankenstein.'" He later muses, "To what height the pulse might have risen with such pictures as 'The Bat,' or 'Frankenstein,' we cannot say." However, Forman has anecdotal evidence for the physiological impact of horror films in the testimony of a trained nurse who ran "children's play-rooms and first-aid rooms in a chain of motion picture theatres in a large mid-western city during a period of two and a half years" and who kept clinical cards to document cinemagoers' responses to specific films. One film in particular generated traumatic reactions, she recalls:

"During 'The Phantom of the Opera' children would scream all over the theatre; many of them would dash out and mothers would leave the theatre with frightened and hysterical children clinging to them. And at times the children would vomit as a result of their emotional condition." . . . [*Phantom*] caused, she declares, eleven faintings and one miscarriage in a single day. Four of the eleven who fainted were men. The average was three or four faintings a day during the run of the picture. Ushers were especially drilled and prepared to deal with cases of faintings and hysterical collapse. "While adults," she adds, "would faint, children would become hysterical."

The nurse also noted the tendency of serial films, which played out over several weeks, to keep children "wrought up" with excitement and of western films to incite excited and violent imitations by young boys.[23]

In a chapter on "Horror and Fright Pictures," Forman elaborates on the nervous physical responses of children to horror films. He provides testimonies from high-school and college students that their childhood viewings of horror films terrified them and instilled irrational fears that they never quite shook: "No effect upon the brain and nerve cells is, as we know, in strict scientific literalness, ever wholly wiped out." An expert outside the Payne Fund survey, Dr. Frederick Peterson, a noted neurologist, offers authoritative testimony regarding the danger that movie "scenes of horror and tense excitement" might instill debilitating nervousness in children:

> If sufficiently strong . . . [such scenes] have an effect very similar to shell-shock, such as soldiers received in war. A healthy child seeing a picture once in a while will suffer no harm. But repeating the stimulation often amounts to emotional debauch. Stimulation, when often repeated, is cumulative. Scenes causing terror and fright are sowing the seeds in the system for future neuroses and psychoses—nervous disorders.[24]

Such notions were not restricted to the Payne Studies: a plethora of articles appeared in publications such as *Commonweal* and *Christian Century*, like Fred Eastman's "The Movies and Your Child's Health," which cited Forman's book in order to conclude that "[t]he excitement of horror pictures—especially if often repeated—may sow the seeds of future nervous disorders."[25]

Dr. Peterson's reference to "shell-shock" mobilizes a public rhetoric that reflected perceptions of modern life as persistently shocking and assaultive. Since Thomas Edison had produced the first lightbulb in 1879 and arc lights began illuminating public spaces in the 1880s, electricity had symbolized technological progress and a modern life of convenience.[26] However, in publications such as George Beard and A. D. Rockwell's *A Practical Treatise on the Medical and Surgical Uses of Electricity* (1871) and Beard's *American Nervousness: Its Causes and Consequences* (1881), electricity also figured the enervations of modern existence. Beard posited a "fixed reservoir of energy" that powered the body and asserted that the physical stimulation of modernity and technology drained this resource: "[Beard's] thinking is prosthetic: as the body is plugged into such external systems as the telegraph and railway, its energy needs rise."[27] Conveniently, electricity also offered the "fix" for this condition; much of *A Practical Treatise* advocated "electro-therapeutics," the use of electricity as a refreshing "tonic" that could replenish the body's energy.[28]

By the 1930s, the conflicting significances of electricity and shock had intensified. The phenomenon of shell shock, for instance, articulated a psychological, even physiological condition caused by the violences of modern life—most obviously, war, but more generally, assaults on the senses by factory machinery, urban noise, and cultural forms. Its symptoms included "paralyses and muscular contractures of the arms, legs, hands and feet, loss of sight, speech and hearing, choreas, palsies and tics, catatonia and obsessive behaviour, amnesia, severe sleeplessness and terrifying nightmares."[29] At the same time, following Beard, doctors and scientists claimed the ability of electricity to cure ills, employing it in diagnostic practices such as electrocardiography and in efforts to ameliorate enervation, fevers, epilepsy, cancer, and paralysis.[30] Shock therapy was used to treat psychological disorders, including shell shock itself. But experiments that used electric shock to induce epileptic convulsions also demonstrated that medically employed shock might cause, rather than cure, disability, a possibility taken to its extreme in the use of electricity as a state instrument for executing condemned criminals.[31] The multivalence of shock thus suggests its conflation of curative and disabling tendencies and, consequently, the instability and medically constructed nature of disability.

The concept of shell shock seemed to acknowledge the powerful shaping effects of culture and environment on bodily and psychological health, although eugenicists sought nonetheless to fit the concept into narratives of heredity and biological determinism.[32] While eugenicists criticized war as a dysgenic event in which members of "the fighting Nordic element" disproportionately sacrificed their lives and their health for their nation, for the most part eugenic discussions of shell shock minimized the role of environmental stimulus and influence.[33] Newspapers reported that in debates at the 1931 International Congress of Military Medicine and Pharmacy at The Hague, Colonel W. F. Lorenz, professor of psychiatry at the University of Wisconsin, declared that there was "no specific mental or nervous condition directly attributable to the effects of artillery fire." Moreover, Lorenz asserted, those who did suffer from neurosis were inherently unfit: "those with weakened nervous systems quickly eliminated themselves."[34] In another article, Colonel Fribourg-Blanc of the French Army supported this notion of inherent weakness, commenting that "the terrors and memories of battle act on nervous systems which were untenable at the start."[35] Thus, while admitting a certain environmental influence, the discourse of shell shock often drew on eugenic language and premises by positing the greater inherited susceptibility of some soldiers to psychological and physical weakness.

Despite eugenic efforts, however, the notion of shock as a formative modern force pervaded public discourse and troubled genetically determinist logic. Concerns about sensory attacks were often articulated around issues of urban living, particularly noise. An editorial in the *Washington Evening Star*, entitled "The Blows of Sound" (September 22, 1929), commended a group of New York citizens who "[i]n the belief that needless loud noises constitute a serious menace to health . . . have organized for the purpose of combating the evil, securing statutory enactments and administrative corrections to lessen the din that constantly assails the ears and rasps the nerves of city dwellers."[36] The same newspaper in 1930 reported a study of industrial workers that "showed that unrhythmic sounds produced a deadening of the hearing in workers who had previously not been affected by any deafness."[37] Such news reinforced medical commentaries on the dangers of modern life to normative bodily health, like a June 1928 report entitled "Death from Heart Disease on Gain: London Professor Blames Emotional Strain of Modern Life for Increase." Along with industrial machinery and fast-paced urban living, film often found itself classed as one of the sensory stimuli to blame for such malaise. The London professor commenting on heart disease, Dr. J. Strickland Goodall, contended that "[t]he form in which we take our pleasures . . . is a direct inversion of nature's demands for adequate rest" and that "the emotional character of modern plays, novels and films, with their appeals to the baser passions, inevitably tends to overstrain, with results which are reflected in the enormously increased number of deaths from heart disease."[38]

But shocking experiences, particularly those of a cinematic nature, were not always understood as negative. In the 1930s, Walter Benjamin drew on Freud to construe the experience of modern life as a parrying of shocks inflicted by external stimuli that were both destructive *and* creative.[39] In "The Work of Art in the Age of Mechanical Reproduction" (1936), Benjamin heralded the technological age of mechanical—photographic and filmic—reproduction for its revolutionary potential. For Benjamin, the soothing illusion of authenticity and transcendence, or "aura," offered by earlier art forms, particularly those attached to elitist social hierarchies, were disrupted by cinema, with its engagement of a collective audience in a shocking and mechanized bodily experience. Film spectatorship constitutes, he suggested, an exemplary engagement with modernity, figured by a surgeon now able to penetrate into the bodily interior ("a different nature opens itself to the camera than opens to the naked eye") and by the mechanization of subjects through urban experience, like the actions of those in Poe's crowd in "The Man of the Crowd," who "act as if they had adapted themselves to the machines and could express themselves only automatically. Their behavior is a reaction to shocks."[40]

Film spectatorship thus approximates and reproduces the everyday shocks of modern sentient experience, acknowledging and valuing the embodied experience of an industrialized world. The cinematic encounter with shock helps counter nostalgic notions of transcendence and disembodiment and models the productive integration of the organic and the technological. But, Benjamin warns, we must nonetheless offset such shocks to some extent, resisting the Futurist embrace of an entirely mechanized existence and the absolute destruction of the organic. As Hal Foster argues, such an embrace tends toward Fascism to the extent that "the (masochistic) drive to self-destruction at its core may also be turned into the (sadistic) drive to master others."[41] Benjamin thus counsels against eliding the organic body through aesthetic or spiritual transcendence *and* against obliterating that body through an absolute mechanization, again suggesting the cinema as a visual technology that, in shocking and engaging viewers, testifies to the modern body's vulnerability and material reality. In the rhetoric of horror-film reception in the 1930s, we find a more anxious perception of the impact of film spectacles on their audiences, ameliorated by efforts to contain bodily vulnerability in moral and religious terms.

## SHOCK HORROR: TRIGGERING DEGENERACY

As already noted, people with disabilities have long been interpreted as signs of God's displeasure or as evil individuals whose moral corruption is manifest. Even in eugenic discourse, conditions such as epilepsy and "feeblemindedness" were conflated with immorality and criminal tendencies. Not surprisingly, then, anxieties about horror films' spectacles of disability and possible debilitating impact were often allied with criticisms of the movies' moral implications and potentially corrupting effects. Criticism and censorship of classic horror film focused primarily on two objectionable elements: gruesomeness and religious blasphemy. Frequent targets were movie elements that merged the two by allying monstrous bodies with artificial or abnormal reproduction: the beautiful woman under monstrous attack, the specter of interspecies/interracial miscegenation, and the scientist who assumes Godlike powers and privileges. Such stock ingredients led to censure of horror films on both moral grounds—based on fears of how such films might warp souls and consciences—and physiological grounds—based on fears of how such films might physically affect their viewers.

Censorial rhetoric in the 1930s increasingly subsumed on-screen and spectatorial disability into a moralistic discourse. Histories of 1930s horror film often link the genre's rising and falling popularity to the attitudes of censors. Tom Johnson depicts the early horror films *Dracula* and *Frankenstein* as sliding under the censors' radar by virtue of their novelty and

*Dr. Jekyll and Mr. Hyde* by virtue of the high standing of Stevenson's novel and critical acclaim for the film. At the time, the MPPDA relied on studios to self-regulate in the interest of good taste and decency; consequently, the Production Code, which had been passed in 1930 and dictated the kinds of elements that films should not exhibit, had few teeth. Studios capitalized on the public's predilection for horror, and the plethora of horror films in 1931 and 1932 contributed to the overall tone of Hollywood in these years, which Johnson describes as "sensational . . . almost *circus maximus.*"[42]

Intriguingly, it is the horror movie with the most realistic display of disabled figures that Johnson blames for increased censorship. With *Freaks*, Johnson suggests, came the beginning of the end for self-regulation: the *Kansas City Star* declared forebodingly, "In *Freaks* the movies make their great step toward national censorship. . . . If they get it, they will have no one to blame but themselves."[43] Writing of *Freaks'* box office failure, Thomas Doherty comments:

> To say that *Freaks* made for a tough sell in 1932 doesn't quite capture the level of revulsion the film incited. The critical reception was not just mixed or negative but downright unnerved. Women seemed particularly repulsed. . . . A directive went out to Paramount theater managers instructing them to follow scrupulously the "special and specific advertising campaign that is being prepared, otherwise great danger will be caused future patronage"—as if *Freaks* were so traumatic as to make an unprepared public swear off movies permanently.[44]

As seen in chapter 2, the reaction to *Freaks* was often cast in physiological terms: Richard Watts, Jr., of the *New York Herald-Tribune* termed *Freaks* "an unhealthy and generally disagreeable work," while *Harrison's Reports* declared, "Not even the most morbidly inclined could possibly find this picture to their liking. Saying that it is horrible is putting it mildly: it is revolting to the extent of turning one's stomach, and only an iron constitution could withstand its effects. . . . Any one who considers this entertainment should be placed in the pathological ward in some hospital."[45] The *Hollywood Reporter* viewed *Freaks* as an "outrageous onslaught upon the feelings, the senses, the brains and the stomachs of an audience."[46] Such responses imitated ostensibly natural reactions of disgust to the freaks' bodies themselves, such as F. Scott Fitzgerald's urge to vomit upon encountering the conjoined Hilton sisters in MGM's dining area.[47] They also imagined that these detrimental effects could damage the reproduction of future generations, as when "a woman who had attended the preview [of *Freaks*] tried to sue the studio, claiming the film had induced a miscarriage."[48]

Faced with the unsettling implication that cultural texts had the capacity to damage individuals and thus the national body, critics of films such as *Freaks* translated physiological threats into moral terms. Some asserted that only those already somehow perverse or deviant could want to see such films: in 1937 British Member of Parliament G. M. Garro-Jones characterized "horrifics" as "films that healthy people have a natural repugnance for."[49] But others worried that the susceptible—children, pregnant women, or the intellectually or physically weak—might also be harmed: Marjorie Ross Davis, a PTA report chairman, complained to the MPPDA that *Dracula* "should be withdrawn from public showing, as children, [the] weakminded and all classes attend motion pictures indiscriminately."[50] Still others felt that everyone was in jeopardy. *Harrison's Reports* encouraged exhibitors of *Freaks* to "[a]nnounce . . . that your theater will remain closed, because you are unwilling to become an instrument of demoralization among the people of your community," while a physician's letter to the editor in the *New York Times* lambasted *Mark of the Vampire* for "the terrible effect that it has on the mental and nervous systems of not only unstable but even normal men, women, and children."[51]

This moralizing discourse reflected the tone of the Production Code, which had been passed in 1930 but was only strictly enforced from July of 1934. The Code imposed on horror-film reception a framework in which certain films' damages to bodily and mental health were also viewed as injuries to the spiritual self. The "Reasons Supporting the Preamble of the Code" asserted that while entertainment had value "in rebuilding the bodies and souls of human beings," it was important to identify whether entertaining texts were "*helpful* or *harmful* to the human race." Art that was "*morally good*" was believed to "*improve* the race, or, at least, to re-create and rebuild human beings exhausted with the realities of life"; art that was "*morally evil* in its effects" tended to "*degrade human beings*, or to lower their standards of life and living." The well-being of the United States, the code declared, depended on proper oversight of film spectacle: "*correct entertainment raises* the whole standard of a nation," it averred, while "[w]*rong entertainment lowers* the whole living condition and moral ideals of a race."[52]

The rhetoric of the Code is intriguing in two respects. First, it conjoins the physiological and the moral or spiritual, linking entertainment to the well-being of "bodies *and* souls" (emphasis added), and it does so in somewhat eugenic language, imagining film's role in terms of improving the "race" or "nation" and offsetting modernity's debilitating effects for those "exhausted with the realities of life." Eugenicists, too, when they considered the dysgenic influence of entertainment, conflated biological and moral health. Davenport declared that once society had failed in "preventing the mating that brings together the antisocial traits of the criminal," its second line of defense lay "in securing the highest development of the good traits and the inhibition of the bad, surrounding the weak protoplasm with the best stimuli and protecting it from harmful stimuli." He continued, "Here is where society must act to cut off the evil suggestions of immoral theaters, yellow journals and other bad literature. These stimulate those who react violently to this kind of suggestion."[53] For Henry Fairfield Osborn, writing in 1931, the cinema was one of several elements contributing to the degeneration of the "race" and was intimately tied to the influx of immoral racial and national others:

> The entire control of the "movie" industry and the larger part of the control of the stage industry in the United States are now in the hands of people of near or remote Oriental origin. . . . Ridiculing religion, modesty and chastity, substituting European for American ideals of love and marriage, grossly decadent and dissolute librettos saved only from obscenity by the occasional hand of the censor, ridiculed as Puritanism, the original American standards are all insidiously tending toward moral decadence.[54]

Thus, when eugenicists were forced to acknowledge a shaping environmental influence, they had recourse to notions of "morality" to marginalize criminals and immigrants; at the same time, film censors adopted notions of racial and national improvement to shore up their conservative moral ethos. In both cases, the subsumption of physiological effects within a moralistic and spiritual discourse legitimated expert intervention in the name of protecting national health.

Second, the rhetoric of the Code's mission statement has remarkable resonance with the projects of the very mad doctors whose activities the Code often condemned. The idea that "good" films would assist in "rebuilding the bodies and souls of human beings" or help to "improve the race, or at least to re-create and rebuild human beings exhausted with the realities of life" recalls the man-making efforts of Frankenstein, the moral uplift espoused by Jekyll, or the ambition of Doctor X's Dr. Wells to "make a crippled world whole again." To prevent the production of harmful films, the Code prohibited a number of elements common to horror films, including sympathetic representations of criminal activity, depictions of violations of "divine" and "natural" or "human" law, illicit sexual activity, and the ridicule of religious subjects.[55] The horror genre, however, in arraying so many of these ingredients within its films, and in depicting as insane professionals who expounded uplifting and "improving" motives, seems to exaggerate and parody the "eugenic" implications of a censorial discourse in which bodily spectacles and effects are always construed as lapses in moral health.

It was precisely the claims of horror's mad doctors and scientists to God-like abilities for the improvement of the human race that drew a good deal of censors' anxiety in the 1930s. In 1932, an as-yet-ineffectual Production Code Administration (PCA) expressed some discomfort with the line in *Island of Lost Souls* (dir. Erle C. Kenton, Paramount) wherein Dr. Moreau (Charles Laughton) asks Edward Parker (Richard Arlen), "Do you know what it means to feel like God?"[56] The line remained in the film, but when *Lost Souls* was banned by several countries and fourteen local censorship boards and screened elsewhere with deletions, Moreau's blasphemous hubris was frequently the target of the greatest censure.[57] When *Bride of Frankenstein* was proffered to the censors' office in 1935, Joseph Breen, then head of the PCA, was particularly concerned by "a number of references to Frankenstein . . . which compare him to God and which compare his creation of the monster to God's creation of Man," proclaiming, "All such references should be deleted."[58] And when Universal sought certification for *Frankenstein*'s rerelease in 1938, the PCA was most anxious about "dialogue in which the name of 'God' is used," including Frankenstein's manic cry, "Now I know what it feels like to be God!"[59] The censors' discomfort derived, certainly, from the blasphemous implications of men seeking to usurp the place of God, but the commonalities between the mad doctors' eugenic visions and those of the Production Code suggest more than a passing resemblance between cinematic doctors building men through medical and scientific technology and cinematic experts seeking to "rebuild" men through the proper application of film technology.

Of course, it was the nature of the "rebuilding" that was at stake, and if American censors aimed to shape men through examples of moral purity, the type of artificial reproduction in most horror films was overtly impure and hybridic: Frankenstein's monster meshed body parts from diverse corpses; Jekyll's creation mutated an upstanding doctor into a darkened bestial creature; and Dr. Moreau's experiments "hastened" evolution to turn animals into "Beast People." Even in the early stages of *Island of Lost Souls'* development, Colonel Joy challenged the film's invocation of this theme, commenting, "I assume that some thought has been given to the possibility of injecting the idea of crossing animals with humans. If this is the case it is my opinion that all such thought should be abandoned, for I am sure you would never be permitted to suggest that sort of thing on the screen."[60] Although the film was released with this theme intact, angry censors soon directed their disapproval toward "the blasphemous suggestion of the character, played by Charles Laughton, wherein he presumes to create human beings out of animals; the obnoxious suggestion of the attempt of these animals to mate with human beings[;] and the general flavor of excessive gruesomeness and horror."[61] When Paramount sought recertification of the film in 1935, Breen demanded several deletions, including Moreau's declaration that "Man is in the present climax of a long process of organic revolution. All animal life is tending toward the human form" and his claim to Godlike status, as well as all dialogue that suggested Moreau's planned liaisons between Parker and the "Panther Woman," Lota (Kathleen Burke), and between Parker's fiancée Ruth (Leila Hyams) and the ape-like Ouran (Hans Steinke).[62]

Again, then, the object of censorial concern was horror's tendency to translate spiritual matters into physiological and organic terms. *Lost Souls* suggests, not least in its title, that man cannot lay claim to a transcendent status that clearly distinguishes him from the carnal beast; the film challenges the notion that man is essentially a spiritual animal whose body forms merely a reflective vessel for his soul. The exchange from the 1941 *Dr. Jekyll and Mr. Hyde* discussed in chapter 4 similarly troubles this assumption. Investigating the case of an apparently insane man injured in a gas explosion, Jekyll (Spencer Tracy) tells a dinner party of his patient's reversion from "fine, solid citizen" to "animal." Expostulates Lanyon (Ian Hunter), "But look here, Harry, we can clearly understand a shock to the nervous system but . . . but what's that got to do with the soul?" Responds Jekyll, "I think the man had been shocked from normal good into complete evil." While using religious terminology, Jekyll insists that the "soul," whatever it might be, is susceptible to shocks experienced by the body and is thus merely an extension of incarnate man. For censors, such a notion is at once horrifying and familiar, being precisely the premise that justifies their protective interventions in cinema content.

Clearly, then, the implication of *Lost Souls* and other horror films that humanity's essence does not necessarily lie somehow beyond or above its embodied existence was threatening to upholders of moral and eugenic discourse alike. And yet the film's promotional materials went out of their way to accentuate precisely these contentious elements. In advertisements for horror film and in the films themselves we find a self-conscious interaction with the moral and eugenic presumptions of censorial rhetoric.

The horror genre's apparent embrace of shocking and "stimulating" bodily effects disavows eugenic and censorial presumptions that the desire for debilitating spectatorship is only harmful and destructive, modeling an organic embrace of the technological, in which viewers transmute daily shocks into pleasurable and painful violations, explore the limits of somatic boundaries, and refuse refuge in the realm of transcendence.

## SELLING SHOCK

It was not uncommon for horror films to explicitly address cultural concerns about the genre's shocking effect on audiences. As noted in chapter 1, *Frankenstein* opens with a warning prologue provided by Edward van Sloan, the film's redoubtable Professor Waldman (see page **80**). Van Sloan's warning that the film might "thrill," "shock," or "horrify" viewers masquerades as a protective and moralistic message intended to counter both religious and medical objections to the film. In reality, it is, as the *New Yorker* reviewer pointed out, "an injunction which naturally holds the audience glued to their seats to the last gasp."[63] The opening warning became a standard gambit, exploited, for instance, in *Mad Love*, which imitates Van Sloan's commentary almost verbatim, and in *Freaks*, where it mimics the freak-show spiel, posing as a prudent caution but actually designed to excite the audience and render them susceptible to the spectacle. Censorial concerns about shocking effects are thus refashioned as salacious invitations to be shocked.

The manner in which horror films were promoted constituted an effort to sensationalize and exploit their dysgenic ingredients. Advertisements for *Island of Lost Souls* presented the specter of monstrous sexual congress as the film's strongest selling point. The majority of posters in Paramount's press book foreground images of Lota, and occasionally both Lota and Parker, with captions such as "OUT OF THE DARK, FANTASTIC MADNESS OF HIS SCIENCE . . . HE CREATED THEM! . . . Pig-Men . . . Wolf-Women . . . Thoughtful Human Apes—And His Masterpiece . . . The Panther Woman . . . Throbbing to the Hot Flush of New Found Love!" And: "THE PANTHER WOMAN lured men on—only to destroy them—body and soul!" The caption of a lobby photo of Lota emphasizes the threatening disjunction between her physical appearance, her innocent nature, and her inner essence: "THE PANTHER WOMAN—the body of a siren—the heart of a child—the soul of a cruel Jungle Killer." The caption both asserts a eugenic narrative in which inner degeneracy is not always apparent on the somatic surface and reminds the audience that the body is not, in fact, a transparent vessel for a determinative soul. That Lota's "Jungle Killer" soul is a construction becomes apparent in the film itself, when, treated kindly by Parker, she falls in love with him and sacrifices her life to secure his reunion with his fiancée. One of the few posters that does not highlight Lota promotes the film's other tale of miscegenation, as savage Ouran menaces blonde Ruth: "TERROR! Stalked the Brush-Choked Island . . . Where Men Who Were Animals Sought the Girl Who Was All-Human!"[64] These ads' fascination with the interrelationship of the animal and the human accentuate again the carnal and bestial elements of human existence and the ways in which embodied interaction with the world—rather than genetic or moral essence—is seen to determine health and identity.

The promotional emphasis on animal-human miscegenation suggests a desire to intensify the anxious and pleasurable spectatorial experience of shock and boundary violation. Berenstein has explained how female classic-horror viewers' performances of screaming and eye-covering and male viewers' performances of bravado and laughter simultaneously affirm and challenge gender conventions, suggesting such behavior as a cover for "perversities" such as homosexuality, cross-gender identifications, male investments in masochism, and female investments in sadism. She also notes that women were the particular targets of promotional stunts, as when a free perm was offered to the woman who would watch *The Invisible Ray* alone, because "[women] were thought to personify the genre's favored affect: fear."[65] But such promotional activities also foregrounded the tantalizing promise of mental and bodily debilitation: advertisements for *Freaks* trumpeted that "children will not be permitted to see this picture and adults not in normal health are urged not to!"[66] Several movie theaters stationed medical personnel inside cinema lobbies, or ambulances outside the cinema, and one planted a female viewer who screamed and fainted at a showing of *Mark of the Vampire*.[67] The suggestions made by MGM for the "exploitation" and promotion of *Mad Love* specifically challenged traditional perceptions of female fragility in the face of sensational spectacle, disparaging beliefs that thrill pictures are hard to sell: "The fact is that most women like them, and they like thrills. This is evidenced by the great turnout of women at boxing and wrestling matches, automobile races and other events where there is a great element of danger or a suggestion of brutality. This is not primarily a horror picture . . . but it may be considered as such. Therefore, appeal directly to women on this picture."[68] Such toying with conventional gender roles and with conservative concerns about the impact of horror films suggests a much more savvy and transgressive audience than self-appointed watchdogs were willing to countenance and emphasizes that the experience of disability was one that horror-film spectators, like the doctors of *Doctor X*, eagerly sought out.

Where medical figures employed by concerned organizations measured the physiological responses to ascertain the damaging effects of film-viewing, horror-film marketers were eager to adapt the same technologies to augment their movies' appeal. In December 1931, *Time* reported a publicity stunt at a Chicago showing of *Frankenstein*:

> 27-year-old Inventor Leonarde Keeler tried out on two members of the audience his "Lie-Detector," which the police have found handy for questioning recalcitrant suspects. The "Lie-Detector" is a device which, by means of arm and chest bands, records on a paper chart changes in blood pressure and pulse action, presumably resulting from emotion. At last week's test, it worked so well when attached to two De Paul University students that Inventor Keeler said: "The results are . . . even more pronounced than in many cases where suspects are being questioned in connection with murders."[69]

The article thus associates measured physiological response with criminal essence, asserting that scientific technology can indeed expurgate moral truth via expert interpretation of the somatic surface. In noting that "[a] live spot in Frankenstein as revealed by the 'Lie-Detector' [is] one in which the ugly face of Frankenstein's dwarfish assistant pops up from behind a graveyard fence," the piece apparently consolidates the conflation of disability, shock, and criminality, invoking spectator's bodily responses as legitimate evidence for the moral corruption signified by physical difference.

But the use of the lie detector also reveals the unreliability of both cinematic spectacle and scientific visual technology, as the article goes on to note that "[d]ead spots" include "the reappearance of the dwarf's face in subsequent scenes when familiarity has made it less frightening." As discussed in chapter 3, this comment suggests that the shocking effects of both disability and horror films are deliberately constructed to elicit certain apparently "natural" effects and that such shocks diminish through frequent encounters. Indeed, reviews of *Island of Lost Souls* suggest an audience already alert to the framing required to generate shocked responses, with the *New York Times* asserting that "the desire to shock the audience is persistently too evident."[70] While the measuring devices at work in the murder-reenactment of *Doctor X* and the screening of *Frankenstein* purport to "reveal" the truth of criminality, we may instead understand their effectiveness in *positioning* and even *re-producing* their subjects *as* criminals. As with the "juveniles" used in the Payne Fund studies, an implicit criminalization renders certain individuals likely subjects for physiological measurement. The lie-detector gimmick simply transposes that criminalization onto audience members, aligning horror-film spectators with criminal suspects whose physiological responses mark their debilitation and, thus, deviance.

At the same time, the event demonstrates the capacity of the horror-film milieu to adapt the diagnostic tools of medical and criminal authorities to a humorous celebration of film's shocking potential:

> Likewise pleased was Universal's publicity department and Universal's General Sales Manager Phil Reisman, who saw in the "Lie-Detector" a mechanical means of forecasting the efficacy of mechanical entertainment. Said he: "Instead of the old hit or miss previews we can now know exactly the emotional effect of any film, can cut out the 'dead' spots, and generally improve the pictures distributed."[71]

The publicist's recognition of the appeal of sensationalistic spectacle cheerfully counters conservative and protective rhetoric about shock, in a manner reminiscent of *Doctor X* itself, where journalist Taylor, in several comic interludes, uses a handheld buzzer to shock unwitting characters. The buzzer also enables him to propel the monstrous Wells out a window ("In the third round I found out he was a little ticklish on a certain spot") and to entertain Joanne as the final scene fades out: while the couple kiss, Taylor turns out an overhead electric light, and in the darkness a buzz sounds, accompanied by Joanne's giggling cry: "Oh, Mr. Taylor!" As well as providing rather awkward laughs, Taylor's shocking habit suggests an effort to mock scientific hubris, as represented by the misuse of electrical technology for physiological diagnosis and "cure." It also belittles conservative philosophies and acts of censorship that seek to protect vulnerable populations from horror, rather than acknowledging the pleasure enabled by even transient identifications with monsters and by spectacles that cause the pulse to race. The buzzer provides, as Benjamin mandates, one way of incorporating the mechanical—and the electrical—within an organic notion of the body that frankly addresses the messy entwinement of comedy and horror in the most mundane of lives and asserts the fun of sensationalism and shocks that do not subscribe to deterministic and eugenic dictates.

Nonetheless, electrical tools perform less salubrious functions within *Doctor X*, mandating our attention once more to the films' implicit criticisms of medical professionals' constructions of horrific and bodily spectacle. Electricity is at work in Xavier's effort to ascertain bodily truth, with one script noting that "[e]lectric cables lead from the machine to the cabinet outside in the hall" and that "[t]here are also four wires—each leading to a chair."[72] As we have seen, however, this apparatus simply intensifies the impairments and debilities of the spectating bodies. Electricity also plays a significant role in Dr. Wells' experiment. The script deliberately notes the importance of "buzzing controls," the "electric casket" from which Wells removes his prosthetic arm, and the process of shock by which Wells animates the synthetic flesh of both his arm and his face:

> Almost terrified he begins to throw the switch of the rheostat. Blue and green electrical flames spit and crackle around the hand. The man seems about to cry out in agony. A gristly [sic] transition takes place. The hand loses its pallor. It lives! . . . Blinding flames encircle the face. The eyes roll with agony. The face changes color. The lips twitch. The nostrils quiver. Lines of pain engrave the mask and perspiration bursts out upon it. With a groan, he casts the wires from him and throws off the power. The monster sits there, breathing—breathing deeply.[73]

The scene brings together the curative and rejuvenating use of electricity and the debilitating and deforming effects of electric shock, thus visually "revealing" that scientific intervention works as much to intensify impairment as it does to mitigate or cure it. The exploitation of the lie detector by a marketing director implicates doctors and scientists as similarly self-serving manufacturers of spectacle carefully designed to elicit shock and horror. But the indication that medical figures seek to experience those responses themselves and are invested in the pleasures and terrors of physiological response to bodily spectacle also indicts and criminalizes the doctor, who cannot escape the deleterious effects of his own medicalizing gaze.

The film still functions to ableist effect: Wells' monstrosity is ultimately explained by his disability, to some extent confirming that the disabled are inherently immoral. At the same time, the film's subjection of the doctors' bodies to their own investigative science and its proliferation of disability to incorporate Wells' one-armed status, Duke's paralysis, Xavier's poor health, and Taylor's enervation suggests, within a logic that persists in linking criminality and disability, that no one is innocent. This insight recalls a more recent fictive engagement with the connections between disability and the shock of spectatorship in Katherine Dunn's novel *Geek Love* (1989). Following the story of a family of deliberately created freaks, the novel attests to the performative nature of disability, most notably when Arty, "The Flipper Boy," has the audiences' seats rigged with electricity in order to further excite them during their viewing experience. Arty becomes a cult leader who inspires "normal" people to reject ordinary life and embrace amputation. Write David T. Mitchell and Sharon L. Snyder, "If the ideal of anonymity in the life of the norms has proven deadening and mundane, the totem of the freak promises rejuvenation. This ironic exposé of the freak's appeal consequently provides Dunn the opportunity to define the side-show as a regenerative model whose mythic packaging and 'technotronic wiring' necessarily responds to an equally devastating cultural dictum."[74] Packaged in this way, both the freak show and the horror film offer that disillusioning shock of materiality envisaged by Benjamin, which counters the banal and destructive cultural insularity that characterizes both eugenics and much censorial justification. At the same time, Arty's performance confronts ableist culture with its disavowed desire for masochistic identification with the freak, something his cult takes to its logical extreme by carving that masochism into the flesh of his spectators. Horror-film spectatorship thus serves a dual function. On the one hand, it offers a productive engagement with—rather than avoidance or denial of—material vulnerability and impairment; horror film intensifies our daily shocks and debilitations. On the other, insofar as such spectatorship is contained within eugenic narratives and moralizing discourse, it fails to acknowledge its complicity in the—medical, scientific, and cultural—construction of disability as a sensationalistic spectacle.

But if we attend closely to horror films, they uncover that complicity in their complicated body politics. Like Arty's followers, the doctors and scientists of horror film are inevitably marked, scarred, and disfigured by the structures of spectatorship that they impose. The marking of scientific practice on the body itself, as an indictment for the medical spectacles enabled by new technology, invokes the X-ray, a technology whose capacities for internal vision were uncovered alongside its faculty for destruction and whose unnamable properties are conveyed in the title of *Doctor X*. Cosmic and death rays preoccupied horror films during the 1930s and offer perhaps the most damning representation of the destructive effects of scientific efforts to cure difference and disability, along with the most bitterly ironic reversal of that infliction on the bodies of those wielding the technology. Horror-film's "monstrification" of doctors and scientists runs parallel to real-life stories of physicians and technicians who suffered consequences of spectatorship far more damaging than the stress on nerves feared by critics of film.

# X-RAYTED: THE DANGERS OF SEEING AND BEING SEEN

On May 15, 1929, the destructive effects of film were revealed in a deadly tragedy at the Cleveland Clinic. Reported the *New York Times* the following day, "Yellow gas fumes, emanating from the X-ray room in the basement of the Cleveland Clinic and following a deafening explosion ended today the lives of 100 patients, doctors, nurses, hospital aides and rescuers in the greatest tragedy in the history of this city."[75] Following the explosion, fire and gas spread throughout the clinic, and rescuers struggled to bring casualties to safety. Many victims died later as a result of lung damage from the gas. The likely cause, reported the newspaper,

> was a mixture of gases coming from many forms of chemicals in the building which were liberated when containers were broken by explosion of celluloid X-ray films. . . . According to general opinion the poisonous gases were due to the burning of X-ray film in large quantities. The photographic film, which has much the same composition as guncotton, in addition to exploding with terrific force when confined, also threw off three kinds of compounds as the result of combustion. These were camphor and carbon monoxide and the gases nitric oxide or other nitrogen compounds.[76]

More than one witness likened the gas and the scene it created to the Great War. The newspaper also noted the bitter irony of the explosion's cause in terms familiar to horror-film fans: "The instrumentalities of advanced science turned against their users, for the greatest cause of death was the gas produced by the burning and explosion of the cellulose and sensitized X-ray and photographic films."[77] A New York fire department official explained that there were two kinds of X-ray film, cellulose acetate and cellulose nitrate, of which the latter was flammable if not stored under proper conditions.[78]

The event tied together many themes evident in the cultural phenomena we have been considering: modern technology, eugenics, medical advances, and concerns around the effects of film. A medical photographic medium, X-ray film, used to penetrate and envision the body's interior in the name of better health, became the combustible source of a violent explosion that destroyed the lives and bodies of doctors and patients alike, while onlookers' reactions cast them in the role of unwilling viewers of horror: "spectators in quivering groups gasped," while a fireman declared, "'I never hope to have to look at anything so horrifying again.'"[79] Moreover, an accompanying *New York Times* article noted, the Clinic's famous cofounder and director, Dr. George W. Crile, hailed as a hero on the occasion of the tragedy, had recently published a book, *The Bipolar Theory of Living Processes* (1926), "in which he propounded the theory that 'man and animals are mechanisms driven by electricity and were originally created and constructed by electrical forces.'" Crile was also known for his invention of the system of blood transfusion, his "successful experiments 'in returning the dead to life' by massage of the heart," and his "nerve block" system of anesthesia, which cordoned off a local area from the brain, thus avoiding the shock damage otherwise inflicted on the nervous system. Popular anxiety about the meanings of such advances—of a procedure in which a part of a patient's body "for the time being, does not belong to the patient . . . and which can be dealt with as the surgeon wishes"—condensed around the explosion and its dysgenic and shocking effects.[80]

Such anxiety, as we have seen, was a staple of much classic horror; but specific 1930s horror films also explicitly invoked X-ray technology in order both to figure the eugenic/dysgenic potential of such invasive picturing techniques and to "talk back" to cultural criticisms of horror films' dysgenic impact by pointing instead to the dangerous specular politics of medicine itself. In *Frankenstein*'s creation scene, Henry excitedly tells Waldman of his discovery that ultraviolet ray is not the highest color in the spectrum: "Here in this machinery I have gone beyond that. I have discovered the great ray that first brought life into the world." In *Island of Lost Souls*, one of the methods used by Laughton's Moreau in his transformative experiments is that of "ray baths." And in 1932's *Chandu the Magician* (dir. William Cameron Menzies and Marcel Varnel, Fox), Bela Lugosi, as the evil Roxor, seeks to steal the death ray invented by Robert Regent (Henry B. Walthall) and to turn the world's populations into easily dominated imbeciles. "Rays" in horror films encapsulate the means through which mad doctors and scientists may transgress against the laws of God and Nature; they also play on the notion of film as a dangerous medium, testifying to the destructive potential of medical technology, particularly that which serves the desire to reveal the inner truths of bodies.

The destructive effects of X-ray were widely reported in both medical and popular forums. The accounts by technicians and doctors considered by Lisa Cartwright read like horror-film scripts that Breen would have severely reprimanded for excessive gruesomeness. As early as 1896, electrician Elihu Thomson conducted X-ray tests on his finger and reported the results: "The whole of the epidermis came away. . . . The skin still comes off in flakes and is very disagreeable and very tender, and there is a burning, smarting sensation every now and then." In 1903, Clarence Dally, who had assisted Thomas Edison's X-ray studies, "had already been afflicted with an X-ray-caused cancer so invasive that his limbs had to be amputated, joint by joint, in an attempt to check its spread." The *Journal of the American Medical Association* reported Edison's own injuries from X-ray use: "His left eye is out of focus, his digestion is upset, and lumps have formed all through the region of his stomach." Decades later, in 1949, the autobiography of "physician, radiologist, and industrialist" Emile Grubbé demonstrated that scientific fascination with X-ray extended to repeated analysis of its effects on the scientific body: "Grubbé coolly outlines in detail the gradual deterioration of his flesh as he subjected his body to X-ray testing. He describes his gradual loss of body parts, beginning with his fingers. . . . [I]n order to analyze more closely the effects of X rays on tissue, he sliced minute bits from his amputated joints and viewed them under the microscope."[81]

X-ray and its effects were widely discussed in the American press. The possibilities for unprecedented insight into the body—for pictures of organs, the heart, and the skeleton, and for motion pictures of the workings of the arteries—were celebrated. The increased capacity for diagnosis—of bone development problems of infants and children, of leprosy, and of cancer—was discussed. And the exciting potential for cure, particularly of various forms of cancer, preoccupied media conversations about X-ray. But X-ray's destructive capacity, particularly for the physicians wielding it, also made the news. In April 1928, Viennese professor Guido Holzknecht, a pioneer in roentgen rays, whose right arm and hand had been rendered useless by "many burnings," had the arm amputated and was reported quite philosophical about the matter: "I still have a highly usable stump to which a number of useful artificial substitutes can be attached." On July 2, 1929, newspapers noted the death of another of Edison's colleagues, electrical engineer William Symes: "He died a martyr to the progress of scientific knowledge, for his death was traceable to the effects of X-ray burns sustained through a prolonged period of investigation thirty-five years ago, when the dangerous properties of X-rays were not understood." In October 1931, the *New York Times* noted the amputation of Dr. E. Mulvaney's left forearm, and in December 1931, on the heels of *Frankenstein*'s success, the *San Francisco Chronicle* reported on Dr. Lawrie B. Morrison of Boston: "His left arm was amputated last Monday, the operation resulting from injuries he had suffered in more than 20 years of studying and working with the x-ray."[82]

At the same time, in late 1931, the public was fascinated and appalled by the scandal of Radithor, "a radium cocktail that enjoyed a vogue as a health tonic among wealthy socialites until its ghastly consequences became all too apparent." A Federal Trade Commission attorney reported a visit to the cocktail's most famous victim, former "playboy industrialist" Eben Mac-Burney Byers: "His head was swathed in bandages. He had undergone two successive jaw operations, and his whole upper jaw, excepting two front teeth, and most of his lower jaw had been removed. All the remaining bone tissue of his body was slowly disintegrating and holes were actually forming in his skull." As Skal points out, "Radium poisoning wasn't restricted to the wealthy; the working-class variant of Byers's sickness was the bone cancer that afflicted female factory workers hired to paint radium watch dials."[83] And in July 1934, radium's most famous pioneer, Marie Curie, died, virtually blinded and suffering leukemia as a result of her work.

X-ray was also linked to eugenic concerns. The successful use of X-ray to alter plants genetically received significant attention, as with the Cornell University experiments that changed an annual plant to a perennial: hence the fascination of horror and science fiction films with the use of X-ray to alter the course of evolution and biological development. But the question of whether X-ray could improve physical condition without significant dysgenic effect remained in doubt: in the journal *Eugenics*, Douglas P. Murphy, noting radium and the X-ray as "extremely valuable therapeutic agents, having perhaps their chief field of usefulness in the treatment of certain diseases peculiar to women," sought to investigate the contention that "irradiation of the generative organs may be followed by the birth of a high percentage of unhealthy or defective young" and that "irradiation of the generative organs *before* conception or fertilization has taken place ... may also have some influence upon the health of the subsequent offspring."[84] Many eugenicists were eager to adopt the X-ray as a weapon against the reproduction of those with hereditary conditions. In 1936, Dr. Marie E. Kopp, newly returned from a study of hereditary diseases in Europe, announced at the Academy of Medicine the advances in sterilizing the "unfit by Germany and the Scandinavian countries"; her paper was followed by comments by Dr. Ira Kaplan, who "explained that sterilization of women by X-rays or radium is now feasible without harmful effects."[85]

In her discussion of X-ray technology in relation to cinema, Cartwright suggests that "the public showed great acuity in recognizing that the X ray was a radically new way of viewing and organizing the body, and in trying to appropriate it as such."[86] Cartwright discusses the use of X-ray photography and X-ray motion pictures as popular spectacle, arguing that the technology was widely seen as particularly transgressive in its stripping away of the body's exterior, signifying "the ultimate violation of the boundaries that define subjectivity and identity, exposing the private interior to the gaze of medicine and the public at large. . . . [T]he X-ray image was regarded as destructive both corporeally and morally."[87] X-ray, then, figured as a kind of spectacle that, like horror film, was deemed at once exciting and physically and morally damaging to its audiences.[88]

But the fact that X-ray was also destructive to its engineers and practitioners reveals its capacity to reshape normative models of medical spectatorship:

> [W]hat can one say about "seeing the body" when the very act of illuminating it destroys it? The discussion of the self-designated "martyrs to the X ray" . . . makes clear the impossibility of identifying the technician, scientist, or physician as the seat of authority in techniques of medical power. Rather, the technician of the gaze occupies an unstable position that at time merges with that of patient and object.[89]

Cartwright's call to rethink the structure of the medical gaze is also relevant for considerations of horror-film spectatorship:

> [T]he tendency has been to think the observer as one who remains psychically removed from the experimental object. And in the analysis of the cinema, the tendency has been to think the observer as one who remains physically distanced from the profilmic object. But here the subject looking is quite literally caught and punished by the surveillant apparatus whose rays do not restrict themselves to the intended object but range out to incorporate the technician.[90]

The horrific bodily effects of X-ray on unwitting doctors and patients resonate with the deformed and doomed doctors and scientists of classic horror and their cinematic spectators. In thus hyperbolizing the effects of film spectatorship as argued by censorial and eugenic discourse, horror films emphasize that such scenarios come much closer, in fact, to the destructive results of medical spectatorship.

The suggestion that scientific spectacle inflicts much greater damage than horror film is evident in *The Invisible Ray* (dir. Lambert Hillyer, Universal, 1936). The film opens with a small group, consisting of Dr. Benet (Bela Lugosi), Sir Francis Stevens (Walter Kingsford), Lady Arabella Stevens (Beulah Bondi), and Lady Stevens' nephew, Ronald Drake (Frank Lawton), arriving at a house and laboratory in the Carpathian mountains, to witness a scientific spectacle staged by unorthodox scientist Dr. Janos Rukh (Boris

Karloff). Having been introduced to Rukh's blind mother (Violet Kemble Cooper) and his wife Diane (Frances Drake), the group proceeds to Rukh's laboratory, where he explains that his telescope will capture a ray from distant Andromeda. Rukh believes in the existence of many rays that have recorded sounds and sights as they travel. The ray, Rukh says, will be "electrically transferred to a projector in my laboratory. There I will re-create what is recorded on that beam of light."

Rukh briefly leaves the room and returns wearing metallic gloves and a contraption like a welding mask. He sets in motion the electrical machinery of his laboratory, which was borrowed from the set of *Frankenstein* and gives off a great deal of humming, crackling, and sparking. Rukh also protects his audience, seating them behind "a new development—barium-crowned glass which will protect you from all dangerous rays" (fig. 5.3). The electrical nature of the imminent display is emphasized by a close-up that focuses on a lightbulb as the filaments spark. The casing of a large orb in the center of the laboratory retracts, revealing a glowing light-source, and the laboratory's domed ceiling becomes a theater screen, filled with a space scene of stars and the moon. Rukh explains the trip they are about to take: "To reproduce what is written upon the beam from Andromeda we must travel out into space upon that ray of light until we reach a point at which we turn and look back upon our own planet." The space scene changes, moving past

**5.3** Dr. Rukh (Boris Karloff) engineers a spectacle for an audience behind "barium-crowned glass" in *The Invisible Ray* (1936).

the dead, ages-old moon revealed by the ray, past Saturn, past the nebula of Orion, to Andromeda, traveling at "the pace of electric magnification." At this point the scene dissolves as the camera turns to look back down the ray. As the audience members view the earth of "a few thousand million years ago," they gasp, seeing a large meteorite spin slowly and then faster down toward Earth, landing with a sudden and resounding crash on the west coast of Africa.

Sir Francis and Dr. Benet congratulate Rukh on proving the existence of the meteor: declares the former, "You have demonstrated something that I have always regarded as an unsupported theory. I am lost for words." But the unhealthy effect of the spectacle is already telling on Rukh, who looks exhausted and seems about to faint. When the group gathers in the parlor for drinks, the viewers' shock is also evident, with Lady Stevens declaring, "Well, I for one am just beginning to recover from what we've seen," and Drake responding, "I don't think I ever shall. It was unbelievable." Because of her blindness, Rukh's mother has not been part of the audience. But when Benet invites Rukh to join them on their trip to Africa, so that he might search for the site of the meteor's landing, she demonstrates her "second sight," predicting that he will not be happy amongst people and urging him to stay and work on his experiments.

The remainder of the film proves rather convoluted. Rukh and Diane accompany the group to Nigeria, but Rukh separates from the others. He finds and experiments with the element deposited by the meteor, which he names Radium X, while Benet carries out his own "astro-chemistry" experiments to prove "that human organisms are all part of astro-chemistry, controlled by radio-forces from the sun." Meanwhile, Diane, who only married Rukh out of loyalty to her father, Rukh's mentor, falls in love with young Drake. Despite Rukh's use of protective clothing, his experiments poison him: he discovers that he glows in the dark and kills whatever he touches. Benet is able to create a counteractive to Rukh's condition, to be taken daily. Concerned about Rukh's focus on Radium X's destructive powers, Benet also insists on revealing Radium X and its healing potential to the scientific community.

When the group returns to Europe, Rukh uses a ray generated by Radium X to cure his mother's blindness. Benet also sets up a clinic and is shown curing a young girl's blindness, while patients flock to his door. Rukh, angered at the theft of his discovery and his wife, and growing increasingly mad from the effects of the counteractive, stages his own death, enabling Diane and Drake to marry. He then begins to murder the group members by delaying taking the medication and rendering himself temporarily poisonous. Killing first Sir Francis and then Lady Stevens, Rukh symbolically marks each death by using his ray to destroy one of the six statues at the church where Diane and Drake were married. Suspecting that Rukh is alive, Drake and Benet stage a lecture on Radium X, hoping to lure the mad scientist and reveal him in all his luminosity by turning off the lights at midnight. Rukh does arrive and, glowing brightly, manages to kill Benet and corner Diane in her room, but the monster cannot bring himself to complete his act of violation and, lurching out of the room, comes face to face with his mother, who righteously smashes to the ground the counteractive he needs to survive. Her son assents, "Yes, you're right—it's better this way. Goodbye, mother." With that, much like the mad Dr. Wells of *Doctor X*, Rukh, who is beginning to smolder, throws himself from a nearby window, bursts into flame, and vanishes before he hits the ground. As Drake and Diane embrace, Mrs. Rukh declares: "Janos Rukh is dead. But part of him will go on for eternity, working *for* humanity."

*The Invisible Ray*, notes Skal, "was the first film to exploit the public interest and anxiety in the alchemical, Faustian aspects of radioactivity." In Mrs. Rukh, Skal finds "the avenging image of Marie Curie herself, returned from the grave to judge the actor most associated in the public mind with the Frankenstein story and its theme of scientific presumption."[91] Even more than the other mad-doctor films we have considered, *The Invisible Ray* insists on environmental influence as determinative. While implications of a neurological link between genius and insanity persist, Rukh's psychological and physical degeneration results directly from his self-exposure to Radium X. Indeed, any form of scientific or medical experimentation is deemed destructive in the film, which punishes even the benign Benet and his financial supporters, the Stevenses. Only Diane and Drake survive, the latter perhaps because, as Lady Stevens announces early in the film, he "doesn't know a thing about science." Drake is redeemed at the moment when he rejects Diane's notion that their marriage is cursed: "We loved each other. We belong to each other. You never belonged to him. And no law of nature or man can make it anything but right for us to have done what we did." The film thus asserts the kind of sentimental morality evident in a film like *Bride of Frankenstein* or *Doctor X*, positing the triumph of love and interpersonal connection—the corruption of which is figured in Rukh's poisonous touch—over biological dictates, the deadly impact of scientific exploitation of nature, and the dangerous consequences of the urge to cure.

X-ray and radium powerfully conjoin the eugenic and the dysgenic, illuminating the potentially monstrous results of the medical and scientific drive to cure or, like the "good" films envisaged by the Production Code, to "improve" the human race. In *The Invisible Ray*, Rukh and Benet both cure patients of blindness: the film displays an article in the International Edition of the *Medical Journal*, which declares: "The miraculous healing power of Radium 'X' has brought thousands of sufferers daily to the doors of Doctor Benet's clinic. Hundreds of maladies have been cured by the marvelous healing powers of this unusual element." But as the *Eugenics* article on uses of irradiation to cure pelvic disease demonstrates, cure can also be damaging: it may deform unborn children and cause sterility.[92] While the most dramatic critique of curative impulses inheres in the film's depiction of Rukh's impairment and insanity, it also resides in more subtle scenes. The paternalist and racist rights eugenic scientists assumed to intervene in individuals' bodies are evident in the benevolent Benet's work in Nigeria. In a conversation with Sir Francis, Benet announces, "See, Stevens, the little creature is going to live!" as he looks down at the table before him. A close-up reveals the "little creature" to be an African baby, whose treatment with solar rays has apparently provided him with a "fresh glow" and greater strength. Benet's treatment of the "creature" as an experimental subject and his indifference as he hands the child back to its anxious mother resonate with the dismissive attitude of the European characters toward the Nigerians who serve them, not to mention Lady Stevens' triumphant comment on her return from hunting, when Drake points out that she has already bagged six rhinos: "Ah, well, they're such nasty-tempered beasts, it's a pleasure to dispose of them." Clearly, then, while the scientists of this film are not in the business of experimenting with genetic makeup or artificially creating life, their use of humans as experimental matter and their drive to perfect and cure have eugenic overtones: Rukh's compulsion to use the ray for destructive purposes reveals the negative and violent underside of eugenics' "positive" drive to improve human "stock." While reveling in the aesthetic effects of physical deviance, horror films castigate the desire to eliminate such difference and homogenize the human race.

*The Invisible Ray* also interweaves in its narrative the dissemination of scientific ideas, emphasizing the popular and sensationalist elements of scientific discovery and discourse that traversed the X-ray motion pictures discussed by Cartwright. The film overtly dramatizes the role of the print media in conveying science to the public. Exposition of Rukh's discovery and Benet's activities are enabled by shots of articles in *World Science*, the *Medical Journal*, and the *Paris Herald*, the last exploiting the more sensationalistic aspects of the case: the murders and the mysterious destruction of the statues. At the same time, horror films like *The Invisible Ray* carry such a strong antiscience and anti-intellectual bias, with such a dramatically reductive physiognomic coding of scientists, that they contribute to the abdication of any popular responsibility for scientific ethics discussed by Pernick in *The Black Stork* and noted in the introduction.

Yet, encoded within the film's narrative itself, lies the inevitable complicity of cinema with the advances of science, with medical uses and abuses of technology, and with the objectification and aestheticization of physical disability. While the print media functions in *The Invisible Ray* to convey information to the public, the cinema is the spectacle that the film repeatedly aligns with the ray and with Radium X itself and thus construes as both curative and potentially destructive. Two scenes in particular explore the power of the camera and the dynamics of vision. The first is, of course, the space spectacle engineered by Rukh. This scene confirms the "motion picture" as a medium that may physically damage its viewers (fig. 5.4): the spectacle is so dangerous that Rukh wears protective gear and seats his audience behind a barrier. Afterwards, he is faint and exhausted, and audience members express shock and disbelief. The destructive effects of this display extend throughout *The Invisible Ray*: by the film's conclusion, four of the six individuals who witness it, including Rukh himself, are dead. Even Drake and Diane must struggle against the destructive influences of the film, saved only by their love. In keeping with Forman's conclusions about

**5.4** The pains of spectatorship: Ronald Drake (Frank Lawton), Diane Rukh (Frances Drake), Dr. Benet (Bela Lugosi), Sir Francis Stevens (Walter Kingsford), and Lady Arabella Stevens (Beulah Bondi) in *The Invisible Ray* (1936).

counteracting the negative effects of film and horror's assertion of morality and environment as forces stronger than eugenics and science, *The Invisible Ray* suggests the healthful effects of love, expressed, of course, within normative marital and family structures.

The second scene exploring the dynamics of the camera and vision occurs after the murder of Sir Francis, who is found lying on his bed, his eyes wide and staring. Lady Stevens asks Benet, "What hideous thing did he see, do you think?" Benet asks for an ultraviolet camera and takes a picture of Sir Francis. Later, in his laboratory, after developing a glass plate, he places it into a viewing machine and sees the face of Rukh reflected in Sir Francis's staring eye (fig. 5.5). But as Benet removes the plate, it breaks, and his visual evidence is destroyed. As in the first scene, and as in X-ray photography and motion pictures, scientific photography is used to reveal a physical truth: in this case, the cause of Sir Francis's death. While it is assumed that the cause of his death was Rukh's poisonous touch— something implicitly proven when Lady Stevens is murdered and Benet reveals Rukh's luminous handprint on her throat—as Lady Stevens intuits, the real cause is something he has witnessed. The ultraviolet camera reveals in Sir Francis's eyes the face of the murderer, confirming that what one sees may kill one. The image recalls H. P. Lovecraft's assertion that the "Italo-Semitico-Mongoloid" inhabitants of Manhattan's Lower East Side "left on the eye . . . a yellow and leering mask with sour, sticky, acid ichors oozing at eyes, ears, nose, and mouth," suggesting that disability and monstrosity imprint on the spectator.[93]

However, both scenes also confirm that the act of revelation is potentially destructive for all parties: the individual who constructs the revelation, those who witness it, and the subject revealed by it. The plate's accidental breakage emphasizes the damaging effects of photographic and cinematic revelation; it also resists the scientific desire to fix truth in spectacular form and forewarns of the deaths of both Rukh and Benet.[94] Only the formerly blind woman, protected from the initial effects of the ray and its cinematic vision, retains a position of innocence from which to judge and sentence. Her former disability entitles her to ameliorate the negative aspects of both ray and cinematic technology and salvage their healing aspects for humanity. But the film indicts the nondisabled spectators for their complicity in scientific spectacle. The film thus models contemporary theories about cinema spectatorship, wherein, Shaviro argues, images "are continually being imprinted upon the retina." Shaviro continues, in terms pertinent to X-ray technology, "Perception is turned back upon the body of the perceiver, so that it affects and alters that body, instead of merely

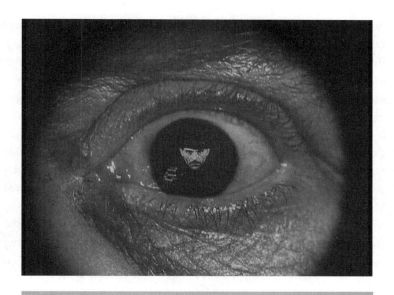

**5.5** Horror imprinted on the eye: Janos Rukh (Boris Karloff) on the eye of his murder victim in *The Invisible Ray* (1936).

constituting a series of representations to be recognized." This insight enables Shaviro to argue that "[c]inema produces real effects *in* the viewer, rather than merely presenting phantasmatic reflections *to* the viewer."[95]

In all, then, the dynamics of shock and X-ray as deployed in cinematic horror confirm the potentially damaging effects of cinematic spectacle. But the greatest destructive power, the films suggest, is reserved for those scientific spectacles that purport to reveal bodily truth and yet are marked with the same desires and perversities that traverse the horror-film spectacle, proving far more deadly than horror film for both physician and patient. In this sense, the films question scientific claims to categorize and reveal bodily deviance, and they persistently relocate such deviance onto the body of the scientist. With parody and slapstick, the horror film also attempts to incorporate the shocking aspects of modern culture and technology; with its affirmation of love and interpersonal connection over scientific objectivity, it models a sentimentalized vision of a healthy society characterized by morality, parental responsibility, and common sense.

However, Shaviro's insistence that films produce effects in their viewers should not be understood as confirmation that viewers are passive victims. In the rhetoric of X-ray and shock mobilized in classic horror films, medical figures and film-viewers alike are revealed as complicit in the eugenic and dysgenic spectacles staged on their behalf. While the physiological drama of horror film may "rebound" on masochistic viewers, audience members nonetheless cooperate in its production; like the medical figure wielding the X-ray, they are at once objects and subjects of the horror film's debilitating gaze. Like the characters in *Geek Love* who seek out freak shows and then sacrifice their limbs to the cult of disability, spectators are at the mercy primarily of their own unacknowledged investments in and desires for disability—and their concomitant ignorance of the political and material implications of their bodily fantasies. As argued in the introduction, the eugenic drama was suppressed because it proved unpleasant for its viewers. Its reincarnation in the horror film proves more palatable, couching eugenic insights within salacious and incredible narratives. But horror's persistent restaging of the scene of its own consumption refuses to exculpate the viewing public from the eugenic imperatives that underwrite the physiognomic logic of the genre. We are all mad doctors, delighted to be impaired and immobilized in our seats as the physiognomic drama unfolds.

# CONCLUSION

n 1927 the United States Supreme Court ruling in the case of Carrie Buck
affirmed the right of states to destroy the reproductive capacities of
those designated "feebleminded" or otherwise congenitally defective.[1]
Expert opinion in the case was provided by Harry H. Laughlin of the Eugenics Record Office (ERO), who, having never met Carrie, her mother, or her
daughter, testified "that Carrie's alleged feeblemindedness was primarily
hereditary."[2] Buck's lawyer protested that salpingectomy, "the opening of
the abdominal cavity and the cutting of the Fallopian tubes with the result
that sterility is produced," violated Buck's "constitutional right of bodily
integrity." He asserted, "The inherent right of mankind to go through life
without mutilation of organs of generation needs no constitutional declaration." However, the opposing lawyer countered that, as in compulsory vaccination, "a surgical operation is required for the protection of the individual
and of society." The opinion of the court, delivered by Justice Oliver Wendell Holmes, affirmed the legality of the sterilization, referencing "An Act
of Virginia, approved March 20, 1924, [which] recites that the health of the
patient and the welfare of society may be promoted in certain cases by the
sterilization of mental defectives, under careful safeguard." Holmes concluded, "It is better for all the world, if instead of waiting to execute degenerate offspring for crime, or to let them starve for their imbecility, society
can prevent those who are manifestly unfit from continuing their kind. The

principle that sustains compulsory vaccination is broad enough to cover cutting the Fallopian tube. . . . Three generations of imbeciles are enough." Predicting the consequences of such a decision, as noted in the introduction, Buck's lawyer declared: "A reign of doctors will be inaugurated and in the name of science new classes will be added, even races may be brought within the scope of such regulation, and the worst form of tyranny practiced."[3]

Some eight years after the Buck ruling, American filmgoers watching *Island of Lost Souls* (dir. Erle C. Kenton, Paramount, 1932) were introduced to the sinister Dr. Moreau (Charles Laughton) who, in his "House of Pain," conducts surgical experimentations without anesthetic on subjugated creatures whom he has turned from animals into humans. His most successful creation is Lota (Kathleen Burke), the Panther Woman. Directed by Moreau to seduce Parker (Richard Arlen), a young man stranded on Moreau's island, Lota fails when Parker glimpses the shocking sight of claws on her hands. Angered, Moreau flings Lota to the ground, where she cowers fearfully as he excoriates the return of her beast flesh and plans to return her to his laboratory, vowing, "This time I'll burn out all the animal in her! I'll make her completely human!" The film thus offers a horrifying and coerced surgical mutilation in the name of bodily integrity, health, and evolutionary advance, reflecting contemporaneous practices of surgical sterilization on the "unfit." The consonance in turn raises the specter of German eugenics: Frank McConnell found in the source text of *Island of Lost Souls*, H. G. Wells' novel *The Island of Doctor Moreau*, "an early, prophetic version of the world of the concentration camp."[4] And reviewer Eric Rhode responded to the 1963 British debut of *Freaks* by observing, "As an attack on complacency, and on the idea of a superior race, *Freaks* is uncommonly forceful[;] one can only wish it had been shown in Nazi Germany."[5]

Rhode's statement retrospectively recognizes in classic horror a dramatic realization of eugenics' pains and perversities. And although Buck's lawyer's vision of widespread tyranny never eventuated in the United States—even as state-sponsored tyranny institutionalized and sterilized countless "unfit" Americans—his response gestures to the link between the American eugenic practices in effect at the time of the rise of classic horror and the horrific genocidal practices carried out in Germany in the 1930s and 1940s. As several histories have documented, not only did American eugenic policies and actions provide a blueprint for Nazi Germany's rounding up of "inferior" groups, medical experiments and torture, and mass killings, but American eugenicists directly collaborated with and praised Germany's embrace of eugenics.[6] Indeed, at the Nuremberg trials, lawyers for Nazi doctors submitted the *Buck* opinion as precedent for their clients' surgeries on the inhabitants of death camps.[7]

The ascendancy of Nazi Germany is typically associated with a decline in the appeal and power of eugenics in the United States. Indeed, since the mid-1920s, American eugenics had been falling from intellectual favor. Scientists criticized its genetic approach, which simplistically connected "unit characters" to physiological traits rather than acknowledging that any given phenotypic characteristic was the result of multiple and variable polygenetic combinations.[8] They also contested its minimization of environmental influence: in 1925, Thomas Hunt Morgan wrote of the "feebleminded" represented in the family studies, "it is obvious that these groups of individuals have lived under demoralizing social conditions that might swamp a family of average persons."[9] Eugenicists themselves forwarded such criticisms: in 1927 biologist Raymond Pearl, a member of the American Eugenics Society and the Galton Society, declared that eugenics had "largely become a mingled mess of ill-grounded and uncritical sociology, economics, anthropology, and politics, full of emotional appeals to class and race prejudices, solemnly put forth as science, and unfortunately accepted as such by the general public."[10]

These views indicated the beginnings of a movement toward "reform" eugenics, where scientists interested in eugenics sought to disentangle race and social "degeneracy" from genetic studies and to explore more fully the complicated relationship between genetics and environment. For instance, British geneticist Lionel Penrose debunked interpretations of Down syndrome, then called "mongolism," as a hereditary condition or a racial category; eugenicists such as R. A. Fisher uncovered connections between blood types and certain diseases; and Otto Klineberg, motivated by anthropologist Franz Boas, a longtime critic of eugenic thought, began investigating the role of environmental influence in the IQ levels of racial groups.[11] The eugenic focus on improving national and racial health was thus recast as a matter of improving human health by advancing medical and genetic knowledge. The reach of "hard-line" eugenics waned: concerned by the ERO's racist associations and unscientific procedures, the Carnegie Institution withdrew its funding, precipitating its permanent closure in December 1939.

At the end of the 1930s, then, as the major phase of the classic horror cycle faded, the horrors of eugenics were, at least publicly, diminishing in the United States as they accelerated in Nazi Germany. This shift is addressed in a handful of late 1930s and early 1940s B horror movies, where, as in Germany, medical experimentation on innocents goes to increasingly horrific extremes. In *The Monster Maker* (dir. Sam Newfield, 1944, PRC), Dr. Igor Markoff (J. Carroll Naish) plans on gaining a wife (Wanda McKay) by capturing her father (Ralph Morgan) and injecting him with acromegaly, which causes enlargement of the bodily extremities.[12] In *The Return of Doctor X* (dir. Vincent Sherman, First National Pictures, 1939), the title character, played by Humphrey Bogart, is brought back to life by Dr. Flegg (John Litel) after being executed for starving a small child in order "to find out how long babies could go without eating." Flegg defends his resurrection of X: "True, in the eyes of society he was a murderer. But he was also a medical genius. And I felt that he had been a martyr to science." But the doctor is forced to acknowledge the folly of his ways as X goes on the prowl for blood to sustain his life, declaring, "My experiments have turned into madness. I've created a monster. May God forgive me." Insane dreams of supermen and themes of fascist conformity preoccupy mad-doctor films such as *Man Made Monster* (dir. George Waggner, Universal, 1941), where Lionel Atwill uses electrical experiments to turn a man into a supercharged and compliant monster, and *The Mad Monster* (dir. Sam Newfield, PRC, 1942), where Dr. Lorenzo Cameron (George Zucco), having used wolf blood to transform his "simple-minded" gardener, Petro (Glenn Strange), into a killer, imagines creating an army out of such creatures. Scientists also carried out nefarious bodily experiments in service to the Nazis in films such as *King of the Zombies* (dir. Jean Yarbrough, Monogram, 1941), *Revenge of the Zombies* (dir. Steve Sekely, Monogram, 1943), *Black Dragons* (dir. William Nigh, Banner Productions, 1942), and the somewhat comic addition to the *Invisible Man* series, *Invisible Agent* (dir. Edwin L. Marin, Frank Lloyd Productions, 1942).

After the war, however, as the extent of and details about the Holocaust became known, horror movies veered away from such eugenic dramatizations, perhaps registering popular discomfort that its fantastical and horrific eugenic visions had come much too close to reality. The genre thus moved in comic or conservative directions and, as Dana Polan has argued, expressed increased faith in medical and political authorities to restore social and bodily order. For instance, in *The House of Dracula* (dir. Erle C. Kenton, Universal, 1945), the Wolfman seeks a cure for his condition and undergoes brain surgery to attain normalcy.[13] Similarly, the prologue added in the late 1940s to *Freaks* by exploitation film distributor Dwain Esper opined, "Never again will such a story be filmed, as modern science and teratology is rapidly eliminating such blunders of nature from the world." Such statements refashioned medical and scientific research as a beneficent enterprise, even as Esper's commentary echoed uncannily the imperatives driving Nazi exterminations of disabled people and undesirable ethnic groups.

Further consideration of postwar horror films is required to understand to what extent they really did turn toward a more conservative body politics, whether they perpetuated eugenic assumptions in more subtle forms, and what connections might be drawn between these developments and the revelations of German atrocities precipitated by eugenic policies. What the increased focus on cure suggests, however, is that if eugenics had been widely and publicly disavowed in the United States, notions of somatic and psychological conformity and aberrance had not. Despite modifications of American eugenics' most egregious and racist elements, some disability scholars have argued that eugenic interpretations of disability and disabled people persisted, insofar as genetic studies continued to assume that physiological and intellectual "defects" were innately bad and to extend the right of medical professionals to shape and dictate concepts of "health," "normalcy," and "disease." In the latter half of the 1930s, commentators like the *New York Times'* Waldemar Kaempffert reflected reformists' move away from racially motivated eugenic studies, affirming that "[e]ach racial type runs the gamut from idiots and criminals to geniuses and statesmen." But the same commentators often took for granted the continuing value of diagnosing and eliminating "defect": wrote Kaempffert, "Genetic research must teach us to identify the hereditary defectives in our midst, whether they are Americans or Chinese, black or white."[14]

Disability scholars such as Anne Kerr and Tom Shakespeare trace this persistent denigration of all kinds of impairment in the genetic developments of the twentieth century. For instance, they contend, as science has developed directive genetic counseling and prenatal diagnostic practices that seek to prevent the reproduction of disabled children, intellectual energy and resources are much less often channeled toward accommodating and providing assistance for already-living disabled people, who continue to face a raft of discriminatory attitudes and actions. Kerr and Shakespeare point out that "we continue to hold contradictory attitudes towards disabled people, largely based on a mixture of fear, suspicion, and pity" and that "[t]here is a widespread view amongst clinicians, scientists, and policy-makers that the birth of a disabled child is a tragedy best avoided"—a claim that could not be made about any other minority group without drawing outrage and censure. As well, Kerr and Shakespeare note, professionals continue to control the nature, application, and regulation of genetic research and services and to make judgments about society's best interests; technological developments continue to be perceived as neutral and inevitable, rather than politically driven; and scientific studies continue to be guided by a principle of progress that has no place for unusual or impaired bodies.[15] Thus, as other marginalized groups have worked to throw off the stigma of disability, it continues to be produced in and on atypical bodies and minds in ways that affirm disabled people as troublesome obstacles to social advancement. Disability also continues to be presented as a medical problem, something that will, as Esper's prologue promised several decades since, soon be reassuringly erased from our sight and our experience.[16]

Classic horror films, then, stand as products of a eugenic era that work against the avowed desire to "look away" from the distasteful image of eugenics. In foregrounding the too-real and evidently impaired body, classic horrors remind us of that the production of disability—on impaired as well as other marginalized bodies—lies at the heart of eugenics. In elucidating the cultural and cinematic conventions of disability representation, classic horrors emphasize the cultural processes that make disability strange and "naturally" repulsive. In drawing attention to the monstrous possibilities of the medical drive for cure and purity, classic horrors suggest that impairment, vulnerability, and bodily and mental imperfections may be less abhorrent aberrations than vital elements of human experience. And in illuminating the desire to see and experience disability that propels the classic horror film, these movies indict viewers for disavowing their investment in disability, a disavowal that allowed the flourishing of both American eugenic practices and the horrors of the Holocaust.

While *Hideous Progeny* has privileged particular classic horror films and, especially, mad-doctor films, we can glimpse the threads of eugenic politics and aesthetics through most movies in the cycle. We can trace eugenic tropes of primitive monstrosity and vitality as threats to the civilized bourgeoisie in several zombie, mummy, hypnosis, and voodoo films, including *Chloe, Love Is Calling You* (1931), *White Zombie* (1932), *The Mummy* (1932), and *The Return of Chandu* (1934). We can locate eugenic anxieties in the conflation of socioeconomic inheritance and physiological heredity that plays out in "old dark house" movies such as *The Old Dark House* (1932), *The Monster Walks* (1932), *The Black Room* (1935), and *Son of Frankenstein* (1939). And we can analyze the knotted intertwining of race and disability, the evolutionary and dysgenic blurring of the animal-human divide, in "bestial" classic horror films such as *Dr. Jekyll and Mr. Hyde* (1931), *Island of Lost Souls* (1932), *The Most Dangerous Game* (1932), *Murders in the Rue Morgue* (1932), and *King Kong* (1933). In each set of films, visible impairment again encodes a host of cultural and pseudoscientific beliefs about disability, using the figure of the monster and of variously disabled characters both to engage and to disintegrate particular biologically deterministic narratives. The endurance and reappearance in our culture of many of these films and their iconographic characters testifies to their continuing appeal to our fears of and desires for disability.

That the relationship of horror film to eugenic notions is, today, still both important and highly charged is suggested in recent public commentaries about eugenics or the Holocaust. For instance, on February 16, 2008, the *New York Times* ran a story about French Prime Minister Nicolas Sarkozy, who was receiving criticism for a proposal that every French fifth-grader be obliged "to learn the life story of one of the 11,000 French children killed by the Nazis in the Holocaust." Critics, the report noted, felt that requiring children to experience this identification could be deeply traumatic. But Jewish historian Serge Klarsfeld demurred, declaring, "To those who say it's too difficult for young children—that's not true. What they see on television or in a horror film is much worse. This is not a morbid mission."[17] In another instance, on March 17, 2008, the University of Minnesota newsletter published a description of the "Deadly Medicine: Creating the Master Race" exhibit being hosted by the Science Museum of Minnesota and the university's Center for Holocaust and Genocide Studies. In the article, director of the Center Stephen Feinstein discussed eugenic activities in the United States in relation to those in Germany and affirmed the exhibit's relevance to contemporary matters of immigration, economic inequities, welfare, and health care. Perhaps in order to encourage potential museum visitors reluctant to peruse a potentially gloomy or disturbing exhibit, Feinstein also added, "I get more scared by horror movies than I do by this stuff."[18]

In both pieces, horror film functions as a yardstick against which to measure the potential effects of eugenic stories on audiences: French schoolchildren, American museum-goers. Like the early-twentieth-century Americans who insisted that eugenic films did not belong in the public sphere, critics of Sarkozy's plan and the reluctant museum visitors imagined by Feinstein find depictions of eugenic extremes harmful and traumatic. But defenders of these projects assert the worth of an intimate engagement with eugenic histories and imply that these histories are both more valuable and less unsettling than the average horror film. As a genre that foregrounds images of bodily violence and generates responses of fear and disgust, horror comes easily to mind as a comparison to texts that convey the monstrous and sickening violence of the Holocaust—or, in the case of "Deadly Medicine," the less extreme but nonetheless egregious crimes of

American eugenics. The comments of Klarsfeld and Feinstein again suggest that we find horror films more palatable because they are fictional but also attest that our familiarity with the shocking spectacles of horror film may in fact steel us for—and enable us to connect with—the real and historical horrors of eugenic actions of the past.

Whether horror films in fact facilitate profound engagements with difficult history or simply aestheticize, commercialize, and numb us to violence and bodily damage is an open question in horror-film scholarship and popular perception. An October 2000 article in the *New York Times* raised the issue with several academic figures. It cited Siegfried Kracauer's thesis about German films' reflection of the rise of authoritarianism and the notion of horror-film directors such as George Romero, John Carpenter, and Tobe Hooper, relayed in the documentary *The American Nightmare* (2000), that 1960s and 1970s horror and gore films enabled "people to process the horrors of real life," including the Vietnam War and violent confrontations over black civil rights. But critics contend that "the graphic images churned out by today's culture make critical thinking more difficult, not less." Geoffrey Hartman, the director of the Fortunoff Video Archive for Holocaust Testimonies at Yale University, asks, "Is this a working-through, or is it a sign that we somehow are in a new phase of culture in which everything gets escalated and violence becomes a necessary ingredient to move us, to stir our emotions?" Or, in the words of the article's author, "is the violence in horror films truly cathartic or just gratuitous pandering?" However, the report suggests, horror films, via their guise as unrealistic genre films, "penetrate the defenses of even the most jaded viewer in a way that straight historical dramas can't." Tom Gunning argues that, unlike horror, a supposedly worthy historical drama such as *Schindler's List* (1993) actually functions to reassure us about historical trauma, "comforting viewers instead of leading them to the abyss."[19]

The idea that horror films might more deeply penetrate our worldviews precisely because of their fantastical and formulaic structures is also advanced by Robin Wood, who declares that films overtly marked as "entertainment" often arrest our consciousness at "the level of plot, action, and character," enabling "the most dangerous and subversive implications [to] disguise themselves and escape attention." Continues Wood, "This is why seemingly innocuous genre movies can be far more radical and fundamentally undermining than works of conscious social criticism." Horror films' fantasies, Wood insists, "are not meaningless," but can constitute radical ways of attempting to address "the unresolved tensions of our lives."[20] More recently, Adam Lowenstein has argued for seeing "the modern horror film as a genre very much engaged with, rather than estranged from, traumatic history," a genre that uses allegory to represent "cruelty, anguish, and horror" in literal images of corpses and "beheadings, dismemberments, and cannibalism." In such shocking spectacles, he suggests, we experience the sudden and explosive "constellation" of past and present that Walter Benjamin called *Jetztzeit*, which "blasts open" and defamiliarizes the "homogenous empty time" of linear, teleological historicism, and opens up new and potentially revolutionary perceptions of both history and the present.[21]

The implications of such a view for this consideration of the eugenic and disability politics of classic horror are twofold. On the one hand, this perspective suggests that, if horror films model ableist narrative dynamics and exploitations of bodily form, the enduring success of the genre may perpetuate eugenic assumptions. Lowenstein notes that "the allegorical moment of *Jetztzeit* is not only disruptive, unpredictable, and open to revision, but also potentially dangerous—it is vulnerable to appropriation by those who wish to manipulate history to oppressive ends."[22] To the extent that some horror scholars have seen in classic horror film only conservative body politics, a view affirmed by several disability scholars, these 1930s films may indeed seem to emulate eugenic narratives, thus perpetuating ableist views of disability as innately "bad" and stigmatizing.

On the other hand, as *Hideous Progeny* has argued, classic horror films can open to contemporary eyes the complex and dynamic imagining of disability that both underwrote and undermined early-twentieth-century genetic determinism and eugenic policy. Classic horror films undeniably exploit the spectacle of the monstrous body for visceral affect and box office gain. But they also call on those who—both within the film and within the theater—gaze at the monster to acknowledge their own investments in that spectacle. Debilitation, these films suggest, is not merely a matter of genetically predestined defect, but an experience of bodily vulnerability we both deny and obsessively pursue, as horror visions of deformed and violated bodies trigger sensory and physiological responses beyond our conscious control. Disability, these films suggest, is something we constantly create—in our responses to unusual bodies and behaviors—and encounter—in our engagement with environmental factors, accidents, and aging processes that we also cannot control.

Consequently, our reading of classic horror films in terms of their disability politics—that is, in terms of their use of aberrant bodies to generate disabling narratives and images—questions the typical historical narrative (Benjamin's historicism), which maps a trajectory ever further away from an offensive and genocidal eugenics toward contemporary benign and objective medical and scientific practices. It suggests that the assumption that disability is something that can and should be eliminated continues to perpetuate the invisibility and denigration of disabled people and to elide their diverse, nuanced, painful, and pleasurable experiences of their bodies and impairments. This assumption also works to disavow the investment our culture and politics have in the rhetoric and imagining of disability. And it covers over the very real possibility that whatever "progress" we make in our genetic and biological studies, we shall never find biological certainty or perfection. A June 12, 2010, *New York Times* article entitled "A Decade Later, Genetic Map Yields Few New Cures" reveals that "[t]en years after President Bill Clinton announced that the first draft of the human genome was complete, medicine has yet to see any large part of the promised benefits." Quoting Clinton's claim in 2000 that the draft would "revolutionize the diagnosis, prevention, and treatment of most, if not all, human diseases," the article notes that this goal "remains largely elusive." The lessons learned by eugenicists in the early twentieth century are repeated: "it has become clear that the genetics of most diseases are more complex than anticipated," and "many of the genetic variants linked to diseases, some scientists have come to fear, could be statistical illusions." Indeed, the piece refers to a report by one medical team that "[t]he old-fashioned method of taking a family history was a better guide."[23]

Perhaps the most profound insight offered by classic horror films, the most challenging way in which they constellate 1930s' eugenics with early-twenty-first century views on disability, is their constant insistence upon the "average" American as deeply imbricated in eugenic politics. As the introduction pointed out, the banishment of eugenic cinema to medical lectures and eugenic society meetings contributed to public withdrawal from eugenic decision-making and practices. Ceding power to professionals, the public was able to surrender responsibility for the hideous operations of eugenics, thus refusing responsibility while passively acquiescing to eugenic premises that demonized and disabled a range of groups and individuals. Classic horror films thus catered to the disavowed desire for eugenic narratives and dysgenic monsters and even facilitated mockery and demonization of the very professionals—the "mad" doctors and scientists—to whom eugenic power had been surrendered.

But the conventions and strategies attached to classic horror narratives and images and explored in *Hideous Progeny* repeatedly frustrate eugenic desires and thus constantly draw attention to spectators' active solicitation and consumption of dysgenic monstrosity. From *Dracula*'s and *Frankenstein*'s presentation of rhetorical eugenic figures—such as the ideal couple, dysgenic blood, and degenerate brains—as empty constructs to *Freaks'* potent and unsettling revelation of the vengeful monster as a convention demanded by thrill-seeking horror-viewers, to the ways in which mad-doctor films and other horror films' spectacles of impairment align spectators with the doctor driven to engineer and experience disability, horror films repeatedly stage the event of their own creation and consumption by American viewers. In so doing, they not only suggest the hypocrisy of public reluctance to confront or participate in eugenic narratives and actions, but they also affirm that our constructions and witnessing of disability inevitably affect our own bodies, exposing them to the impairment that eugenics worked so hard to contain within clearly marked others and intimating a widespread desire to connect with and experience disability, albeit in a controlled, fictional, and fleeting manner.

# NOTES

## INTRODUCTION: DISABILITY, EUGENICS, AND CLASSIC HORROR FILMS

1 Jason S. Joy to B. P. Schulberg, Dec. 1, 1931, Motion Picture Producers and Distributors of America (MPPDA) Case File on *Dr. Jekyll and Mr. Hyde*, Special Collections, Margaret Herrick Library, Academy of Motion Picture Arts and Sciences, Los Angeles, CA (hereafter, AMPAS); Jason S. Joy to Will H. Hays, Dec. 5, 1931, MPPDA Case Files, Special Collections, AMPAS.

2 On horror as a "body genre," see, for example, Linda Williams, "Film Bodies: Gender, Genre, and Excess" (1991), in Leo Braudy and Marshall Cohen, eds., *Film Theory and Criticism*, 727–41: Carol Clover, *Men, Women, and Chain Saws: Gender in the Modern Horror Film*; and Joan Hawkins, *Cutting Edge: Art-Horror and the Horrific Avant-Garde*.

3 For "gruen," see the *Middle English Dictionary*, accessed through the Middle English Compendium database, Marriott Library of the University of Utah, Jan. 31, 2011; for "horror," see *The Compact Edition of the Oxford English Dictionary* (Oxford: Oxford UP, 1971).

4 Rosemarie Garland-Thomson, "Introduction: From Wonder to Error—A Genealogy of Freak Discourse in Modernity," in Garland-Thomson, ed., *Freakery: Cultural Spectacles of the Extraordinary Body*, 3.

5 David T. Mitchell and Sharon L. Snyder, *Narrative Prosthesis: Disability and the*

*Dependencies of Discourse*, 65; see also Leslie Fiedler, *Freaks: Myths and Images of the Secret Self*, 20–21.

6    Garland-Thomson, "Introduction," 3.

7    Bacon, *Novum Organum*, translated by R. Ellis and James Spedding, Aphorism XXIX, 228; and Isidore Geoffroy Saint-Hilaire, *Histoire générale et particulière des anomalies de l'organisation chez l'homme et les animaux*.

8    French statistician Adolphe Quetelet idealized his *l'homme moyen*, or "average man," as the future of a progressing species, declaring, "The more that enlightenment is propagated, the more will deviations from the norm diminish. . . . The perfectibility of the human species is derived as a necessary consequence of all our investigations. Defects and monstrosities disappear more and more from the body." Quoted in Lennard J. Davis, *Enforcing Normalcy: Disability, Deafness, and the Body*, 28.

9    Mitchell and Snyder, *Narrative Prosthesis*, 58, 65. As Michel Foucault argues in *The Birth of the Clinic*, even with increasing practices of corpse dissection and the subsequent rise of pathological anatomy, which opened up "the tangible space of the body" and enabled a new "anatomo-clinical gaze," the material surface remained a locus of truth, as in the form of the tissue surfaces studied by Marie-François-Xavier Bichat: the bodily interior, now expurgated, offered a decipherable text for doctors and scientists. Foucault, *The Birth of the Clinic: An Archaeology of Medical Perception*, 122, 146, 124–48 *passim*.

     For more on the medical gaze and its pertinence to classic horror cinema, see chapter 4 in this book. On the emergence of the concept of the "norm," see Davis, *Enforcing Normalcy*, esp. ch. 2.

10   Garland-Thomson, *Extraordinary Bodies: Figuring Physical Disability in American Culture and Literature*, 13.

11   This concept was articulated in 1975, when the Union of the Physically Impaired Against Segregation (UPIAS) declared, "In our view, it is society which disables physically impaired people. Disability is something imposed on top of our impairments, by the way we are unnecessarily isolated and excluded from full participation in society." Union of the Physically Impaired Against Segregation, "Fundamental Principles of Disability," 3 (website accessed May 15, 2008: see bibliography).

     This approach inspired Michael Oliver's outline of the "social model" of disability in his 1983 book *Social Work with Disabled People* and in his *The Politics of Disablement: A Sociological Approach*. See also Simi Linton, *Claiming Disability: Knowledge and Identity*, for a clear discussion of the social model.

12   Davis, *Enforcing Normalcy*, 129.

13   Mitchell and Snyder, *Narrative Prosthesis*, 47–48.

14   Mitchell and Snyder, *Narrative Prosthesis*, 47; de Baecque, quoted in ibid., 63.

15  Ibid., 63.

16  Davis, *Enforcing Normalcy*, 49.

17  "[F]irst, a deviance or marked difference is exposed to a reader; second, a narrative consolidates the need for its own existence by calling for an explanation of the deviation's origins and formative consequences; third, the deviance is brought from the periphery of concerns to the center of the story to come; and fourth, the remainder of the story rehabilitates or fixes the deviance in some manner." Mitchell and Snyder, *Narrative Prosthesis*, 53–54.

18  Mitchell and Snyder, *Narrative Prosthesis*, 54–57, 53, 49, 48.

19  Davis, *Enforcing Normalcy*, 48.

20  Disability studies encompasses a variety of methodologies and subjects in its exploration of legal, social, and cultural constructions of disability. It includes, but is not limited to, histories and analyses of disability policy; sociological and psychological studies of attitudes toward and/or experiences of disability; autobiographical writings on experiences of disability; "the new disability history" that seeks to write the overlooked histories of the disabled, disability, and disability activism; and cultural, textual, and philosophical studies of disability representations.

   *Hideous Progeny* draws much of its inspiration from texts in the last category, including Alan Gartner and Tom Joe, eds., *Images of the Disabled: Disabling Images*; David Hevey, *The Creatures Time Forgot: Photography and Disability Imagery*; David T. Mitchell and Sharon L. Snyder, eds., *The Body and Physical Difference: Discourses of Disability*; Mitchell and Snyder, *Narrative Prosthesis*; Snyder and Mitchell, *Cultural Locations of Disability*; Rosemarie Garland-Thomson, *Extraordinary Bodies*; Jennifer Terry and Jacqueline Urla, eds., *Deviant Bodies: Critical Perspectives on Difference in Science and Popular Culture*; Lennard J. Davis, ed., *The Disability Studies Reader*; Robert McRuer, *Crip Theory: Cultural Signs of Queerness and Disability*; Ato Quayson, *Aesthetic Nervousness: Disability and the Crisis of Representation*; Tobin Siebers, *Disability Theory*; and Susan Wendell, *The Rejected Body: Feminist Philosophical Reflections on Disability*.

21  Mitchell and Snyder, *Narrative Prosthesis*, 7, 8 (italics in original).

22  Quayson, *Aesthetic Nervousness*, 27, 19, 18, 17–18.

23  "Survival of the fittest" was first used by Herbert Spencer in his 1864 *Principles of Biology*, where he stated, "This survival of the fittest, which I have here sought to express in mechanical terms, is that which Mr. Darwin has called 'natural selection', or the preservation of favoured races in the struggle for life." Spencer, *The Principles of Biology* 1:444–45.

   Darwin approved of the term, using it in a chapter title for his fifth edition of *The Origin of Species* (1869), and discussing it in his introduction as an acceptable alternative to "natural selection." Spencer combined evolutionary notions with

Malthusian principles to imagine racial development as a continual struggle for limited resources.

24  Texts central to "degeneration" theory included Georges-Louis Leclerc, Comte de Buffon's *Histoire naturelle, générale et particulière* (1749–1788), which hypothesized that species removed from their natural and original homes would degenerate and weaken; French doctor Bénédict Morel's *Traité des dégénérescences* (1857), which took "cretinism"—the physical and mental impairments caused by hypothyroidism—as the exemplary manifestation of widespread hereditary degeneration; Max Nordau's *Degeneration* (1892), which imagined a civilization growing fatigued and hysterical; and American Eugene S. Talbot's *Degeneracy: Its Causes, Signs, and Results* (1898). For an examination of these and other degeneration theorists, see Daniel Pick, *Faces of Degeneration: A European Disorder, c.1848–c.1918*.

25  Cesare Lombroso, "Introduction," in *Criminal Man*, ed. Gina Lombroso-Ferrero, xi–xx.

26  See Mary Gibson and Nicole Hahn Rafter, "Editors' Introduction," in Lombroso, *Criminal Man*, 13–15.

27  Galton, *Inquiries into Human Faculty and Its Development*, 17n1.

28  On the role of Weismann and Mendel's thought in eugenics, see, for example, Donald Pickens, *Eugenics and the Progressives*, 42–50; and Daniel J. Kevles, *In the Name of Eugenics: Genetics and the Uses of Human Heredity*.

29  See Susan M. Schweik, *The Ugly Laws: Disability in Public*.

30  Alexander Graham Bell, *Memoir Upon the Formation of a Deaf Variety of the Human Race*.

31  Paul A. Lombardo, *Three Generations, No Imbeciles: Eugenics, the Supreme Court, and Buck v. Bell*, 39.

32  See Henry Cabot Lodge, "The Restriction of Immigration," in *Speeches and Addresses, 1884–1909*, 245–266.

33  For histories and cultural studies of American eugenics, see, for example, Mark H. Haller, *Eugenics: Hereditarian Attitudes In America*; Pickens, *Eugenics and the Progressives*; Kenneth Ludmerer, *Genetics and American Society: A Historical Appraisal*; Allan Chase, *The Legacy of Malthus: The Social Costs of the New Scientific Racism*; Kevles, *In the Name of Eugenics*; Marouf A. Hasian Jr., *The Rhetoric of Eugenics in Anglo-American Thought*; Elazar Barkan, *The Retreat of Scientific Racism: Changing Concepts of Race in Britain and the United States Between the World Wars*; Edward J. Larson, *Sex, Race, and Science: Eugenics in the Deep South*; Wendy Kline, *Building a Better Race: Gender, Sexuality, and Eugenics from the Turn of the Century to the Baby Boom*; Nancy Ordover, *American Eugenics: Race, Queer Anatomy, and the Science of Nationalism*; Martin S. Pernick, *The Black Stork: Eugenics and the Death of "Defective" Babies in American Medicine and Motion Pictures since 1915*; Edwin Black, *War Against the Weak: Eugenics and America's Campaign to Create a Master Race*; Alexandra Minna Stern,

*Eugenic Nation: Faults and Frontiers of Better Breeding in Modern America*; and Steven Selden, *Inheriting Shame: The Story of Eugenics and Racism in America*.

34  Davenport, *Heredity in Relation to Eugenics*, 1.

35  Ibid., 222

36  Hasian, *The Rhetoric of Eugenics in Anglo-American Thought*, 82.

37  Madison Grant, *The Passing of the Great Race: Or, The Racial Basis of European History*, 193, 27, 29. On Grant's aesthetic depiction of Nordic stock see Betsy Nies, *Eugenic Fantasies: Racial Ideology in the Literature and Popular Culture of the 1920's*, 28–29 and much of ch. 3.

38  Mary K. Coffey, "The American Adonis: A Natural History of the 'Average American' (Man), 1921–1932," in Currell and Cogdell, eds., *Popular Eugenics: National Efficiency and American Mass Culture in the 1930s*, 190–91.

39  Coffey, "The American Adonis," 196.

40  Snyder and Mitchell, *Cultural Locations of Disability*, 30.

41  "Union of the Splendidly Developed Dancer Ruth St. Denis and Edwin Shawn, 'the Handsomest Man in America,' May Produce Results of Great Value to the Science of Race Betterment," 1922, in the Image Archive on the American Eugenics Movement (IAAEM), #855 (accessed Sept. 10, 2010; www.eugenicsarchive.org). The newspaper source is uncertain, although a handwritten annotation suggests "N.Y. American?"

42  Davenport to the ABA, 1911, quoted in Black, *War Against the Weak*, 39.

43  Black, *War Against the Weak*, 58.

44  E. R. Johnstone, "Stimulating Public Interest in the Feeble-Minded," 1916, in IAAEM, #1447 (accessed Aug. 31, 2010). Johnstone attributed this quotation to an unnamed representative of the National Committee for Mental Hygiene.

45  Howe, quoted in Sam Smith, "Harvard Scientist Wants Married Couples Bonded" (orig. in *Boston Sunday Post*, June 10, 1928), in IAAEM, #271 (accessed June 20, 2010).

46  Lucien Howe, "The Control by Law of Hereditary Blindness," ca. 1928, in IAEEM #279 (accessed June 20, 2010; emphasis added).

47  Smith, "Harvard Scientist Wants Married Couples Bonded." For overviews of eugenics' beliefs and aims from eugenicists' perspectives, see Davenport, *Heredity in Relation to Eugenics*; Paul Popenoe and Roswell Hill Johnson, *Applied Eugenics* (1918); Albert Edward Wiggam, *The New Decalogue of Science* (1922); and American Eugenics Society, "Practical Eugenics: Aims and Methods of the American Eugenics Society," 1938, in folder 9, *AES Printing Orders*, APS.

48  The first such "family study," which preceded American eugenics and emphasized environmental factors shaping social delinquency, was Richard L. Dugdale's *The Jukes: A Study in Crime, Pauperism, Disease, and Heredity* (1875). Eugenic family studies included Henry Goddard's *The Kallikak Family: A Study in the Heredity of Feeble-Mindedness* (1912); Arthur H. Estabrook's *The Jukes in 1915* (1916); and

the collection of studies now available in Nicole Hahn Rafter's *White Trash: The Eugenic Family Studies, 1877–1919*. For more on the studies, see John David Smith, *Minds Made Feeble: The Myth and Legacy of the Kallikaks*; and Nicole Hahn Rafter, *Creating Born Criminals*.

**49** Grant, *The Passing of the Great Race*, xix, 89, 20. Other eugenic texts that empha-sized the threat of immigration to the United States included Lothrop Stoddard, *The Rising Tide of Color Against White World Supremacy* (1920); Henry Pratt Fairch-ild, *The Melting-Pot Mistake* (1926); and Madison Grant, ed., *The Alien in Our Midst* (1930).

**50** Davenport, "Race Crossing in Man," ca.1920, in IAAEM, #447 (accessed Aug. 23, 2010); Charles Davenport and Morris Steggerda, *Race Crossing in Jamaica*, 471; Davenport, "The Effects of Race Intermingling," in *Proceedings of the American Philosophical Society* 56 (1917), 367. For another Davenport work on interracial-ity, see Davenport and Florence Harris Danielson, *Heredity of Skin Color in Negro-White Crosses*.

For other eugenic texts focused on racial mixing or purity, see Stoddard, *The Rising Tide of Color*; Earnest Sevier Cox, *White America* (1923); Arthur H. Esta-brook and Ivan E. McDougle, *Mongrel Virginians: The WIN Tribe* (1926); and Wal-ter Ashby Plecker, "Virginia's Attempt to Adjust the Color Problem," *The Ameri-can Journal of Public Health* 15 (Feb. 1925): 111–15.

**51** Grant, *The Passing of the Great Race*, 51.

**52** For eugenic views on sterilization see, for example, Harry H. Laughlin, *Eugenical Sterilization in the United States*; Human Betterment Foundation, "Human Steril-ization," in IAAEM, #1753 (accessed Aug. 18, 2010); and E. S. Gosney and Paul B. Popenoe, *Sterilization for Human Betterment: A Summary of Results of 6,000 Opera-tions in California, 1909–1929*. For histories of forced sterilization in the United States or of the Carrie Buck case, see many of the eugenic histories already listed, as well as John David Smith and K. Ray Nelson, *The Sterilization of Carrie Buck*; Harry Bruinius, *Better for All the World: The Secret History of Forced Sterilization and America's Quest for Racial Purity*; Lombardo, *Three Generations, No Imbeciles*; Phil-lip R. Reilly, *The Surgical Solution: A History of Involuntary Sterilization in the United States*; and Mark A. Largent, *Breeding Contempt: The History of Coerced Sterilization in the United States*. On the continuation of legalized sterilization into the 1970s see, for example, Reilly, *The Surgical Solution*, ch.10.

**53** Mitchell and Snyder, *Narrative Prosthesis*, 2–3.

**54** Black, *War Against the Weak*, 53, 55.

**55** See Stephen Neale, *Genre*, 20–21.

**56** Pernick, *The Black Stork*, 133. As Pernick points out, anti-eugenic films were also an early staple of the cinema, as in Thomas Edison's satirical *The Strenuous Life, or Anti-Race Suicide* (1904).

57 Haiselden allowed six "defective" babies to die between 1915 and 1918. Fisher wrote Haiselden to hope that "the time may come when it will be a commonplace [that] defective babies be allowed to die" and Davenport criticized doctors who "unduly restrict the operation of what is one of Nature's greatest racial blessings—death." Fisher and Davenport quoted in Pernick, *The Black Stork*, 84.

58 Pernick, *The Black Stork*, 144, 56–57. As Pernick documents, the 1916 version of *The Black Stork* now exists only as a paper print. The film was reissued, in revised form, in 1927, whereupon the slave girl was replaced by a white servant girl, for fear that, in the wake of *The Birth of a Nation* (1915), "any mention of race could be inflammatory to someone and that any depiction of miscegenation would outrage southern whites." Pernick, *The Black Stork*, 56–57; subsequent references to this work are cited in the text.

59 "Eugenics in Church Class," *New York Times*, Oct. 20, 1913, 5.

60 Hasian, *The Rhetoric of Eugenics in Anglo-American Thought*, 31.

61 Pernick, *The Black Stork*, 53.

62 Jim Marshall, "The Observer" (orig. in the Portland [OR] *News*, Nov, 7, 1927), in the Leon F. Whitney Eugenics Scrapbook, American Eugenics Society (AES) Collection, American Philosophical Society Library (APS), 2; "What Will the Children Be?" (orig. in the San Francisco *Call*, Nov. 15, 1928), in the Leon F. Whitney Eugenics Scrapbook #1, AES Collection, APS, 1; and "Strange, but True" (orig. in the Minneapolis *Evening Tribune*, Feb. 29, 1928), in the Leon F. Whitney Eugenics Scrapbook #1, AES Collection, APS, 1.

63 Pernick, *The Black Stork*, 121–22, 122–23, 123, 127.

64 For Pernick, the history of Haiselden, *The Black Stork*, and eugenics more generally is valuable "because it makes so dramatically visible the cultural value judgments that are inevitably part of defining any human difference as a disease or a disability and identifying any specific factors as 'the' cause." Pernick, "Defining the Defective: Eugenics, Aesthetics, and Mass Culture in Early-Twentieth-Century America," in Mitchell and Snyder, eds., *The Body and Physical Difference*, 89–110 (90).

65 Pernick, *The Black Stork*, 123–24, 103.

66 Pernick's research shows that the 1927 version of *The Black Stork* received an "adults only" permit in Chicago and indicates that it was banned in Pennsylvania. Ibid., 158.

67 United States Supreme Court, "Buck v. Bell Superintendent," in Carl Jay Bajema, ed., *Eugenics: Then and Now*, 158.

68 Texts that examine popular cultural manifestations of eugenics include Nies, *Eugenic Fantasies*; Tamsen Wolff, *Mendel's Theatre: Heredity, Eugenics, and Early Twentieth-Century American Drama*; Robert Rydell, *World of Fairs: The Century-of-Progress Expositions*; Christina Cogdell, *Eugenic Design: Streamlining America in the 1930s*; and Currell and Cogdell, eds., *Popular Eugenics*.

**69** "The Circus Side Show," *New York Times*, July 9, 1932, 7.

**70** Mary Shelley, "Author's Introduction to the Standard Novels Edition (1831)," in *Frankenstein*, 5.

**71** Shelley, "Author's Introduction," 9.

**72** Ibid., 10.

**73** The issue of *Frankenstein*'s authorship is further muddied, of course, by the significant contributions and changes made by Percy Shelley, traced, for instance, in Charles E. Robinson, ed., *The Original Frankenstein*, and by continuing allegations that Percy is, in fact, the novel's primary author, as in John Lauritsen, *The Man Who Wrote Frankenstein*.

**74** Shelley's capacious understanding of origins encourages contemplation of horror film's many "hideous progenitors," each with its own body politics: not just the Gothic novel, but also Eadweard Muybridge's late-nineteenth-century motion photography, which featured both non-disabled and disabled bodies; the early "cinema of attractions" described by Tom Gunning, which flaunted its artificiality by self-consciously confronting and shocking audience members who, in turn, suspended disbelief to embrace the thrills of such shock; German Expressionist cinema, whose surrealistic, distorted sets and chiaroscuro lighting manifested the workings of mad or uneasy minds; and the silent films of Lon Chaney, whose body was repeatedly and famously contorted in the name of disability performance.

See Muybridge's photography in *The Human Figure in Motion*; *Animal Locomotion*; and *The Male and Female Figure in Motion*. For a disability perspective on Muybridge's images, see Joseph Grigely, "Postcards to Sophie Calle," in Susan Crutchfield and Marcy Epstein, eds., *Points of Contact: Disability, Art, and Culture*, 31–58. On the "cinema of attractions," see Tom Gunning, "An Aesthetic of Astonishment: Early Film and the [In]Credulous Spectator" (1989), in Braudy and Cohen, eds., *Film Theory and Criticism*, 862–76. For a reading of German Expressionist films such as *The Cabinet of Dr. Caligari* (1920) that tie their visual dynamics to the ascendance in Germany of medical and political totalitarianism, see Siegfried Kracauer, *From Caligari to Hitler: A Psychological History of the German Film*, 63–67; for a rereading of *Dr. Caligari* in terms of epistemological uncertainty rather than medical and political authority, see S. S. Prawer, *Caligari's Children: The Film as Tale of Terror*, 195; and for a critique of Kracauer's interpretation, see Thomas Elsaesser, *Weimar Cinema and After: Germany's Historical Imaginary*, esp. Part I.

We should note also that several key Expressionist directors and actors made their way to Hollywood, often as a result of the rise of German eugenic policies, including Paul Leni (*The Cat and the Canary* [1927], *The Man Who Laughs* [1928]); Fritz Lang, who made mainly crime dramas and films noir in Hollywood; F. W. Murnau, killed in a car accident in 1931; Karl Freund, director of photography for *Dracula* and director of *The Mummy* (1932) and *Mad Love* (1935); and Peter Lorre, who starred in *Mad Love* (1935), *The Face Behind the Mask* (1941), and *The Beast with Five Fingers* (1946). Important studies of Chaney's bodily performances include Martin F. Norden, ch. 3, "Man of a Thousand Disabilities and His Brethren," in his *Cinema of Isolation: A History of Physical Disability in the Movies*; and Gaylyn Studlar, ch. 4, "Sideshow Oedipus: Lon Chaney and Film's Freak Possibilities," in *This Mad Masquerade: Stardom and Masculinity in the Jazz Age*. See also Robert G. Anderson, *Faces, Forms, Films: The Artistry of Lon Chaney*; and Michael F. Blake, *A Thousand Faces: Lon Chaney's Unique Artistry in Motion Pictures*.

75  Judith Halberstam, *Skin Shows: Gothic Horror and the Technology of Monsters*, 2–4, 39.

76  *Dr. Jekyll and Mr. Hyde* was released in 1931, but just barely, premiering on the final day of the year. For this reason, it is sometimes referred to as a 1932 film.

77  Halberstam, *Skin Shows*, 3, 39.

78  Chris Baldick, *In Frankenstein's Shadow: Myth, Monstrosity, and Nineteenth-century Writing*, 5.

79  Halberstam, *Skin Shows*, 3.

80  Isabel Cristina Pinedo, *Recreational Terror: Women and the Pleasures of Horror Film Viewing*, 22. As Neale has shown, any genre text portrays "the interruption of an initial equilibrium and the tracing of the dispersal and refiguration of its components." In horror, according to Neale, that interruption occurs when a monstrous body "initiates a series of acts of murder and destruction which can only end when it itself is either destroyed or becomes normalised." Neale, *Genre*, 20–21. Rick Altman somewhat complicates this linear pattern, suggesting that genre films such as horror "offer a process of intensification and release," as cultural norms are increasingly eluded, only to conclude with a pleasurable reversal. Rick Altman, *Film/Genre*, 154.

81  See, for instance, Rhona J. Berenstein, *Attack of the Leading Ladies: Gender, Sexuality, and Spectatorship in Classic Horror Cinema*, 14–15. On the fall of the Laemmle empire at Universal, see Michael Brunas, John Brunas, and Tom Weaver, *Universal Horrors: The Studio's Classic Films, 1931–1946*, 3.

82  See, for example, David J. Skal, *The Monster Show: A Cultural History of Horror*, 206.

83  This periodization is observed in studies such as Brunas, Brunas, and Weaver, *Universal Horrors*, and Rick Worland, *The Horror Film: An Introduction*.

84  Andrew Tudor, *Monsters and Mad Scientists: A Cultural History of the Horror Movie*, 102–104 and ch. 10.

85  Robin Wood, *Hollywood from Vietnam to Reagan . . . and Beyond*, 78.

86  Pinedo, *Recreational Terror*, 22.

87  Halberstam, *Skin Shows*, 24, 27.

88  Mitchell and Snyder, *Narrative Prosthesis*, 33; see also Snyder and Mitchell, *Cultural Locations of Disability*, 17.

89  Neale, *Genre*, 21–22.

90  See, for instance, Roger Dadoun, "Fetishism and the Horror Film," *Enclitic* 1.2 (1979): 39–63.

91  Sigmund Freud, "The Uncanny" (1919), in *The Standard Edition of the Complete Psychological Works of Sigmund Freud*, vol. 17, ed. and trans. James Strachey, 243.

92  Walter Evans, "Monster Movies: A Sexual Theory," in Barry Keith Grant, ed., *Planks of Reason: Essays on the Horror Film*, 54. Horror movies' narrative engagement with and dispensation of such monsters is seen, in such readings, to reinforce conventional sexuality and identity: James B. Twitchell asserts that the Freudian lessons of horror film help induct adolescent audiences into normative reproductive sexuality. See Twitchell, *Dreadful Pleasures: An Anatomy of Modern Horror*.

93  See Margaret Tarratt, "Monsters from the Id" (1970), in Barry Keith Grant, ed., *Film Genre Reader II*, 330–349.

94  Robin Wood, "An Introduction to the American Horror Film," 1979, in Barry Keith Grant, ed., *Planks of Reason*, 169–70.

95  Gendered and sexual frameworks for horror-film interpretations predominate, for example, in important horror-film texts such as Barry Keith Grant, ed., *The Dread of Difference: Gender and the Horror Film*; Pinedo, *Recreational Terror*; and Tania Modleski, "The Terror of Pleasure: The Contemporary Horror Film and Postmodern Theory," in Modleski, ed., *Studies in Entertainment: Critical Approaches to Mass Culture*, 155–66. An influential reading of monster-as-woman occurs in Linda Williams, "When the Woman Looks," in Barry Keith Grant, ed., *The Dread of Difference*, 15–34, while a sustained reading of horror films in relation to the abject, drawing on Julia Kristeva's theories in *Powers of Horror*, is Barbara Creed's *The Monstrous-Feminine: Film, Feminism, Psychoanalysis*. For queer readings, see Halberstam, *Skin Shows*; Berenstein, *Attack of the Leading Ladies*; Harry M. Benshoff, *Monsters in the Closet: Homosexuality and the Horror Film*; and a number of studies on sexuality and vampire films, such as Andrea Weiss, *Vampires and Violets: Lesbians in the Cinema*. On the hystericized male in horror film, see Linda Badley, *Film, Horror, and the Body Fantastic*; see also Clover's discussion of male spectatorship and identification with the victimized woman in horror film in *Men, Women, and Chain Saws*.

96  On the Romero films see, for example, Badley, *Film, Horror, and the Body Fantastic*, esp. ch. 3; Steve Beard, "No Particular Place to Go," *Sight and Sound* 3.4 (Apr. 1993): 30–31; and Steven Shaviro, *The Cinematic Body*, esp. ch. 2. On the "redneck" and his class (and racial) implications, see Clover, *Men, Women, and Chain Saws*, ch. 3. On *Invasion of the Body Snatchers*, see Katrina Mann, "You're Next! Postwar Hegemony Besieged in *Invasion of the Body Snatchers* (1956)," *Cinema Journal* 44.1 (Fall 2004): 49–68.

**97** On class in the Frankenstein films, see Robin Wood, "An Introduction to the American Horror Film," and Peter O'Flinn, "Production and Reproduction: The Case of *Frankenstein*." On queerness in the Frankenstein films, see Benshoff, *Monsters in the Closet*, and Berenstein, *Attack of the Leading Ladies*. On race and gender in the films, see Elizabeth Young, "Here Comes the Bride: Wedding Gender and Race in *Bride of Frankenstein*," in Barry Keith Grant, ed., *The Dread of Difference*, 309–337. Young expands on this reading in the wide-ranging *Black Frankenstein: The Making of an American Metaphor*.

**98** Young, "Here Comes the Bride," 325–26.

**99** Halberstam, *Skin Shows*, 84.

**100** One essay that confronts the bodily politics of the horror-monster on its own terms is Pete Boss's "Vile Bodies and Bad Medicine," which, while pessimistic about the progressive potential of images of bodily "ruination," valuably insists that a Foucauldian "political technology of the body" should inform analyses of contemporary horror; such a focus is also pertinent to contextual studies of classic films. Pete Boss, "Vile Bodies and Bad Medicine," *Screen* 27.1 (1986): 18, 19.

**101** Robert Bogdan et al., "The Disabled: Media's Monster," *Social Policy* 13.2 (Fall 1982): 33.

**102** Norden, *The Cinema of Isolation*, 113. Norden here refers to characters such as Fritz (Dwight Frye), the hunchbacked assistant in *Frankenstein*, and Ygor (Bela Lugosi), the monster's misshapen friend in *Son of Frankenstein*.

**103** Mitchell and Snyder, *Narrative Prosthesis*, 98; Davis, *Enforcing Normalcy*, 183n76.

**104** An exception as a disability analysis of early horror films is Ian Olney, "The Problem Body Politic, or 'These Hands Have a Mind All Their Own!': Figuring Disability in the Horror Film Adaptations of Renard's *Les mains d'Orlac*," *Literature/Film Quarterly* 34.4 (2006): 294–302. One of those adaptations, *Mad Love*, is discussed in chapter 3 of *Hideous Progeny*.

**105** Nöel Carroll, *The Philosophy of Horror or Paradoxes of the Heart*. Carroll draws on Mary Douglas' anthropological text *Purity and Danger: An Analysis of Concepts of Pollution and Taboo*, a significant source also for Julia Kristeva's theory of the abject in *Powers of Horror*. Carroll's ideas about the physical and cultural boundary transgressions of monsters as the center of their fascinating and repulsive effects echo similar discussions of monstrosity's violation of ontological divisions in, for instance, Jeffrey Jerome Cohen's "Monster Culture (Seven Theses)," in Cohen, ed., *Monster Theory: Reading Culture*, 3–25.

**106** Carroll, *The Philosophy of Horror*, 33, 27.

**107** Ibid., 44.

**108** Quoted in ibid., 45.

109 Francis Galton, "Composite Portraits," orig. 1878, in IAAEM, #2193 and #2194; Galton, "Illustrations of Composite Portraiture, The Jewish Type" (orig. in *The Photographic News*, Apr. 17, 1885), in IAAEM, #2217; all accessed Sept. 12, 2009.

110 Carroll, *The Philosophy of Horror*, 45.

111 Wood, "An Introduction," 175.

112 Quayson, *Aesthetic Nervousness*, 15.

113 Eugenics should be seen as only one of several disability discourses operative in this historical moment. The first few decades of the twentieth century in the United States saw several conflicting and overlapping disability discourses, including those related to surrealism, scientific management, disabled veterans, and the carefully managed disabled body of President Franklin Delano Roosevelt. Future projects, it is to be hoped, will take up the connections of these variant disability discourses to the classic horror genre.

## 1. EUGENIC REPRODUCTION: CHIMERAS IN *DRACULA* AND *FRANKENSTEIN*

1 Nicholas Wade, "Chimeras on the Horizon, but Don't Expect Centaurs," *The New York Times* (hereafter, *NYT*), May 3, 2005 (accessed June 10, 2009).

2 John Donne, sermon preached at the funeral of Sir William Cokayne, Knight Alderman of London (Dec. 12, 1626): 9 (accessed Apr. 25, 2008).

3 Claire Ainsworth, "The Stranger Within," *New Scientist* (Nov. 11, 2003): 34–37 (accessed Sept. 15, 2010).

4 Harry H. Laughlin, "American History in terms of [Human] Migration" (1928), quoted in Harry H. Laughlin, *Immigration and Conquest: A Report of the Special Committee on Immigration and Naturalization of the Chamber of Commerce of the State of New York*, 31.

5 Lovecraft, quoted in Michel Houellebecq, *H. P. Lovecraft: Against the World, Against Life*, 106–107.

6 Madison Grant, *The Passing of the Great Race*, 20, 92.

7 D. E. McBroom, quoted in Snyder and Mitchell, *Cultural Locations of Disability*, 83.

8 Grant, *The Passing of the Great Race*, 16, 51–52.

9 Skal, *The Monster Show*, 159.

10 Walter J. Hadden, Charles H. Robinson, and Mary R. Melendy, *The Science of Eugenics and Sex-Life, Love, Marriage, Maternity*, v.

11 Girard and von Wlislocki, quoted in David J. Skal, *Hollywood Gothic: The Tangled Web of "Dracula" from Novel to Stage to Screen*, 80. Skal cites Emily Gerard, "Transylvanian Superstitions," *The Nineteenth Century* (July 1885): 128–44; and Heinrich von Wlislocki, "Torturing Spirits in Romanian Popular Belief," *Am Ur-Quell* 6 (1896): 108–109.

12   Von Wlislocki, quoted in Skal, *Hollywood Gothic*, 81.

13   Davenport, *Heredity in Relation to Eugenics*, 1–2.

14   Ibid., iv.

15   At the same time, Harker's figurative impotence in the face of Dracula's "seduction" of Mina sets in place the genre's stock characterization of the endangered woman's male partner. His weakness when confronted by the dysgenic threat dramatizes the eugenic fear that civilization has domesticated and enervated its "normal," or better, classes. As we shall see, *Frankenstein* elaborates this concept in its representation of the nervous Dr. Frankenstein.

16   Berenstein, *Attack of the Leading Ladies*, 84–85. Berenstein here draws on Lea Jacobs' discussion in *The Wages of Sin* of the period prior to the more stringent enforcement of the Production Code.

17   Berenstein, *Attack of the Leading Ladies*, 66.

18   The sexual element of this scene is even more apparent in the Spanish *Drácula* (dir. George Melford, 1931), filmed concurrently: Mina's Spanish counterpart, Eva (Lupita Tovar), comments, "The next morning, I felt very weak, as if I had lost my virginity."

19   Brunas, Brunas, and Weaver, *Universal Horrors*, 16.

20   Writes Daryl Jones, "From its very beginnings as a literary trope, vampirism has always been used as a vehicle for more-or-less encoded articulations of sexuality and desire (as a way of writing about sex without writing about sex), and importantly (though not exclusively) of articulating homosexual desire, thus operating on a dialectic of vampirism as dissident or deviant." Quoted in Kendall R. Phillips, *Projected Fears: Horror Film and American Culture*, 29. Writes Elaine Showalter, "While most film versions of *Dracula* have been heterosexual, nevertheless, homosexuality is strongly represented in the films, coded into the script and images in indirect ways." Showalter, *Sexual Anarchy: Gender and Culture at the Fin De Siècle*, 182–83.

21   Laemmle, quoted in Skal, *The Monster Show*, 126.

22   Benshoff, *Monsters in the Closet*, 48; Skal, *Hollywood Gothic*, 198–99. Even reviewers of the period found Dracula's weirdness "queer": Mordaunt Hall termed the vampire a "queer genius" and noted that the film featured "all sorts of queer noises, such as the cries of wolves and the hooting of owls." Hall, "'Dracula' as a Film," *NYT*, Feb. 22, 1931, 98; Hall, "Bram Stoker's Human Vampire," *NYT*, Feb. 13, 1931, 21.

23   Writes Phillips, "She has . . . become a vision—albeit a distorted one—of the traditional, maternal wife; a bride in white in pursuit of a child." Phillips, *Projected Fears*, 30–31.

24   In the 1914 movie *For Those Unborn*, for instance, consumptive Blanche Sweet declines two marriage offers, while in *Married in Name Only* (1917), a couple

"agree[s] to a platonic marriage" when the husband discovers "a family history of insanity." Martin S. Pernick notes the convention in pro-eugenic films of rewarding such selfless actions with revelations of misdiagnosis. Pernick, *The Black Stork*, 135.

The notion of such sacrifice was common in eugenic texts: for instance, Hadden, Robinson, and Melendy asserted that should young men or women "discover themselves vitally defective, even if the marriage day has been set," they must "for the sake of their own offspring and for the upbuilding of the race, control their emotions and affections so effectively as to step back into their single and respective paths of life; thus to bless the world with their own lives while heroically refraining from cursing the succeeding generation with their unhappy and unfortunate offspring." Hadden, Robinson, and Melendy, *The Science of Eugenics*, viii.

**25** Neale, *Genre*, 22.

**26** David Starr Jordan, *The Blood of the Nation: A Study of the Decay of Races Through the Survival of the Unfit*, 7, 9.

**27** Theodore Roosevelt, Letter to C. Davenport about "degenerates reproducing," Jan. 3, 1913, in the Image Archive on the American Eugenics Movement (IAAEM), #1242; www.eugenicsarchive.org (accessed Sept. 6, 2010).

**28** Eugenics Record Office, "Eugenics Seeks to Improve the Natural, Physical, Mental and Temperamental Qualities of the Human Family," ca. 1927, in IAAEM, #249 (accessed Aug. 5, 2010).

**29** Phillips, *Projected Fears*, 26.

**30** In the words of Daniel J. Kevles, Galton saw the professional classes as "the prime repository of ability and civic virtue" and "the keystone of a biological program designed to lead to the creation of a conservative meritocracy." Kevles, *In the Name of Eugenics*, 8.

**31** Francis Galton, *Hereditary Genius: An Inquiry into Its Laws and Consequences*, 131–40.

**32** Davenport, *Heredity in Relation to Eugenics*, 198.

**33** On Dracula as "sanguinary capitalist," see Skal, *The Monster Show*, 159. On Marxism and vampire imagery, see Baldick, *In Frankenstein's Shadow*, esp. ch. 6. That the vampire is a vital metaphor for both the aristocracy and capitalism suggests the ways in which the new capitalist order, from the point of view of its critics, adopts and adapts the exploitative excesses of the inequitable feudal system that it displaces.

**34** William Starr Myers, "Political Aspects of Immigration," in Madison Grant, ed., *The Alien in Our Midst*, 201.

**35** Davenport, *Heredity in Relation to Eugenics*, 198.

**36** Brunas, Brunas, and Weaver, *Universal Horrors*, 8.

**37** Fairchild, *The Melting-Pot Mistake*, 107, 110–11.

**38** Other factors also contributed to the immigration restrictions of the 1920s, including organized labor's fears that an influx of immigrants would lower wages and deprive Americans of employment. Mae Ngai notes that the "racial and ethnic remapping of the nation in the 1920s," of which the 1924 Immigration Act was one part, "took place in mutually constituting realms of demography, economics, and law." Ngai, "The Architecture of Race in American Immigration Law: A Reexamination of the Immigration Act of 1924," in the *Journal of American History* 86.1 (June 1999): 71. Nevertheless, in the move toward restrictions, economic and other concerns were repeatedly presented through or alongside eugenic rhetoric and imperatives, as in the 1911 report of the Dillingham Immigration Commission which incorporated and approved Johann Blumenbach's racial hierarchy in *The Anthropological Treatises of Johann Friedrich Blumenbach*; further, eugenicists were extremely influential in the development and realization of the restrictions, as in the case of Harry H. Laughlin's submissions to the House Committee on Immigration and Naturalization. For more on the prominent role of eugenicists in the creation of immigration restrictions, see Matthew Frye Jacobson, *Whiteness of a Different Color: European Immigrants and the Alchemy of Race*, esp. 78–83.

**39** Davenport, *Heredity in Relation to Eugenics*, 219.

**40** Lothrop Stoddard, "The Permanent Menace from Europe," in Madison Grant, ed., *The Alien in Our Midst*, 227.

**41** John E. Edgerton, "The Effect of Recent Immigration upon the Future of this Country," in Madison Grant, ed., *The Alien in Our Midst*, 8.

**42** Fairchild, *The Melting-Pot Mistake*, 114.

**43** Laughlin, *Immigration and Conquest*, 31; Pickens, *Eugenics and the Progressives*, 67.

**44** Fairchild, *The Melting-Pot Mistake*, 111, 123, 124, 123.

**45** Fred Botting, *Gothic*, 146.

**46** For instance, see the glossary in the Prestwick House Literary Touchstone edition of Bram Stoker's *Dracula*, 349. Skal is skeptical of this etymological connection and considers it more likely that Emily Gerard, from whom Stoker took the term "nosferatu," incorrectly transcribed the Romanian *nesuferit*, meaning "insufferable" or "plaguesome." Skal, *Hollywood Gothic*, 80. Peter Hutchings represents the novel "as a kind of invasion narrative in which the vampire, a mysterious figure from the East, threatens to invade both British society—via the proliferating infectiousness of vampirism—and the British body." Hutchings, *The Horror Film*, 45. In *Nosferatu, eine Symphonie des Grauens* (1922), the vampire, visually encoded as Jewish, brings plague and pestilence from Transylvania to Germany.

**47** Halberstam, *Skin Shows*, 78.

**48** Grant, "Closing the Floodgates," in Madison Grant, ed., *The Alien in Our Midst*, 16; Kenneth L. Roberts, "Mexican Immigration in the Southwest," in Grant, ed., *The*

*Alien in Our Midst*, 214, 218; Albert Johnson, "The Opponents of Restricted Immigration," in Grant, ed., *The Alien in Our Midst*, 10.

49  Robert Wickliffe Woolley, "The South's Fight for Race Purity" (orig. in *Pearson's Magazine*, n.d. [ca. 1910], 206–207), in Eugenics Record Office Files, MSC77, series I, box 38, A:3174, at the American Philosophical Society Library (APS). Also available in IAAEM, #676 (accessed Sept. 17, 2010).

50  Charles Davenport, "Eugenics: The Science of Human Improvement by Better Breeding" (1910), in IAAEM, #1714 (accessed June 9, 2010).

51  Quoted in Hasian, Jr., *The Rhetoric of Eugenics*, 67.

52  Hutchings, *The Horror Film*, 45–46.

53  For a sustained critique of Dracula's failings in these areas, see Brunas, Brunas, and Weaver, *Universal Horrors*, 7–19.

54  Roy Huss, "Vampire's Progress: Dracula from Novel to Film via Broadway," in Roy Huss and T. J. Ross, eds., *Focus on the Horror Film*, 56.

55  Berenstein, *Attack of the Leading Ladies*, 119.

56  Skal, *Hollywood Gothic*, 198.

57  Ibid., 223; Arthur Lennig, *The Immortal Count: The Life and Films of Bela Lugosi*, 118.

58  Lyndon W. Joslin, *Count Dracula Goes to the Movies: Stoker's Novel Adapted, 1922–2003*, 31.

59  Joslin expresses an exceptional level of frustration with Dracula's offscreen location of "action" including "Lucy's blood transfusions, her death, and even the wounds on her throat," her "career as a vampire," "[t]he Count's appearance as a wolf," and his "forcing Mina to drink some of his blood from a cut on his arm." Joslin's exasperation speaks to the ways that earlier scenes develop expectations—of "action" and spectacles of degeneracy—that later scenes stymie. Like many scholars, Joslin attributes such deficiencies to the film's origins as "a play, and an underproduced one at that, with characters staring off into the wings of the stage to describe what they purportedly see there." In effect, if not in intent, then, the film refuses to satisfy viewers' desires for blood and visible monstrosity, instead drawing attention to the instability and ephemerality of visible signs of deviance, which are always just out of sight and often "purported" rather than evidentiary. See Joslin, *Count Dracula Goes to the Movies*, 31.

60  It seems consistent with the film's evaporations of blood and, thus, of biological proof, that its epilogue, borrowed from the stage play, has also disappeared. In the film's initial release, Van Helsing appeared against the cinema proscenium and addressed the film audience: "Just a moment, ladies and gentlemen! Just a word before you go. We hope the memories of Dracula and Renfield won't give you bad dreams, so just a word of reassurance. When you get home tonight and the lights have been turned out and you are afraid to look behind the curtains and

you dread to see a face appear at the window—why just pull yourself together and remember that after all there are such things." Skal, *Hollywood Gothic*, 189.

The epilogue thus again asserted the reality of the vampire, the bogeyman, the dysgenic monster. According to David J. Skal and Elias Savada, the epilogue was cut for the film's 1938 rerelease in order to "avoid giving offense to religious groups" by claiming the reality of vampires. Skal and Savada, *Dark Carnival: The Secret World of Tod Browning, Hollywood's Master of the Macabre*, 151. Once excised, then, the missing epilogue forms another of the vanishings central to the film's narrative of blood-loss and slippery somatic proof.

**61** As discussed in the introduction, the question of procreative origins is also inscribed in nuanced ways in Mary Shelley's own representation, in her 1831 introduction, of the novel's conception and authorship. See Shelley, "Author's Introduction" (1831), in *Frankenstein*, 5–10.

**62** Shelley, *Frankenstein*, 36; Pickens, *Eugenics and the Progressives*, 55.

**63** Pickens, *Eugenics and the Progressives*, 55; Shelley, *Frankenstein*, 139.

**64** Like Richard Brinsley Peake's 1823 theatrical adaptation *Presumption: or, The Fate of Frankenstein*, the film dispenses with the novel's epistolary outer layers and the narrator-character of Robert Walton, refashions the monster as a mute creature whose violent actions thus appear somewhat inexplicable and malevolent, and contributes a deformed laboratory assistant. Like Thomas Edison's 1910 short film *Frankenstein*, the 1931 version portrays its titular character's scientific work as an improper distraction from his normative romantic relationship. In its use of a deformed laboratory assistant, 1931's *Frankenstein* borrowed from both Peake's and Edison's texts, while in its representation of Karloff's monster as large, awkward, and lumbering, it drew from German expressionist cinema, notably Carl Boese and Paul Wegener's *Der Golem* (1920) and Robert Wiene's *The Cabinet of Dr. Caligari* (1920). Finally, according to Susan Lederer, the film, in visualizing lightning to galvanize Frankenstein's creation in place of the novel's "working of some powerful engine," imitated the use of electrical apparatus for the same purpose in the American theatrical farce *The Last Laugh* (1913). Lederer, *Frankenstein: Penetrating the Secrets of Nature*, 36.

**65** On the altered ending, see Brunas, Brunas, and Weaver, *Universal Horrors*, 26–27.

**66** Skal credits screenwriter John Russell with this emendation as does Lederer, who cites the American Film Institute's (AFI) catalog. But Carlos Clarens attributes it to Robert Florey. See Skal, *Screams of Reason: Mad Science and Modern Culture*, 128; Lederer, *Frankenstein*, 39; Clarens, "Children of the Night," in Stephen Prince, ed., *The Horror Film*, 60.

**67** Martin Tropp, *Mary Shelley's Monster: The Story of Frankenstein*, 87; Skal, *Screams of Reason*, 128.

**68** Baldick, *In Frankenstein's Shadow*, 5. See also David Pirie, who castigates the change as "ridiculous," and Paul M. Jensen, who presents it as the film's "main weakness." Pirie, *A Heritage of Horror: The English Gothic Cinema, 1946–1972*, 69; Jensen, *Boris Karloff and His Films*, 44.

**69** As Peter O'Flinn points out, the device of the "abnormal" brain makes perfect sense within the film's ideology, which counters the "radical political implications" of Shelley's sympathies for working-class uprisings as products of social conditions; the film "instead sees violence as rooted in personal deficiencies, to be viewed with horror and to be labelled, literally, ABNORMAL and so sub-human." O'Flinn, "Production and Reproduction," 211. As seen below, though, I contend that the film also counters such essentialism with gestures toward social and environmental influence.

**70** Laughlin, "Analysis of America's Modern Melting Pot," testimony before the House Committee on Immigration and Naturalization, 1922, in IAAEM, #1128 (accessed June 9, 2010).

**71** Rafter, *Creating Born Criminals*, 138. Rafter is here summarizing the conclusions of Goddard's article "Four Hundred Feeble-Minded Children Classified by the Binet Method," *Journal of Psycho-Asthenics* 15 (1910): 17–30.

**72** Goddard, "Four Hundred Feeble-Minded Children," 29–30.

**73** W. E. Fernald, "The Burden of Feeble-Mindedness," address to the Massachusetts Medical Society, in *Journal of Psycho-Asthenics* 17.3 (Mar. 1912): 91.

**74** Snyder and Mitchell, *Cultural Locations*, 88.

**75** Ibid., 78.

**76** C. F. Dight, "Eugenics Society President Replies to Questions" (orig. Letter to the Editor, in [Minneapolis] *Journal*, Apr. 29, 1928), in Leon F. Whitney Eugenics Scrapbook #2, AES Collection, APS.

**77** Anderson, quoted in Snyder and Mitchell, *Cultural Locations*, 88.

**78** Goddard, *The Kallikak Family*, 53.

**79** See also the collection of family studies edited by Nicole Hahn Rafter, entitled *White Trash*.

**80** Goddard, *The Kallikak Family*, 71.

**81** See Donald A. MacKenzie, *Statistics in Britain, 1865–1930: The Social Construction of Scientific Knowledge*; and Rafter's introduction to her *White Trash*, esp. 12–17. Among the sponsors of such studies were Mrs. E. H. Harriman and John D. Rockefeller.

**82** The accompanying explanation read, "Every 48 seconds a person is born in the United States who will never grow up mentally beyond that stage of a normal 8 year old boy or girl. . . . Every 7 1/2 minutes a high grade person is born in the United States, who will have ability to do creative work and be fit for leadership." "Some People are Born to Be a Burden on the Rest," AES Scrapbook, APS.

83 "Massachusetts Department of Mental Diseases Exhibits Pictures of 59 Criminal Brains" (1921), in IAAEM, #567 (accessed June 10, 2010).

84 Pierce, quoted in "Oh, You Beautiful Monster," *NYT*, Jan. 29, 1939, X4.

85 Skal, *The Monster Show*, 130; Donald F. Glut, *The Frankenstein Legend: A Tribute to Mary Shelley and Boris Karloff*, 100.

86 "Oh, You Beautiful Monster," X4. On Pierce's makeup, see also Brunas, Brunas, and Weaver, *Universal Horrors*, 24; Skal, *The Monster Show*, 130; Cynthia A. Freeland, *The Naked and the Undead: Evil and the Appeal of Horror*, 46; and Lederer, *Frankenstein*, 40–42.

87 McBroom, quoted in Snyder and Mitchell, *Cultural Locations*, 83.

88 Lederer, *Frankenstein*, 32, 35.

89 Wood, "An Introduction," 171. In the 1930s, the Frankenstein monster, often referred to simply as "Frankenstein," continued to provide an image for insubordinate or dangerous working classes, as in a 1935 *New York Times* article discussing a nationwide movement in which company unions in various industries were seeking the status of autonomous unions. Wrote Louis Stark, "Industrialists here recall the words of General Johnson, [an] NRA administrator, who told them in 1933 that their feverish haste in organizing company unions to circumvent Section 7a of the Recovery Act would react [*sic*] in the form of a 'Frankenstein that will ultimately override you.'" Stark, "Industry Alarmed by Company Unions," *NYT*, Oct. 27, 1935, 16. Intriguingly, while O'Flinn contends that the film erases both the novel's sympathy for the Monster and his symbolic representation of an oppressed class, he overlooks the class connotations of the Monster's attire and the degraded social status implicit in the film's depiction of the Monster as, in O'Flinn's own words, a "shambling goon with a forehead like a brick wall." O'Flinn, "Production and Reproduction," 212.

90 Stoddard, *The Revolt Against Civilization*, 94.

91 Elizabeth Young's article on *Bride of Frankenstein*'s monster points to similar characteristics—his "[d]elinquency, criminality, inferiority, subhumanity"— as evidence that he embodies another stereotype, that of the "black 'brute.'" Young, "Here Comes the Bride," 322. As noted in the introduction, her reading, although focused on the Monster's racial connotations, reminds us that eugenic and related discourses enacted classist, racist, and other prejudiced policies by means of overlapping categorizations based on the perception of behavioral, psychological, intellectual, and physical dysfunction.

92 The phrase "manifestly unfit" was used by Justice Oliver Wendell Holmes in justifying the 1927 U.S. Supreme Court decision to sterilize Carrie Buck, deemed "feebleminded" by experts from the Eugenics Record Office. See United States Supreme Court, "Buck v. Bell Superintendent," in Bajema, ed., *Eugenics*, 156–208.

93  Indeed, Lennard J. Davis has suggested that the movie's monster is in fact "disabled," insofar as "disability" constitutes "a disruption in the visual, auditory, or perceptual field as it relates to the power of the gaze," for he "is inarticulate, somewhat mentally slow, and walks with a kind of physical impairment." Davis, *Enforcing Normalcy*, 129, 144.

94  Clarens, "Children of the Night," 60.

95  Karloff, quoted in Skal, *Screams of Reason*, 129.

96  Davis, *Enforcing Normalcy*, 183n76.

97  Pernick, "Defining the Defective," 98. See also Pernick, *The Black Stork*, and Hasian, *The Rhetoric of Eugenics*. Such popular interpretations anticipated, and perhaps even contributed to, the development of reform eugenics in the late 1920s and 1930s. For more on this topic, see the conclusion.

98  F. S. N., "At the Roxy [*The Bride of Frankenstein*]," *NYT*, May 11, 1935, 21.

99  Andre Sennwald, "Reading the Log for April and May," *NYT*, June 2, 1935, X3.

100 Galton, "Eugenics: Its Definition, Scope, and Aims," in *American Journal of Sociology* 10 (July 1904) (accessed Sept. 8, 2010).

101 Christine Rosen, *Preaching Eugenics: Religious Leaders and the American Eugenics Movement*, 122.

102 For Pomeroy's comments, see "Sterilization Laws Praised," *Los Angeles Times*, Jan. 26, 1928; Leon F. Whitney, "A Charity to Lessen Charity" (ca. 1925), in AES, *Reprints of Eugenic-Related Works, 1923–1963*, box 1, Leon Whitney Collection, APS.

103 Rosen, *Preaching Eugenics*, 140.

104 Fr. Francis J. Connell, "The Catholic Church and Eugenics," in *American Eugenics Society: Conference on the Relation of Eugenics and the Church* (May 8, 1939): 1–6. AES Files, APS.

105 Kevles, *In the Name of Eugenics*, 119. Such anti-eugenic sentiment came to the fore within the Church on December 31, 1930, when Pope Pius XI issued an encyclical on marriage that dealt with eugenic proposals to prevent the marriage or propagation of certain types of individuals. Pius declared, "Public magistrates have no direct power over the bodies of their subjects, therefore, where no crime has taken place and there is no cause present for grave punishment, they can never directly harm, or tamper with the integrity of the body, either for the reasons of eugenics or any other reason." Quoted in Rosen, *Preaching Eugenics*, 159. This encyclical was interpreted by the Catholic press as a condemnation of eugenic methods and even as a call to actively prevent sterilization legislation in the United States.

106 Rosen, *Preaching Eugenics*, 22.

107 Gary Morris, "Sexual Subversion: *The Bride of Frankenstein*" (1993), reprinted in *Bright Lights Film Journal* 19 (July 1997) (accessed Sept. 13, 2010).

108 Gerald Gardner, *The Censorship Papers: Movie Censorship Letters from the Hays Office, 1934–1968*, 65.

109 George Beard, *American Nervousness: Its Causes and Consequences*, vi. See also Tom Lutz, *American Nervousness, 1903: An Anecdotal History*.

110 Gail Bederman, *Manliness and Civilization: A Cultural History of Gender and Race in the United States, 1880–1917*, 84–5; Beard, *American Nervousness*, 26.

111 William Thomas Councilman, *Disease and Its Causes*, 67 (Project Gutenberg E-Book PDF; accessed Sept. 15, 2010).

112 Davenport, "Eugenics: The Science of Human Improvement."

113 Wiggam, *The New Decalogue of Science*, 22, 25, 26.

114 Beard, *American Nervousness*, vi.

115 Quoted in Councilman, *Disease and Its Causes*, 157. Councilman attributes this quotation to "a well-known medical writer."

116 Colin Clive's unfortunate offscreen life modeled a dysgenic narrative of neurasthenic behavior and eventual degeneration, aided by one of the "race poisons" some eugenicists feared. James Curtis documents Clive's anxiety, alcoholism, and premature death in *James Whale: A New World of Gods and Monsters*.

117 Nordau, *Degeneration*, 15, 39–40, 40.

118 See for instance, the *New York Times* article "'Frankenstein' Finished," which reproduces a letter wherein Whale refers to Fritz as "the Dwarf." "'Frankenstein' Finished," *NYT*, Oct. 11, 1931, X5.

119 Frye, quoted in Brunas, Brunas, and Weaver, *Universal Horrors*, 15.

120 Freeland, *The Naked and the Undead*, 137–38.

121 Tony Williams, *Hearths of Darkness: The Family in American Horror Film*, 38.

122 This pattern was repeated in the conclusion for *Bride of Frankenstein*. Writes Curtis, "Only days before its April 19 opening in San Francisco, Whale decided to alter the ending to allow Henry and Elizabeth—both of whom had perished in the preliminary cut—to survive the explosion. Colin Clive, Valerie Hobson, and Boris Karloff were recalled for additional shots, but it was too late to re-shoot the entire collapse of the lab, in which Clive is clearly visible." Curtis, *James Whale*, 250.

123 Tony Williams, *Hearths of Darkness*, 38.

124 As Rick Worland comments, if we applied the classical narrative structure too closely to the film, "then the hopelessly dull Victor Moritz might have been the film's center of interest. That is, to regard the ending as a categorical endorsement of the status quo we must forgive and forget a lot about Henry Frankenstein." Worland, *The Horror Film*, 174.

125 Evans, "Monster Movies," 59.

126 Thanks are due to Richard Preiss for pointing this out.

1   Norbert Lusk, "'Dracula' Hit on Broadway," *Los Angeles Times*, Feb. 22, 1931, Sec. 3: 9.

2   Drawing on documents from the 1955 antitrust case *U.S. v. 20th Century Fox Film Corporation*, Skal puts *Dracula*'s domestic gross at the end of 1931 at nearly $700,000, almost twice its investment, and its international take by 1936 at $1,012,189.42. Skal, *Hollywood Gothic*, 204.

3   "U Has Horror Cycle All to Self," *Variety*, Apr. 8, 1931, 2.

4   Freud, "The Uncanny," 219, 220, 220–26, 231, 241–45.

5   Davis, *Enforcing Normalcy*, 142.

6   Violet and Daisy Hilton performed in vaudeville rather than in freak shows. For a history and analysis of the Hilton sisters, see Allison Pingree, "The 'Exceptions That Prove the Rule': Daisy and Violet Hilton, the 'New Woman,' and the Bonds of Marriage," in Garland-Thomson, ed., *Freakery*, 173–84.

7   Skal, *The Monster Show*, 148.

8   See, for example, Hawkins, *Cutting Edge*, 151; and Méira Cook, "None of Us: Ambiguity as Moral Discourse in Tod Browning's *Freaks*," in Christopher R. Smit and Anthony Enns, eds., *Screening Disability: Essays on Cinema and Disability*, 49–50.

9   Cook, "None of Us," 51.

10  The "monstering" of Cleo operates also in the film's formal elements. In the scenes in which Cleo administers poison to a bedridden Hans, she is portrayed, through body posture, mise-en-scène, and camera angle, as too-big and awkwardly hunched over. See Cook, "None of Us," 52; and Hawkins, *Cutting Edge*, 152. The use of such physical and visual cues both resorts to eugenic assumptions that inner monstrosity is always visually revealed, demonstrating classic horror film reliance on an impoverished physiognomic vocabulary, and suggests that monstrosity is only in the eye of the beholder, that its representation in visual terms is not transparent but determined by cultural and textual conventions.

11  "*Freaks*," *Variety*, July 12, 1932, 16.

12  Sally Chivers, "The Horror of Becoming 'One of Us': Tod Browning's *Freaks* and Disability," in Smit and Enns, eds., *Screening Disability*, 61.

13  See, for example, John Brosnan, *The Horror People*, 65–66; Martin F. Norden and Madeleine A. Cahill, "Violence, Women, and Disability in Tod Browning's *Freaks* and *The Devil Doll*," *Journal of Popular Film and Television* 26.2 (Summer 1998): 86–94; Nicole Markotic, "Disabling the Viewer: Perceptions of Disability in Tod Browning's *Freaks*," in Smit and Enns, eds., *Screening Disability*, 71; Cook, "None of Us," 50–51; Hawkins, *Cutting Edge*, 157–158.

14  As Oliver Gaycken points out, "the freaks' revenge is in an important sense as humanizing a gesture as the earlier parts of the film where they are shown going

about their daily business. . . . What this penultimate sequence tells us is that the freaks are just as human as the other revenge-obsessed protagonists of Browning's films." Gaycken, "Tod Browning and the Monstrosity of Hollywood Style," in Smit and Enns, eds., *Screening Disability*, 79.

**15** The shooting script also called for the revelation of Hercules singing soprano nearby, indicating that the freaks had punished him with castration; the scene was either never filmed or cut from the final release. See *"Freaks,"* in Patricia King Hanson and Alan Gevinson, eds., *The American Film Institute Catalog: Feature Films, 1931–1940*, 700; Skal and Savada, *Dark Carnival*, 174; Norden and Cahill, "Violence, Women, and Disability," 90.

**16** For Hawkins, the punishment that transforms Cleo "into a physical 'monstrosity' seems to affirm that physical difference can be the tangible sign of inner depravity. And it is this possibility that serves to partially blunt the progressive edge of the film." Moreover, as Hawkins notes, the film's pervasive misogyny culminates in the attack, which bears connotations of rape, and which, in rendering Cleo incapable of attracting other men, is implicitly a punishment for her inappropriate expression of sexuality. Hawkins, *Cutting Edge*, 158, 162. For another nuanced reading of the film in gendered and sexual terms, see Rachel Adams, ch. 3, in *Sideshow U.S.A.: Freaks and the American Cultural Imagination*.

**17** Muriel Babcock, "'Freaks' Rouse Ire and Wonder," *Los Angeles Times*, Feb. 14, 1932, 9.

**18** Numerous changes were made to *Freaks* after the January 1932 preview, as detailed by Skal and Savada, reducing the film's running time by half an hour with cuts of "the horrifying details of the mud-dripping freaks swarming over the tree-pinned Olga Baclanova and pouring into a circus wagon to castrate her lover," of comic scenes "including one of the turtle girl being amorously pursued by a seal," and of most of the epilogue set in "Tetrallini's Freaks and Music Hall." The barker's prologue and the reconciliation of Hans and Frieda were added at this point. Skal and Savada, *Dark Carnival*, 174–75.

**19** David J. Skal, "Alternate Endings," *Freaks*, DVD (Burbank, CA: Turner Entertainment and Warner Bros., 2004).

**20** Marx, quoted in Skal and Savada, *Dark Carnival*, 168. An anecdote frequently related in association with these events has F. Scott Fitzgerald responding negatively to his encounter with the conjoined Hilton sisters: "Scenarist Dwight Taylor recounted having lunch with a distraught Fitzgerald the week before he was fired. Fitzgerald and Taylor had no sooner seated themselves than they were joined at the same table by the Siamese twins. 'One of them picked up the menu and, without even looking at the other, asked, "What are you going to have?" Scott turned pea-green and, putting his hand to his mouth, rushed for the great outdoors.'" Ibid., 168.

21  Babcock, "'Freaks' Rouse Ire and Wonder," 9; Skal and Savada, *Dark Carnival*, 174.

22  Trade advertisement reprinted in Skal, *The Monster Show*, 157; *Washington Post* advertisement reprinted in Skal and Savada, *Dark Carnival*, 177.

23  Skal and Savada, *Dark Carnival*, 178; "Freaks," *Variety*, July 12, 1932, 16.

24  "The Circus Side Show," *New York Times*, July 9, 1932, 7; "'Freaks' Arrives," *New York Times*, July 17, 1932, X3.

25  J. C. M, "The Current Cinema [*Freaks*]," *The New Yorker*, July 16, 1932, 45; Lewis, quoted in Skal and Savada, *Dark Carnival*, 180; Parsons, quoted in Skal, *The Monster Show*, 155.

26  Richard Watts Jr., "Freaks," *New York Herald-Tribune*, July 9, 1932, 6; "Freaks," *Harrison's Reports*, July 16, 1932, 114; "Freaks," *Harrison's Reports*, Feb. 27, 1932, 35.

27  Mrs. Alonzo Richardson, letter to Will H. Hays, quoted in Skal and Savada, *Dark Carnival*, 178; Moffitt, quoted in Skal and Savada, *Dark Carnival*, 178.

28  On the film's removal from theaters and poor box office, see Skal and Savada, *Dark Carnival*, 181; Hawkins, *Cutting Edge*, 143; and Robin Larsen and Beth A. Haller, "Public Reception of Real Disability: The Case of Freaks," *Journal of Popular Film and Television* 29.4 (2002): 167.

29  Skal and Savada, *Dark Carnival*, 182.

30  Garland-Thomson, "Introduction: From Wonder to Error," 5.

31  David Gerber, "The 'Careers' of People Exhibited in Freak Shows: The Problem of Volition and Valorization," in Garland-Thomson, ed., *Freakery*, 45; Robert Bogdan, *Freak Show: Presenting Human Oddities for Profit and Amusement*, 23. On the American freak show and its changing fortunes see also Fiedler, *Freaks*; the introduction and essays in Garland-Thomson, ed., *Freakery*; Garland-Thomson, ch. 3 in *Extraordinary Bodies*; and Adams, *Sideshow U.S.A.* For an intriguing discussion of the uses and problems of the term "disability" in historical studies of freak shows, see Nadja Durbach, *Spectacle of Deformity: Freak Shows and Modern British Culture*, 14–21.

32  "The Circus Side Show," 7; "The Pay-Off," *Motion Picture Daily*, Apr. 11, 1932, 2; Mrs. Ambrose Nevin Diehl, letter to William H. Hays, quoted in Skal and Savada, *Dark Carnival*, 176. J. C. M. in the *New Yorker* offered a counterview, suggesting that "if the poor things themselves can be displayed in the basement of Madison Square Garden, pictures of them might as well be shown in the Rialto." J. C. M., "The Current Cinema [*Freaks*]," 45.

33  Heffernan, quoted in Elias Savada, "The Making of *Freaks*" (orig. in *Photon* 23 [1973]), *The Freaks Show: Exhibit 3* (2004) (accessed July 5, 2010).

34  J. C. M., "The Current Cinema [*Freaks*]," 45.

35  *Boston Herald* and *Boston Evening Transcript* quoted in Skal and Savada, *Dark Carnival*, 178–79; "'Freaks' Arrives," X3.

36  Fiedler, *Freaks*, 22, 23, 18, 24.

**37** Responses to Fiedler demonstrate the complex freak-show interplay of the mythic, the individual, and the sociocultural. Robert Bogdan criticizes Fiedler's mystification and naturalization of a constructed category, the freak, and his implied suggestion that "human beings have a deep, psychic fear of people with specific abnormalities." He distinguishes disabled individuals and freaks, declaring, " 'Freak' is a way of thinking, of presenting, a set of practices, an institution—not characteristic of an individual. Freak shows can teach us not to confuse the role a person plays with who that person really is." Bogdan, *Freak Show*, 7, 10. In turn, David Gerber suggests that Bogdan minimizes considerations of constraint and social inequality, presenting freakery as a freely chosen performance rather than exploitation. Gerber, "The 'Careers' of People Exhibited in Freak Shows," 44–45. Adams offers an insightful critique of how Fiedler's work, along with the writing of counterculture figures such as Abbie Hoffman and Jerry Rubin, enacts an "identification with freaks [that] lays claim to the marginality of a white masculine self as his authority is threatened by the rising voices of disenfranchised coalitions." Adams, *Sideshow U.S.A.*, 19. Despite Fiedler's homage to Browning, then, I argue that *Freaks* can be read in ways that contest Fiedler's exoticization of freaks and assert a much greater overlap than he is willing to acknowledge amongst monsters, freaks, and people with disabilities.

**38** The term "enfreakment" is borrowed from David Hevey, *The Creatures Time Forgot*, 53.

**39** Wood, "An Introduction," 182; John Swales, *Genre Analysis: English in Academic and Research Settings*, 49.

**40** Ludwig Wittgenstein, *Philosophical Investigations*, 4th ed., ed. and trans. P. M. S. Hacker and Joachim Schulte, 64.

**41** Swales, *Genre Analysis*, 50, 51.

**42** For these points and more on most of the freak performers in *Freaks*, see "Freaks: The Sideshow Cinema," *Freaks*, DVD (Burbank, CA: Turner Entertainment and Warner Bros., 2004).

**43** The Hilton subplot—and, indeed, much of the film (as indicated in n. 16)—also invokes a specific set of gender politics. Pingree has explored the lives of Daisy and Violet Hilton as vaudeville performers, suggesting that their doubleness both aggravated fears about independent, monstrous New Women and challenged the conventions of marriage. Pingree, "The 'Exceptions That Prove the Rule,'" 177. Certainly, gender transgression seems evident in Violet's headstrong disregard for Roscoe's commands and in Roscoe's own stuttering ineffectuality, compounded by his role in the circus as a Roman lady.

**44** Thomas Schatz, *Hollywood Genres: Formulas, Filmmaking, and the Studio System*, 16, 18, 12.

**45** Edward Buscombe, "The Idea of Genre in the American Cinema" (1970), in Barry Keith Grant, ed., *Film Genre Reader II*, 21; Schatz, *Hollywood Genres*, 22.

**46** Neale, *Genre*, 50.

**47** Buscombe, "The Idea of Genre," 21; Neale, *Genre*, 50.

**48** This chapter thus implicitly draws on recent film-genre theories attentive to the fluctuating and contextual status of genre categories and to the interdependent roles in genre creation played by producers, promoters, and audiences. See, particularly, Altman, *Film/Genre*.

**49** "91.1 Per Cent of Kindergarten and First-Grade Pupils Found with Physical Imperfections," in *Washington Evening Star*, Aug. 25, 1928, 1–2; and "Some People are Born to Be a Burden on the Rest," Image of State Fair Display, American Eugenics Society Scrapbook, APS.

**50** "Farmer Uprisings More Frequent," *New York Times*, Jan. 22, 1933, sec. 4: 7.

**51** "Battle of Washington," *Time*, Aug. 8, 1932, 5.

**52** J. Hoberman and Jonathan Rosenbaum, *Midnight Movies*, 307.

**53** Ibid.

**54** Larsen and Haller, "Public Reception of Real Disability," 167 (Bret Wood's work, "Tod Browning," remains unpublished at this writing).

**55** Mitchell and Snyder, *Narrative Prosthesis*, 7, 8; Quayson, *Aesthetic Nervousness*, 19.

**56** Bordwell, "The Classical Hollywood Style, 1917–1960," in David Bordwell, Janet Staiger, and Kristin Thompson, *The Classical Hollywood Cinema: Film Style and Mode of Production to 1960*, 8.

**57** Bordwell, "The Classical Hollywood Style," 19–21, 22, 23, 22.

**58** Gaycken, "Tod Browning and the Monstrosity of Hollywood Style," 77.

**59** Ibid.

**60** Our discussion of *Freaks'* prosthetic politics confronts the tendency, noted by Vivian Sobchack, of academic discourse to employ "the prosthetic" as "a sexy, new metaphor" describing "a vague and shifting constellation of relationships among bodies, technologies, and subjectivities." Such tropology, Sobchack argues, displaces the literal function of the prosthesis and "the experience and agency of those who . . . actually use prostheses without feeling 'posthuman.'" Sobchack contests objectifying views that assume the wholeness and naturalness of the pre-prosthetic body and that inscribe the prostheticized body as at once lacking something and sporting an artificial supplement. Instead, she privileges the disabled person's willful incorporation of the prosthetic as part of the bodily ensemble. In the same way, *Freaks'* combination of silent and sound elements, while it may be perceived by scholars as a freakish grafting of the unnatural onto the normal—a problematic stance insofar as, as we shall see, neither silent nor sound can be situated comfortably on either side of that divide—in fact insists on the possibility of what Sobchack sees as the organic relationship between and "reversibility" of the prosthetic and the body. Moreover, the film refuses to elide the literal body in the name of a meta-phorical statement about cinema, modernity, or humanity, instead foregrounding the materiality of those bodies usually envisaged only as grounds for intellectual and cultural metaphors. See Vivian Sobchack, *Carnal Thoughts: Embodiment and Moving Image Culture*, 205–215.

**61**  A similar intermingling of sound and silent conventions is also present in Brown-ing's *Dracula*. As Skal and Savada note, although Universal cut several silent sequences from *Dracula* prior to its release, the film is notable for its limited dia-logue and dearth of music; moreover, a silent version was produced "[a]s a con-cession to theaters not yet equipped for sound." Skal and Savada, *Dark Carnival*, 152, 155.

**62**  Skal, *The Monster Show*, 158.

**63**  Rudolf Arnheim, "Sound Film," in *Film Essays and Criticism*, 30.

**64**  Potamkin, quoted in Tim Armstrong, *Modernism, Technology, and the Body*, 231–32; Betts, quoted in ibid., 230.

**65**  Ibid., 233, 232.

**66**  Robert Spadoni, *Uncanny Bodies: The Coming of Sound Film and the Origins of the Horror Genre*, 13, 14.

**67**  Robert Spadoni, "The Uncanny Body of Early Sound Film," *The Velvet Light Trap* 51 (Spring 2003): 11.

**68**  Spadoni, *Uncanny Bodies*, 17; Jonathan Culler, *On Deconstruction: Theory and Criti-cism After Structuralism*, 103.

**69**  Spadoni, "The Uncanny Body of Early Sound Film," 8. In the feast scene, we watch and hear Hercules drunkenly laughing to Cleopatra, "They're going to make you one of them, my peacock!" The line is repeated, identically, on the soundtrack moments later, while the camera lingers on the increasingly furious Cleo.

**70**  John Thomas, "*Freaks*," *Film Quarterly* 17.3 (Spring 1964): 60–61.

**71**  Howard, quoted in Armstrong, *Modernism, Technology, and the Body*, 231.

**72**  Horace, *To the Pisos (The Art of Poetry)* in *The Epistles of Horace*, 152.

**73**  Gaycken, "Tod Browning and the Monstrosity of Hollywood Style," 79.

**74**  "The Pay-Off," 2.

**75**  "'Freaks' Arrives," X3.

**76**  The preamble's addition is attributed to Esper by Skal and Savada, *Dark Car-nival*, 223. Most sources draw on Skal and Savada in this respect, but a few instead attribute the appended text to an effort by Irving Thalberg to revive the film in the mid-1930s: writes Martin F. Norden, "After adding a new pro-logue . . . and rechristening the movie *Nature's Mistakes*, [Thalberg] used a posi-tive comment by the Hearst papers' Louella Parsons as the cornerstone for a new marketing campaign. Unfortunately for all concerned, however, the rein-vented film sank about as quickly as Thalberg's executive authority at MGM."

Norden, *The Cinema of Isolation*, 119. See also Stephen L. Hanson, *"Freaks,"* in Frank N. Magill, ed., *Magill's Survey of Cinema: English Language Films, Second Series*, vol. 2: 842.

77  Skal and Savada, *Dark Carnival*, 223.

78  Eric Schaefer, *Bold! Daring! Shocking! True!: A History of Exploitation Films, 1919–1959*, 5.

79  David F. Friedman, *A Youth in Babylon: Confessions of a Trash-Film King*, 63.

80  Fiedler, *Freaks*, 297–98.

81  Skal and Savada, *Dark Carnival*, 215.

82  Fiedler, *Freaks*, 298. For documentation of locations where Freaks had midnight runs, see Hoberman and Rosenbaum, *Midnight Movies*, 1983.

83  Fiedler, *Freaks*, 14; Hoberman and Rosenbaum, *Midnight Movies*, 295

84  Milne, quoted in Skal and Savada, *Dark Carnival*, 223–24; Andrew Sarris, *"You Ain't Heard Nothin' Yet": The American Talking Film, History and Memory, 1927–1949*, 81; Sarris, *The American Cinema: Directors and Directions, 1929–1968*, 229.

85  Durgnat, quoted in Hawkins, *Cutting Edge*, 150; Christian Oddos, *Le Cinéma Fantastique*, 165; I am indebted to Anne Jamison for this translation from the French.

86  Thomas, *"Freaks,"* 59, 60.

87  Hutchings, *The Horror Film*, 27. Similarly, Hanson writes that *Freaks* "is, in most respects, the antithesis of the conventional horror film." Hanson, *"Freaks,"* 843.

88  Thomas, *"Freaks,"* 59.

89  Program note on *Freaks* in the Pacific Film Archive series "Received Images: A Reading of Disability in Cinema," July 8, 1990; www.bampfa.berkeley.edu/film/FN8310 (accessed July 6, 2010).

90  The PFA commentary is particularly unconvincing in indicting Browning's authorial choices as it cites the "original prologue," which was neither Browning's nor part of the original film's release.

91  Hawkins, *Cutting Edge*, 159. In similar terms, Markotic asserts that "the film reinscribes the essentialism it purports to challenge." Markotic, "Disabling the Viewer," 71.

92  Norden, *The Cinema of Isolation*, 122; Cook, "None of Us," 50. It seems clear that the first revival of *Freaks* occurred at the Venice Film Festival, in September 1962. Skal confirms that his archival research has proven its appearance there (e-mail with the author, July 6, 2010). Still, in 1960s sources such as Thomas's review, this festival screening became confused with the Cannes Film Festival, which occurred earlier that year, in May. Many sources have repeated this error and the statement that *Freaks* appeared there in the horror category, often in order to contest such categorization of the film. See for example, Thomas, *"Freaks,"* 59; Hanson, *"Freaks,"* 843.

93  Claude Beylie, *Ecran* 73 (July–Aug. 1973); Oddos, *Le Cinéma Fantastique*, 165. Thanks again to Anne Jamison for translation assistance.

94  Wood, "An Introduction," 175.

95  Chivers, "The Horror of Becoming 'One of Us,'" 59.

96  Ralph Cohen, "History and Genre," *New Literary History* 17.2 (Winter 1986): 204.

97  Schatz, *Hollywood Genres*, 38.

98  Kent L. Brintnall, "The Moral Demand of the 'Loving Cup': The Presence of the Abject Body in Tod Browning's *Freaks* and the Christian Eucharist," *Golem* 1.1 (Spring 2006): 20–21 (accessed July 15, 2010).

## 3. REVELATIONS AND CONVULSIONS: SPECTACLES OF IMPAIRMENT IN CLASSIC HORROR FILM

1  Sophocles, *Oedipus the King*, 86.

2  See, for instance, Lucien Howe, "Response to Charles Davenport and Harry Laughlin, about Sterilization, Marriage and Blindness" (1923), in Image Archive on the American Eugenics Movement (www.eugenicsarchive.org), IAAEM, #325; and Howe, "The Control by Law of Hereditary Blindness" (ca. 1928), in IAAEM, #275 (both accessed June 20, 2010).

3  "*Dark Eyes of London*," *Motion Picture Herald*, November 18, 1939, 49.

4  *Freaks*, of course, *does* deploy some characters/actors with real and identifiable disabilities and, as argued in chapter 2, suggests the necessity of relating classic horror films' mythic and fictional monsters to more quotidian social understandings of impairment, a task this chapter begins to undertake.

5  Mitchell and Snyder, *Narrative Prosthesis*, 181n4. See also ibid., chapter 4, which explores in greater depth scholarly and theatrical efforts to accurately diagnose the impairments of Richard III in the name of authentic performance.

6  A comprehensive index of these files, now held by the American Philosophical Society Library, is available at www.amphilsoc.org/mole/view?docId=ead/Mss.Ms.Coll.77-ead.xml (accessed June 20, 2010).

7  "Hereditary Disorders," in IAAEM (accessed Aug 12, 2010).

8  See Howe, "Response to Davenport and Laughlin"; Howe, "The Control by Law of Hereditary Blindness"; and Howe's interview in Sam Smith, "Harvard Scientist Wants Married Couples Bonded" (all accessed June 20, 2010). The processes of projection and fear of loss of identity that structure the encounter of the seeing with the blind shadow Howe's paranoid comments on the proliferation of the blind: "if [the average man] had worked in an eye clinic day after day for a little over 50 years, as I have, he would begin to think that the whole world was blind,

or nearly blind." Howe also asserts the eugenically logical extension of such legislation toward other, associated, dysgenic conditions: "[Howe] goes further and says that it would be a good idea if couples were also required to bond themselves against bringing into the world insane or epileptic children." Smith, "Harvard Scientist." On matters of projection and identity in relation to blindness, see Michael E. Monbeck, *The Meaning of Blindness: Attitudes Toward Blindness and Blind People*.

**9**  Shelley Tremain, "On the Government of Disability," *Social Theory and Practice* 27.4 (Oct. 2001): 632.

**10**  Some disability scholars express concern that social and Foucauldian models of disability, in emphasizing "social construction" of impairment, risk eliding or leaving untheorized individual experiences of embodiment and impairment. See, for instance, Liz Crow, "Including All of Our Lives: Renewing the Social Model of Disability," in Colin Barnes and Geof Mercer, eds., *Exploring the Divide: Illness and Disability*, 55–72; Bill Hughes and Kevin Paterson, "The Social Model of Disability and the Disappearing Body: Towards a Sociology of Impairment," *Disability & Society* 12 (1997): 325–40; and Tobin Siebers, "Disability in Theory: From Social Constructionism to the New Realism of the Body," in Davis, ed., *The Disability Studies Reader* (2006), 173–83.

**11**  Mordaunt Hall, "A Fantastic Melodrama," *New York Times* (hereafter, *NYT*), Sept. 12, 1925, 15.

**12**  "*Frankenstein*," *Time*, Dec. 14, 1931, 2.

**13**  See Blumenbach, *The Anthropological Treatises of Johann Friedrich Blumenbach*.

**14**  Pick, *Faces of Degeneration*, 113.

**15**  Hasian, *The Rhetoric of Eugenics*, 18.

**16**  Lombroso, "Introduction," xiv–xv.

**17**.  Quoted in Pick, *Faces of Degeneration*, 52.

**18**  "Cranium of Murderer Like Anthropoid Ape's," *NYT*, Jan. 25, 1930, 6.

**19**  Schweik, *The Ugly Laws*, 68.

**20**  Snyder and Mitchell, *Cultural Locations*, 30, 40–41.

**21**  Wiggam and Haiselden quoted in Pernick, *The Black Stork*, 61, 64.

**22**  Jan Witkowski, "Traits Studied by Eugenicists," in IAAEM (accessed June 25, 2010).

**23**  Davenport, *Heredity in Relation to Eugenics*, 241, 240; Davenport, *Guide to Anthropometry and Anthroposcopy*.

**24**  "Syllabus of Lectures Given to Field Workers" (1921), in IAAEM, #1105 (accessed June 26, 2010).

**25**  "Heredity of Harelip and Cleft Palate," in IAAEM, #566; "The Catlin Mark: The Inheritance of an Unusual Opening in the Parietal Bone," in IAAEM, #565; "Pedigree of Red Hair Family," in IAAEM, #828; "A.B.W. Family: Musical, Literary, and Inventive Ability," IAAEM, #885; "Single-trait Sheet: Wanderlust," in IAAEM, #691;

and "Form for Studying the Inheritance of Pauperism and Criminality," in IAAEM, #100 (all accessed Aug. 10, 2010).

26 Morel, quoted in Pick, *Faces of Degeneration*, 51–52.

27 Gibson and Rafter, "Editors' Introduction," in Lombroso, *Criminal Man*, 23.

28 Witkowski, "Traits Studied by Eugenicists."

29 United States Public Health Service, *Manual of the Mental Examination of Aliens* (1918), in IAAEM, #1530 (accessed June 20, 2010).

30 Pick, *Faces of Degeneration*, 52.

31 Linda Williams, "When the Woman Looks," 20.

32 Ibid.

33 Studlar, *This Mad Masquerade*, 248.

34 Ibid., 223.

35 Williams, "When the Woman Looks," 19.

36 Christian Metz, "The Impersonal Enunciation or the Site of the Film: In the Margin of Recent Works on Enunciation in Cinema," in Warren Buckland, ed., *The Film Spectator: From Sign to Mind*, 149.

37 "*Frankenstein*," *Time*, 2.

38 Freud, "The Uncanny," 226, 231.

39. Norden, *The Cinema of Isolation*, 52.

40 Fairchild, *The Melting-Pot Mistake*, 29.

41 Florence also echoes the popular misnaming of the monster after his creator that Henry's nephew would petulantly bemoan in *Son of Frankenstein* (1939).

42 Norden, *The Cinema of Isolation*, 115.

43 Susan Stewart, "The Epistemology of the Horror Story," *Journal of American Folklore* 95.375 (1982): 48, 44.

44 See Norden, *The Cinema of Isolation*, 14–17.

45 Jean Baudrillard, "Simulacra and Simulations," in *Jean Baudrillard: Selected Writings*, ed. Mark Poster, 170–71.

46 Ibid., 171.

47 See Erving Goffman, *The Presentation of Self in Everyday Life*; Judith Butler, "Imitation and Gender Insubordination," in Diana Fuss, ed., *Inside/Out: Lesbian Theories, Gay Theories*, 13–31; and Judith Butler, *Bodies That Matter: On the Discursive Limits of Sex*.

48 Butler, "Imitation and Gender Insubordination," 28.

49 McRuer, *Crip Theory*.

50 Carrie Sandahl and Philip Auslander, "Introduction: Disability Studies in Commotion with Performance Studies," in Sandahl and Auslander, eds., *Bodies in Commotion: Disability and Performance*, 2–3.

51 Goffman's consideration of daily performance encompasses the "management" of stigma in a formative pre-disability studies text, *Stigma: Notes on the Manage-*

*ment of a Spoiled Identity*. His work is taken up in disability-studies considerations of disability "passing" in texts such as Tobin Siebers' *Disability Theory*, esp. ch. 4, "Disability as Masquerade."

52  Butler, *Bodies That Matter*, 129.

53  Petra Kuppers, "Bodies, Hysteria, Pain: Staging the Invisible," in Sandahl and Auslander, eds., *Bodies in Commotion*, 151, 148.

54  Sandahl and Auslander, "Introduction," 10, 3.

55  Owsei Temkin, *The Falling Sickness: A History of Epilepsy from the Greeks to the Beginnings of Modern Neurology*, 7–9.

56  Hippocrates, "The Sacred Disease," in *The Medical Works of Hippocrates*, 179–80. As Temkin notes, the author of the text in fact remains unknown, since "[h]e is one of the many anonymous physicians whose writings go under the name of Hippocrates." Temkin, *The Falling Sickness*, 5.

57  Hippocrates, "The Sacred Disease," 182, 184, 185.

58  Lisa Cartwright, *Screening the Body: Tracing Medicine's Visual Culture*, 178n21.

59  Allan H. Ropper and Robert H. Brown, *Adams and Victor's Principles of Neurology*, 273.

60  Ibid., 277.

61  Ibid.

62  Henderson, quoted in Schweik, *The Ugly Laws*, 89.

63  Philip Brophy, "Horrality—the Textuality of Contemporary Horror Films," *Screen* 27.1 (1986): 9.

64  Freud, "Dostoevsky and Parricide" (ca. 1927), in *The Standard Edition of the Complete Psychological Works of Sigmund Freud* 21:177–94, ed. and trans. James Strachey.

65  Dennis Patrick Slattery, "Seized by the Muse: Dostoevsky's Convulsive Poetics in *The Idiot*," in *Literature and Medicine* 18.1 (1999): 61.

66  Ibid., 75.

67  The subcommittees on heredity dealt with feeblemindedness, insanity, epilepsy, criminality, and deaf-mutism. See "Description of the American Breeders Association" (ca. 1909), in IAAEM, #412 (accessed June 20, 2010).

68  See, for instance, "Heredity in Epilepsy," IAAEM, #570, which includes pedigree charts entitled "Syphilis and Epilepsy" and "Epilepsy and Feeblemindedness: A Forced Marriage"; and Charles B. Davenport and D. Weeks, "Poorhouse Type of Source of Defectives: Pedigree of Epilepsy and Feeblemindedness" (1911), in IAAEM, #1696 (accessed June 20, 2010).

69  D. A. Thom and G. S. Walker, "Epilepsy in Offspring of Epileptics" (orig. in *American Journal of Psychiatry* 10.4 [Apr. 1922]: 613), in IAAEM, #372 (accessed June 21, 2010).

70  C. W. Burr, "Heredity in Epilepsy: Study of One Thousand Four Hundred and Forty Nine Cases," (orig. in *Archives of Neurology and Psychiatry* 7.6 [June 1922]: 721), in IAAEM, #372 (accessed June 21, 2010).

71  For the statistics and surgical operations, see "Operates on Brain to Treat Epilepsy," *NYT*, Dec. 28, 1929, 7. On diet, see "Linking Up Man's Diet and Character," *NYT*, Apr. 14, 1929, sec. 5: 3. This notion retains some validity today; Ropper and Brown note that despite a lack of controlled trials, past tests suggest the ketogenic diet "can be effective in cases of refractory epilepsy in childhood." Ropper and Brown, *Adams and Victor's Principles of Neurology*, 299.

72  Cartwright, *Screening the Body*, 63, 64, 66, 67, 65, 71.

73  Ibid., 60, 61. Dercum also used electrical stimulus to mechanically generate certain facial expressions in his subjects. See Cartwright, *Screening the Body*, 60. On experiments by Ivan Pavlov and other Russian physiologists that induced epileptic convulsions through electric shock, see Judith A. Overmier and John Edward Senior, *Books and Manuscripts of the Bakken*, 331.

74  Cartwright, *Screening the Body*, 61–2.

75  The term "cultural performance" derives from sociologist Ronald Frankenberg in "Sickness as Cultural Performance: Drama, Trajectory, and Pilgrimage Root Metaphors and the Making Social of Disease," *International Journal of Health Services* 16 (November 1986): 603–625.

76  Robert Louis Stevenson, *The Strange Case of Dr. Jekyll and Mr. Hyde* (1886), in Leonard Wolf, ed., *The Essential Dr. Jekyll and Mr. Hyde*, 119, 133.

77  Wolf, *The Essential Dr. Jekyll and Mr. Hyde*, 133n75.

78  Skal, *The Monster Show*, 141.

79  Toba Schwaber Kerson and Lawrence A. Kerson, "Implacable Images: Why Epileptiform Events Continue to be Featured in Film and Television," in *Epileptic Disorders* 8.2 (2006): 103, 105; and Jennie F. Kerson, Toba Schwaber Kerson, and Lawrence A. Kerson, "The Depiction of Seizures in Film," in *Epilepsia* 40.8 (1999): 1167.

80  Kerson and Kerson, "Implacable Images," 104, 109–110.

81  See "Heredity in Epilepsy," in IAAEM, #570 (accessed June 10, 2010), which includes pedigree charts entitled "Syphilis and Epilepsy" and "Epilepsy and Feeblemindedness: A Forced Marriage."

82  This use of visual connotations of syphilis is discussed in "The Many Faces of Jekyll/Hyde" on the 2001 Kino International DVD production of the Robertson/Barrymore *Dr. Jekyll and Mr. Hyde*.

83  Halberstam, *Skin Shows*, 78.

84  Ibid., 93. It is even possible that Barrymore's use of "rubber appliances" to extend his fingertips influenced Max Schreck's costume, a Jewish caricature, in *Nosferatu* the following year. Skal, *The Monster Show*, 141.

**85**  Davenport, *Heredity in Relation to Eugenics*, 2, 83.

**86**  Lydston, quoted in ibid., 82.

**87**  Hasian, *The Rhetoric of Eugenics*, 34. In his discussion of eugenic arguments around Prohibition, Hasian draws on John Kobler, *Ardent Spirits: The Rise and Fall of Prohibition*.

**88**  Jordan, *The Blood of the Nation*, 38–39.

**89**  Pick, *Faces of Degeneration*, 230–31.

**90**  Skal, *The Monster Show*, 142. The creation or cure of deformity and disability was central to this cinematic effect: Skal notes it was "originally devised by camera-man Karl Strauss for *Ben Hur* where, used in reverse, it created the miraculous 'healing' of lepers."

**91**  Mamoulian explained these techniques in an interview: "I had the camera revolve around on its axis 360 degrees, the first time this was done on the screen. One cameraman had to sit on the floor, and the man handling the focus—luckily a very small guy who looked like a jockey—was tied with ropes on the top of the camera box, so that he could control it from the top. Because the camera revolved, the whole set had to be lighted which was a real tough job." On the creation of the discordant sound, Mamoulian recalls: "I thought the only way to match the event and create this incredible reality would be to concoct a mélange of sounds that do not exist in nature, that a human ear cannot hear. I said, 'Let's photograph light.' We photographed the light of a candle in various frequencies of intensity, directly transforming light into sound. Then I said, 'Let's record the beat of a gong, cut off the impact, run it backwards.' And we recorded other things like that. But when we ran it the whole thing lacked rhythm. . . . I ran up and down the stairway for a few minutes, and then I put a microphone to my heart and said, 'Record it.' And that's what is used as the basic rhythm in the scene—the thumping noise which is like no drum on earth because it's the heart beat, my own heartbeat." Rouben Mamoulian, "An Interview with Rouben Mamoulian," by Thomas R. Atkins (1973), in Harry M. Geduld, ed., *The Definitive "Dr. Jekyll and Mr. Hyde" Companion*, 180.

**92**  Virginia Wright Wexman, "Horrors of the Body: Hollywood's Discourse on Beauty and Rouben Mamoulian's *Dr. Jekyll and Mr. Hyde*," in William Veeder and Gordon Hirsch, eds., *Dr. Jekyll and Mr. Hyde After One Hundred Years*, 289.

**93**  Mamoulian, "An Interview with Rouben Mamoulian," 177.

**94**  In its animalistic iconography, and in the spectacle of human transformation into bestial form, *Dr. Jekyll and Mr. Hyde* belongs to a subgenre of classic horrors that I term the "bestial" horror film, which includes *Murders in the Rue Morgue*, *Island of Lost Souls*, *The Most Dangerous Game*, *Murders in the Zoo*, *King Kong*, and *Werewolf of London*. These films, which are not examined in detail in the current study, conjoin eugenic, evolutionary, racial, and disability discourses in complicated and powerful ways, something I hope future studies will demonstrate.

95  Wexman, "Horrors of the Body," 296.

96  The link between the candles' form and that of Jekyll/Hyde is suggested by a remark from reviewer Mordaunt Hall, who commended the "camera wizardry" that caused "Dr. Jekyll's finely chiseled face to melt slowly into the bestial face of Hyde." Hall, "Fine Photography in 'Jekyll and Hyde,'" *NYT*, Jan. 10, 1932, X4.

97  Siebers, "Disability in Theory," 175, 177, 177, 180, 173.

98  Skal, *The Monster Show*, 65, 66, 68, 65. Lon Chaney was also the child of deaf parents.

99  Ibid., 141.

100  On Barrymore's highs and lows, see John Kobler, *Damned in Paradise: The Life of John Barrymore*.

101  "Now You See Him: The Invisible Man Revealed," on Universal's Legacy Collection DVD of *The Invisible Man*.

102  Norden, *The Cinema of Isolation*, 17.

103  Siebers, *Disability Theory*, 116.

104  Skal and Savada, *The Dark Carnival*, 48–51, 88; Skal, *Hollywood Gothic*, 179.

105  Béla Balázs, *Theory of the Film: Character and Growth of a New Art*, 63, 55, 56. Balázs' use of the term "microphysiognomics" indicates the affinities his view of facial expression might have with eugenic concerns, particularly considered alongside his references to racial physiognomies and his belief that film microphysiognomics might have "an important scientific function, supplying invaluable material to anthropology and psychology." Ibid., 83.

106  Siegfried Kracauer, *Theory of Film: The Redemption of Physical Reality*, 47. Subsequent references to this work are cited in the text.

107  See, for instance, Kracauer's comments on *The Cabinet of Dr. Caligari* in *From Caligari to Hitler: A Psychological History of the German Film*, 63–67

108  Walter Benjamin, "The Work of Art in the Age of Mechanical Reproduction" (1936), in *Illuminations: Essays and Reflections*, ed. Hannah Arendt, 228–32.

109  Shaviro, *The Cinematic Body*, 43–44, 51, 52.

110  Siebers, "Disability in Theory," 176.

## 4. MAD MEDICINE: DISABILITY IN THE MAD-DOCTOR FILMS

1  Ian Conrich, "Horrific Films and 1930s British Cinema," in Steve Chibnall and Julian Petley, eds., *British Horror Cinema*, 65.

2  Quoted in Skal, *The Monster Show*, 195.

3  "Horror Films Taken off U Sked," *Variety*, May 6, 1936, 7.

4  Berenstein, *Attack of the Leading Ladies*, 15.

**5** Universal's horror film cycles were built around particular, identifiable monsters (or, in some cases, types of monsters). After 1936, they called again on vampires in *Son of Dracula* (1943); Frankenstein's monster in *Son of Frankenstein* (1939) and *The Ghost of Frankenstein* (1942); invisible characters in *The Invisible Man Returns* (1940), *The Invisible Woman* (1940), *Invisible Agent* (1942), and *The Invisible Man's Revenge* (1944); mummies in *The Mummy's Hand* (1940), *The Mummy's Tomb* (1942), *The Mummy's Ghost* (1944), and *The Mummy's Curse* (1944); lycanthropes in 1941's *The Wolf Man*; and several of these monsters at once in films such as *Frankenstein Meets the Wolf Man* (1943), *House of Frankenstein* (1945), *House of Dracula* (1945), and the *Abbott and Costello Meet . . .* series of the 1940s and early 1950s.

**6** "Horror on the Screen: The Demon Surgeon," *The Times* (London), Aug. 4, 1936, 8.

**7** Davis, *Enforcing Normalcy*, 48.

**8** Foucault, *The Birth of the Clinic*, 166.

**9** Michel Foucault, *Discipline and Punish: The Birth of the Prison*, 170–71.

**10** Sander Gilman, *Seeing the Insane*, 194.

**11** Kuppers, "Bodies, Hysteria, Pain," 149.

**12** Gilman, "The Image of the Hysteric," in Sander L. Gilman et al., *Hysteria Beyond Freud*, 346.

**13** Kuppers, "Bodies, Hysteria, Pain," 149, 151.

**14** The performative elements of images of hysterical women also underline the nature of hysteria itself as a condition where the psychological, the cultural, and the physical mutually inform one another. As Elizabeth Grosz points out, "Lacan argues that instead of observing and following the neurological connections in organic paralyses, hysterical paralyses reproduce various naïve or everyday beliefs about the way the body functions. In an hysterical paralysis, it is more likely that the limbs which are immobilised are unable to move from a joint, whereas in organic paralyses, the immobility extends further upwards and encompasses many nerve and muscle connections not apparent to the lay observer." Grosz, quoted in Kuppers, "Bodies, Hysteria, Pain," 159–60n1.

**15** Foucault, *Discipline and Punish*, 55, 39, 202, 19, 203.

**16** Ibid., 16, 202–203, 30.

**17** Vollin's insight is akin to that advanced by New Zealand–British plastic surgery pioneer Sir Harold Delf Gillies who, in dealing with the facial injuries of World War I veterans, commented: "We noticed that if we made a poor repair for a wretched fellow, the man's character was inclined to change for the worse. He would be morose, break rules and give trouble generally. Conversely, if we made a good repair, the patient usually became a happy convalescent and soon regained his old character and habits. This seems to emphasise again the powerful influence that our physical appearance wields over our character." Quoted in David

Fisher, "Plastic Fantastic," *The Listener* (Wellington, New Zealand), Jan. 17–23, 2009, 26.

18  A similar representation of criminality resulting from ableist responses to facial deformity plays out in *The Face Behind the Mask* (1941), starring Peter Lorre.

19  Foucault, *Discipline and Punish*, 272, 277.

20  Indeed, Rollo declares that his skill with knives was learned and honed with practice, rather than coming naturally.

21  "*Mad Love*," *Daily Variety*, June 27, 1935, 3.

22  To this extent, the films anticipate contemporary disability scholarship, particularly works such as Susan Wendell's chapter "Feminism, Disability, and Transcendence of the Body" in her book *The Rejected Body*.

23  Foucault, *Discipline and Punish*, 202, 204.

24  H. G. Wells, *The Invisible Man*, 142. Subsequent references to this work are cited in the text.

25  Whale, quoted in Skal, *Screams of Reason*, 146.

26  Wells would pick up on this notion in his 1904 short story "The Country of the Blind," where an explorer becomes stranded in an isolated community of blind people and believes that he will prove the truth of the maxim "In the Country of the Blind, the One-eyed Man is King." Instead, he has difficulty in adapting to the community's worldviews and environment and finds himself treated as abnormal and mad.

27  Foucault, *Discipline and Punish*, 214.

28  Richard Dyer, *White*, 1, 3.

29  Ralph Ellison, *Invisible Man*, 197.

30  Toni Morrison, *Playing in the Dark: Whiteness and the Literary Imagination*, 38–39.

31  bell hooks, "Representations of Whiteness in the Black Imagination," in *Black Looks: Race and Representation*, 169. As Richard Dyer notes in using this quotation, a printing error in hooks's *Black Looks* makes it seem as if this sentence is part of a quotation from Dyer, but the words are her own. See Dyer, *White*, 232n2.

32  Writes Foucault of the Panopticon's cells, "Full lighting and the eye of a supervisor capture better than darkness, which ultimately protected. Visibility is a trap." Foucault, *Discipline and Punish*, 200.

33  On the simultaneous development of photographic representations of disability and the removal of people with disabilities from public view, see Rosemarie Garland-Thomson, "Seeing the Disabled: Visual Rhetorics of Disability in Popular Photography," in Paul K. Longmore and Lauri Umansky, eds., *The New Disability History: American Perspectives*, 337–38; see also this concept expanded in Garland-Thomson, *Staring: How We Look*. The trope of the invisibility of people with disabilities was evident in a 1999 statement by the Disabled Peoples' International and other international disability rights' groups, which condemned the United

Nations' failure to improve "the lives of people with disabilities, especially women and girls with disabilities, who remain the most invisible of all disadvantaged groups." "Beijing Declaration on the Rights of People with Disabilities in the New Century," adopted on March 12, 2000, at the World NGO Summit on Disability (accessed July 1, 2008).

Although disability is frequently represented in most media, stereotyping and strategic elisions register the presumed inability of people with disabilities to stand in for (to represent) the normative citizen or society at large. For instance, Harlan Hahn notes that advertising images construct a picture of "acceptable forms of human appearance" that delineates those who are economically and socially valuable and, by inscribing their absence, renders people with disabilities invisible. Hahn, "Advertising the Acceptably Employable Image: Disability and Capitalism" (1995), in Davis, ed., *The Disability Studies Reader* (1997), 176. The titles of many articles on disability and media recognize this invisibility: see, for example, Jack A. Nelson, "The Invisible Cultural Group: Images of Disability," in P. Lester, ed., *Images That Injure: Pictorial Stereotypes in the Media*, 119–25; and Brent Hardin et al., "Missing in Action? Images of Disability in *Sports Illustrated for Kids*," *Disability Studies Quarterly* 21.2 (Spring 2001) (accessed Sept. 13, 2010). Such representational invisibility is complicit with the political and economic marginalization addressed in the "Beijing Declaration."

34 Rose Galvin, "The Making of the Disabled Identity: A Linguistic Analysis of Marginalisation," *Disability Studies Quarterly* 23.2 (Spring 2003) (accessed Sept. 13, 2010).

35 On associations of whiteness with death, see Dyer, ch. 6, "White Death," in his book *White*. Dyer explores how the connotations of spirituality and disembodiment that attach to whiteness lead also to notions of nonexistence and death. He also notes that literary and cinematic instances of "extreme whiteness" figure the ideals and extremes to which whiteness aspires but also sediment, by their exceptionality and marked status, the assumption of a contrastive "ordinary" whiteness that does not see itself as "white." Griffin certainly seems to perform this function, rendering white scientific power so extreme that more "ordinary" characters, including other scientists, may disassociate themselves from his exceptionally "white" status and the violence and monomania it entails.

36 "*Mad Love*," *Daily Variety*, June 27, 1935, 3.

37 Jacques Lacan, "The Mirror Stage . . . " (1949), in *Écrits: A Selection*, 1–7.

38 Davis, *Enforcing Normalcy*, 141.

39 Lacan's work makes clear that the separation between a subject's embodied experience and his perceived mirror image inscribes an enduring "split" or "lack" at the heart of subjectivity, a duality that haunts our reflections. Elizabeth Grosz emphasizes that the lure of the mirror image derives from "a narcissistic delight

at the shape of our own externality, which is always inaccessible to us by direct means and is achievable only if we occupy the perspective others have on us." She points out, however, that the mirror image also "threatens to draw us into its spell of spectral doubling, annihilating the self that wants to see itself reflected." See Grosz, "Intolerable Ambiguity, Freaks as/at the Limit," in Garland-Thomson, ed., *Freakery*, 65.

40  Metz, "The Impersonal Enunciation or the Site of the Film," 149.

41  See Michel Foucault, *The Order of Things: An Archaeology of the Human Sciences*, ch. 1.

42  Peggy Phelan, *Mourning Sex: Performing Public Memories*, 23–24.

43  Ibid., 27.

44  Such moments remind us, as Tom Gunning has argued, that early film's aesthetics of astonishment endures in the spectacular moments of otherwise predominantly narrative films. Gunning, "An Aesthetic of Astonishment," 870.

45  The convincing special effects were undoubtedly a significant part of the film's astounding appeal. Michael Brunas, John Brunas, and Tom Weaver report that "[t]he film broke house records at New York's immense Roxy Theater for the 1932–1933 season, shattering a three-year record. Eighty thousand patrons saw the film in four days; a whopping $42,000 was collected during the first week, prompting the theater to hold the film over for a second. *The Invisible Man* singlehandedly revived the fortunes of the financially ailing studio." Brunas , Brunas, and Weaver, *Universal Horrors*, 73. Fulton's work in sequels to *The Invisible Man* drew critical commendation and three Academy Award nominations.

46  As well as the multiple printings and combinations required, some scenes also required retouching by hand: Fulton estimates that about 4,000 feet of film received retouching of some kind. For an extensive discussion of the process involved, see reproductions of parts of Fulton's September 1934 interview with *The American Cinematographer* in Brunas, Brunas, and Weaver, *Universal Horrors*, 72–73. See also Rudy Behlmer's comments in "Now You See Him: The Invisible Man Revealed" on Universal's Legacy Collection DVD of *The Invisible Man*.

47  Phelan, *Mourning Sex*, 27.

48  The fact that "admiring colleagues and producers" nicknamed Fulton "The Doctor" suggests an overlap between medical and cinematic abilities to manipulate bodily appearances. On "The Doctor" nickname, see Brunas, Brunas, and Weaver, *Universal Horrors*, 72.

49  Johnson Cheu, "Performing Disability, Problematizing Cure," in Sandahl and Auslander, eds., *Bodies in Commotion*, 138–39.

50  The music is from *Bach's Toccata and Fugue in D Minor*. As indicated by the positioning of Jekyll's hands on different keyboards, the nature of the fugue composition is contrapuntal, featuring two or more relatively independent melodies

played at the same time. Visually and aurally, then, this shot conveys the divid-edness that will inform the Jekyll-Hyde narrative, just as the shadow that Jekyll casts across his music sheet anticipates the dark monster within.

51 Virginia Wright Wexman gives a compelling reading of the ways this film's aes-thetic politics, evident in elements such as the white statuary, forward a utopian vision of beauty that casts racial and sexual difference as signifiers of decay and death. See Wexman, "Horrors of the Body," 283–312. The contrast between these white statues and the black demon statue next to the mirror in which Hyde first appears, noted by Wexman, suggests the interaction between—and inextrica-bility of—the concepts of classical and grotesque bodies explored by Mikhail Bakhtin in *Rabelais and His World* and expanded by Mary Russo in *The Female Gro-tesque: Risk, Excess and Modernity*.

52 Halberstam, *Skin Shows*, 60, 60, 64, 64, 66.

53 Stephanie Brown Clark makes a similar point when she says that this mirror scene "points to the instability of [Jekyll's] identity as merely a representation," although I would suggest there is nothing "mere" or necessarily immaterial about such a representation. See Clark, "Frankenflicks: Medical Monsters in Classic Horror Films," in Lester D. Friedman, ed., *Cultural Sutures: Medicine and Media*, 138.

54 See V. S. Ramachandran, D. C. Rogers-Ramachandran, and S. Cobb, "Touching the Phantom," in *Nature* 377 (1995): 489–90; and V. S. Ramachandran and D. C. Rogers-Ramachandran, "Synaesthesia in Phantom Limbs Induced with Mirrors," *Proceedings of the Royal Society of London* 263.1369 (1996): 377–86.

55 Sobchack, *Carnal Thoughts*, 193.

56 Ibid., 194–95.


## 5. SHOCK HORROR AND DEATH RAYS: DISABLING SPECTATORSHIP

1 *Doctor X* Script, Mar. 10, 1932, in the *Doctor X* Collection, at the Warner Bros. Archive, University of Southern California, Los Angeles.

2 Clover, *Men, Women, and Chain Saws*. This interpretation resonates with the ear-lier scene in which Duke has a "hysteria reaction," a bodily experience of psycho-logical trauma persistently associated with women and ancient theories of the "wandering womb" or *hystera*.

3 Berenstein, *Attack of the Leading Ladies*, 127.

4 Jean-Louis Baudry, "The Apparatus: Meta-Psychological Approaches to the Impression of Reality in Cinema" (1970), in Braudy and Cohen, eds., *Film Theory and Criticism*, 209–10; Baudry, "Ideological Effects of the Basic Cinematographic Apparatus" (1970), in Braudy and Cohen, eds., *Film Theory and Criticism*, 364.

5   Baudry, "Ideological Effects," 364.

6   See Christian Metz, *The Imaginary Signifier: Psychoanalysis and the Cinema*; and Laura Mulvey, "Visual Pleasure and Narrative Cinema," *Screen* 16.3 (1975): 6–18.

7   Gary K. Wolf, science fiction and horror literature critic, quoted in David G. Hartwell, "Introduction," in Hartwell, ed., *Foundations of Fear: An Exploration of Horror*, 10.

8   *The Compact Edition of the Oxford English Dictionary* (Oxford: Oxford UP, 1971; 2d ed. 1989).

9   Carroll, *The Philosophy of Horror*, 24.

10   Williams, "Film Bodies," 729, 730, 730, 731.

11   Creed, *The Monstrous-Feminine*, 14.

12   Pinedo, *Recreational Terror*, 41.

13   Davis, *Enforcing Normalcy*, 48.

14   Morris Dickstein, "The Aesthetics of Fright," 1980, in Barry Keith Grant, ed., *Planks of Reason*, 68.

15   King, quoted in Badley, *Film, Horror, and the Body Fantastic*, 10.

16   Fairchild, *The Melting-Pot Mistake*, 69–70.

17   Williams, "Film Bodies," 736.

18   Shaviro, *The Cinematic Body*, 56, 61.

19   Sobchack, *Carnal Thoughts*, 57.

20   Ibid., 76–77.

21   Henry James Forman, *Our Movie Made Children*, 16. Titles of the Payne Fund books included *Motion Pictures and Youth: A Summary*; *Motion Pictures and the Social Attitudes of Children*; *The Emotional Responses of Children to the Motion Picture Situation*; and *Motion Pictures and Standards of Morality*. For more on the Payne Fund studies, see Garth S. Jowett, Ian C. Jarvie, and Kathryn H. Fuller, *Children and the Movies: Media Influence and the Payne Fund Controversy*.

22   Forman, *Our Movie Made Children*, 73, 82, 84, 7, 95, 96, 101.

23   Ibid., 98–99, 101, 90, 91, 92.

24   Ibid., 107, 104.

25   Fred Eastman, "The Movies and Your Child's Health," *Christian Century*, May 10, 1933, 622.

26   For a social history of electricity in America, see David E. Nye, *Electrifying America: Social Meanings of the New Technology, 1880–1940*.

27   Armstrong, *Modernism, Technology, and the Body*, 17–18. Armstrong here cites George Beard's use, in *American Nervousness*, of the image of the electric lamp to depict stress on the body's energy resources. Beard argued that "Edison's electric light is now sufficiently advanced in an experimental direction to give us the best possible illustration of the effects of modern civilization on the nervous system. . . . The nervous system of man is the centre of the nerve-force supplying all

the organs of the body.... [W]hen new functions are interposed in the circuit, as modern civilization is constantly requiring us to do, there comes a period, sooner or later ... when the amount of force is insufficient to keep all the lamps actively burning; those that are weakest go out entirely, or ... burn faint and feebly ... this is the philosophy of modern nervousness." Beard, *American Nervousness*, 98–99.

**28** See Beard and A. D. Rockwell, *A Practical Treatise on the Medical and Surgical Uses of Electricity*, 253; Armstrong, *Modernism, Technology, and the Body*, 18.

**29** Pick, *Faces of Degeneration*, 231–32.

**30** On medical uses of electricity, see Margaret Rowbottom and Charles Susskind, *Electricity and Medicine: History of Their Interaction*.

**31** On experiments by Ivan Pavlov and other Russian physiologists that induced epileptic convulsions through electric shock, see Overmier and Senior, *Books and Manuscripts of the Bakken*, 331. The first use of electricity for capital punishment came in the 1890 New York execution of William Kemmler. For a description of this event, see Armstrong, *Modernism, Technology, and the Body*, 13–14.

**32** For a history of shell shock, see Ben Shephard, *A War of Nerves: Soldiers and Psychiatrists in the Twentieth Century*. For a history of "trauma" in this period, see Mark S. Micale and Paul Lerner, eds., *Traumatic Pasts: History, Psychiatry, and Trauma in the Modern Age, 1870–1930*, including Caroline Cox, "Invisible Wounds: The American Legion, Shell-Shocked Veterans, and American Society, 1919–1924," 280–305.

**33** On the dangers of war to the "fighting Nordic element," see Madison Grant, *The Passing of the Great Race*, 73–4.

**34** "Shellshock Hit as Popular Fancy by World Doctors," *Washington Evening Star*, July 31, 1931, B1.

**35** "Memories of War Afflict Veterans," *Washington Evening Star*, August 2, 1931, A6.

**36** "The Blows of Sound," *Washington Evening Star*, Sept. 22, 1929, sec. 2: 2.

**37** "Workers Fatigued by Factory Noises," *Washington Evening Star*, Nov. 17, 1930, A15. Beard represented as one of the contributing causes to neurasthenia the noises of civilization "that are unrhythmical, unmelodious and therefore annoying, if not injurious." See Beard, *American Nervousness*, 106, and the entire section, "Effect of Noise on the Nerves," 106–112.

**38** "Death from Heart Disease on Gain: London Professor Blames Emotional Strain of Modern Life for Increase," *Washington Evening Star*, June 17, sec. 1: 40.

**39** Walter Benjamin, "On Some Motifs in Baudelaire" (1939), in *Illuminations: Essays and Reflections*, ed. Hannah Arendt, 155–200.

**40** Benjamin, "The Work of Art in the Age of Mechanical Reproduction," 217–51, 236–37; Benjamin, "On Some Motifs in Baudelaire," 176.

**41** Hal Foster, "Prosthetic Gods," *Modernism/Modernity* 4.2 (1997): 26.

**42** Tom Johnson, *Censored Screams: The British Ban on Hollywood Horror in the Thirties*, 162.

43  John C. Moffitt, *Kansas City Star*, quoted in Skal and Savada, *Dark Carnival*, 178.

44  Thomas Doherty, *Pre-Code Hollywood: Sex, Immorality, and Insurrection in American Cinema*, 318.

45  Richard Watts Jr., "Freaks," *New York Herald-Tribune*, July 9, 1932, 6; "Freaks," *Harrison's Reports*, July 16, 1932, 114.

46  "MGM 'Freaks' Repellent: Appeal Mainly to Morbid," *The Hollywood Reporter*, Jan. 12, 1932, 3.

47  See note 20 of chapter 2, and Skal and Savada, *Dark Carnival*, 168.

48  Skal and Savada, *Dark Carnival*, 174.

49  Jones, quoted in Johnson, *Censored Screams*, 144.

50  Davis, quoted in Skal, *The Monster Show*, 125.

51  "What to Do with 'Freaks,'" in *Harrison's Reports*, Apr. 9, 1932, 60; William J. Robinson, "Concerning Horror Films" (Letter to the Screen Editor), *New York Times* (hereafter, *NYT*), July 28, 1935, X2.

52  "Appendix 1: The Text of the Production Code," in Thomas Doherty, *Hollywood's Censor: Joseph I. Breen and the Production Code Administration*, 347–59, 347–48 (italics in original).

53  Davenport, *Heredity in Relation to Eugenics*, 266.

54  Henry Fairfield Osborn, "Shall We Maintain Washington's Ideal of Americanism?" in Madison Grant, ed., *The Alien in Our Midst*, 208.

55  "Appendix 1: The Text of the Production Code," 351, 355, 359.

56  Jason S. Joy, letter to Mr. Harold Hurley at Paramount, Sept 26, 1932, in *Island of Lost Souls* Production Code File, AMPAS. On Dec 8, James Wingate, Joy's successor at the Production Code Administration, also mentioned the line as a possible source of concern but was otherwise delighted with the film, declaring it "a splendid job . . . which should not only meet with a great deal of success, but which should also cause very little difficulty from a censorable standpoint." Wingate later described the film to General Hays as "one of the best of the horror stories that have been brought to the screen." See James Wingate, letter to Mr. John Hammell, Dec. 8, 1932; and Wingate, letter to General Hays, Dec. 9, 1932, both in the *Island of Lost Souls* Production Code File, AMPAS.

57  See Joseph Breen, letter to John Hammell, Paramount, Sept. 18, 1935; and Breen, letter to Luigi Luraschi, Mar. 4, 1941, which lists the cuts required to "eliminate from the picture the suggestion that Moreau considers himself on a par with God as a creator." See also the "Local Censorship Boards" figures, which, along with the letters, are included in the *Island of Lost Souls* Production Code File, AMPAS.

58  Breen, quoted in Gerald Gardner, *The Censorship Papers: Movie Censorship Letters from the Hays Office, 1934–1968*, 66.

59  "Frankenstein," in Patricia King Hanson and Alan Gevinson, *The American Film Institute Catalog, Feature Films, 1931–1940*, 699.

**60** Jason S. Joy, letter to Mr. B. P. Schulberg, June 3, 1932, *Island of Lost Souls* Production Code File, Margaret Herrick Library, AMPAS.

**61** Breen, letter to Luigi Luraschi, Mar. 4, 1941. Thomas Doherty notes that early horror films benefited from a pre-Code "'censorial oversight' regarding what was called 'the quality of 'gruesomeness'" and cites a 1931 issue of *Variety*: "There is no provision, it is officially conceded, in any censor law which rules on the quality or extent of gruesomeness." Again, like eugenic films, horror films forced a reconceptualization of aesthetic politics and their deployment of disability. See Doherty, *Pre-Code Hollywood*, 297.

**62** Luigi Luraschi, letter to Joseph Breen, Mar. 15, 1941, *Island of Lost Souls* Production Code File, AMPAS.

**63** J. C. M., "The Current Cinema [*Frankenstein*]," *The New Yorker*, Dec. 12, 1931, 80.

**64** See the *Island of Lost Souls* Press Book, AMPAS.

**65** Berenstein, *Attack of the Leading Ladies*, 72.

**66** Advertisement, *NYT*, July 9, 1932, 7.

**67** Berenstein, *Attack of the Leading Ladies*, 70–73.

**68** "*Mad Love* Advertising Approach," in the *Mad Love* Core Collection Production File, Margaret Herrick Library, AMPAS.

**69** "Frankenstein," *Time*, Dec. 14, 1931, 25.

**70** "The Island of Dr. Moreau," *NYT*, Jan. 22, 1933, X5.

**71** "Frankenstein," *Time*, 25.

**72** *Doctor X* Script.

**73** Ibid.

**74** Mitchell and Snyder, *Narrative Prosthesis*, 156–57.

**75** "Poison Gas Kills 100 in Cleveland Clinic," *NYT*, May 16, 1929, 1. For more on the Cleveland Clinic disaster, see John Stark Bellamy, II, *They Died Crawling and Other Tales of Cleveland Woe*; and J. D. Clough, ed., *To Act as a Unit: The Story of the Cleveland Clinic*. The latter gives the final death toll as 123, a number that included one of the clinic's four founders, Dr. John Phillips. The disaster led to the nationwide revision of regulations for storage of nitro-cellulose film and to a shift toward the use of acetate film.

**76** "Experts Divided on Nature of Gas," *NYT*, May 16, 1929, 1.

**77** "Poison Gas Kills 100," 1.

**78** "Strict Rules Guard Hospital Film Here," *NYT*, May 16, 1929, 1.

**79** "Poison Gas Kills 100," 1.

**80** "Crile Famous for Medical Work," *NYT*, May 16, 1929, 3.

**81** Cartwright, *Screening the Body*, 127, 110, 109, 127–28.

**82** "Loses Arm in X-Ray Work," *NYT*, Apr. 28, 1931, 4; "W. S. Andrews Dies: An Edison Pioneer," *NYT*, July 2, 1929, 27; "X-Ray Experiments Cost Doctor an Arm," *NYT*,

Oct. 16, 1929, 31; and "X-Ray Specialist Loses Arm Due to Practice," *Washington Evening Star*, Dec. 28, 1931, A12.

83 Skal, *Screams of Reason*, 158–59.

84 Douglas P. Murphy, "The Eugenical Aspects of Pelvic Irradiation Therapy," *Eugenics* 1.1 (Oct. 1928): 22–23. Studying the health of children born to women irradiated for pelvic disease, some while they were pregnant and some prior to conception, Murphy concludes from the large number of children with "microcephalic idiocy" born to the former group that "irradiation of the growing embryo is extremely detrimental to its normal development," but "concerning the influence of maternal pelvic irradiation, when given before conception, it would seem that such treatment has little or no damaging influence upon the health of subsequent children." See also L. Goldstein and D. P. Murphy, "Etiology of the Ill-Health in Children Born After Maternal Pelvic Irradiation," *American Journal of Roentgenology* 22 (1929): 322–31.

85 "3% Found Victims of Hereditary Ills," *NYT*, Nov. 25, 1936, 21.

86 Cartwright, *Screening the Body*, 121.

87 Ibid.

88 For a history of X-ray technology, see Alan G. Michette and Slawka Pfauntsch, *X-rays: The First Hundred Years*.

89 Cartwright, *Screening the Body*, 125.

90 Ibid., 129.

91 Skal, *Screams of Reason*, 157, 158.

92 Murphy, "The Eugenical Aspects of Pelvic Irradiation Therapy," 22–23.

93 Lovecraft, quoted in Houellebecq, *H. P. Lovecraft*, 106–107.

94 The destruction of the plate also invokes the impermanence of X-ray film discussed above, asserting, once again, the transient and unstable nature of medical spectacle despite scientific claims to truth and certainty.

95 Shaviro, *The Cinematic Body*, 51.

## CONCLUSION

1 For the full history of Buck's case, see, for example, Smith and Nelson, *The Sterilization of Carrie Buck*; and Paul A. Lombardo, *Three Generations, No Imbeciles*.

2 Kevles, *In the Name of Eugenics*, 110.

3 United States Supreme Court, "Buck v. Bell Superintendent" (1927), in Bajema, ed., *Eugenics*, 157, 158, 161, 161, 163, 158.

4 Frank McConnell, *The Science Fiction of H. G. Wells*, 104.

5   Rhode, quoted in Tom Johnson, *Censored Screams*, 69–71.

6   See, for instance, Stefan Kühl, *The Nazi Connection: Eugenics, American Racism, and German National Socialism*; and Black, *War Against the Weak*.

7   Lombardo, *Three Generations, No Imbeciles*, xii–xiii.

8   Kevles, *In the Name of Eugenics*, 145–46.

9   Thomas Hunt Morgan, *Evolution and Genetics*, 201; excerpt in IAEEM, #1918 (accessed Sept. 8, 2010).

10  Pearl, quoted in Hasian, *The Rhetoric of Eugenics*, 50. Kevles notes a 1935 comment by American geneticist Hermann J. Muller which conveys a similar sentiment: Muller declared that "eugenics had become 'hopelessly perverted' into a pseudoscientific façade for 'advocates of race and class prejudice, defenders of vested interests of church and state, Fascists, Hitlerites, and reactionaries generally.'" Kevles, *In the Name of Eugenics*, 164.

11  Anne Kerr and Tom Shakespeare, *Genetic Politics: From Eugenics to Genome*, 63–64. For general discussions of the move from hard-line to reform eugenics, see most recent histories of eugenics, including Kevles, *In the Name of Eugenics*; Diane B. Paul, *Controlling Human Heredity: 1865 to the Present*; Kühl, *The Nazi Connection*; and Anne Kerr and Tom Shakespeare, *Genetic Politics*.

12  The film incorrectly presents acromegaly as a communicable disease rather than a hormonal disorder often caused by a tumor on the pituitary gland. The disorder's disfiguring effects produce a form well-suited to the horror genre's physical conception of monstrosity. Many individuals with acromegaly have made livings in the entertainment sphere, most notably as wrestlers (Andre the Giant, Paul Wight/"The Big Show"), but also as horror actors: Rondo Hatton starred in horror films *House of Horrors* (dir. Jean Yarbrough, Universal, 1946) and *The Brute Man* (dir. Jean Yarbrough, Universal, 1946) as the disfigured "Creeper"; Ted Cassidy played Lurch in the 1960s' TV series *The Addams Family*; and Matthew McGrory featured in independent films such as *The Dead Hate the Living!* (dir. Rob Parker, 2000), *House of 1000 Corpses* (dir. Rob Zombie, 2003), and *The Devil's Rejects* (dir. Zombie, 2005).

13  Dana Polan, *Power and Paranoia: History, Narrative, and the American Cinema, 1940–1950*, 174–76.

14  Waldemar Kaempffert, "The Week in Science: Theories of the Eugenists," *New York Times* (hereafter, *NYT*), June 7, 1936, XX6.

15  Kerr and Shakespeare, *Genetic Politics*, 179, 180, 180–81, 181.

16  Other texts examining the persistence of American eugenic ideas in contemporary genetic science include Paul, *Controlling Human Heredity*; and Troy Duster, *Backdoor to Eugenics*. It is not just eugenic ableism that persists: post-eugenic research and medical conventions still target racial and other minority groups, as in the 1970s practice, in some American regions, of performing unwanted tubal

ligations or hysterectomies on black women, discussed, for instance, in Dorothy Roberts, *Killing the Black Body: Race, Reproduction, and the Meaning of Liberty*. Rather, this perspective argues that while such racist biology is no longer widely and publicly validated, even as it is still practiced in some spaces, ableist biological views continue to permeate our culture, as disability, disease, and genetic "defect" are still seen as "naturally" troubling and undesirable.

**17** Klarsfeld, quoted in Elaine Sciolino, "By Making Holocaust Personal to Pupils, Sarkozy Stirs Anger," *NYT*, Feb 16, 2008 (accessed May 17, 2008).

**18** Feinstein, quoted in Pauline Oo, "In Search of the Perfect Human: U Explores International Eugenics Movements with Science Museum of Minnesota," *UMN News*, Mar. 17, 2008 (accessed May 17, 2008).

**19** Shaila K. Dewan, "Do Horror Films Filter the Horrors of History?" *NYT*, Oct. 14, 2000 (accessed May 18, 2008).

**20** Wood, "An Introduction," 174.

**21** Adam Lowenstein, *Shocking Representation: Historical Trauma, National Cinema, and the Modern Horror Film*, 10, 13–14. See Walter Benjamin, "Theses on the Philosophy of History" (1968), in *Illuminations: Essays and Reflections*, ed. Hannah Arendt, 253–64.

**22** Lowenstein, *Shocking Representation*, 14.

**23** Nicholas Wade, "A Decade Later, Genetic Map Yields Few New Cures," *NYT*, June 12, 2010 (accessed Sept. 20, 2010).

# BIBLIOGRAPHY

## PRIMARY TEXTS

### ABBREVIATIONS

AES      American Eugenics Society records

AMPAS      Margaret Herrick Library, Academy of Motion Pictures Arts and Sciences, Los Angeles

APS      American Philosophical Society Library, Philadelphia

ERO      Eugenics Record Office records (at APS)

IAAEM      Image Archive on the American Eugenics Movement (www.eugenicsar-chive.org/eugenics and click on "Enter the Archive")

(Each document page or image has its own identifying number, rendered as #.)

"3% Found Victims of Hereditary Ills." *New York Times*, Nov. 25, 1936, 21.

"91.1 Per Cent of Kindergarten and First-Grade Pupils Found with Physical Imperfections." *Washington Evening Star*, Aug. 25, 1928, 1–2.

"A.B.W. Family: Musical, Literary, and Inventive Ability." In IAAEM, #885 (accessed Aug. 10, 2010).

Ainsworth, Claire. "The Stranger Within." *New Scientist* (Nov. 11, 2003): 34–37. Academic Search Premier, EBSCOhost (accessed Sept. 15, 2010).

American Eugenics Society. "Practical Eugenics: Aims and Methods of the American Eugenics Society" (1938). Folder 9, *AES Printing Orders*, APS.

*American Eugenics Society Scrapbook*. AES, APS.

"Appendix 1: The Text of the Production Code." In Thomas Doherty, *Hollywood's Censor: Joseph I. Breen and the Production Code Administration*, 351–63. New York: Columbia UP, 2007.

Babcock, Muriel. "'Freaks' Rouse Ire and Wonder." *Los Angeles Times*, Feb. 14, 1932, 9.

Bacon, Francis. *Novum Organum* (1620). Trans. R. Ellis and James Spedding. New York: Routledge, 1900.

"Battle of Washington." *Time*, Aug. 8, 1932, 5.

Beard, George. *American Nervousness: Its Causes and Consequences* (1881). New York: Arno Press, 1972.

Beard, George and A. D. Rockwell. *A Practical Treatise on the Medical and Surgical Uses of Electricity: Including Localized and General Faradization, Localized and Central Galvanization, Electrolysis and Galvano-Cautery* (1871). 2d ed. New York, W. Wood, 1875.

Bell, Alexander Graham. *Memoir Upon the Formation of a Deaf Variety of the Human Race*. Washington D.C.: National Academy of Sciences, 1884.

"The Blows of Sound." *Washington Evening Star*, Sept. 22, 1929, sec. 2: 2.

Blumenbach, Johann Friedrich. *The Anthropological Treatises of Johann Friedrich Blumenbach* (1865). Boston : Longwood Press, 1978.

Breen, Joseph. Letter to John Hammell, Sept. 18, 1935. Production Code File for *Island of Lost Souls*, AMPAS.

——. Letter to Mr. Luigi Luraschi, Mar. 4, 1941. Production Code File for *Island of Lost Souls*, AMPAS.

Buffon, Georges-Louis LeClerc, Count. *Histoire naturelle, générale et particulière*. Paris: Imprimeries royale, 1749–1788.

Burr, C. W. "Heredity in Epilepsy: Study of One Thousand Four Hundred and Forty Nine Cases" (orig. in *Archives of Neurology and Psychiatry* 7.6 [June 1922]: 721). In IAAEM, #372 (accessed June 21, 2010).

"The Catlin Mark: The Inheritance of an Unusual Opening in the Parietal Bone." In IAAEM, #565 (accessed Aug. 10, 2010).

"The Circus Side Show." *New York Times*, July 9, 1932, 7.

Connell, Fr. Francis J. "The Catholic Church and Eugenics." *American Eugenics Society: Conference on the Relation of Eugenics and the Church* (May 8, 1939), 1–6. AES Files, APS.

Councilman, William Thomas. *Disease and Its Causes*. New York: Henry Holt, 1913. Project Gutenberg E-Book PDF; http://manybooks.net/titles/councilman w15281528315283–8.html (accessed Sept. 15, 2010).

Cox, Earnest Sevier. *White America* (1923). Richmond, VA: White America Society, 1937.

"Cranium of Murderer Like Anthropoid Ape's." *New York Times*, Jan. 25, 1930, 6.

"Crile Famous for Medical Work." *New York Times*, May 16, 1929, 3.

Crile, George Washington. *The Bipolar Theory of Living Processes*. New York, Macmillan, 1926.

"*Dark Eyes of London.*" *Motion Picture Herald*, Nov. 18, 1939, 49, 52.

Darwin, Charles. *On the Origin of Species by Means of Natural Selection* (1857). New York, Heritage Press, 1963.

Davenport, Charles B. "The Effects of Race Intermingling." *Proceedings of the American Philosophical Society* 56 (1917): 364–68.

——. "Eugenics: The Science of Human Improvement by Better Breeding" (1910). In IAAEM, #1714 (accessed June 9, 2010).

——. *Guide to Anthropometry and Anthroposcopy*. Eugenics Research Association Handbook Series. New York: Cold Spring Harbor, 1927.

——. *Heredity in Relation to Eugenics*. New York: Holt, 1911.

——. "Race Crossing in Man" (ca.1920), in IAAEM, #447 (accessed Aug. 23, 2010).

Davenport, Charles B. and D. Weeks. "Poorhouse Type of Source of Defectives: Pedigree of Epilepsy and Feeblemindedness" (1911). In IAAEM, #1696 (accessed June 20, 2010).

Davenport, Charles B. and Florence Harris Danielson. *Heredity of Skin Color in Negro-White Crosses*. Washington, D.C.: Carnegie Institution of Washington, 1913.

Davenport, Charles B. and Morris Steggerda. *Race Crossing in Jamaica*. Washington, D.C.: Carnegie Institution of Washington, 1929.

"Death from Heart Disease on Gain: London Professor Blames Emotional Strain of Modern Life for Increase." *Washington Evening Star*, June 17, 1928, sec. 1: 40.

"Description of the American Breeders Association" (ca. 1909). In IAAEM, #412 (accessed June 20, 2010).

Dewan, Shaila K. "Do Horror Films Filter the Horrors of History?" *New York Times*, Oct. 14, 2000; www.nytimes.com/2000/10/14/movies/do-horror-films-filter-the-horrors-of-history.html?emc=eta1 (accessed May 18, 2008).

Dight, C. F. "Eugenics Society President Replies to Questions." Letter to the Editor, (Minneapolis) *Journal*, Apr. 29, 1928. In Leon F. Whitney Scrapbook #2, AES Collection, APS.

*Doctor X* Script (Mar. 10 1932). *Doctor X* Collection. Warner Bros. Archive, University of Southern California, Los Angeles.

Donne, John. Sermon preached at the funerals of Sir William Cokayne, Knight Alderman of London, Dec. 12, 1626; http://contentdm.lib.byu.edu/cdm4/document.php?CISOROOT=/JohnDonne&CISOPTR=3230&REC=2 (accessed Apr. 25, 2008).

Dugdale, Richard L. *The Jukes: A Study in Crime, Pauperism, Disease and Heredity* (1875). 4th ed. New York: Putnam's, 1910.

Dunn, Katherine. *Geek Love*. New York: Warner Books, 1989.

Eastman, Fred. "The Movies and Your Child's Health." *Christian Century*, May 10, 1933, 620–22.

Ellison, Ralph. *Invisible Man* (1952). New York: Modern Library, 1994.

Estabrook, Arthur H. *The Jukes in 1915*. Washington, D.C.: Carnegie Institution, 1916.

Estabrook, Arthur H. and Ivan E. McDougle. *Mongrel Virginians: The WIN Tribe*. Baltimore: Williams & Wilkins, 1926.

"Eugenics in Church Class." *New York Times*, Oct. 20, 1913, 5.

Eugenics Record Office. "Eugenics Seeks to Improve the Natural, Physical, Mental and Temperamental Qualities of the Human Family" (ca. 1927). In IAAEM, #249 (accessed Aug. 5, 2010).

"Experts Divided on Nature of Gas." *New York Times*, May 16, 1929, 1–2.

F. S. N. "At the Roxy [*The Bride of Frankenstein*]." *New York Times*, May 11, 1935, 21.

Fairchild, Henry Pratt. "Immigration and National Unity." In Madison Grant, ed., *The Alien in Our Midst*, 105–110.

——. *The Melting-Pot Mistake*. Boston: Little, Brown, 1926.

"Farmer Uprisings More Frequent." *New York Times*, Jan. 22, 1933, sec. 4: 7.

Fernald, W. E. "The Burden of Feeble-Mindedness." Address to the Massachusetts Medical Society, *Journal of Psycho-Asthenics* 17.3 (Mar. 1912): 85–111.

"Finds Western Vices Increase Epilepsy." *New York Times*, June 2, 1931, 2.

"Form for Studying the Inheritance of Pauperism and Criminality." In IAAEM, #100 (accessed Aug. 10, 2010).

Forman, Henry James. *Our Movie Made Children*. New York: Macmillan, 1933.

"Frankenstein." *Time*, Dec. 14, 1931, 25.

"'Frankenstein' Finished." *New York Times*, Oct. 11, 1931, X5.

"Freaks." *Harrison's Reports*, Feb. 27, 1932, 35.

"Freaks." *Harrison's Reports*, July 16, 1932, 114.

"Freaks." *Variety*, July 12, 1932, 16.

"'Freaks' Arrives." *New York Times*, July 17, 1932, X3.

Galton, Francis. "Composite Portraits" (1878). In IAAEM, #2193 and #2194 (accessed Sept. 12, 2009).

——. *Essays in Eugenics* (1909). New York: Garland, 1985.

——. "Eugenics: Its Definition, Scope, and Aims." *American Journal of Sociology* 10 (July 1904); http://galton.org/essays/1900–1911/galton-1904-am-journ-soc-eugenics-scope-aims.htm (accessed Sept. 8, 2010).

——. *Hereditary Genius: An Inquiry into Its Laws and Consequences* (1869). New York: Horizon, 1952.

——. "Illustrations of Composite Portraiture, The Jewish Type." Orig. in *The Photographic News*, Apr. 17, 1885. In IAAEM, #2217 (accessed Sept. 12, 2009).

——. *Inquiries into Human Faculty and Its Development*. New York: Macmillan, 1883.

Geoffroy Saint-Hilaire, Isidore. *Histoire générale et particulière des anomalies de l'organisation chez l'homme et les animaux*. Brussels: Établissement Encyclographique, 1837.

Gerard, Emily. "Transylvanian Superstitions." *The Nineteenth Century* (July 1885): 128–44.

Goddard, Henry. "Four Hundred Feeble-Minded Children Classified by the Binet Method." *Journal of Psycho-Asthenics* 15 (1910): 17–30.

——. *The Kallikak Family: A Study in the Heredity of Feeble-Mindedness*. New York: Macmillan, 1912.

Goldstein L. and D. P. Murphy. "Etiology of the Ill-Health in Children Born After Maternal Pelvic Irradiation." *American Journal of Roentgenology* 22 (1929): 322–31.

Gosney, E. S. and Paul B. Popenoe. *Sterilization for Human Betterment: A Summary of Results of 6,000 Operations in California, 1909–1929*. New York: Macmillan, 1929.

Grant, Madison. "Closing the Floodgates." In Madison Grant, ed., *The Alien in Our Midst*. 13–24.

——. *The Passing of the Great Race: Or, The Racial Basis of European History* (1916). 4th ed. New York: Scribner's, 1921.

Grant, Madison, ed. *The Alien in Our Midst*. New York: Galton, 1930.

Hadden, Walter J., Charles H. Robinson, and Mary R. Melendy. *The Science of Eugenics and Sex-Life, Love, Marriage, Maternity* (1914). New York: Martin and Murray, 1927.

Hall, Mordaunt. "Bram Stoker's Human Vampire," *New York Times*, Feb. 13, 1931, 21.

——. "'Dracula' as a Film." *New York Times*, Feb. 22, 1931, 98.

——. "A Fantastic Melodrama." *New York Times*, Sept. 7, 1925, 15.

——. "Fine Photography in 'Jekyll and Hyde.'" *New York Times*, Jan. 10, 1932, X4.

——. "Fredric March in a Splendidly Produced Pictorial Version of 'Dr. Jekyll and Mr. Hyde.'" *New York Times*, Jan. 2, 1932, 14.

"Hereditary Disorders." In IAEEM; www.eugenicsarchive.org/html/eugenics/index2 .html?tag=271, then click on "Topics" (accessed Aug. 12, 2010).

"Heredity in Epilepsy." In IAAEM, #570 (accessed June 10, 2010).

"Heredity of Harelip and Cleft Palate." In IAAEM, #566 (accessed Aug. 10, 2010).

Hippocrates. "The Sacred Disease." In *The Medical Works of Hippocrates*, 179–93. Trans. John Chadwick and W. N. Mann. Oxford: Blackwell Scientific, 1950.

"Horror Films Taken off U Sked." *Variety*, May 6, 1936, 7.

"Horror on the Screen: The Demon Surgeon." *The Times* (London), Aug. 4, 1936, 8.

Howe, Lucien. "The Control by Law of Hereditary Blindness" (ca. 1928), in IAEEM, #279 (accessed June 20, 2010).

——. "Response to Charles Davenport and Harry Laughlin, about Sterilization, Marriage and Blindness" (1923), in IAAEM, #325 (accessed June 20, 2010).

Human Betterment Foundation. "Human Sterilization." Pasadena, CA: The Human Betterment Foundation, 1934. In IAAEM, #1753 (accessed Aug. 18, 2010).

"The Island of Dr. Moreau." *New York Times*, Jan. 22, 1933, sec. 9: 5.

*Island of Lost Souls* Press Book. AMPAS.

J. C. M. "The Current Cinema [*Frankenstein*]." *The New Yorker*, Dec. 12, 1931, 79–80.

——. "The Current Cinema [*Freaks*]." *The New Yorker*, July 16, 1932, 45.

Johnson, Albert. "The Opponents of Restricted Immigration." In Madison Grant, ed., *The Alien in Our Midst*, 9–12.

Johnstone, E. R. "Stimulating Public Interest in the Feeble-Minded" (1916). In IAAEM, #1447, accessed Aug 31, 2010.

Jordan, David Starr. *The Blood of the Nation: A Study of the Decay of Races Through the Survival of the Unfit*. Boston: American Unitarian Association, 1902.

Joy, Jason S. Letter to B. P. Schulberg, Dec. 1, 1931. MPPDA Case File on *Dr. Jekyll and Mr. Hyde*, Special Collections, AMPAS.

——. Letter to Mr. B. P. Schulberg, June 3, 1932. *Island of Lost Souls* Production Code File, AMPAS.

——. Letter to Mr. Harold Hurley, Sept. 26, 1932. *Island of Lost Souls* Production Code File, AMPAS.

——. Letter to Will H. Hays, Dec. 5, 1931. MPPDA Case Files, Special Collections, AMPAS.

Kaempffert, Waldemar. "The Week in Science: Theories of the Eugenists." *New York Times*, June 7, 1936, XX6.

Laughlin, Harry H. "Analysis of America's Modern Melting Pot." Testimony before the House Committee on Immigration and Naturalization (1922). In IAAEM, #1128 (accessed June 9, 2010).

——. *Eugenical Sterilization in the United States*. Chicago: Psychopathic Laboratory of the Municipal Court of Chicago, 1922.

——. *Immigration and Conquest: A Report of the Special Committee on Immigration and Naturalization of the Chamber of Commerce of the State of New York* (Carnegie Institution of Washington). New York, 1939.

"Linking Up Man's Diet and Character." *New York Times*, Apr. 14, 1929, sec. 5: 3.

Lodge, Henry Cabot. "The Restriction of Immigration." In *Speeches and Addresses, 1884–1909*, 245–66. Boston: Houghton Mifflin, 1909.

Lombroso, Cesare. *Criminal Man* (1876). Ed. and trans. Mary Gibson and Nicole Hahn Rafter. Durham, NC: Duke UP, 2006.

——. "Introduction." In *Criminal Man*, ed. Gina Lombroso-Ferrero, xi—xx. New York: Putnam's, 1911.

"Loses Arm in X-Ray Work." *New York Times*, Apr. 28, 1931, 4.

Luraschi, Luigi. Letter to Joseph Breen, Mar. 15, 1941. *Island of Lost Souls* Production Code File, AMPAS.

Lusk, Norbert. "'Dracula' Hit on Broadway." *Los Angeles Times*, Feb. 22, 1931, sec. 3: 9.

"*Mad Love*," *Daily Variety*, June 27, 1935, 3.

"*Mad Love* Advertising Approach." *Mad Love* Core Collection Production File, AMPAS.

Marshall, Jim. "The Observer." Portland (OR) *News*, Nov. 7, 1927. AES: Leon F. Whitney Eugenics Scrapbook #2, AES Collection, APS.

"Massachusetts Department of Mental Diseases Exhibits Pictures of 59 Criminal Brains" (1921). In IAAEM, #567 (accessed June 10, 2010).

"Memories of War Afflict Veterans." *Washington Evening Star*, Aug. 2, 1931, A6.

"MGM 'Freaks' Repellent: Appeal Mainly to Morbid." *The Hollywood Reporter*, Jan. 12, 1932, 3.

Morgan, Thomas Hunt. *Evolution and Genetics*. Princeton, NJ: Princeton UP, 1925.

Morel, Bénédict Augustin. *Traité des dégéneréscences physiques, intellectuelles et morales de l'espèce humaine*. Paris: Baillière, 1857.

Murphy, Douglas P. "The Eugenical Aspects of Pelvic Irradiation Therapy." *Eugenics* 1.1 (Oct. 1928): 22–24.

Muybridge, Eadweard. *Animal Locomotion*. New York: Da Capo Press, 1969.

——. *The Human Figure in Motion*. New York: Dover, 1955.

——. *The Male and Female Figure in Motion*. New York: Dover, 1984.

Myers, William Starr. "Political Aspects of Immigration." In Madison Grant, ed., *The Alien in Our Midst*, 200–203.

Nordau, Max (1892–93). *Degeneration*. Lincoln: U of Nebraska P, 1993.

"Oh You Beautiful Monster." *New York Times*, Jan. 29, 1939, X4.

Oo, Pauline. "In Search of the Perfect Human: U Explores International Eugenics Movements with Science Museum of Minnesota." *UMN News*, Mar. 17, 2008; www1.umn.edu/umnnews/Feature_Stories/In_search_of_the_perfect_human .html (accessed May 17, 2008)

"Operates on Brain to Treat Epilepsy." *New York Times*, Dec. 28, 1929, 7.

Osborn, Henry Fairfield. "Shall We Maintain Washington's Ideal of Americanism?" In Madison Grant, ed., *The Alien in Our Midst*, 204–209.

Paré, Ambroise. *On Monsters and Marvels* (1573). Trans. Janis Pallister. Chicago: U of Chicago P, 1982.

"The Pay-Off." *Motion Picture Daily*, Apr. 11, 1932, 2.

"Pedigree of Red Hair Family." In IAAEM, #828 (accessed Aug. 10, 2010).

Plecker, Walter Ashby. "Virginia's Attempt to Adjust the Color Problem." *The American Journal of Public Health* 15 (Feb. 1925): 111–15.

"Poison Gas Kills 100 in Cleveland Clinic." *New York Times*, May 16, 1929, 1.

Popenoe, Paul and Roswell Hill Johnson. *Applied Eugenics*. New York: Macmillan, 1918.

Roberts, Kenneth L. "Mexican Immigration in the Southwest." In Madison Grant, ed., *The Alien in Our Midst*, 214–19.

Robinson, William J. "Concerning Horror Films" (Letter to the Screen Editor). *New York Times*, July 28, 1935, X2.

Roosevelt, Theodore. Letter to C. Davenport about "degenerates reproducing," Jan. 3, 1913. In IAAEM, #1242 (accessed Sept. 6, 2010).

Sciolino, Elaine. "By Making Holocaust Personal to Pupils, Sarkozy Stirs Anger." *New York Times*, Feb. 16, 2008; www.nytimes.com/2008/02/16/world/europe/16france.html?emc=eta1 (accessed May 17, 2008).

Sennwald, Andre. "Reading the Log for April and May." *New York Times*, June 2, 1935, X3.

Shelley, Mary. "Author's Introduction to the Standard Novels Edition (1831)." In Maurice Hindle, ed., *Frankenstein*, 5–10.

——. *Frankenstein*. Ed. Maurice Hindle. New York: Penguin, 1992; rev. ed., 2003.

"Shellshock Hit as Popular Fancy by World Doctors." *Washington Evening Star*, July 31, 1931, B1.

"Single-trait Sheet: Wanderlust." In IAAEM, #691 (accessed Aug. 10, 2010).

Smith, Sam. "Harvard Scientist Wants Married Couples Bonded" (orig. in *Boston Sunday Post*, June 10, 1928). In IAAEM, #271 (accessed June 20, 2010).

"Some People are Born to Be a Burden on the Rest." Image of State Fair Display, AES Scrapbook, APS.

Sophocles. *Oedipus the King*. Trans. Stephen Berg and Diskin Clay. New York: Oxford UP, 1978.

Spencer, Herbert. *The Principles of Biology*. Vol. 1. New York: Appleton, 1888.

Stark, Louis. "Industry Alarmed by Company Unions." *New York Times*, Oct. 27, 1935, 16.

"Sterilization Laws Praised." *Los Angeles Times*, Jan. 26, 1928.

Stevenson, Robert Louis. *The Strange Case of Dr. Jekyll and Mr. Hyde* (1886). In Wolf, ed., *The Essential Dr. Jekyll and Mr. Hyde*, 31–136.

Stoddard, Lothrop. "The Permanent Menace from Europe." In Madison Grant, ed., *The Alien in Our Midst*, 225–29.

——. *The Revolt Against Civilization: The Menace of the Under Man*. New York: Scribner's, 1922.

——. *The Rising Tide of Color Against White World Supremacy*. New York: Scribner's, 1920.

Stoker, Bram. *Dracula* (1897). Clayton, DE: Prestwick House Literary Touchstone Classics, 2006.

"Strange, but True." *Minneapolis Evening Tribune*, Feb. 29, 1928. In Leon F. Whitney Eugenics Scrapbook #1, AES Collection, APS.

"Strict Rules Guard Hospital Film Here." *New York Times*, May 16, 1929, 1–2.

"Syllabus of Lectures Given to Field Workers" (1921). In IAAEM, #1105 (accessed June 26, 2010).

Talbot, Eugene S. *Degeneracy: Its Causes, Signs and Results* (1898). New York: Scribner's, 1901.

Thom, D. A. and G. S. Walker. "Epilepsy in Offspring of Epileptics" (orig. in *American Journal of Psychiatry* 10.4 [Apr. 1922]: 613). In IAAEM, #372 (accessed June 21, 2010).

"U Has Horror Cycle All to Self." *Variety*, Apr. 8, 1931, 2.

Union of the Physically Impaired Against Segregation (UPIAS). "Fundamental Principles of Disability." London: Union of the Physically Against Segregation, 1975; www.leeds.ac.uk/disability-studies/archiveuk/UPIAS/fundamental%20principles.pdf (accessed May 15, 2008).

"Union of the Splendidly Developed Dancer Ruth St. Denis and Edwin Shawn, 'the Handsomest Man in America,' May Produce Results of Great Value to the Science of Race Betterment" (1922). In IAAEM, #855 (accessed Sept. 10, 2010).

United States Public Health Service. *Manual of the Mental Examination of Aliens* (1918). In IAAEM, #1530 (accessed June 20, 2010).

United States Supreme Court. "Buck v. Bell Superintendent" (1927). In Carl Jay Bajema, ed., *Eugenics: Then and Now*, 156–208. Stroudsburg, PA: Dowden, Hutchinson & Ross, 1976.

"W. S. Andrews Dies: An Edison Pioneer." *New York Times*, July 2, 1929, 27.

Wade, Nicholas. "Chimeras on the Horizon, but Don't Expect Centaurs." *New York Times*, May 3, 2005; www.nytimes.com/2005/05/03/science/03chim.html?emc=eta1 (accessed June 10, 2009).

——. "A Decade Later, Genetic Map Yields Few New Cures," *New York Times*, June 12, 2010; www.nytimes.com/2010/06/13/health/research/13genome.html?emc=eta1 (accessed Sept. 20, 2010).

Watts Jr., Richard. "*Freaks.*" *New York Herald-Tribune*, July 9, 1932, 6.

Wells, H. G. *The Invisible Man* (1897). New York: Signet Classic, 2002.

——. *The Island of Doctor Moreau* (1896). New York Dover, 1996.

"What to Do with 'Freaks.' " *Harrison's Reports*, Apr. 9, 1932: 60.

"What Will the Children Be?" San Francisco *Call*, Nov. 15, 1928. Leon F. Whitney Eugenics Scrapbook #1, AES Collection, APS.

Whitney, Leon F. "A Charity to Lessen Charity." New Haven, CT: American Eugenics Society (ca. 1925). In AES: *Reprints of Eugenic-Related Works, 1923–1963*, box 1, Leon F. Whitney Collection, APS.

Wiggam, Albert Edward. *The New Decalogue of Science.* Indianapolis: Bobbs-Merrill, 1922.

Wingate, James. Letter to Mr. John Hammell, Dec. 8, 1932. *Island of Lost Souls* Production Code File, AMPAS.

——. Letter to General Hays, Dec. 9, 1932. *Island of Lost Souls* Production Code File, AMPAS.

von Wlislocki, Heinrich. "Torturing Spirits in Romanian Popular Belief." *Am Ur-Quell* 6 (1896): 108–109.

Woolley, Robert Wickliffe. "The South's Fight for Race Purity." *Pearson's Magazine*, n.d. (ca. 1910), 206–213. ERO: MSC77, series I, box 38, A:3174 (APS). Also available in IAAEM, #676.

"Workers Fatigued by Factory Noises." *Washington Evening Star*, Nov. 17, 1930, A15.

"X-Ray Experiments Cost Doctor an Arm." *New York Times*, Oct. 16, 1929, 31.

"X-Ray Specialist Loses Arm Due to Practice." *Washington Evening Star*, Dec. 28, 1931, A12.

## SECONDARY TEXTS

Adams, Rachel. *Sideshow U.S.A.: Freaks and the American Cultural Imagination*. Chicago: Chicago UP, 2001.

Altman, Rick. *Film/Genre*. London: British Film Institute, 1999.

Anderson, Robert G. *Faces, Forms, Films: The Artistry of Lon Chaney*. New York: A. S. Barnes, 1971.

Armstrong, Tim. *Modernism, Technology, and the Body*. Cambridge: Cambridge UP, 1998.

Arnheim, Rudolf. "Sound Film" (1928). In *Film Essays and Criticism*, 29–51. Trans. Brenda Benthien. Madison: U of Wisconsin P, 1997.

Badley, Linda. *Film, Horror, and the Body Fantastic*. Westport, CT: Greenwood Press, 1995.

Bakhtin, Mikhail. *Rabelais and His World*. Trans. Helene Iswolsky. Bloomington: Indiana UP, 1984.

Balázs, Béla. *Theory of the Film: Character and Growth of a New Art*. New York: Arno, 1972.

Baldick, Chris. *In Frankenstein's Shadow: Myth, Monstrosity, and Nineteenth-century Writing*. Oxford: Clarendon Press, 1987.

Barkan, Elazar. *The Retreat of Scientific Racism: Changing Concepts of Race in Britain and the United States Between the World Wars*. Cambridge: Cambridge UP, 1992.

Baudrillard, Jean. "Simulacra and Simulations" (1981). In *Jean Baudrillard: Selected Writings*, 166–84. Ed. Mark Poster. Stanford: Stanford UP, 1988.

Baudry, Jean-Louis. "The Apparatus: Meta-Psychological Approaches to the Impression of Reality in Cinema" (1970). Trans. Jean Andrews and Bernard Augst. In Braudy and Cohen, eds., *Film Theory and Criticism*, 206–223.

——. "Ideological Effects of the Basic Cinematographic Apparatus" (1970). Trans. Alan Williams. In Braudy and Cohen, eds., *Film Theory and Criticism*, 355–65.

Beard, Steve. "No Particular Place to Go." *Sight and Sound* 3.4 (Apr. 1993): 30–31.

Bederman, Gail. *Manliness and Civilization: A Cultural History of Gender and Race in the United States, 1880–1917*. Chicago: U of Chicago P, 1995.

"Beijing Declaration on the Rights of People with Disabilities in the New Century." Adopted on March 12, 2000, at the World NGO Summit on Disability; www.icdri .org/News/beijing_declaration_on_the_right.htm (accessed July 1, 2008).

Bellamy, John Stark II. *They Died Crawling and Other Tales of Cleveland Woe*. Cleveland: Gray & Company, 1995.

Benjamin, Walter. "On Some Motifs in Baudelaire" (1939). In *Illuminations: Essays and Reflections*, 155–200. Ed. Hannah Arendt. Trans. Harry Zohn. New York: Schocken, 1968.

——. "Theses on the Philosophy of History" (1968). In *Illuminations: Essays and Reflections*, 253–64. Ed. Hannah Arendt. Trans. Harry Zohn. New York: Schocken, 1968.

——. "The Work of Art in the Age of Mechanical Reproduction" (1936). In *Illuminations: Essays and Reflections*, 217–51. Ed. Hannah Arendt. Trans. Harry Zohn. New York: Schocken, 1968.

Benshoff, Harry M. *Monsters in the Closet: Homosexuality and the Horror Film*. Manchester: Manchester UP, 1997.

Berenstein, Rhona J. *Attack of the Leading Ladies: Gender, Sexuality, and Spectatorship in Classic Horror Cinema*. New York: Columbia UP, 1996.

Beylie, Claude. "*Freaks*, or the Monstrous Parade." *Ecran* 73.17 (July–Aug. 1973).

Black, Edwin. *War Against the Weak: Eugenics and America's Campaign to Create a Master Race*. New York: Four Walls Eight Windows, 2003.

Blake, Michael F. *A Thousand Faces: Lon Chaney's Unique Artistry in Motion Pictures*. New York: Vestal Press, 1995.

Bogdan, Robert. *Freak Show: Presenting Human Oddities for Profit and Amusement*. Chicago: U of Chicago P, 1998.

Bogdan, Robert, Douglas Biklen, Arthur Shapiro, and David Spelkoman. "The Disabled: Media's Monster." *Social Policy* 13.2 (Fall 1982): 32–35.

Bordwell, David. "The Classical Hollywood Style, 1917–1960." In David Bordwell, Janet Staiger, and Kristin Thompson, *The Classical Hollywood Cinema: Film Style and Mode of Production to 1960*, 1–84. New York: Columbia UP, 1985.

Boss, Pete. "Vile Bodies and Bad Medicine." *Screen* 27.1 (1986): 14–24.

Botting, Fred. *Gothic*. New York: Routledge, 1996.

Braudy, Leo and Marshall Cohen, eds. *Film Theory and Criticism*. 6th ed. New York: Oxford UP, 2004.

Brintnall, Kent L. "The Moral Demand of the 'Loving Cup': The Presence of the Abject Body in Tod Browning's *Freaks* and the Christian Eucharist." *Golem* 1.1 (Spring 2006): 1–26; www.golemjournal.org/Spring_2006_Issue/Brintnall_Freaks_S06 .pdf (accessed July 15, 2010).

Brophy, Philip. "Horrality—the Textuality of Contemporary Horror Films." *Screen* 27.1 (1986): 2–13.

Brosnan, John. *The Horror People*. New York: St. Martin's, 1976.

Bruinius, Harry. *Better for All the World: The Secret History of Forced Sterilization and America's Quest for Racial Purity*. New York: Vintage, 2007.

Brunas, Michael, John Brunas, and Tom Weaver. *Universal Horrors: The Studio's Classic Films, 1931–1946*. Jefferson, NC: McFarland, 1990.

Buscombe, Edward. "The Idea of Genre in the American Cinema" (1970). In Barry Keith Grant, ed., *Film Genre Reader II*, 11–25.

Butler, Ivan. *Horror in the Cinema*. New York: A. S. Barnes/Zwemmer, 1970.

Butler, Judith. *Bodies That Matter: On the Discursive Limits of Sex*. New York: Routledge, 1993.

——. "Imitation and Gender Insubordination." In Diana Fuss, ed., *Inside/Out: Lesbian Theories, Gay Theories*, 13–31. New York: Routledge, 1991.

Carroll, Noël. *The Philosophy of Horror, or Paradoxes of the Heart*. New York: Routledge, 1990.

Cartwright, Lisa. *Screening the Body: Tracing Medicine's Visual Culture*. Minneapolis: U of Minnesota P, 1995.

Chase, Allan. *The Legacy of Malthus: The Social Costs of the New Scientific Racism*. New York: Knopf, 1977.

Cheu, Johnson. "Performing Disability, Problematizing Cure." In Sandahl and Auslander, eds., *Bodies in Commotion*, 135–46.

Chivers, Sally. "The Horror of Becoming 'One of Us': Tod Browning's *Freaks* and Disability." In Smit and Enns, eds., *Screening Disability*, 57–64.

Clarens, Carlos. "Children of the Night" (1967). In Stephen Prince, ed., *The Horror Film*, 58–69. New Brunswick: Rutgers UP, 2004.

Clark, Stephanie Brown. "Frankenflicks: Medical Monsters in Classic Horror Films." In Lester D. Friedman, ed., *Cultural Sutures: Medicine and Media*, 129–48. Durham, NC: Duke UP, 2004.

Clough, J. D., ed. *To Act as a Unit: The Story of the Cleveland Clinic*. Cleveland: The Cleveland Clinic Foundation, 1996.

Clover, Carol. *Men, Women, and Chain Saws: Gender in the Modern Horror Film*. Princeton, NJ: Princeton UP, 1992.

Coffey, Mary K. "The American Adonis: A Natural History of the 'Average American' (Man), 1921–1932." In Currell and Cogdell, eds., *Popular Eugenics*, 185–216.

Cogdell, Christina. *Eugenic Design: Streamlining America in the 1930s*. Philadelphia: U of Pennsylvania P, 2004.

Cohen, Jeffrey Jerome. "Monster Culture (Seven Theses)." In Cohen, ed., *Monster Theory: Reading Culture*, 3–25. Minneapolis: U of Minnesota P, 1996.

Cohen, Ralph. "History and Genre." *New Literary History* 17.2 (Winter 1986): 203–218.

Conrich, Ian. "Horrific Films and 1930s British Cinema." In Steve Chibnall and Julian Petley, eds., *British Horror Cinema*, 58–70. New York: Routledge, 2001.

Cook, Méira. "None of Us: Ambiguity as Moral Discourse in Tod Browning's *Freaks*." In Smit and Enns, eds., *Screening Disability*, 47–56.

Cox, Caroline. "Invisible Wounds: The American Legion, Shell-Shocked Veterans, and American Society, 1919–1924." In Micale and Lerner, eds., *Traumatic Pasts*, 280–305.

Creed, Barbara. *The Monstrous-Feminine: Film, Feminism, Psychoanalysis*. New York: Routledge, 1993.

Crow, Liz. "Including All Of Our Lives: Renewing the Social Model of Disability." In Colin Barnes and Geof Mercer, eds., *Exploring the Divide: Illness and Disability*, 55–72. Leeds: The Disability Press, 1996.

Culler, Jonathan. *On Deconstruction: Theory and Criticism After Structuralism*. Ithaca, NY: Cornell UP, 1982.

Currell, Susan and Christina Cogdell, eds. *Popular Eugenics: National Efficiency and American Mass Culture in the 1930s*. Athens: Ohio UP, 2006.

Curtis, James. *James Whale: A New World of Gods and Monsters*. Boston: Faber and Faber, 1998.

Dadoun, Roger. "Fetishism in the Horror Film." *Enclitic* 1.2 (1979): 39–63.

Davis, Lennard J. *The Disability Studies Reader*. New York: Routledge, 1997; 2d ed., New York: Routledge, 2006.

——. *Enforcing Normalcy: Disability, Deafness, and the Body*. 2d ed. New York: Routledge, 2006.

Dickstein, Morris. "The Aesthetics of Fright" (1980). In Barry Keith Grant, ed., *Planks of Reason*, 65–78.

Doherty, Thomas. *Pre-Code Hollywood: Sex, Immorality, and Insurrection in American Cinema*. New York: Columbia UP, 1999.

Douglas, Mary. *Purity and Danger: An Analysis of Concepts of Pollution and Taboo*. London: Routledge & K. Paul, 1966.

Durbach, Nadja. *Spectacle of Deformity: Freak Shows and Modern British Culture*. Berkeley: U of California P, 2010.

Duster, Troy. *Backdoor to Eugenics*. New York : Routledge, 1990.

Dyer, Richard. *White*. New York: Routledge, 1997.

Edgerton, John E. "The Effect of Recent Immigration upon the Future of this Country." In Madison Grant, ed., *The Alien in Our Midst*, 4–8.

Elsaesser, Thomas. *Weimar Cinema and After: Germany's Historical Imaginary*. New York: Routledge, 2000.

Evans, Walter. "Monster Movies: A Sexual Theory" (1973). In Barry Keith Grant, ed., *Planks of Reason*, 53–64.

Fiedler, Leslie. *Freaks: Myths and Images of the Secret Self*. New York: Simon and Schuster, 1978.

Fisher, David. "Plastic Fantastic." *The Listener* (Wellington, New Zealand), Jan. 17–23, 2009, 24–30.

Foster, Hal. "Prosthetic Gods." *Modernism/Modernity* 4.2 (1997): 5–38.

Foucault, Michel. *The Birth of the Clinic: An Archaeology of Medical Perception*. Trans. A. M. Sheridan Smith. New York: Pantheon, 1973.

——. *Discipline and Punish: The Birth of the Prison*. Trans. Alan Sheridan. New York: Random House, 1977.

——. *The Order of Things: An Archaeology of the Human Sciences*. New York: Vintage, 1994.

Frankenberg, Ronald. "Sickness as Cultural Performance: Drama, Trajectory, and Pilgrimage Root Metaphors and the Making Social of Disease." *International Journal of Health Services* 16 (Nov. 1986): 603–625.

"*Frankenstein*." In Patricia King Hanson and Alan Gevinson, eds., *The American Film Institute Catalog: Feature Films, 1931–1940*, 698–99. Berkeley: U of California P, 1993.

"*Freaks*." In Patricia King Hanson and Alan Gevinson, eds., *The American Film Institute Catalog: Feature Films, 1931–1940*, 700. Berkeley: U of California P, 1993.

Freeland, Cynthia A. *The Naked and the Undead: Evil and the Appeal of Horror*. Boulder, CO: Westview Press, 2000.

Freud, Sigmund. "Dostoevsky and Parricide" (ca. 1927). *The Standard Edition of the Complete Psychological Works of Sigmund Freud* 21:177–94. Ed. and trans. James Strachey. London: Hogarth Press, 1961.

——. "The Uncanny" (1919). In *The Standard Edition of the Complete Psychological Works of Sigmund Freud* 17:219–52. Ed. and trans. James Strachey. London: Hogarth Press, 1953.

Friedman, David F. *A Youth in Babylon: Confessions of a Trash-Film King*. Buffalo, NY: Prometheus, 1990.

Galvin, Rose. "The Making of the Disabled Identity: A Linguistic Analysis of Marginalisation." *Disability Studies Quarterly* 23.2 (Spring 2003); www.dsq-sds.org/article/viewFile/421/590 (accessed Sept. 13, 2010).

Gardner, Gerald. *The Censorship Papers: Movie Censorship Letters from the Hays Office, 1934–1968*. New York: Dodd, Mead, 1987.

Garland-Thomson, Rosemarie. *Extraordinary Bodies: Figuring Physical Disability in American Culture and Literature*. New York: Columbia UP, 1997.

——. "Introduction: From Wonder to Error —A Genealogy of Freak Discourse in Modernity." In Garland-Thomson, ed., *Freakery*, 1–19.

——. "Seeing the Disabled: Visual Rhetorics of Disability in Popular Photography." In Paul K. Longmore and Lauri Umansky, eds., *The New Disability History: American Perspectives*, 335–74. New York: New York UP, 2001.

——. *Staring: How We Look*. New York: Oxford UP, 2009.

Garland-Thomson, Rosemarie, ed. *Freakery: Cultural Spectacles of the Extraordinary Body*. New York: New York UP, 1996.

Gartner, Alan, and Tom Joe, eds. *Images of the Disabled: Disabling Images*. New York: Praeger, 1987.

Gaycken, Oliver. "Tod Browning and the Monstrosity of Hollywood Style." In Smit and Enns, eds., *Screening Disability*, 73–85.

Gerber, David A. "The 'Careers' of People Exhibited in Freak Shows: The Problem of Volition and Valorization." In Garland-Thomson, ed., *Freakery*, 38–54.

Gibson, Mary and Nicole Hahn Rafter. "Editors' Introduction." In Cesare Lombroso, *Criminal Man*, 1–36. Ed. and trans. Gibson and Rafter. Durham, NC: Duke UP, 2006.

Gilman, Sander. "The Image of the Hysteric." In Sander L. Gilman, Helen King, Roy Porter, G. S. Rousseau, and Elaine Showalter, *Hysteria Beyond Freud*, 345–52. Berkeley: U of California P, 1993.

——. *Seeing the Insane*. New York: John Wiley, 1982.

Glut, Donald F. *The Frankenstein Legend: A Tribute to Mary Shelley and Boris Karloff*. Metuchen, NJ: Scarecrow Press, 1973.

Goffman, Erving. *The Presentation of Self in Everyday Life*. New York: Doubleday, 1959.

——. *Stigma: Notes on the Management of a Spoiled Identity*. Englewood Cliffs, NJ: Prentice Hall, 1963.

Grant, Barry Keith, ed. *The Dread of Difference: Gender and the Horror Film*. Austin: U of Texas P, 1996.

——, ed. *Film Genre Reader II*. Austin: U of Texas P, 1996.

——, ed. *Planks of Reason: Essays on the Horror Film*. Metuchen, NJ: Scarecrow Press, 1984.

Grigely, Joseph. "Postcards to Sophie Calle." In Susan Crutchfield and Marcy Epstein, eds., *Points of Contact: Disability, Art, and Culture*, 31–58. Ann Arbor: U of Michigan P, 2000.

Grosz, Elizabeth. "Intolerable Ambiguity: Freaks as/at the Limit." In Garland-Thomson, ed., *Freakery*, 55–66.

Gunning, Tom. "An Aesthetic of Astonishment: Early Film and the [In]Credulous Spectator" (1989). In Braudy and Cohen, eds., *Film Theory and Criticism*, 862–76.

Hahn, Harlan. "Advertising the Acceptably Employable Image: Disability and Capitalism" (1995). In Davis, ed., *The Disability Studies Reader* (1997), 172–86.

Halberstam, Judith. *Skin Shows: Gothic Horror and the Technology of Monsters*. Durham: Duke UP, 1995.

Haller, Mark H. *Eugenics: Hereditarian Attitudes In American Thought*. New Brunswick, NJ: Rutgers UP, 1963.

Hanson, Stephen L. "*Freaks.*" In Frank N. Magill, ed., *Magill's Survey of Cinema: English Language Films, Second Series*, vol. 2: 842–46. Englewood Cliffs, NJ: Salem Press, 1981.

Hardin, Brent, Marie Hardin, Susan Lynn, and Kristi Walsdorfet. "Missing in Action? Images of Disability in *Sports Illustrated for Kids*." *Disability Studies Quarterly* 21.2 (Spring 2001); www.dsq-sds-archives.org/_articles_pdf/2001/Spring/dsq_2001_Spring_04.pdf (accessed Sept. 13, 2010).

Hartwell, David G. "Introduction." In Hartwell, ed., *Foundations of Fear: An Exploration of Horror*, 1–11. New York: Tor, 1992.

Hasian, Jr., Marouf A. *The Rhetoric of Eugenics in Anglo-American Thought*. Athens, GA: U of Georgia P, 1996.

Hawkins, Joan. *Cutting Edge: Art-Horror and the Horrific Avant-Garde*. Minneapolis: U of Minnesota P, 2000.

Hevey, David. *The Creatures Time Forgot: Photography and Disability Imagery*. London: Routledge, 1992.

Hoberman, J. and Jonathan Rosenbaum. *Midnight Movies*. New York: Harper and Row, 1983.

hooks, bell. "Representations of Whiteness in the Black Imagination." In *Black Looks: Race and Representation*, 165–78. Boston: South End Press, 1992.

Horace. *To the Pisos (The Art of Poetry)* in *The Epistles of Horace*, 151–54. Trans. David Ferry. New York: Farrar, Straus, and Giroux, 2001.

Houellebecq, Michel. *H. P. Lovecraft: Against the World, Against Life* (1991). Trans. Dorna Khazeni. San Francisco: Believer Books, 2005.

Hughes, Bill and Kevin Paterson. "The Social Model of Disability and the Disappearing Body: Towards a Sociology of Impairment." *Disability & Society* 12 (1997): 325–40.

Hutchings, Peter. *The Horror Film*. Harlow, Eng.: Pearson Education, 2004.

Huss, Roy. "Vampire's Progress: *Dracula* from Novel to Film via Broadway." In Roy Huss and T. J. Ross, eds., *Focus on the Horror Film*, 50–57. Englewood Cliffs, NJ: Prentice Hall, 1972.

Jacobs, Lea. *The Wages of Sin: Censorship and the Fallen Woman Film, 1928–1942*. Madison: U of Wisconsin P, 1991.

Jacobson, Matthew Frye. *Whiteness of a Different Color: European Immigrants and the Alchemy of Race*. Cambridge: Harvard UP, 1998.

Jensen, Paul M. *Boris Karloff and His Films*. South Brunswick, NJ: A. S. Barnes, 1974.

Johnson, Tom. *Censored Screams: The British Ban on Hollywood Horror in the Thirties*. Jefferson, NC: McFarland, 1997.

Joslin, Lyndon W. *Count Dracula Goes to the Movies: Stoker's Novel Adapted, 1922–2003*. 2d ed. Jefferson, NC: McFarland, 2006.

Jowett, Garth S., Ian C. Jarvie, and Kathryn H. Fuller, *Children and the Movies: Media Influence and the Payne Fund Controversy*. Cambridge: Cambridge UP, 1996.

Kerr, Anne and Tom Shakespeare, *Genetic Politics: From Eugenics to Genome*. Cheltenham, Eng.: New Clarion Press, 2002.

Kerson, Jennie F., Toba Schwaber Kerson, and Lawrence A. Kerson. "The Depiction of Seizures in Film." *Epilepsia* 40.8 (1999): 1163–67.

Kerson, Toba Schwaber and Lawrence A. Kerson. "Implacable Images: Why Epileptiform Events Continue to be Featured in Film and Television." *Epileptic Disorders* 8.2 (2006): 103–113.

Kevles, Daniel J. *In the Name of Eugenics: Genetics and the Uses of Human Heredity*. New York: Knopf, 1985.

Kline, Wendy. *Building a Better Race: Gender, Sexuality, and Eugenics from the Turn of the Century to the Baby Boom*. Berkeley: U of California P, 2001.

Kobler, John. *Ardent Spirits: The Rise and Fall of Prohibition*. New York: Putnam, 1973.

——. *Damned in Paradise: The Life of John Barrymore*. New York: Atheneum, 1977.

Kracauer, Siegfried. *From Caligari to Hitler: A Psychological History of the German Film*. Princeton, NJ: Princeton UP, 1947.

——. *Theory of Film: The Redemption of Physical Reality*. Princeton, NJ: Princeton UP, 1997.

Kristeva, Julia. *Powers of Horror: An Essay on Abjection*. Trans. Leon S. Roudiez. New York: Columbia UP, 1982.

Kühl, Stefan. *The Nazi Connection: Eugenics, American Racism, and German National Socialism*. New York: Oxford UP, 1994.

Kuppers, Petra. "Bodies, Hysteria, Pain: Staging the Invisible." In Sandahl and Auslander, eds., *Bodies in Commotion*, 147–62.

Lacan, Jacques. "The Mirror Stage as Formative of the I as Revealed in Psychoanalytic Experience" (1949). In *Écrits: A Selection*, 1–7. Trans. Alan Sheridan. New York: Norton, 1977.

Largent, Mark A. *Breeding Contempt: The History of Coerced Sterilization in the United States*. New Brunswick, NJ: Rutgers UP, 2008.

Larsen, Robin and Beth A. Haller. "Public Reception of Real Disability: The Case of *Freaks*." *Journal of Popular Film and Television* 29.4 (2002): 164–72.

Larson, Edward J. *Sex, Race, and Science: Eugenics in the Deep South*. Baltimore: John Hopkins UP, 1995.

Lauritsen, John. *The Man Who Wrote Frankenstein*. Pagan Press, 2007.

Lederer, Susan. *Frankenstein: Penetrating the Secrets of Nature*. New Brunswick, N.J.: Rutgers UP, 2002.

Lennig, Arthur. *The Immortal Count: The Life and Films of Bela Lugosi*. Lexington: UP of Kentucky, 2003.

Linton, Simi. *Claiming Disability: Knowledge and Identity*. New York: New York UP, 1998.

Lombardo, Paul A. *Three Generations, No Imbeciles: Eugenics, the Supreme Court, and Buck v. Bell*. Baltimore: Johns Hopkins UP, 2008.

Lowenstein, Adam. *Shocking Representation: Historical Trauma, National Cinema, and the Modern Horror Film*. New York: Columbia UP, 2005.

Ludmerer, Kenneth. *Genetics and American Society: A Historical Appraisal*. Baltimore: Johns Hopkins UP, 1972.

Lutz, Tom. *American Nervousness, 1903: An Anecdotal History*. Ithaca, NY: Cornell UP, 1991.

MacKenzie, Donald A. *Statistics in Britain, 1865–1930: The Social Construction of Scientific Knowledge*. Edinburgh: Edinburgh UP, 1981.

Mamoulian, Rouben. "An Interview with Rouben Mamoulian," by Thomas R. Atkins (1973). In Harry M. Geduld, ed., *The Definitive "Dr. Jekyll and Mr. Hyde" Companion*, 174–82. New York: Garland, 1983.

Mann, Katrina. "You're Next! Postwar Hegemony Besieged in *Invasion of the Body Snatchers* (1956)." *Cinema Journal* 44.1 (Fall 2004): 49–68.

Markotic, Nicole. "Disabling the Viewer: Perceptions of Disability in Tod Browning's *Freaks*." In Smit and Enns, eds., *Screening Disability*, 65–72.

McConnell, Frank. *The Science Fiction of H. G. Wells*. New York: Oxford UP, 1981.

McRuer, Robert. *Crip Theory: Cultural Signs of Queerness and Disability*. New York: New York UP, 2006.

Metz, Christian. *The Imaginary Signifier: Psychoanalysis and the Cinema*. Trans. Celia Britton, Annwyl Williams, Ben Brewster, and Alfred Guzzetti. Bloomington: Indiana UP, 1982.

——. "The Impersonal Enunciation or the Site of the Film: In the Margin of Recent Works on Enunciation in Cinema." In Warren Buckland, ed., *The Film Spectator: From Sign to Mind*, 140–63. Amsterdam: Amsterdam UP, 1995.

Micale, Mark S. and Paul Lerner, eds., *Traumatic Pasts: History, Psychiatry, and Trauma in the Modern Age, 1870–1930*. New York: Cambridge UP, 2001.

Michette, Alan G., and Slawka Pfauntsch. *X-rays: The First Hundred Years*. New York: John Wiley, 1996.

Mitchell, David T. and Sharon L. Snyder. *Narrative Prosthesis: Disability and the Dependencies of Discourse*. Ann Arbor: U of Michigan P, 2000.

Mitchell, David T. and Sharon L. Snyder, eds. *The Body and Physical Difference: Discourses of Disability*. Ann Arbor: U of Michigan P, 1997.

Modleski, Tania. "The Terror of Pleasure: The Contemporary Horror Film and Postmodern Theory." In Modleski, ed., *Studies in Entertainment: Critical Approaches to Mass Culture*, 155–66. Bloomington: Indiana UP, 1986.

Monbeck, Michael E. *The Meaning of Blindness: Attitudes Toward Blindness and Blind People*. Bloomington: Indiana UP, 1973.

Morris, Gary. "Sexual Subversion: *The Bride of Frankenstein*" (1993). Repr. in *Bright Lights Film Journal* 19 (July 1997); www.brightlightsfilm.com/19/19_bride_1.html (accessed Sept. 13, 2010).

Morrison, Toni. *Playing in the Dark: Whiteness and the Literary Imagination*. Cambridge: Harvard UP, 1992.

Mulvey, Laura. "Visual Pleasure and Narrative Cinema." *Screen* 16.3 (1975): 6–18.

Neale, Stephen. *Genre*. London: British Film Institute, 1980.

Nelson, Jack A. "The Invisible Cultural Group: Images of Disability." In P. Lester, ed.,

*Images That Injure: Pictorial Stereotypes in the Media*, 119–25. Westport, CT: Praeger, 1996.

Ngai, Mae. "The Architecture of Race in American Immigration Law: A Reexamination of the Immigration Act of 1924." *Journal of American History* 86.1 (June 1999): 67–92.

Nies, Betsy L. *Eugenic Fantasies: Racial Ideology in the Literature and Popular Culture of the 1920's*. New York: Routledge, 2002.

Norden, Martin F. *The Cinema of Isolation: A History of Physical Disability in the Movies*. New Brunswick: Rutgers UP, 1994.

Norden, Martin F. and Madeleine A. Cahill. "Violence, Women, and Disability in Tod Browning's *Freaks* and *The Devil Doll*." *Journal of Popular Film and Television* 26.2 (Summer 1998): 86–94.

Nye, David E. *Electrifying America: Social Meanings of the New Technology, 1880–1940*. Cambridge: MIT Press, 1990.

Oddos, Christian. *Le Cinéma Fantastique*. Paris: G. Authier, 1977.

O'Flinn, Paul. "Production and Reproduction: The Case of *Frankenstein*." *Literature and History* 9.2 (1983): 194–213.

Oliver, Michael. *The Politics of Disablement: A Sociological Approach*. New York: St. Martin's, 1990.

—— *Social Work with Disabled People*. Basingstoke, Eng.: Macmillan, 1983.

Olney, Ian. "The Problem Body Politic, or 'These Hands Have a Mind All Their Own!': Figuring Disability in the Horror Film Adaptations of Renard's *Les mains d'Orlac*." *Literature/Film Quarterly* 34.4 (2006): 294–302.

Ordover, Nancy. *American Eugenics: Race, Queer Anatomy, and the Science of Nationalism*. Minneapolis: U of Minnesota P, 2003.

Overmier, Judith A. and John Edward Senior. *Books and Manuscripts of the Bakken*. Metuchen, NJ: Scarecrow Press, 1992.

Paul, Diane B. *Controlling Human Heredity: 1865 to the Present*. Atlantic Highlands, NJ: Humanities Press, 1995.

Pernick, Martin S. *The Black Stork: Eugenics and the Death of "Defective" Babies in American Medicine and Motion Pictures Since 1915*. New York: Oxford UP, 1996.

——. "Defining the Defective: Eugenics, Aesthetics, and Mass Culture in Early-Twentieth-Century America." In Mitchell and Snyder, eds., *The Body and Physical Difference*, 89–110.

Phelan, Peggy. *Mourning Sex: Performing Public Memories*. New York: Routledge, 1997.

Phillips, Kendall R. *Projected Fears: Horror Film and American Culture*. Westport, CT: Praeger, 2005.

Pick, Daniel. *Faces of Degeneration: A European Disorder, c. 1848–c. 1918*. New York: Cambridge UP, 1989.

Pickens, Donald. *Eugenics and the Progressives*. Nashville, TN: Vanderbilt UP, 1969.

Pinedo, Isabel Cristina. *Recreational Terror: Women and the Pleasures of Horror Film Viewing*. New York: SUNY Press, 1997.

Pingree, Allison. "The 'Exceptions That Prove the Rule': Daisy and Violet Hilton, the 'New Woman,' and the Bonds of Marriage." In Garland-Thomson, ed., *Freakery*, 173–84.

Pirie, David. *A Heritage of Horror: The English Gothic Cinema, 1946–1972*. New York: Equinox, 1973.

Polan, Dana. *Power and Paranoia: History, Narrative, and the American Cinema, 1940–1950*. New York: Columbia UP, 1986.

Prawer, S. S. *Caligari's Children: The Film as Tale of Terror*. New York: Da Capo, 1980.

Quayson, Ato. *Aesthetic Nervousness: Disability and the Crisis of Representation*. New York: Columbia UP, 2007.

Rafter, Nicole Hahn. *Creating Born Criminals*. Urbana: U of Illinois P, 1997.

——. *White Trash: The Eugenic Family Studies, 1877–1919*. Boston: Northeastern UP, 1988.

Ramachandran, V. S. and D. C. Rogers-Ramachandran. "Synaesthesia in Phantom Limbs Induced with Mirrors." *Proceedings of the Royal Society of London* 263.1369 (1996): 377–86.

Ramachandran, V. S., D. C. Rogers-Ramachandran, and S. Cobb. "Touching the Phantom." *Nature* 377 (1995): 489–90.

Reilly, Philip R. *The Surgical Solution: A History of Involuntary Sterilization in the United States*. Baltimore: Johns Hopkins UP, 1991.

Roberts, Dorothy. *Killing the Black Body: Race, Reproduction, and the Meaning of Liberty*. New York: Pantheon, 1997.

Robinson, Charles E., ed. *The Original Frankenstein*. New York: First Vintage Classics Edition, 2009.

Ropper, Allan H. and Robert H. Brown. *Adams and Victor's Principles of Neurology*. 8th ed. Blacklick, OH: McGraw-Hill, 2005.

Rosen, Christine. *Preaching Eugenics: Religious Leaders and the American Eugenics Movement*. New York: Oxford UP, 2004.

Rowbottom, Margaret and Charles Susskind. *Electricity and Medicine: History of Their Interaction*. San Francisco: San Francisco Press, 1984.

Russo, Mary. *The Female Grotesque: Risk, Excess and Modernity*. New York: Routledge, 1995.

Rydell, Robert. *World of Fairs: The Century-of-Progress Exposition*. Chicago: U of Chicago P, 1993.

Sandahl, Carrie and Philip Auslander. "Introduction: Disability Studies in Commotion with Performance Studies." In Sandahl and Auslander, eds., *Bodies in Commotion*, 1–15.

Sandahl, Carrie and Philip Auslander, eds. *Bodies in Commotion: Disability and Performance*. Ann Arbor: U of Michigan P, 2005.

Sarris, Andrew. *The American Cinema: Directors and Directions, 1929–1968*. New York: Dutton, 1968.

——. *"You Ain't Heard Nothin' Yet": The American Talking Film, History and Memory, 1927–1949*. New York: Oxford UP, 1998.

Savada, Elias. "The Making of *Freaks*" (orig. in *Photon* 23 [1973]). In *The "Freaks" Show: Exhibit 3* (2004); www.olgabaclanova.com/the_making_of_freaks.htm (accessed July 5, 2010).

Schaefer, Eric. *Bold! Daring! Shocking! True!: A History of Exploitation Films, 1919–1959*. Durham, NC: Duke UP, 1999.

Schatz, Thomas. *Hollywood Genres: Formulas, Filmmaking, and the Studio System*. Philadelphia: Temple UP, 1981.

Schweik, Susan M. *The Ugly Laws: Disability in Public*. New York: New York UP 2009.

Selden, Steven. *Inheriting Shame: The Story of Eugenics and Racism in America*. New York: Teachers College Press, 1999.

Shaviro, Steven. *The Cinematic Body*. Minneapolis: U of Minnesota P, 1993.

Shephard, Ben. *A War of Nerves: Soldiers and Psychiatrists in the Twentieth Century*. Cambridge: Harvard UP, 2001.

Showalter, Elaine. *Sexual Anarchy: Gender and Culture at the Fin De Siècle*. New York: Penguin, 1990.

Siebers, Tobin. "Disability in Theory: From Social Constructionism to the New Realism of the Body." In Davis, ed., *The Disability Studies Reader* (2006), 173–83.

——. *Disability Theory*. Ann Arbor: U of Michigan P, 2008.

Skal, David J. *Hollywood Gothic: The Tangled Web of "Dracula" from Novel to Stage to Screen* (1990). Rev. ed., New York: Faber and Faber, 2004.

——. *The Monster Show: A Cultural History of Horror*. New York: Norton, 1993.

——. *Screams of Reason: Mad Science and Modern Culture*. New York: Norton, 1998.

Skal, David J. and Elias Savada. *Dark Carnival: The Secret World of Tod Browning, Hollywood's Master of the Macabre*. New York: Anchor, 1995.

Slattery, Dennis Patrick. "Seized by the Muse: Dostoevsky's Convulsive Poetics in *The Idiot*." *Literature and Medicine* 18.1 (1999): 60–81.

Smit, Christopher R. and Anthony Enns, eds. *Screening Disability: Essays on cinema and Disability*. New York: UP of America, 2001.

Smith, John David. *Minds Made Feeble: The Myth and Legacy of the Kallikaks*. Rockville, MD: Aspen Systems Corp., 1985.

Smith, John David and K. Ray Nelson. *The Sterilization of Carrie Buck*. Far Hills, NJ: New Horizon Press, 1989.

Snyder, Sharon L. and David T. Mitchell. *Cultural Locations of Disability*. Chicago: U of Chicago P, 2006.

Sobchack, Vivian. *Carnal Thoughts: Embodiment and Moving Image Culture*. Berkeley: U of California P, 2004.

Spadoni, Robert. *Uncanny Bodies: The Coming of Sound Film and the Origins of the Horror Genre*. Berkeley: U of California P, 2007.

——. "The Uncanny Body of Early Sound Film." *The Velvet Light Trap* 51 (Spring 2003): 4–16.

Stern, Alexandra Minna. *Eugenic Nation: Faults and Frontiers of Better Breeding in Modern America*. Berkeley: U of California P, 2005.

Stewart, Susan. "The Epistemology of the Horror Story." *Journal of American Folklore* 95.375 (1982): 33–50.

Studlar, Gaylin. *This Mad Masquerade: Stardom and Masculinity in the Jazz Age*. New York: Columbia UP, 1996.

Swales, John. *Genre Analysis: English in Academic and Research Settings*. Cambridge: Cambridge UP, 1990.

Tarratt, Margaret. "Monsters from the Id" (1970). In Barry Keith Grant, ed., *Film Genre Reader II*, 330–49.

Temkin, Owsei. *The Falling Sickness: A History of Epilepsy from the Greeks to the Beginnings of Modern Neurology*. 2d ed. Baltimore: Johns Hopkins UP, 1971.

Terry, Jennifer and Jacqueline Urla, eds. *Deviant Bodies: Critical Perspectives on Difference in Science and Popular Culture*. Bloomington: Indiana UP, 1995.

Thomas, John. "*Freaks*." *Film Quarterly* 17.3 (Spring 1964): 60–61.

Tremain, Shelley. "On the Government of Disability." *Social Theory and Practice* 27.4 (Oct. 2001): 617–36.

Todorov, Tzvetan. *The Fantastic: A Structural Approach to a Literary Genre*. Trans. Richard Howard. Cleveland: P of Case Western Reserve U, 1973; rpt., Ithaca, NY: Cornell UP, 1975.

Tropp, Martin. *Mary Shelley's Monster: The Story of Frankenstein*. Boston: Houghton Mifflin, 1976.

Tucker, William H. *The Science and Politics of Racial Research*. Urbana: U of Illinois P, 1994.

Tudor, Andrew. *Monsters and Mad Scientists: A Cultural History of the Horror Movie*. Cambridge, MA: Basil Blackwell, 1989.

Twitchell, James B. *Dreadful Pleasures: An Anatomy of Modern Horror*. New York: Oxford UP, 1985.

Weiss, Andrea. *Vampires and Violets: Lesbians in the Cinema*. London: Jonathon Cape, 1992.

Wendell, Susan. *The Rejected Body: Feminist Philosophical Reflections on Disability*. New York: Routledge, 1996.

Wexman, Virginia Wright. "Horrors of the Body: Hollywood's Discourse on Beauty and Rouben Mamoulian's *Dr. Jekyll and Mr. Hyde*." In William Veeder and Gordon

Hirsch, eds., *Dr. Jekyll and Mr. Hyde After One Hundred Years*, 283–312. Chicago: U of Chicago P, 1988.

Williams, Linda. "Film Bodies: Gender, Genre, and Excess" (1991). In Braudy and Cohen, eds., *Film Theory and Criticism*, 727–41.

——. "When the Woman Looks" (1983). In Barry Keith Grant, ed., *The Dread of Difference*, 15–34.

Williams, Tony. *Hearths of Darkness: The Family in American Horror Film*. London: Associated UP, 1996.

Witkowski, Jan. "Traits Studied by Eugenicists." In IAAEM; www.eugenicsarchive.org/html/eugenics/essay4text.html (accessed June 25, 2010).

Wittgenstein, Ludwig. *Philosophical Investigations* (1953). Ed. P. M. S. Hacker and Joachim Schulte. Trans. G. E. M. Anscombe, P. M. S. Hacker, and Joachim Schulte. 4th ed. Chichester, U.K.: Wiley-Blackwell, 2009.

Wolf, Leonard, ed. and introduction. *The Essential Dr. Jekyll and Mr. Hyde*. New York: Penguin, 1995.

Wolff, Tamsen. *Mendel's Theatre: Heredity, Eugenics, and Early Twentieth-Century American Drama*. New York: Palgrave Macmillan, 2009.

Wood, Robin. *Hollywood from Vietnam to Reagan . . . and Beyond*. Rev. ed. New York: Columbia UP, 2003.

——. "An Introduction to the American Horror Film" (1979). In Barry Keith Grant, ed., *Planks of Reason*, 164–200.

Worland, Rick. *The Horror Film: An Introduction*. Malden, MA: Blackwell, 2007.

Young, Elizabeth. *Black Frankenstein: The Making of an American Metaphor*. New York: New York UP, 2008.

——. "Here Comes the Bride: Wedding Gender and Race in *Bride of Frankenstein*." In Barry Keith Grant, ed., *The Dread of Difference*, 309–337.

# SELECTED FILMS

*Almost Married.* Dir. William Cameron Menzies. Fox Film Corp., 1932.

*The American Nightmare.* Dir. Adam Simon. Minerva Pictures, 2000.

*The Beast with Five Fingers.* Dir. Robert Florey, Warner Bros., 1946.

*The Black Cat.* Dir. Edgar G. Ulmer, Universal, 1934.

*Black Dragons.* Dir. William Nigh. Banner Productions, 1942.

*The Black Room.* Dir. Roy William Neill. Columbia, 1935.

*The Black Stork* (aka *Are You Fit to Marry?*). Dir. Leopold and Theodore Wharton. Wharton Inc., 1916. Revised and rereleased, Quality Amusement Corp., 1927.

*The Bride of Frankenstein.* Dir. James Whale. Universal, 1935.

*The Brute Man.* Dir. Jean Yarbrough. Universal, 1946.

*The Cabinet of Dr. Caligari.* Dir. Robert Wiene. Decla-Bioscop, 1920.

*Chandu the Magician.* Dir. William Cameron Menzies and Marcel Varnel. Fox Film Co., 1932.

*Chloe, Love Is Calling You.* Dir. Marshall Nieman. Pinnacle Productions, 1931.

*The Dark Eyes of London* (aka *The Human Monster*). Dir. Walter Summers. John Argyle Productions (UK), 1939.

*The Devil-Doll.* Dir. Tod Browning. MGM, 1936.

*Doctor X.* Dir. Michael Curtiz. First National/Warner Bros., 1932.

*Dr. Jekyll and Mr. Hyde.* Dir. John S. Robertson. Famous Players–Lasky Corporation, 1920.

*Dr. Jekyll and Mr. Hyde.* Dir. Rouben Mamoulian. Paramount, 1931.

*Dr. Jekyll and Mr. Hyde*. Dir. Victor Fleming. MGM, 1941.

*Dracula*. Dir. Tod Browning. Universal, 1931.

*Drácula*. Dir. George Melford. Universal, 1931.

*Dracula's Daughter*. Dir. Lambert Hillyer. Universal, 1936.

*The Face Behind the Mask*. Dir. Robert Florey. Columbia, 1941.

*Frankenstein*. Dir. James Whale. Universal, 1931.

*Freaks*. Dir. Tod Browning. MGM, 1932.

*The Hills Have Eyes*. Dir. Wes Craven. Blood Relations, Co., 1977.

*The House of Dracula*. Dir. Erle C. Kenton. Universal, 1945.

*House of Horrors*. Dir. Jean Yarbrough. Universal, 1946.

*The Hunchback of Notre Dame*. Dir. Wallace Worsley. Universal, 1923.

*Invasion of the Body Snatchers*. Dir. Don Siegel. Walter Wanger Productions, 1956.

*Invisible Agent*. Dir. Edwin L. Marin. Frank Lloyd Productions, 1942.

*The Invisible Man*. Dir. James Whale. Universal, 1933.

*The Invisible Ray*. Dir. Lambert Hillyer. Universal, 1936.

*Island of Lost Souls*. Dir. Erle Kenton. Paramount, 1932.

*King Kong*. Dir. Merian C. Cooper and Ernest B. Schoedsack. RKO, 1933.

*King of the Zombies*. Dir. Jean Yarbrough. Monogram, 1941.

*Mad Love*. Dir. Karl Freund. MGM, 1935.

*The Mad Monster*. Dir. Sam Newfield. PRC, 1942.

*Man Made Monster*. Dir. George Waggner. Universal, 1941.

*The Man Who Changed His Mind* (aka *The Man Who Lived Again*). Dir. Robert Stevenson.
    Gainsborough Pictures (UK), 1936.

*Mark of the Vampire*. Dir. Tod Browning. MGM, 1935.

*The Monster Maker*. Dir. Sam Newfield. PRC, 1944.

*The Monster Walks*. Dir. Frank Strayer. Ralph M. Like Productions and Action Pictures,
    1932.

*The Most Dangerous Game*. Dir. Ernest B. Schoedsack and Irving Pichel. RKO, 1932.

*The Mummy*. Dir. Karl Freund. Universal, 1932.

*Murders in the Rue Morgue*. Dir. Robert Florey. Universal, 1932.

*Murders in the Zoo*. Dir. A. Edward Sutherland. Paramount, 1933.

*The Mystery of the Wax Museum*. Dir. Michael Curtiz. Warner Bros., 1933.

*Nosferatu, eine Symphonie des Grauens*. Dir. F. W. Murnau. Prana-Film, 1922.

*The Old Dark House*. Dir. James Whale. Universal, 1932.

*The Penalty*. Dir. Wallace Worsley. Eminent Authors Pictures, 1920.

*The Phantom of the Opera*. Dir. Rupert Julian. Universal, 1925.

*Psycho*. Dir. Alfred Hitchcock. Shamley Productions. Distr. Paramount Pictures, 1960.

*The Raven*. Dir. Louis Friedlander. Universal, 1935.

*The Return of Chandu*. Dir. Ray Taylor. Sol Lesser Productions (as Principal Pictures
    Corp.), 1934.

*The Return of Doctor X*. Dir. Vincent Sherman. First National Pictures, 1939.

*Revenge of the Zombies*. Dir. Steve Sekely. Monogram, 1943.

*Scanners*. Dir. David Cronenberg. Canadian Film Development Corporation. Distr. MGM, 1981.

*The Silence of the Lambs*. Dir. Jonathan Demme. Orion Pictures Corporation, 1991.

*Son of Dracula*. Dir. Robert Siodmak. Universal, 1943.

*Son of Frankenstein*. Dir. Rowland V. Lee. Universal, 1939.

*The Texas Chain Saw Massacre*. Dir. Tobe Hooper. Vortex, 1974.

*Werewolf of London*. Dir. Stuart Walker. Universal, 1935.

*White Zombie*. Dir. Victor Halperin. Halperin Productions. Distributed United Artists, 1932.

*The Wolf Man*. Dir. George Waggner, Universal, 1941.

# INDEX

Titles of films are in *italic*. **Bold** numbers indicate illustrations. Initial articles in all languages (e.g., The, L', Le) are ignored in sorting titles, and numbers are sorted as spelled out in English. Notes are indicated by n.

Baudrillard, Jean, 133–34, 144,

Baudry, Jean-Louis, 198

Bazin, André, 159

Beard, George, 74, 75, 205, 206, 285n27, 286n37

*The Beast with Five Fingers* (1946), 155, 253n74

Belázs, Béla, 157

Bell, Alexander, 9, 10

Benjamin, Walter, 159, 207–208, 217, 219, 241

Berenstein, Rhona, 43, 56–57, 197, 215

Beresford, Harry, 195, **197, 199**

Bergman, Ingrid, 152, **153**

Bertillon, Alphonse, 64

Beylie, Claude, 115–16

*The Birth of a Nation* (1915), 251n58

Black, Edwin, 13, 16

*The Black Cat* (1934), 23

*Black Dragons* (1942), 236

*The Black Room* (1935), 238

blindness: in *Bride of Frankenstein*, 70, 72, 119; cultural views of, 119; of Marie Curie, 223; in *Dark Eyes of London*, 119, 161–62, 164, 166; in *The Devil-Doll*, 119; as eugenic target, 13–14, 15, 119, 120; in *The Invisible Man* (novel), 178; in *The Invisible Ray*, 119, 225–28, 230; psychoanalytic view of, 25; of Claude Rains, 156

blood: as chimerical, 34; in *Dracula*, 35, 38, 39, 41, 43–47, 48, 50–53, 56, 68, 83, 163; in eugenic rhetoric, 9, 13, 40, 41, 47–51, 54–55; in *The Return of Doctor X*, 236

Blumenbach, Johann, 122–23, 131, 259n38

Boas, Franz, 235

Boese, Carl, 261n64

Bogdan, Robert, 269n37

Bondi, Beulah, 224, **229**

Bordwell, David, 105

brain: a chimera in, 34; in epilepsy, 136–37, 140; in eugenic rhetoric, 63–66; in *Frankenstein*, 35, 38, 39–40, 60–63, **62**, 66–68, 73–76, 96; in *The House of Dracula*, 236; in nineteenth-century medico-scientific discourse, 123–24, 166; responses to bodily illusion, 192. *See also* "feeblemindedness"; neurasthenia

Breen, Joseph, 212, 213, 221

*Bride of Frankenstein* (1935), 23; altered ending of, 265n122; blindness in, 70, 72, 119; censorship of, 212; class politics in, 26; classic horror conclusion of, 96, 116; criminality in, 72, 263n91; "feeblemindedness" in, 72; gender in, 77; hysterical "eugenic" woman in, 77; marriage in, 73; nurture and nature in, 39, 69–73, **71**, 227; queerness in, 73; race and disability in, 27, 149, 263n91; sexuality in, 73, 96

Brouillet, André, 183–84

Brunas, John (with Michael Brunas and Tom Weaver), 45, 253n81, 253n83, 283n45

Brunas, Michael (with John Brunas and Tom Weaver), 45, 253n81, 253n83, 283n45

Browning, Tod: director of *Dracula*, 41, 57; director of *Freaks*, 83, 86, 94, 95, 105–106, 113, 114–16, 118; disability of, 156–57; use of trickery, 105–106

*Buck vs. Bell* decision, 15, 21, 233–35, 263n92

*The Cabinet of Dr. Caligari* (1920), 261n64

Carnegie Institution, 10, 235

Carroll, Noël, 28–29, 199

criminality: in *Bride of Frankenstein*, 72, 263n91; in *Doctor X*, 218; eugenic views of, 11, 13–15, 19, 29, 30, 38, 64–66, 71–72, 102, 125, 208, 211, 276n67; executions and, 206; and facial disfigurement, 131, 158, 171–72; Foucault on, 170–71; in *Frankenstein*, 39, 63, 66–68, 76–81, 131; in *Freaks*, 87, 88, 92; in horror-film spectatorship, 216–17; Lombroso's studies of, 7–8, 29, 63–64, 123–25, 131; in *Mad Love*, 172–75; in *The Mystery of the Wax Museum*, 131; in *The Phantom of the Opera*, 127, 131; and the Production Code, 211; and *The Raven*, 171–72, 175; religious views of, 72; and responses to film, 208, 211, 216–17

Curie, Marie, 246, 251

Curtiz, Michael, 142

Dade, Frances, 41, **43, 44**

*The Dark Eyes of London* (aka *The Human Monster*, 1939), 119, 161–62, 164–66

Darwin, Charles, 7, 8. *See also* social Darwinism

Davenport, Charles: description of eugenics/genetics, 10–11; on entertainment, 211; as eugenics leader, 10; on eugenics as ancient knowledge, 40–41; fear of aristocratic breeding practices, 48; on genetic transmission, 11, 40, 55; in relation to Harry Haiselden, 17; on immigration, 49; in newspaper, 12–13; on neurasthenia, 74; on racial-mixing, 14–15; on sexual diseases and alcoholism, 146; study of physical features, 125, 126

Davis, Lennard, 5–6, 28, 68, 86, 138, 165, 183, 264n93

*Dawn of the Dead* (1978), 26

deafness: in *Dark Eyes of London*, 162; eugenic views of, 9, 13, 15, 38, 276n67; and hearing damage due to urban life, 207; in *The Mystery of the Wax Museum*, 132

degeneration/degeneracy: in *The Black Stork*, 18; cinema as degenerate, 211; in classic horror advertising, 214–15; in the classic horror genre, 56, 119–20, 126–27, 128, 158, 242–43; in the *Dr. Jekyll and Mr. Hyde* films, 144–47, 149–51, 154, 158, 183; in *Dracula*, 26, 38, 43, 45, 48–49, 52, 57, 58, 60; and epilepsy, 140, 142, 147, 149; in eugenic thought, 11, 13, 36, 37, 55, 65, 101, 119, 125–26, 144, 211, 233–35; in *Frankenstein*, 38, 61, 62–63; in Gothic texts, 147; in *The Invisible Man*, 178; in *The Invisible Ray*, 227; and neurasthenia, 76; and *The Phantom of the Opera*, 127; and race, 145; theory of, 7–8, 54, 125, 145

the Depression, 110–11

*The Devil-Doll* (1936), 23, 119

Dione, Rose, **84**, 87

disability: "cure" of, 4, 5, 160, 168, 169, 171–73, 189, 191–92, 206, 217–19, 222, 226, 227–28, 236–38, 278n90; definitions of, 4–5; in degeneration discourse, 7–8; in eugenic film *The Black Stork*, 17–19; in *Geek Love*, 218–19; historical views of, 3–4, 208; impairment and, 4–5, 121; in *The Invisible Man* (novel), 176–77, 181; materiality of, 121, 134, 154–60, 167–68, 193; medicalized views of, 4, 94, 238; as "naturally" repugnant, 2, 3, 15, 20, 21, 36, 86, 200, 238; 1930s disability discourses, 256n113; politics, policy, and activism, 102, 246n11, 281–82n33; as "real" limitation, 15–16, 96, 110; in silent/sound film experience, 106–108; simulation or performance of, 109–110, 121, 133–36, 140–60, 167, 188–89, 192–93, 219; social/textual construction of, 4–6, 16, 63, 86, 90, 95–96, 99–100, 102, 103–104, 110, 119–21, 127–28, 139, 171–74, 184–85, 216 (*see also Freaks*, framing and de/familiarization in); stereotypes of, 131, 133; visibility and invisibility of, 180–81. *See also* blindness; deafness; degeneration/degeneracy; disease; epilepsy; facial deformity and revelations; "feeblemindedness"; neurasthenia; physiognomic logic; prosthesis

disability studies, 6, 274n10, 275n51, 281n22

disease: and definition of horror, 198–99; as element of disability, 4; as evidence of degeneration, 7, 54; in eugenic films, 18, 20; eugenic views on, 11, 13, 15, 40–41, 54–55, 65, 74, 124, 139, 146; in *Dr. Jekyll and Mr. Hyde* (1920), 144–45; in *Dracula*, 26, 39, 55–58, 78, 163–64; epilepsy as, 136, 139–40; heart disease as result of modern life, 207; hopes for genetic cures of, 242; in *The Invisible Man*, 177; and medical gaze, 165; misrepresentation of acromegaly as, 290n12; racist views of, 54; in reform eugenics, 235; in vampire texts, 54; x-ray as treatment for, 223, 228

*Doctor X* (1932), 23, 84, 114, 211, 227; criminality in, 218; disabled characters in, 182; disabling spectatorship in, 196–99, **197, 199**, 201–202, 216;

facial deformity and revelations in, 195, 218; gender in, 196–97; madness in, 196; medical gaze in, 165, **197, 199**, 198–99, 218; sentimental morality in, 227; sexuality in, 196–97, 201; shock in, 217–18; X-ray in, 219

Doherty, Thomas, 209, 288n61

*Dr. Jekyll and Mr. Hyde* (1920), 165, 177; class politics in, 145; disabling effects on John Barrymore, 156; disease in, 144–45; eliciting response in spectator, 159; epilepsy and convulsions in, 142–45, **143**, 158; immigration in, 145; madness in, 147; materiality of body in, 155; mirrors in, 183; race in, 145, 153–54; sexual disease in, 144–45; substance abuse in, 145–47

*Dr. Jekyll and Mr. Hyde* (1931), 95, 165, 177, 204; aesthetic and bodily politics of, 150–51; awards and critical acclaim, 23, 84; as "bestial" film, 238–39, 278n94; censorial response to, 1–2, 208–209; class politics in, 150, 154; critique of sexual repression, 150; doctor as healer/producer of disability, 191–92; effects and trickery in, 147–48, 191; eliciting response in spectator, 159; epilepsy and convulsions in, 147–49, **149**, 158; facial deformity and revelations in, 148–50, 279n96; gender in, 192; link to eugenic films, 21; madness in, 151, 153; marriage in, 150; materiality of body in, 155; medical gaze in, 165, 191–94; mirror and performative identity in, 189–92; racial implications of, 149–50; release date of, 253n76; sexuality in, 142, 149, 150, 284n51; transforming effect of substances in, 150

medical gaze (*continued*)
231–32; in *The Invisible Man*, 175–82, 189; in *Mad Love*, 168–70, 175; in mad-doctor films, 30–31, 160, 165, 166, 175, 182, 198; in *The Raven*, 168–70, **169**, 171–72, 175. *See also* X-ray

Melendy, Mary R. (with Walter J. Hadden and Charles H. Robinson), 256n10, 258n24

*Las Meninas* (1656), 186–88

Metz, Christian, 128, 198

MGM film studio, 86, 93, 111, 209–10, 215

Mitchell, David T. (with Sharon L. Snyder): on "diagnosis" of literary characters, 273n5; on disability as "natural" stigma, 15–16, 253n88; on "feeblemindedness," 262n74; on *Geek Love*, 219; on historical views of disability, 245–46n5, 246n9; on horror films, 28; on idealized eugenic body, 12–13; on materiality of metaphor, 5; on narrative prosthesis, 5–6, 104; on ugly laws, 124

monster: as chimera, 33–35; in classic horror film, 24–25, 96, 280n5; definition, 3; as disabled or impaired, 25, 27–29, 30, 35, 96–97, 157, 159, 160, 165; as dysgenic figure, 37–38, 58, 168, 242; eugenic production of, 40, 57; as figure for Others, 25–27; and freaks, 95–96; in Gothic literature, 22–23; historical views of, 3–4; in horror-film formula 35–36, 116, 168; horror film's visualization of, 23–24, 96, 107; in mad-doctor films, 163–65, 175, 182, 190; in postmodern horror, 24–25; psychoanalytic readings of, 25–26; spectators' identification with or production as, 194, 199, 201, 217, 241–43. *See also* classic horror

subgenres, "bestial"; and discussion of specific monsters under *Dark Eyes of London, Doctor X, Dr. Jekyll and Mr. Hyde* (all versions), *Dracula, Frankenstein, Freaks, The Invisible Man, The Invisible Ray, The Mad Monster, Man Made Monster, The Monster Maker, The Mystery of the Wax Museum, The Phantom of the Opera, The Return of Doctor X*

*The Monster Maker* (1944), 236

*The Monster Walks* (1932), 238

Morgan, Thomas Hunt, 235

Morel, Bénédict, 125, 248n24

Morrison, Toni, 179

*The Most Dangerous Game* (1932), 23, 238, 278n94

Motion Picture Producers and Distributors of America (MPPDA), 1, 209, 210. *See also* Production Code

Mulvey, Laura, 198

*The Mummy* (1932), 23, 84, 238, 252n74

*Murders in the Rue Morgue* (1932), 23, 238, 278n94

*Murders in the Zoo* (1933), 23, 278n94

Murnau, F. W., 54, 252n74

Muybridge, Eadweard, 141, 252n74

*The Mystery of the Wax Museum* (1933), 23, 114; criminality in, 131; disability simulation in, 133–34; facial deformity and revelation in, 129–34, **130**; madness in, 131; race in, 131

Nation, Carrie, 146

Nazi Germany, 31, 164, 223, 234–37, 239–40, 252n74

Neale, Stephen, 25, 46, 99, 253n80

neurasthenia, 74, 76; eugenic views of, 38, 74–75; in *Frankenstein*, 75–76, 257n15

Newfield, Sam, 236

Nigh, William, 236

*Night of the Living Dead* (1968), 24

Nordau, Max, 54, 76, 248n24

Norden, Martin, 27–28, 115, 117, 131, 132, 133, 156, 271n76

*Nosferatu, eine Symphonie des Grauens* (1922), 54, 55, 259n46, 277n84

Oddos, Christian, 114, 116

*The Old Dark House* (1932), 23, 238

Osborn, Henry Fairfield, 10, 211

Paramount film studio, 1, 209, 213, 214

Parsons, Louella, 94, 271n76

Payne Film Studies, 202–205, 217

Pearl, Raymond, 235

*The Penalty* (1920), 155

Penrose, Lionel, 235

Pernick, Martin, 17–21, 124, 229, 251n64, 258n24

*The Phantom of the Opera* (1925): criminality in, 127, 131; debilitating effects of makeup, 156; facial deformity and revelation in, 121–22, **123**, 127–28, 131, 158; viewer response to, 204

Philbin, Mary, 121, **123**

physiognomic logic, 4, 12–13; in composite portraits, 29; of criminals, 8, 63–64; in *Dr. Jekyll and Mr. Hyde* (1920), 145; in *Dr. Jekyll and Mr. Hyde* (1931), 149–50; in eugenic studies, 125–26; in film melodrama, 13–14; in film theory, 157; in *Frankenstein*, 66, 78, 122; in *Freaks*, 92, 101, 118; in Gothic literature, 147; in mad-doctor films, 229, 232; in *Mad Love*, 182; in *The Phantom of the Opera*, 127; of skulls, 7–8, 122–24, 131, 135, 182

Pick, Daniel, 147, 274n14, 274n17, 275n26, 275n30, 286n29

Pickens, Donald, 50, 261n62, 261n63

*The Picture of Dorian Gray* (1891), 22

Pierce, Jack, 66

Pinedo, Isabel Cristina, 24, 200

Polan, Dana, 236

Pomeroy, Hugh, 71–72

*Presumption, or the Fate of Frankenstein* (1823 play), 261n64

Production Code, 1, 21, 43, 77, 209, 210–13, 227–28

prosthesis: in cultural narratives, 5–6, 118; in *Doctor X*, 195, 196, 218; in film experience, 107, 198, 201–202; in *Freaks*, 104, 106, 108, 110, 118; modern technology as, 205; in theory, 154, 192–93, 270–71n62

*Psycho* (1960), 24

Quayson, Ato, 6, 29–30, 104

queerness: in *Bride of Frankenstein*, 73; in classic horror film readings, 26; in *Dracula*, 45–47; in *Frankenstein*, 78, 80; monstrosity as queer category, 25

Quetelet, Adolphe, 64, 246n8

race: in "bestial" classic horror films, 238–39, 278n94; in *The Black Stork*, 18; in *Bride of Frankenstein*, 27, 149, 263n91; censoring of interraciality in film, 208; and composite portraits, 29; and degeneration/degeneracy, 145; and disability, 14, 15–16, 18, 27, 29, 150, 153–54, 181, 235; and disease, 54–55, 145; in *Dr. Jekyll and Mr. Hyde* (1920), 145, 153–54; in *Dr. Jekyll and Mr. Hyde* (1931), 149–50, 153–54, 284n51; in *Dracula*, 49, 50–51; and

race (*continued*)
    epilepsy, 145; in eugenic thought
    and policy, 7, 9, 10, 11, 12, 13, 14–15,
    21, 36, 47, 48, 49, 50–51, 54–55, 74, 131,
    133, 200–201, 210–11, 234, 235, 237,
    290n16; in *Frankenstein*, 27, 131; in
    Gothic texts, 22–23, 147; in horror
    film interpretations, 26, 27, 96; in
    *The Invisible Man* (film), 179–81; in
    *The Invisible Man* (novel), 181; in
    *The Invisible Ray*, 228; in *Island of
    Lost Souls*, 219; in *The Mystery of the
    Wax Museum*, 131; and physiognomy,
    122–23, 131; and "race poisons," 19,
    146–47, 265n116; in social Darwinism,
    7; in Victorian ideology, 54, 145; and
    whiteness, 179–80, 181
Rains, Claude, 156, 177, **187**, 188
*The Raven* (1935), 23; British censorial
    response to, 162; criminality in,
    171–72, 175; facial deformity and rev-
    elation in, 171–72, **173**; gender in, 169;
    madness in, 161–62; medical gaze in,
    168–70, **169**, 171–72, 175; production
    of disability in, 170–72
*The Return of Chandu* (1934), 238
*The Return of Doctor X* (1939), 236
*Revenge of the Zombies* (1943), 236
Robbins, Tod, 86
Roberts, Kenneth L., 54
Robertson, John S., 142, 147, 183,
    277n82
Robinson, Charles H. (with Mary R.
    Melendy and Walter J. Hadden),
    256n10, 258n24
Rockefeller family, 10, 262n81
Rockwell, A. D., 205
Romero, George, 26, 240,
Roosevelt, Franklin Delano, 256n113
Roosevelt, Theodore, 10, 47

Rosen, Christine, 72, 264n101, 264n105,
    264n106
Rosenbaum, Jonathan (with J. Hober-
    man), 270n52, 272n83

Sacks, Oliver, 192
Sandahl, Carrie (with Philip Auslander),
    135
Sarkozy, Nicolas, 239
Sarris, Andrew, 113
Savada, Elias (with David J. Skal): on
    *Dracula*, 261n60, 270n60; on *Freaks*,
    112, 267n18, 267n20, 271n76
*Scanners* (1981), 138
Schaefer, Eric, 112
Schatz, Thomas, 99, 117
*Schindler's List* (1993), 240
Schweik, Susan, 124
scientific management, 256n113
sexual reproduction: in *Dracula*, 42–43,
    45, 47, 50–51, 52, 55–59; in eugenics, 8,
    18, 37, 46, 50, 54–55; in *Frankenstein*,
    60, 61, 76, 80. *See also* sexuality
sexuality: in *Bride of Frankenstein*, 73,
    96; in classic horror films, 23–24,
    38; and disability, 15–16, 25–26, 28,
    134–135; in *Doctor X*, 196–97, 201;
    in *Dr. Jekyll and Mr. Hyde* (1920),
    144–45; in *Dr. Jekyll and Mr. Hyde*
    (1931), 142, 149, 150, 284n51; in *Dr.
    Jekyll and Mr. Hyde* (1941), 152–53;
    in *Dracula*, 39, 42–43, 45, 168; in
    eugenics, 64, 144, 146; in *Freaks*,
    92, 98, 111, 112, 267n16; in Gothic
    literature, 22–23; in horror-film
    interpretations, 26; in horror-film
    spectatorship, 215; in *Island of Lost
    Souls*, 214–15; and the medical gaze,
    166–67. *See also* queerness; sexual
    reproduction

Shakespeare, Tom (with Anne Kerr), 237–38

Shaviro, Steven, 159, 201, 230–31

Shelley, Mary, 22, 23, 59, 63, 66, 95

Shelley, Percy, 22, 252n73

shock: in classic horror films, 122, 127–28, 132, 151, 181, 196, 198, 213, 217–18, 226, 229–30; and film spectatorship, 158–59, 207–208, 252n74; and horror as emotion, 2, 198–99; and medical experiments, 221; as method of execution, 206; as product of modern environment, 151, 153, 205–208; as response to disability/horror film, 80, 112–14, 121, 128, 132, 198, 208, 214–16, 218, 219, 231–32, 240–41; shell shock, 205–206; as treatment or therapy, 206; used to induce seizures, 167, 206

Siebers, Tobin, 154–55, 156, 159, 275n51

*The Silence of the Lambs* (1991), 24–25

Skal, David J.: on alternative reproduction in class horror, 38; on *Dr. Jekyll and Mr. Hyde* (1920), 143; on *Dracula*, 45, 266n2; on *Frankenstein*, 63, 261n66; on *Freaks*, 92, 106, 108; on *The Invisible Ray*, 227; on Lon Chaney, 156; on "nosferatu," 259n46; on radium poisoning, 223

—with Elias Savada: on *Dracula*, 261n60, 270n60; on *Freaks*, 112, 267n18, 267n20, 271n76

Snyder, Sharon L. (with David T. Mitchell): on "diagnosis" of literary characters, 273n5; on disability as "natural" stigma, 15–16, 253n88; on "feeblemindedness," 262n74; on *Geek Love*, 219; on historical views of disability, 245–46n5, 246n9; on horror films, 28; on idealized eugenic body,

12–13; on materiality of metaphor, 5; on narrative prosthesis, 5–6, 104; on ugly laws, 124

Sobchack, Vivian, 192–93, 201–202, 270–71n62

social Darwinism, 7, 142, 247n23

*Son of Frankenstein* (1939), 24, 163, 238, 255n102, 275n41

Spadoni, Robert, 107–108

spectatorship. *See* cinema, spectatorship; classic horror film, spectatorship in; horror film, spectatorship of; horror film, spectatorship as disabling; madness, spectatorial; medical gaze; monster, spectators' identification with or production as; shock, and film spectatorship

Spratling, William, 140, 150

sterilization: as eugenic measure, 2, 13, 14, 15, 36, 37, 65, 67, 139, 234; religious response to, 264n105; and ugly laws, 124; and X-ray, 223. *See also Buck vs. Bell* decision

Stevenson, Robert Louis. *See The Strange Case of Dr. Jekyll and Mr. Hyde* (1886)

Stoddard, Lothrop, 10, 49, 67

Stoker, Bram. *See Dracula* (1897 novel)

*The Strange Case of Dr. Jekyll and Mr. Hyde* (1886), 22, 141–42, 190–91, 209

Studlar, Gaylyn, 128

surrealism, 256n113; in the *Dr. Jekyll and Mr. Hyde* films, 147–49, 152, 153–54, 159; in German Expressionism, 252n74

survival of the fittest. *See* social Darwinism

Swales, John, 97

*The Texas Chain Saw Massacre* (1974), 24, 26

# FILM AND CULTURE

A series of Columbia University Press

Edited by John Belton